ESSENTIAL SKILLS OF
SOCIAL WORK
PRACTICE

Related books of interest

Second Edition

ESSENTIAL SKILLS OF SOCIAL WORK PRACTICE

Assessment, Intervention, and Evaluation

THOMAS O'HARE
Boston College

LYCEUM
BOOKS, INC.

5758 South Blackstone Avenue
Chicago, Illinois 60637

© 2016 by Lyceum Books, Inc.
Published by
LYCEUM BOOKS, INC.
5758 S. Blackstone Avenue
Chicago, Illinois 60637
773-643-1903 fax
773-643-1902 phone
lyceum@lyceumbooks.com
www.lyceumbooks.com

6   5   4   3   2   1   14   15   16   17   18

ISBN 978-1-935871-78-1

Printed in the United States of America.

The painting on the cover, The Insomniac's Bible, was created by noted Chicago artist, Leslie Baum, using watercolor on paper.

Library of Congress Cataloging-in-Publication Data

O'Hare, Thomas.
    Essential skills of social work practice : assessment, intervention, evaluation / Thomas O'Hare, MSW, Ph.D.—Second Edition.
        pages   cm
    Revised edition of the author's Essential skills of social work practice, 2009.
    Includes bibliographical references and index.
    ISBN 978-1-935871-78-1 (pbk. : alk. paper)
    1. Psychiatric social work.   2. Social service.   3. Social work education.   I. Title.
HV689.O42   2015
361.3′2—dc23   2015005274

Contents

Preface to the Second Edition

In 2009, *Essential Skills of Social Work Practice* was published as an effort to help social work students learn the basics of effective psychosocial practice and learn how to use informed critical thinking to advance their skills over a professional lifetime. The basic intent and structure of this second edition are in line with the original edition. Most changes reflect updates in the best available literature on effective practice as well as changes to reflect modifications in the recently published DSM-5.

Learning basic practice skills is important for two reasons: first, they are necessary for working effectively with clients who experience mild-to-moderate psychosocial distress; second, they provide the building blocks for learning advanced evidence-based practices that are now required for working with more seriously troubled clients. As such, this book serves as both a foundation practice text as well as a bridge to learning advanced social work practices. The literature on advanced interventions is more thoroughly reviewed and described in *Evidence-Based Practices for Social Workers: An Interdisciplinary Approach, Second Edition* (O'Hare, 2015).

This text is divided into three sections. Part I includes three chapters that address the core foundations of social work practice. Chapter 1 provides an overview of the three interrelated functions of effective practice: assessment, intervention, and evaluation. It also examines how different theoretical models have contributed to the evolution of essential skills over the past several decades. Chapter 2 explores how research and practice are linked as well as how critical thinking informs social work practice. Chapter 3 examines the basic ethical and liability concerns of social work practitioners and emphasizes how using knowledge supported by evidence can help maintain high ethical practice standards and avoid malpractice lawsuits.

Part II contains four chapters that explain and describe essential practice skills in greater detail. Chapter 4 examines how to conduct comprehensive assessments and utilize evaluation methods, two closely related functions. Chapter 5 provides an overview of *supportive skills,* those core aspects of the intervention that build the working relationship and facilitate client engagement in the intervention process. Chapter 6 describes *cognitive-behavioral skills,* those more action-oriented skills that enhance the client's ability to cope with cognitive, emotional, and behavioral challenges and build on their own adaptive strengths. Chapter 7 examines *case management skills,* those practice activities essential for working with multiproblem clients and coordinating complex intervention plans. Collectively, the chapters in Part II outline a coherent and testable model of social work practice that incorporates contributions from many approaches.

Part III contains six chapters, five of which explain how essential skills can be combined and applied to specific problems and disorders experienced by individuals, couples, children, and families. Each of these five chapters includes a brief case study with an illustrative psychosocial assessment, intervention, and evaluation plan. These cases are fictional illustrations, but inspired by real clients seen by the author over many years of social work practice. Students should critique these treatment plans, strive to improve upon them, and apply them thoughtfully with clients in their field placements or practice. In Chapter 8, the author addresses serious mental illnesses and anxiety disorders in adults. Chapter 9 covers substance abuse and personality disorders. Chapter 10 focuses on skills utilized with distressed couples. Chapter 11 explains how to work in the context of family interventions with children who are experiencing internalizing disorders (i.e., depression, anxiety). Chapter 12 does the same for externalizing disorders (i.e., conduct disorders and ADHD). Although not exhaustively inclusive of all psychosocial problems, these chapters describe essential skills and interventions that can, with some modification, be readily applied to most problems that social workers encounter in direct practice settings. Collectively, these are the competencies that social workers now need to master in order to help clients solve problems, enhance their adaptive capabilities, and cope optimally with serious psychosocial challenges in their everyday lives. Finally, Chapter 13 briefly examines the links between essential skills and evidence-based practice, arguments for and against evidence-based practice, and the interconnected roles of researchers, administrators, educators, consumers, and practitioners with respect to advancing evidence-based practice.

The book also contains several appendices. These are designed to be useful aids for beginning practitioners. They include a copy of the Psychosocial Intervention Scale (PSIS) (Appendix A) developed by the author to help practitioners conduct an inventory of the skills and interventions they utilize with their clients, critically consider their rationale for selecting a particular combination of skills, and monitor how their skill selection changes over time with each client. Appendix B contains a copy of the Comprehensive Service Plan designed to help beginning practitioners collect, summarize, and synthesize qualitative assessment information, make quantitative ratings of client well-being across multiple domains, and make informed recommendations for their intervention based on a complete multidimensional/functional assessment. The plan also encourages the development of simple evaluation indexes to monitor client progress. Lastly, Appendix C outlines basic research guidelines to help students become better consumers of human behavior research and outcome studies, a major benchmark for validating social work's professional knowledge base. Together, these three tools are intended to help students develop competence in social work assessment, intervention, and evaluation.

The content of this text is based on best evidence gleaned from the best practice research across the helping professions. As beginning social workers develop their knowledge and skills through both classroom learning and practice experience, it is this author's hope that they will go beyond this text and learn advanced evidence-based practices relevant to their chosen field. By mastering the essentials, social work students will be better prepared to continue their professional development, keep abreast of advances in practice research, and remain active critical learners throughout their careers.

Tom O'Hare
Charlestown, R.I.

PART ONE

Conceptual Foundations of Essential Social Work Practice Skills

CHAPTER ONE

Overview: Defining and Linking Assessment, Intervention, and Evaluation

THE TEACHING OF BASIC, or essential, skills has a long tradition in social work and the allied helping professions. The sources that have influenced the development of the essential skills curriculum in social work programs over the last century include: theory, practice wisdom and tradition, and, more recently, empirical research on the processes of psychosocial interventions and their relationships to client outcomes (e.g., Compton & Galaway, 1999; Fischer, 1981; Hill & O'Brien, 2004; O'Hare, 2015; O'Hare & Collins, 1997; Orlinsky, Grawe, & Parks, 1994; Perlman, 1957; Richmond, 1918; Rogers, 1951; Shulman, 1999; Truax & Carkhuff, 1967; Woods & Hollis, 1999). Many other practice scholars have contributed to the vast body of literature on how to help people in serious psychosocial distress; they are too numerous to name here. Until recently, however, little work has been done to provide a conceptual model of social work practice that incorporates a broad array of these interdisciplinary influences from social work, counseling, clinical psychology, and the other allied helping professions with an emphasis on those skills and interventions (i.e., combinations of skills) that are supported by the preponderance of current process and outcome research.

Building on these previous accomplishments, the current chapter does the following: (1) outlines a conceptual model of social work practice skills that is informed by practice experience, tested through research methods, and provides a foundation for constructing evidence-based practices in contemporary social work; and (2) incorporates essential assessment and evaluation skills into that model. As such, this chapter outlines the framework for the rest of this text.

Practitioners who work with individuals, couples, families, and small groups experiencing psychosocial difficulties and disorders are primarily concerned with three key professional functions: assessment, intervention, and evaluation. *Assessment* requires that the practitioner have a competent grasp of the relevant knowledge base pertinent to their client's presenting problems as well as a keen understanding of the client's difficulties, deficits, and adaptive strengths as conceptualized from each client's unique point of view. *Interventions* are comprised of combinations of essential skills drawn from three major categories: (1) *supportive skills* that engage the client in a working relationship and facilitate the intervention process; (2) *cognitive-behavioral coping skills* that enhance the client's ability to cope with life's stressors, reduce symptoms of serious disorders, and solve problems; and (3) *case management skills* that are used to improve social and instrumental supports and coordinate complex services. An intervention plan is ideally developed by consulting the relevant practice research (now summarized in various texts) and implementing the approach with some flexibility to fit the client's unique needs and circumstances. *Evaluation* of the intervention is conducted by employing key measures of the client's difficulties at assessment, and repeating those measures at key intervals during the intervention, at termination, and, if possible, within six months to one year following the termination of services (only if the client provides informed consent). Those measures should include quantitative and qualitative indicators of the client's problems (e.g., depression) or intervention goals (e.g., improved relationship with parents, reduction in alcohol use) and are used to monitor client progress and determine the degree to which the intervention was successful.

Below (Figure 1) is a model representing the reciprocal and iterative relationships among assessment, intervention, and evaluation.[1]

As depicted in the figure, assessments are grounded in human behavior research, guide treatment selection, and provide a baseline for evaluating one's own practice. Choice of intervention is guided by the preponderance of practice outcome research (evidence-based practices, or EBPs), but implementation is flexibly adapted to individual client's problems, needs, and circumstances. Interventions across all treatment modalities are comprised of combinations of supportive, coping, and case management skills. The client's progress is then monitored and treatment is evaluated over time by using both qualitative and quantitative measures. Ongoing client change then further informs the assessment. This process continues in a cumulative and interactive manner until termination of the case.

---

[1] O'Hare, T. (2015). *Evidence-based practices for social workers*. Chicago, IL: Lyceum Books, Inc.

FIGURE 1. ESSENTIAL SKILLS OF SOCIAL WORK PRACTICE: ASSESSMENT, INTERVENTION, EVALUATION

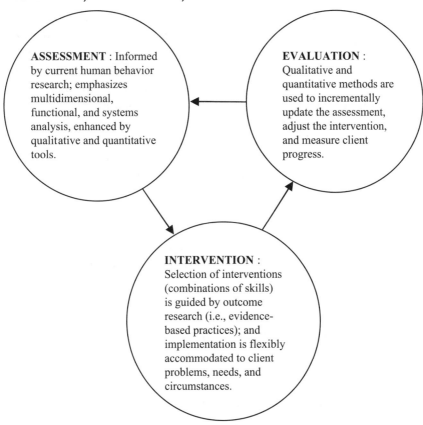

The combination of skills utilized for conducting assessment, intervention, and evaluation ranges from the simple to the complex. Becoming an effective advanced practitioner means learning the essentials first, and then applying them to more challenging and complex problems over time as one gains additional knowledge and experience. This chapter will briefly describe each of these essential aspects of practice and how they are interrelated. But, first, a brief review of prominent practice theories is in order for two main reasons: first, to understand how each approach relates human behavior theory to practice; and second, to understand how much each practice theory has contributed to contemporary evidence-based practices.

A Review of Practice Theories

Many practice scholars would agree that a few major practice models have guided social work over the second half of the twentieth century and into the twenty-first: psychodynamic theories and practices; social cognitive theory and cognitive-behavioral interventions; various family systems theories and methods; a collection of relatively atheoretical phenomenological approaches known as humanistic, constructivist, narrative, solution-focused, existential, and client-centered approaches; and, more recently, anti-oppression and empowerment theories. Some of these approaches have had important influences on contemporary practice, yet each, by itself, provides an inadequate foundation for understanding human behavior, conducting a comprehensive assessment, explaining the processes (i.e., psychosocial mechanisms) of change in treatment, or offering intervention methods that are universally effective. In addition, some intervention models have been more thoroughly tested than others, yet some models offer little to no evidence of effectiveness but continue to be promoted in schools of social work.

Practice theory (aka orientation, school of thought) is really a catch-all phrase that represents a collection of different types of theories and assumptions associated with a general intervention approach. A sound "practice theory" should actually incorporate three separate but related dimensions of practice: (1) assumptions and theories about human behavior in the social environment that are supported by a body of research (i.e., scientifically grounded human behavior theory), (2) assumptions and theories about how people change as a result of the intervention (i.e., change process theory), and (3) a collection of observable practice skills, techniques, and strategies designed to help people reduce psychosocial distress, alleviate symptoms of psychological disorders, and improve coping capabilities (i.e., enhance strengths and improve adaptive capabilities). Collectively, these activities are referred to as an "intervention." Below (Figure 2) is a simple graphic description of the components of a complete practice theory.

The first dimension of a practice theory addresses the questions: Why do people behave as they do? How do human beings develop into happy and productive members of society or become unhappy or troublesome to others? What biological, psychological, social, cultural, and environmental factors influence people's behavior over time, and how do these risk and resilience factors interact resulting in positive or negative adaptation in life? Obviously, such questions are complex, and the research methods

FIGURE 2. OVERVIEW OF THE TRADITIONAL PRACTICE THEORY MODEL

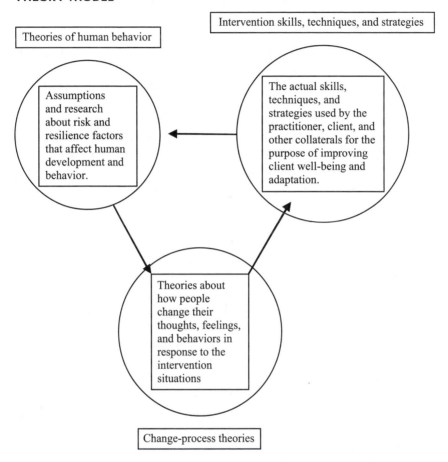

utilized to answer them can be complicated as well. Nevertheless, a considerable amount of knowledge has been developed and catalogued that does help us understand some of the factors that contribute to major mental illnesses, addictions, childhood disorders, domestic violence, and so forth. The scientific knowledge base of human behavior in the social environment is derived from the findings of multivariate research and provides a foundation for conducting informed assessments with our clients. *Human behavior theories* are now understood to be complex and multivariate, and they incorporate a range of biopsychosocial influences. Thus, human behavior theories that overemphasize one factor or another (e.g., bad genes, bad mothering, bad learning experiences, dysfunctional thinking, stressful environment, oppression, etc.) provide an inadequate basis for explaining the causes of human problems. Therefore, they cannot be relied on to support a valid assessment.

Human development is influenced by the complex interactions of both risk and resilience factors over time. Risks and resiliencies can originate from and be expressed as biological, psychological, social, and environmental factors. Although some have found it fashionable to reject a "deficit" or "pathology" view in favor of only considering "strengths," such an approach is scientifically untenable. Conducting assessment and intervention with a client by ignoring deficits and focusing exclusively on strengths suggests some degree of professional malpractice. Since biopsychosocial risk and resilience factors do exist, they must all be considered in order to achieve a more complete understanding of complex human problems. Risk and resiliency factors associated with biological heredity, cognition, and behavior in a sociocultural context can often be conceptualized as two ends of a continuum that represent the influences of both psychosocial pathology and adaptive strengths. For example, if a genetic predisposition to depression or substance abuse is a risk factor, having parents with no such history or parents who have modeled how to successfully cope with depression and anxiety can be considered a form of resilience or an adaptive strength. The same can be said of positive versus negative psychosocial modeling of one's parents (e.g., prosocial vs. criminal behavior), quality of education, or other social or socioeconomic influences on one's life. As these examples imply, both risks and resiliencies can also be categorized as causal factors, change-process factors (i.e., mediating factors), or developmental or treatment outcomes. Biopsychosocial risks and resiliencies can affect human development (e.g., ability to handle stress), affect the process of change in treatment (e.g., ability to handle critical feedback and try new behaviors), or can be the outcome of healthy psychosocial development or result of an intervention (e.g., the degree to which a client learns to cope with bouts of depression or utilize social supports). Obviously, any and all of these forms of behavior can be considered a risk or resilience factor depending on how, to what degree, and under what circumstances they are expressed by the individual. Risk and resilience can also be value-laden concepts, the interpretation of which may be in the eye of the beholder.

The second area of knowledge required to support a practice theory is derived from research on *human change processes*. This category of theory development addresses questions such as the following: What are the psychosocial mechanisms by which people change their behavior or their situation for the better? What personal or environmental factors affect how people change? What are the biopsychosocial mechanisms that must be activated in order for people to achieve lasting change with or without formal psychosocial intervention? Can change processes be activated by broader societal changes? Answers to these questions can help us understand how people achieve success over their addictions, improve self-esteem, reduce impulsive behaviors such as self-mutilation, reduce symptoms of depression or psychosis, gain confidence to conquer anxieties and other fears, or simply become better communicators, problem solvers, better parents, and more loving partners.

Change process theories are human behavior theories that focus on how people change and, as with human behavior theories in general, are likely to include contributions from the biological, psychological, and other social sciences. A change process theory can suggest both deficits and adaptive capabilities that can be targeted by an intervention in order to bring about successful treatment outcomes. Depending on the practice theory employed, change has been shown to result from a number of processes: feeling understood in response to a social worker's empathic responses; feeling increased self-efficacy (i.e., confidence that one can cope successfully with a difficult situation) as a result of gradually confronting a problem; improved school performance as a result of positive reinforcement; improved mood brought about by exercise or medication; or improved quality of life as a result of a change in finances, a positive relationship, spiritual enlightenment, or the removal of some externally oppressive force. The reasons why and how people change are complex and not well understood within the behavioral sciences. Although theories abound, evidence to support specific change process theories remains inconclusive at best. How these change processes can be activated to help our clients overcome problems and enhance their adaptive capabilities is the main purpose of psychosocial interventions. However, although it is well known that some psychosocial interventions are effective and that some are more effective than others for specific problems, much less is currently known about *how* these approaches help people change.

The third dimension of a practice theory, the actual *intervention methods used,* is defined by the activities of the practitioner, the client, and other collaborators. Collectively, practitioner, client, and other collaborators can help a client solve a problem or improve their overall adaptive strengths by activating some or all of the biological, psychological, behavioral or social change processes discussed above. Interventions constitute a collection of skills, intervention techniques, and overall strategies to help the client move toward their goals. Practice skills, collectively, are those efforts that actually constitute the intervention. *Although underlying human behavior and change process theories are critically important matters for research and further understanding, it is the actual combination of skills (i.e., the intervention) that can be more readily defined, taught, supervised, tested, and evaluated to see if they are effective in helping clients reduce symptoms, enhance coping abilities, and improve overall life circumstances.* Thus, it is important when adopting a "practice theory" to clearly distinguish these three separate but related parts: *human behavior theory* (i.e., what factors cause the problem), *change process theory* (i.e., what factors explain how people change), and the actual *intervention* (i.e., what skills the practitioner uses to help the client). Evidence for effective practice is based on research that tests the third component of a practice theory: the actual intervention.

The Current State of Prominent Practice Theories

Although many practice theories and models have made positive contributions to effective social work practice, their relative contributions to current evidence-based practices are highly disproportionate. Some of the problems with practice theories still taught in schools of social work are these: (1) the human behavior theory associated with the approach is not supported by scientific evidence; (2) the intervention methods have not been adequately tested or, if tested, not shown to be effective with certain problems or conditions; and (3) the approach is not broad-based enough to support a comprehensive approach for a wide range of psychosocial problems and psychiatric disorders. Some social work practice theory texts do not even utilize a critical framework to help students judge the relative validity of these theories or effectiveness of the interventions, but rather present practice theories as though they are all, more or less, equal and should be evaluated on their intuitive appeal to the student or the instructor. However, professional practice in all helping professions now demands a more critical stance with regard to selecting interventions. Although a thorough critique of each of these practice models is well beyond the scope of this text, what follows is a brief overview and summary critique of the more prominent practice theories utilized in social work practice today.

Psychodynamic Theory and Practice

Psychodynamic theory has long been a mainstay for practitioners due to its intuitive appeal and ostensible explanatory power regarding how people develop psychologically (human behavior theory), how they change (change process theory), and how practitioners attempt to help them (the intervention techniques). Human behavior theory (according to psychoanalytic theories) is somewhat complex (e.g., Freud, 1938; Kernberg, 1976;

Kohut, 1971). More recently, some psychodynamic social work practitioners have shown interest in "relational theory" (Johnson, 2007), a reconstituted form of psychodynamic theory that also borrows from Bowlby's (1980) and Mahler, Pine, and Bergman's (1975) theories on childhood attachment. In brief, most psychodynamic practitioners work on the assumption that people develop internal representations of themselves and adaptive capacities (ego functioning, defenses) largely as a result of early childhood experiences that are presumably caused by interactions with their primary caretakers, particularly their mothers. These internal representations and ego functions (i.e., psychological coping mechanisms) affect the way they deal with human relationships and other environmental stressors over time. Presumably, as a result of these early influences, people develop interpersonal relations that are generally growth enhancing or increasingly problematic. Much of the theoretical emphasis in psychoanalytic theory and its variants (e.g., ego psychology, object relations theory, self-psychology, attachment theory, relational theory, etc.) is on the way early childhood experiences establish relationship patterns (internalized models) that in large part determine interpersonal functioning over the life span. Assuming that clients are having difficulties in intrapsychic and interpersonal functioning, they may seek treatment.

Although psychodynamic theorists and practitioners have rightly stressed the importance of early childhood development, the core assumption that specific disorders can be predicted as a function of the timing and type of developmental disruption has not survived scientific scrutiny. Early disruptions in nurturance have not been shown to accurately predict the development of major mental illnesses, substance abuse, or specific emotional and behavioral disorders. Cross-sectional and, more importantly, longitudinal studies have, however, supported the conclusion that, to one degree or another, these problems are largely a result of the combined effects of genetic predisposition, early childhood experiences (e.g., that affect learning, cognitive development, emotion regulation, social behavior), and familial, social, environmental, and cultural influences that interact and reverberate over time. Thus, the important contributions of psychodynamic theoreticians and researchers have been greatly modified and incorporated into a more multivariate developmental framework grounded in the developmental behavioral sciences including more recent advances in neurology.

Regarding intervention methods, psychodynamic practitioners have made important contributions to effective practice by emphasizing the importance of developing and maintaining a sound working alliance and creating a therapeutic environment whereby the client can work through psychological injuries incurred in previous relationships. By using therapeutic techniques such as explanation and interpretation of "transference," practitioners attempt to help their clients better understand (through the change processes of "insight" and a "corrective emotional experience") how their past experiences affect them in the present. Through explanation and interpretation, practitioners attempt to help the client better understand their difficulties and learn to cope with current relationships in a more enlightened and fulfilling way. Although the evidence supporting the efficacy of transference interpretations is scarce (Clarkin, Levy, Lenzenweger, & Kernberg, 2007; Weiss, 1995), emotion-focused therapy (Johnson, 2007), rooted in attachment theory, has emphasized improving couples relations by enhancing emotional communication and understanding. Whether the positive outcomes associated with this approach have any causal connection to early attachment experiences is unknown. Regardless of speculation about theoretical causality, a contemporary model of evidence-based practice now emphasizes both the development of a sound working alliance and improving communication skills that focus on emotion-based content, important areas emphasized by psychodynamic practitioners.

Social-Cognitive Theory and Cognitive-Behavioral Therapy

Cognitive-behavioral therapy (CBT) is primarily built upon social-cognitive theory, which evolved from three sources: scientific approaches to reasoning and cognition, classical and operant behavior theories, and social learning theory (e.g., modeling) (Bandura, 1986, 1999; Beck, 1976, 1996). Aaron Beck's cognitive theory of depression has had a substantial impact on the evolution of CBT. For cognitive therapists, cognition is "primary." Thus, for people to change their distressing thoughts about themselves, others, the world about them, and the future, they need to question and refute dysfunctional (i.e., irrational) ways of thinking. For example: "If someone doesn't like me, then it must be that I am no good"; "If I don't get into the school of my choice, I'm never going to be a success"; "I saw some students talking and laughing in the cafeteria . . . they must be making fun of me"; "If she leaves me, I will have to kill myself"; and so forth.

By way of intervention technique, cognitive-behavioral therapists guide the client in a critical examination of the inherent thinking flaws (see "critical thinking" in Chapter 2). The crux of the gentle inquiry is to challenge the client to answer the question "Where is the evidence to support your view that (for example) you can't live without her," or "Everyone is laughing at you," and so forth. However, the goal of CBT is not simply to help the client reason their way out of their dilemma but to set up real world tests to "disconfirm" or "debunk" the irrational belief (i.e., a process known as *behavioral disconfirmation*). The result of disconfirming dysfunctional beliefs can be highly reinforcing, and with increased self-confidence (i.e., self-efficacy), clients feel that they can continue to make progress with their particular difficulties.

Although cognitive practitioners focus on helping clients challenge irrational beliefs through critical thinking, traditional behaviorists emphasize gradually changing behaviors in order to positively reinforce change (i.e., increase the likelihood of change). Although behavioral interventions showed generally positive results, they were unsatisfying for some because they tended to downplay the cognitive component, or the "client's view." Theoretically, behavioral models fell short because research showed that external reinforcement procedures, although facilitative of change, were not always necessary or sufficient for producing change. Neo-behaviorists and, later, social-cognitive theorists like Albert Bandura began to take a more explicit scientific interest in the role of cognition in relationship to behavior and reinforcement. Social-cognitive theory incorporated cognitive and behavioral theories but emphasized the role of learning without immediate external reinforcement and also stressed the importance of increasing self-efficacy, bolstering the belief that one can cope with challenging situations. Social-cognitive theory provides a somewhat integrated model for human behavior in that it emphasizes the interrelatedness of modifying cognitions, regulating physiological responses (e.g., anxiety reduction), and activating behavior change within the client's day-to-day social environment.

As a result of the combined influences of research in cognition, conditioning theories, and social-cognitive theory, change processes in cognitive-behavioral interventions now emphasize changing dysfunctional thinking, anxiety-reduction methods, and reducing dysfunctional thinking through behavioral disconfirmation (i.e., practice in real life), with a resulting increase in one's belief that one can successfully cope with similar problems in the future (i.e., increased self-efficacy). Intervention methods utilized by cognitive-behavioral therapists are quite eclectic, depending on the problem, and include the following: directly addressing cognitive distortions through critical examination of those thoughts (i.e., Socratic questioning) and challenging their veracity; direct modification of physiological arousal to reduce anxiety and improve mood (e.g., exercise, relaxation, and meditation techniques); using covert (i.e., in the imagination) and in vivo (i.e., live) rehearsal, role play, and practice of new behaviors; coaching clients in problem-solving and communication skills; and teaching the use of reinforcement techniques to improve one's own or another's (e.g., a child's) behavior.

By way of illustrating the combined influences of cognitive, physiological, and behavioral change efforts, consider the scenario of the young woman who suffers from severe shyness and general lack of self-confidence. After critically analyzing "the evidence" (or lack thereof) to support her opinion that "no one likes me" and "everyone is laughing at me," the young woman and the practitioner collaboratively plan weekly tasks to initiate brief conversations with some people in her class. The practitioner helps the client reduce her social anxiety through simple breathing techniques and provides guidance through role modeling and rehearsal to work on improving her conversation skills. She is also asked to imagine, for five minutes every evening at home, how she will initiate a conversation with someone at school while controlling her breathing to reduce anxiety. After a few attempts in vivo (i.e., actual real-life "experiments"), she is likely to have had one or two successful conversations, and the expectation that people are always talking about or ridiculing her begins to dissipate. As a result of these reinforcing experiences, she becomes less concerned with being ridiculed, and grows in self-confidence (i.e., achieves greater self-efficacy). This confidence causes others to respond to her more positively.

CBT has spawned a wide array of effective interventions that have influenced and been combined with other practice approaches for major mental illnesses, depression, anxiety disorders (including panic disorder with agoraphobia, obsessive compulsive disorder and PTSD), eating disorders, substance abuse and the addictions, borderline personality disorder, and the full range of childhood emotional and behavioral disorders. No other intervention methods can rival the totality of clinical outcome research that supports cognitive-behavioral therapies.

Until recently, CBT practitioner-researchers often gave short shrift to the importance of the therapeutic relationship despite the evidence underscoring its importance as an effective dimension of psychosocial interventions. Studies of CBT now incorporate more engagement factors and have placed a greater emphasis on motivational interviewing efforts. Although change process research has not clearly supported some theoretical assertions regarding how or why people change, "psychological mechanisms" are now more frequently the focus of practice research. In the past, CBT was typically presented as an individually focused treatment. Now couples and family work often incorporates CBT methods including when the main focus of the intervention is a child or adolescent. CBT has also been incorporated into more broad-based care that addresses key environmental barriers as in the case of Assertive Case Management, supported housing, and supported employment programs for people with severe mental illness and incorporating parent skills training into child welfare interventions. Thus, cognitive-behavioral interventions have become increasingly eclectic in that they combine the three categories of essential skills (i.e., support, coping, case management) to address a wide range of psychosocial problems and psychiatric disorders. CBT research has also set the standard for methodologically sound clinical outcome research. Evidence-based practices today are primarily driven by research on cognitive-behavioral therapy.

Phenomenological Therapies

Since the 1950s, a variety of relatively atheoretical therapies evolved, to some extent, as a counterweight to the dominant approach at the time—psychodynamic therapy—and, more recently, as a reactionary response to empirically supported interventions to some degree. These include existential (e.g., Frankl, 1963; May, 1969), narrative (e.g., Berg, 1999), humanist (e.g., Goldstein, 1986), solution-focused (e.g., O'Hanlon & Weiner-Davis, 1989), strength-based (e.g., Saleeby, 1996), and other similar phenomenological and experiential approaches. The term *phenomenological* generally refers to an attempt to describe the pure experience of the client, unfiltered and unfettered by psychological theories, research findings, or the practitioner's perspective. These approaches attempt to engage the client on their own psychological turf, and work with their own inner experience (i.e., phenomenology) to define the problem and seek solutions. To varying degrees, phenomenological practitioners generally avoid, diminish, or reject outright theory-driven research on human behavior, and feel that practice research somehow distorts or sullies the creativity and spontaneity of the client's change experience. This position might be considered a limitation in the current professional environment since practitioners are expected to provide research-based justification for their choice of intervention.

As for practice methods, these approaches generally incorporate a range of counseling techniques and pragmatic problem-solving approaches to help clients express their own unique view of problems and construct potential solutions for them. Sometimes expressive, creative, or otherwise experiential techniques are employed to aid in this process. These techniques might include drawing, poetry, keeping diaries or journals, dramatic demonstration, or other "creative" modes of expression. How these methods are arrived at is, perhaps, somewhat spontaneous or intuitive, and clear or testable guidelines for implementation are usually not provided.

In fact, these approaches are often difficult to define, and few research-based guidelines are available to either clarify or justify the use of these methods with specific problems. However, a key strength of phenomenological approaches is the emphasis on exploring and understanding the client's experience from their unique perspective and working with the client's strengths to develop intervention methods rather than simply imposing interventions on the client.

Client-centered therapy (person-centered therapy; Raskin & Rogers, 1995; Rogers, 1951) was also developed as a relatively atheoretical approach to interpersonal helping that focused on the client's inner experience. However, counseling and psychotherapy process researchers later refined and further developed its key concepts over many years. As a result, client-centered therapy stands apart from other phenomenological approaches in that it has spawned the research foundation of modern psychotherapy process-outcome research. Rogers and his colleagues emphasized the inherent transformational abilities of the client and the practitioner's capacities to express empathy, authenticity, positive regard, and respect for the client. Developing the working relationship based on these principles remains a cornerstone of the psychosocial helping professions to this day. Client-centered counseling has made unique and long-standing contributions to psychosocial practice as a result of the hundreds of studies conducted to define, measure, and test the efficacy of his basic helping concepts. Thus, the evidence for the essential role of the working relationship and the core helping skills of client-centered practice remains quite strong (Hill & O'Brien, 2004; O'Hare, Tran, & Collins, 2002; Orlinsky et al. 1994; Truax & Carkhuff, 1967).

In summary, proponents of narrative, existential, solution-focused, and other atheoretical approaches emphasize understanding the clients' inner experience and helping the client to use their innate abilities, skills, and strengths to find lasting solutions to their difficulties. As such, they provide an important foundation for working with a wide array of clients but, due to the lack of clear treatment guidelines, must often be complemented with evidence-based approaches especially when working with clients who have moderate to severe psychosocial difficulties and disorders. Evidence-based approaches have increasingly incorporated these basic counseling skills as an essential component of effective interventions.

Family Therapies

Family therapies are actually a diverse group of practices designed to treat individual, couple, or family problems by including some or all members of the family in the intervention. However, family therapies vary widely in both theoretical foundation and intervention methods. Thus, family therapy is not really a coherent theoretical approach as much as it is a framework within which various theories and practices are applied to understanding and dealing with families in distress. To be more specific, it makes more sense to stipulate which type of family therapy is the focus of interest: psychodynamic family therapy, behavioral family therapy, humanistic family therapy, and so on. As this is the case, judging the efficacy of each type of family therapy will coincide with research on individual approaches that are rooted in the same practice theory. Thus, research on the effectiveness of psychodynamic family therapy or narrative family therapies (and similar approaches) is rather thin.

Nevertheless, there appear to be some broad assumptions common among family therapies (Becvar & Becvar, 2009; Nichols & Schwartz, 2006). First, working with family members is often a more effective approach because the practitioners can see how family members interact as a system, and can better understand how those interactions affect the problems of the "identified client" (i.e., the person, usually a child, who is presented as having or expressing the problem of immediate concern). Second, changes in the behavior of one family member tend to cause changes in other members. Third, the family system is made up of subsystems (e.g., parents, siblings, or other alliances) that help to maintain problems or could be keys to solving them. Fourth, changing the way the whole family behaves can help to maintain changes over time. Helping family members learn to reinforce prosocial and constructive behaviors can make for lasting change. However, it is hard for individuals to change within a family or for family life to improve if other members are undermining those changes, deliberately or unintentionally. Last, family problems often have a way of being transferred from one generation to the next.

Cognitive-behavioral family therapy has been extensively studied and shown to be effective for a variety of vulnerable clients, including families with a member who suffers from schizophrenia, substance use disorders in a parent or adolescent, emotional and behavioral disorders in children and adolescents, ADHD, eating disorders, anxiety, and depression, among others. The formal titles of these approaches have varied over the years in the literature: behavioral family therapy, behavioral couples therapy, psycho-education, and behavior family therapy. However, with some variation, they are based on common social-cognitive learning principles, and most include cognitive and behavioral techniques within a broader family systems framework to one degree or another.

CBT-oriented family practitioners emphasize the identification and examination of problem behaviors, a functional assessment of how family members interact within the family system, track the positive and negative consequences of those behaviors, and help family members change the way they communicate and problem-solve in order to resolve difficulties and reinforce more constructive forms of interaction. These approaches incorporate basic family therapy principles (e.g., interactions, subsystems, etc.) but also use core cognitive and behavioral approaches: cognitive examination of beliefs and faulty thinking, practicing new behaviors in the consulting office and at home, promoting mutually reinforcing behaviors among family members, focusing on clear goals, and evaluating outcomes. Cognitive-behavioral family therapies have also been used to work with families where one member has a serious disorder such as a major mental illness or addiction to alcohol or other drugs. Evidence to support cognitive-behavioral family and couples therapies is substantial for addressing emotional and behavioral disorders with children and adolescents (Fabiano et al., 2009; Northey, Wells, Silverman, & Bailey, 2003), substance abuse problems (O'Farrell & Fals-Stewart, 2003; Stanton & Shadish, 1997), and severe mental illness (Dixon, Adams, & Lucksted, 2000; Kreyenbuhl, Buchanan, Dickerson, & Dixon, 2010), among other family-related problems. Beyond working with the immediate family, CBT family work has also been applied within a broader ecosystems model whereby the practitioner works with the family as well as other members of the community: law enforcement, the schools, and other important collaterals that have a vested interest in improving the welfare of the family. Multisystemic therapy (Henggeler, Schoenwald, Borduin, Rowland, & Cunningham, 1998; Henggeler, Schoenwald, Borduin, Rowland, & Cunningham, 2009) is one exemplary evidence-based approach.

Anti-Oppressive and Empowerment Social Work Practice

As social workers, many of us give high priority in our practice to people who confront structural, organizational, and institutional barriers every day both in Western societies as well as most other parts of the world. Poverty, physical and sexual abuse, discrimination due to one's race, religion, gender, and sexual orientation, and social stigma due to one's mental or physical disability, no doubt, oppress many people over the life span. Pressures associated with various personal identity factors (e.g., race and gender) can also intersect and interact, thus, multiplying the effects of oppression (Collins, 2000). Although there is an array of social theories (e.g., feminist theory, structural theories) that address various social inequities, they can generally be categorized under the umbrella of *anti-oppressive theories of social work practice*. Anti-oppressive social work focuses primarily on social, political, and economic structures as well as psychosocial processes that cause and maintain oppression (Robbins, 2011).

Efforts to bring about large-scale social change and increase social and economic justice are primarily the province of macrosocial workers, legislators, political activists, policymakers, economists, and applied social scientists, among others. However, articulating goals and interventions for oppressed clients in direct practice social work requires specificity with respect to defining the problem, selecting effective interventions, and defining realistic goals for an individual, family, small group, or even an organization such as a school or social service agency. Anti-oppressive interventions can take many forms for the expressed purpose of empowering our clients (Gutierrez, 1990). For example: providing psycho-education for young women with bulimia-nervosa regarding idealized body image to improve self-esteem and reduce harmful eating habits; leading discussion groups in high schools to reduce homophobia; advocating for mentally ill people with their potential employers to reduce stigma and discrimination; working with community groups to reduce hostility toward a local African-American Muslim group planning to build a mosque in the neighborhood; and using cognitive-behavioral treatment with a depressed Hispanic woman who has been in an abusive marriage for years and has a drinking problem. Oppression is a likely causal factor in all of these cases, and clients could benefit from direct intervention of some kind.

However, keeping in mind the difference between causal theories and interventions, one must ask the following questions in each case: First, what intervention is designed to alleviate oppression or the consequences of oppression in a given situation? Second, what evidence is currently available to support the proposed intervention? Eating disorders might be, in part, caused by a particular culture's prevailing view of the ideal female body type, but there are no controlled studies to show that explaining this social bias to young women with eating disorders results in clinically significant improvements. However, there are evidence-based practices available for some eating disorders (i.e., cognitive-behavioral therapy and interpersonal psychotherapy). For the depressed, abused woman with a drinking problem, another social worker might decide that, in addition to offering psycho-education with regard to the psychological impact of physical abuse, she should also make a referral for a medication consult, use a brief motivational intervention to reduce her alcohol use, and refer the client to a support group for battered women. For the mentally ill young man, a supported employment model (e.g., interview rehearsal, rapid job search, ongoing support and advocacy) could help him obtain and keep a job in a local business resulting in a boost to his feelings of self-efficacy and improved social skills. In short, while anti-oppressive *theories* might help us to understand those social factors that contribute to vulnerable people's psychosocial problems, the effectiveness of *practices that can reduce the consequences of oppression* must be supported by intervention research in order to ethically justify their use. Many evidence-based practices can be empowering, but they are unlikely to be labeled as "empowerment interventions."

The main problem in the empowerment therapy literature is that the term "empowerment" is also often used in a way that fails to distinguish causes (i.e., oppression causes disempowerment), from the intervention (i.e., the use of empowering intervention skills), or from the intended goals or outcomes (i.e., clients feeling more empowered as a result of the intervention). When an empowerment intervention is applied to community organizing, however, it is often intended to help a larger group leverage influence over local power structures in order to advance some aspect of social justice. When applied to individuals, efforts to "empower" a client are usually defined by psycho-educational, behaviorally oriented, and advocacy-based approaches that lead to clients feeling and (perhaps) being more empowered (e.g., increased confidence, self-efficacy, ability to cope, etc.). Thus, there is currently no substantial body of research that supports empowerment therapy, but there are many evidence-based practices that result in people becoming more empowered.

Although a review of the literature going back ten years reveals little sound empirical work testing the efficacy of anti-oppressive interventions, a search of the term empowerment over the same time period yields more results. However, the research is methodologically weak, overall, making it hard to judge whether empowerment interventions are effective. Part of the problem lies in the varying definitions of the term "empowerment." Some researchers use the term to describe a *characteristic of the client*, some use it to define the actual *intervention process*, and some use the term as a *treatment goal or outcome* (i.e., feeling more empowered). For example, cognitive-behavioral intervention was shown to be effective at reducing depression for a sample of poor women in Pakistan who were described as not being empowered financially in their households (i.e., not allowed to handle household budgets) (Rahman et al., 2012). In this case, level of empowerment was a moderator (a client characteristic), not the intervention or the outcome. One meta-analysis (Kerrigan, Fonner, Stromdahl, & Kennedy, 2013) of ten studies referred to empowerment approaches to help female sex workers in low- and middle-income countries avoid contracting HIV/AIDS. The interventions, generally, consisted of education about sexually transmitted disease, promotion of free condom use, and access to medical screening and treatment for sexually transmitted diseases. The authors defined empowerment, not as a goal, but as process by which the sex workers were also helped to *organize and challenge power structures* (i.e., the intervention) in order to obtain social legitimacy for their work and obtain better health care. Although results regarding overall reductions in sexually transmitted diseases were mixed, it appeared that there was some reduction in HIV/AIDS. However, the authors concluded that any conclusions were tentative due to the methodological weakness of the studies selected for the meta-analysis. One could not determine whether the reduction in HIV/AIDS was due to "leveraging power structures" or increasing access to free condoms.

In another study with consumers diagnosed with severe mental illnesses, self-reported feelings of empowerment (a "mediator") were correlated with a recovery treatment orientation (the intervention) and consumer satisfaction (the outcome) (Barrett, Young, Teague et al., 2010). Although one would normally expect consumer choice to correlate with consumer satisfaction, it is not known if an empowerment approach (i.e., self-directed care) yielded better outcomes than (more-or-less) practitioner-directed care since there was no such comparison group.

Given the lack of sound research and unreliable definitions of the term empowerment, it is difficult to determine what an empowerment intervention is, much less whether it is effective for specific problems. When an empowerment intervention *is* shown to be effective, it is usually due to a previously known evidence-based practice. For example, one randomized controlled trial with depressed women (Crisp, Griffiths, MacKinnon, & Bennett, 2014) offered an Internet support group, psycho-education, and a combination of the two treatments compared with a waitlist control group. Women in the three treatment conditions did better than controls showing increases in both empowerment (an outcome) and quality of life. In this case, the intervention consisted of a behaviorally oriented psycho-educational approach, with increased empowerment being one of the intended treatment goals. Thus, one can tentatively conclude that behavioral interventions could be empowering for depressed women.

In the coming chapters, many evidence-based approaches to working with a wide range of psychosocial problems will be described and illustrated. Although more research is needed with oppressed and otherwise vulnerable groups, the research literature is replete with practices that have been shown to be effective with many people who suffer from various forms of oppression. It is the ethical obligation of every social worker to use interventions that have been well defined and shown to be effective, especially with our most vulnerable clients.

An Interdisciplinary Evidence-Based Approach to Social Work Practice

Various schools of practice have made important contributions to contemporary effective social work. The combination of a sound working alliance, a knowledge-based understanding of their psychosocial deficits and strengths, the use of effective coping skills, and case management strategies collectively provide a coherent and effective social work practice framework for a wide array of psychosocial problems. Given that no individual practice model is sufficiently comprehensive to provide a complete understanding of our clients' difficulties or fully inform effective interventions, a more systematic interdisciplinary framework is needed to guide effective social work practice. The approaches applied within this framework, however, must now be supported with evidence from controlled practice research. What follows is a brief overview of the essential assessment, intervention, and evaluation skills now required for effective social work practice. These skills will be examined in greater depth in Part II of this book, and how these skills can be flexibly combined to form evidence-based practices will be addressed in Part III.

Assessment

A Range of Assessment Strategies

Assessment in social work practice is a general term that refers to a range of strategies used to describe, analyze, categorize, measure, and otherwise help practitioners understand their client's difficulties and capabilities (Bellack & Hersen, 1998; Franklin & Jordan, 2003; O'Hare, 2015; Sadock & Sadock, 2003). There is a wide and varied literature on assessment, but little agreement regarding what assessment is. For example, in conducting an assessment with a very depressed client (Bob), a practitioner may do one or more of the following:

- Qualitatively describe Bob's difficulties based solely on his own perception and understanding of the problem (Bob might say, "I feel like I'm being crushed by the weight of the world").
- Apply a psychiatric diagnosis (major depressive disorder, 296.00).
- Rate the severity of Bob's problems in one or more areas of

his life (on a scale from 0 to 4: 0 = none, 1 = mild, 2 = moderate, 3 = serious, 4 = severe).

- Analyze a sample of Bob's daily behavior in detail to identify factors that seem to be associated with his depression. For example, after discussing Bob's day-to-day struggles at length, the practitioner may try to help him "connect the dots" by pointing out the following: "It appears that you feel worse after you have consumed a lot of alcohol over the course of a couple of weeks, you've missed work, and your wife is angry at you for neglecting her and your children. Your kids don't sound too happy with you either. Could your depression be, at least in part, a consequence of heavy drinking and the consequences related to drinking?"

- Observe the interactions of family members to determine how problems are caused or maintained. In a family visit, the family expresses their feelings to one another about Bob's drinking and neglect of his obligations at home and work. The social worker observes the communication patterns, body language, the tone of their expression, and so forth.

All of these methods of assessment have useful qualities to recommend them, and they all have limitations because, as described earlier, the human behavior theories upon which they are based all have limited explanatory power. Therefore, to apply only one form of assessment is likely to prove inadequate in most cases. Thus, a pragmatic approach to assessment would combine some of the more useful aspects of different methods, and capitalize on the guidance of research literature when relevant.

The Role of Personal Identity Factors and Culturally Competent Practice

Although practitioners should approach assessment with the understanding that all clients and their circumstances are unique, one should also consider the important role of gender, age, race, ethnicity, culture, language, socioeconomic level, sexual orientation, and other client identifying characteristics that are often grouped as "demographics," but what this author prefers (for lack of a better phrase) to call "personal identity factors." In the context of human behavior theory and research (in addition to some degree of common sense), these factors often provide important clues regarding variation in types and severity of problems by both individuals as well as client groups. For example: on average, men consume a lot more alcohol than women; women are much more likely to meet diagnos-tic criteria for clinical depression than men; clients from racial minorities are more likely to feel reluctant to engage in treatment in an agency staffed predominantly by whites; recent immigrants to their new host country may have little understanding of what behavioral norms are expected in a "therapy" clinic; and so on. Although one should avoid stereotyping people when noting personal identity factors, they can be helpful in guiding the assessment by signaling known risk and resilience factors that *on average* may be representative of some groups of clients more so than others. How-ever, these factors should be determined by research findings and in-depth appreciation for the unique person's experience of each client, not by con-ventional wisdom or solely the practitioner's own personal experience. Cli-ents with similar racial, ethnic, or cultural backgrounds, for examples, may have very different personal views on the meaning of these characteristics.

Sensitivity and knowledge regarding identity factors is closely related to the growing interest in culturally competent practice. Although all prac-titioners want to provide services that are seen by the client as respectful and congruent with their own cultural background and beliefs, the concept of culturally competent practice remains largely theoretical and relatively untested. For starters, terms such as race, ethnicity, and culture are hetero-geneous terms that preclude an easy one-to-one match-up between a client and a specific approach to assessment and treatment. Although culturally informed engagement processes (i.e., good listening skills, working alli-ance) used early on in the intervention may be critical to engendering client participation in treatment, there is currently no body of empirical evidence available to guide practitioners to be culturally competent in a way that measurably improves current evidence-based practices. However, practices shown to be effective in controlled research (such as many cognitive-behavioral treatments) often work comparably well across racial, ethnic, and cultural lines (Waley & Davis, 2007). In addition, it remains unclear what practitioners would do differently given certain racial or cul-tural characteristics of the client. One study showed that practitioners receiving multicultural training and more experienced practitioners were both equally likely to make practice decisions based on the individual cli-ent's problems and circumstances rather than based on the client's refer-ence group (Seghal, Young, Gillem, et al. 2011). Although many published treatment studies do include people from various racial and cultural back-grounds, there is a pressing need to recruit more people of color in practice research to determine whether intervention modifications with different groups can, indeed, improve practice outcomes.

Despite the lack of controlled research on culturally competent practice, it stands to reason that one can enhance the working relationship with clients and better engage them in treatment if they feel that their cultural perspective is understood and respected by the practitioner. Being a culturally competent practitioner is, in part, about educating oneself about a client's cultural background and using skills in a way that is culturally congruent with client expectations (Sue, 2005). It also refers to possessing a genuine awareness of one's own cultural background, strengths, limitations, and biases as well as learning about client assimilation and acculturation challenges in the host country: how specific policies affect the client's reference group, what services are available to them, and what experiences they have had with racism and discrimination (Lum, 2007). Given the current state of the knowledge, practitioners can be culturally competent by engaging clients during the assessment around matters of cultural identity (i.e., what their cultural identity means to them) and by implementing practices that have been shown to be effective in the current outcome research with the understanding that most clients are likely to respond well to these. In a similar way, these treatment engagement considerations extend to other personal identity factors as well: sexual orientation, religious/spiritual beliefs and practices, and so on. By utilizing the supportive, therapeutic coping and case management skills in this text in a culturally sensitive and informed way, practitioners can become truly culturally competent. How to engage clients on these important issues will be more thoroughly addressed as part of "assessment" in Chapter 4.

Sources of Assessment Information and Methods for Gathering It

A comprehensive assessment strategy requires the gathering of salient information, ideally, from multiple sources using multiple methods. *Sources of assessment information* refer to those persons or databases that provide information that helps the practitioner to better understand the client's problems, strengths, and other salient facts about their situation. Other people who provide assessment information directly (e.g., a teacher) or indirectly (e.g., physician's record) are referred to as treatment collaterals or collaborators. Sources include the client, family members or other relatives, school personnel, law enforcement/criminal justice, and other medical or human service professionals, among others. Relevant information about the client can be provided by intervention collaborators verbally or obtained from relevant reports.

The *method of information gathering* refers to those techniques employed to obtain the information from various sources. The most commonly employed method for gathering assessment information is the *face-to-face interview* based primarily on the client's self-report. This method may be relatively unstructured, but most interviewers have some key information that they plan to examine, such as the client's mental status, quality of relationships with family or others in the community, general health status, use of alcohol or other drugs, and so forth. Given that the interview is somewhat structured, it is referred to as a *semistructured interview*. Since a large amount of essential assessment data can be gathered in the semistructured format, the practitioner wants to "hit all the main points" but can do so with considerable flexibility in order to accommodate to the client's pacing, priorities, style of communication, and other unexpected disclosures. With practice, a skilled social worker can amass a considerable amount of important qualitative information in a fairly short period of time. Different aspects of interviewing techniques will be addressed in Chapter 4.

Other information-gathering methods include *direct observation* of clients (e.g., social worker observing a child with a behavioral problem in school or a treatment facility) and the use of *clinical rating scales* and similar quantitative *instruments* (to be discussed below). For a behaviorally troubled child or adolescent, obtaining various points of view from several family members as well as teachers and an attending physician or the child's tutor or coach is likely to give a more complete assessment picture. In addition, combining large amounts of qualitative information from semistructured interviews and quantitative information from clinical rating scales can provide a rich and useful assessment and basis for ongoing monitoring and evaluation of each case. Above all, practitioners must remember that no client or collaborator is interviewed without the informed consent of the client (or guardian), and when the data are collected, every effort is made to protect the client's confidentiality. These matters will be discussed further in Chapter 3.

Making Sense of Assessment Information

A practitioner may gather pages of assessment information from interviews with the client, family members, and collaborators, along with data from direct observation, as well as the use of forms, scales, and other measurement tools. What to make of all this information, however, is another matter. As was noted earlier, there are several approaches to assessment, and all are informed by somewhat different theoretical frameworks. These different approaches are based upon different assumptions about the nature of clients' problems (e.g., a disease, a behavior problem, dysfunctional thinking, the result of oppression, or just the client's raw experience). Yet, considering all the different models of assessment, this author has argued that there are three major overarching themes that encompass them:

1. Clients' problems are caused by multiple biopsychosocial influences, both past and present, and these problems manifest themselves in multiple areas of a client's life: psychological, social, physical, and economic, among others. These characteristics of problems (i.e., having multiple causes and manifesting multiple psychosocial effects) constitute the concept of *multidimensionality*.

2. Although clients with similar problems (e.g., addictions, depression) manifest similar characteristics and difficulties, each client experiences those problems in a unique way. This uniqueness becomes evident when practitioners conduct detailed assessments into the client's day-to-day life. A detailed analysis of an individual client's thoughts, feelings, behaviors, and situational factors that influence their behavior will reveal a complex interplay of vulnerabilities and strengths that affect the problem. These factors do not occur randomly but tend to follow a pattern. Even clients with major mental illnesses have good days and bad days, strengths, and deficits that appear to coincide with improvements or decline in their condition. Troubled families where conflict is frequent and intense also experience times of relative tranquility where parents and siblings seem to get along, some affection and cooperation is apparent, and serious problems abate. These patterns revealing both problematic and more adaptive experiences need to be identified, so practitioners and their clients can reinforce adaptive behaviors and try to diminish behaviors that seem to maintain problems or precipitate crises. This unique patterning and sequencing of behaviors and related factors addresses the *functionality* dimension of an assessment. The detailed analysis of factors that seem related to a client's daily experiences is referred to as *functional analysis* because the purpose is to tentatively determine and better understand how the problem functions (i.e., how it works).

3. Although the concept of interaction is implicit in both the multidimensional view and functional analysis, it is important to emphasize that individual functioning must be understood within a social context. How the client is affected by others in his

family, community, work environment, and so forth, and how he reciprocally affects them must be seen within a *systemic social context.*

Taken together, we refer to contemporary assessment that is informed by both current research and client experience as *multidimensional-functional-systems (MFS) assessment* (O'Hare, 2015). How to conduct an MFS assessment will be examined in greater detail in Chapter 4.

Using Clinical Rating Scales and Other Measurement Tools for Assessment and Evaluation

Although it may seem like we're jumping ahead to evaluation prematurely, in fact, the foundation for conducting evaluation of every case is put into place during the assessment phase. Although the rationale for evaluation and the use of various evaluation designs will be discussed further in this chapter, it is important at this point to discuss the use of indexes and scales. What follows is a brief overview of the different types of instruments employed in everyday practice to enhance qualitative assessment and to lay a quantitative foundation for monitoring client progress.

Measurement instrument is, perhaps, the most generic term that encompasses a range of tools for measuring the frequency, intensity, or duration of various client problems. These tools range from the simple (e.g., counting the number of swear words Johnny uses each day) to the complex (e.g., scales that measure quality of life). They may also measure one or more *domains of client experience* (i.e., thoughts, feelings, or behaviors). Measurement tools are not intended to be used as a substitute for a comprehensive qualitative assessment but serve as a useful adjunct to provide a quantitative baseline of client well-being in one or more areas (e.g., level of depression, anxiety, etc.). Scales also serve as a handy monitoring tool to gauge client progress during and after the intervention. Measurement tools also have some advantages over qualitative assessment in that the data collected from many clients in the same program can be aggregated and used for program evaluation, something that is much less practical with large volumes of qualitative reports. When used repeatedly on large numbers of clients, these data can provide important tracking information to determine if a client or group of clients within the same program are improving, staying about the same, or getting worse. In addition, most measurement tools can be tested for two critical qualities: the *consistency* with which they measure some aspect of human behavior (i.e., reliability) and the *accuracy* with which they measure that same phenomenon (i.e., validity). These matters will be discussed more in depth in Chapter 4.

There are generally four types of measurement tools that practitioners can use in everyday practice: (1) diagnosis, (2) simple indexes, (3) unidimensional scales, and (4) multidimensional scales. Although *diagnosis* is generally not thought of as a form of measurement, in fact, it is. Categorization is a basic and somewhat useful form of measurement (i.e., nominal measurement), and the DSM-5 (American Psychiatric Association [APA], 2013) also allows for measuring the severity of the condition. Although diagnosis is an important part of an assessment, there are considerable limitations to psychiatric diagnosis, and diagnosis is no substitute for a complete assessment.

Simple *indexes* may be among the simplest and most useful tools for quick assessment and continuous monitoring of client progress. Assuming accurate self-report by the client or observational report by others, indexes provide straightforward, useful information and are generally considered to be reliable and accurate with most clients (unless there is good reason to believe that the client has motive to dissemble or deny a problem). Some examples include number of drinks consumed daily, number of "good" days reported by a distressed couple, number of days a young person attends class (or number of days truant), a student's overall grade point average, number of times a young woman with schizophrenia initiates a conversation in the community, the level of intensity of panic attacks, intensity of depression on any given day, duration of time-out for an oppositional child, number of days sober for a mom trying to regain custody of her child, and so on. As one can see, the variety of measures one can create to specifically suit a client's needs or situation is limitless. One needs only to accurately define a problem of concern and decide whether the best way is to measure its *frequency* (i.e., how often it occurs), *intensity* (i.e., severity of the problem), or *duration* (i.e., how long it lasts). Sometimes these indexes are referred to as *self-anchored scales* when they measure the client's subjective report (e.g., severely depressed) rather than an observable measure (days absent from work).

Unidimensional scales are instruments that use multiple items to measure the same concept. Scale development is a branch of the social sciences that requires considerable expertise and links theory development with empirical measures of people's thoughts, feelings, and behaviors. Valid scales are typically developed by interviewing a representative sample of people that includes those who do and those who do not experience the given problem to one degree or another. For example, a scale for measuring depression may contain twenty items some of which might include "I feel blue," "I don't know if I can go on living," "I have little interest in things that I used to enjoy," "I don't sleep very well," "I feel guilty," and so on. These items have been shown to correlate statistically with a diagnosis of clinical depression. Depending on the purpose of the scale, these items may be measured by frequency (e.g., all of the time, most of the time, some of the time, seldom, none of the time), by intensity (e.g., extremely, moderately, a little), or by duration (a day, a week, a month, a year). In most scales, all the items are measured using the same rating system, although that is not always the case. In addition, some scales contain items that are scored in the opposite direction (e.g., "I feel happy" may be an item in a depression scale). If the client rated that item as "seldom," then that item would indicate some degree of depression for that client. The benefit of scales is that they use multiple items that enhance *reliability* (consistency) and *validity* (accuracy). The client's level of depression is not gauged on their response to one item, but many items. In addition, the use of a scale improves the likelihood that practitioners will not forget to address key items, such as one that measures the frequency or intensity of suicidal thoughts. In this way, the adjunctive use of a scale improves the consistency and accuracy of assessments by indicating client responses to potentially high-risk behaviors.

Multidimensional scales share the same qualities as unidimensional scales, except that they measure multiple aspects of a problem. As with unidimensional scales, they are designed and tested to optimize reliability and validity but are used to measure more complex problems. A scale that measures quality of life, for example, may use five items to measure each of the following: their satisfaction with their living situation, health, psychological well-being, relationships, spirituality, and work. For ten domains of living, a total of fifty items may be used (five for each). Each domain can be scored individually to measure a specific domain (e.g., family satisfaction), and an overall Global Life Satisfaction score might be used by combining all subscale measures. In addition to several quality-of-life scales, multidimensional scales have been designed to measure psychiatric symptoms, addiction severity, posttraumatic stress, childhood disorders, and many other areas relevant to social work practice.

Practitioners may decide to use only one type of measurement, or may use a combination of measures. The selection of instruments may vary from client to client, or a program may use one uniform instrument package for routine client assessment, during the intervention and at termination in order to conduct evaluation of a program. Some instruments are proprietary, that is, they can only be used with the permission of the scale creator (often for a fee), but there is a growing array of scales that are readily available in the public domain for no cost. Practitioners can locate these fairly easily since they are often compiled in reference books in the library or can be found on various websites. Practitioners should also place a high value on *utility* (practical use) of the scale. In addition to being reliable and valid, they should also be relatively brief so they can be incorporated into routine assessment/evaluation without placing undue demand on the client or on agency staff.

Assessment, overall, is both a qualitative and quantitative effort. A competent MFS assessment must be thorough, grounded in current human behavior research, describe the unique aspects of the client's day-to-day experiences, and attempt to understand the client's problems and strengths within their broader social system. Scales should be used to augment the assessment and lay a foundation for evaluation. Summarizing assessment data succinctly is a challenge, and linking this information to the overall service plan requires further knowledge regarding effective practices, the subject to which we now turn.

Intervention

Defining Effective Interventions

Interventions are combinations of skills applied by practitioners, their clients, and, often, collateral participants (e.g., family members, teachers, etc.) implemented for the purpose of reducing symptoms, resolving problems, enhancing adaptive capabilities, and improving the overall psychosocial well-being of the client. Interventions include skills and combinations of skills that help clients achieve important intervention goals (e.g., lower depression, enhance couple's communication, increase prosocial behavior in behaviorally disordered children, improve school performance, reduce symptoms of psychosis, etc.). In later chapters, practice skills and their application to specific psychosocial problems and psychiatric disorders will be examined in greater detail.

In brief, hundreds of studies by clinician-researchers over the past few decades have resulted in a body of practice knowledge now known as evidence-based practices (Barlow, 2008; Lambert & Bergin, 1994; O'Hare, 2015; Orlinsky, Grawe, & Parks, 1994; Orlinsky & Howard, 1986). These practices are largely comprised of a common set of practice skills that will be examined in greater detail in later chapters:

- *Supportive/facilitative skills:* These include those efforts to engage clients in a therapeutic relationship, enhance motivation, and facilitate client change.

- *Therapeutic coping skills:* These are predominantly cognitive-behavioral techniques shown to effectively help clients to enhance their understanding of and change troubling thoughts, feelings, and behaviors in order to reduce problems and enhance adaptive (coping) skills.
- *Case management skills:* These are efforts that help clients deal with social and environmental barriers, gain access to needed resources, enhance social supports, and coordinate the efforts of various service providers.

As with other professional activities, beginning or basic interventions may be composed of one or two key skills to address mild to moderate problems, whereas more complex and advanced interventions are likely to be made up of combinations of skills that have been shown to be effective in controlled practice research. *Thus, the emphasis in this text is on learning those basic or essential skills that alone or in eclectic combinations provide the best chance of ameliorating a client's psychosocial distress and improving their problem-solving and coping abilities over time.* Combinations of skills shown in controlled practice research to be effective with moderate to severe psychosocial problems and disorders are now referred to as *evidence-based practices* (Barlow, 2008; Goodheart, Kazdin, & Sternberg, 2006; Nathan & Gorman, 2007; O'Hare, 2015; Stout & Hayes, 2005; Thyer, 2004).

Supportive, coping, and case management skills are applied in unique ways depending on the client's problems, challenges, and needs. For example, the application of empathic listening (a supportive skill) with a seriously thought-disordered person will be quite different than when used with a person experiencing a normal but difficult grief reaction. Using role play, problem solving, or graduated exposure (therapeutic coping skills) to help a young man reduce obsessive-compulsive rituals is quite different than using the same techniques to help a couple improve their communication and parenting skills. Coordinating the efforts of several providers and advocating for a client (case management skills) take on a unique character whether one is working on a child-abuse case or attempting to help a severely disabled elderly person. Essential skills in social work practice share a common research and practice base but take on unique application depending on the client's problems and needs. *Defining a coherent set of skills that can be utilized individually and in combination is essential for teaching, implementing, supervising, evaluating, and researching social work interventions.*

Optimally Combining Essential Skills

Although essential practice skills can be used individually for discrete problems, they are often combined as evidence-based practices. For example, after employing supportive and facilitative skills to engage a troubled couple who have been fighting bitterly and are considering divorce, the practitioner may use both supportive and therapeutic coping skills: help them examine their interactions with each other in a more calm and less reactive manner; have them take turns listening carefully to each other without interrupting; and ask them to show that they can identify one another's needs, communicate their own thoughts and feelings in a more sensitive manner, and work on sharing household and other responsibilities. Case management activities may not be required at all in such a case. On the other hand, for a young mentally ill mother who recently had her two children removed from her home under suspicion of neglect, using supportive and facilitative skills may be more challenging given the client's suspicions and other cognitive distortions related to her illness. Therapeutic coping skills might include psycho-education about her illness, the importance of taking medication to ameliorate her symptoms, coaching her in better parenting skills, and teaching stress management skills to help her deal better with trauma-related anxiety and depression. Case management skills would also likely be required to help the client maintain her benefits and access to mental health care, to coordinate services, help her manage her money, and to advocate for her with the courts and child welfare department. Most, if not all, cases will employ some combination of essential supportive, coping, and case management skills, but these skills will be applied in very different ways depending on the individual challenges facing the client. How these skills are combined and implemented is guided by both clinical outcome research and the use of practitioner judgment.

However, to simply recommend "tailoring the treatment to client needs" means little if there are no empirical practice guidelines to plan the intervention. Although practice typically includes some "trial and error" efforts, relying exclusively on "practice wisdom" or "creativity" is not sufficient for professional social work practice. Evidence-based practice guidelines can help practitioners reduce some of the guesswork in treatment planning with clients who are struggling with a wide array of problems from major mental illnesses, to addictions, eating disorders, anxiety, traumatic reactions, depression, and emotional and behavioral problems in children, among other problems. EBPs are made up of varying configurations of essential skills. These configurations of skills have been packaged and often "manualized" to provide practitioners with research-supported intervention guidelines to better serve their clients. However, before practitioners can effectively learn evidence-based practices, they must master the essential supportive, cognitive-behavioral coping, and case management skills explained within the chapters of this text. The Psychosocial Intervention Scale will be described at the end of this chapter to help practitioners evaluate their own use of essential social work practice skills and consider how to combine them to help different clients.

Applying Essential Skills to Family Interventions

The term *treatment modality* refers primarily to the configuration and relationship of clients who participate in the intervention. The traditional service modalities are individual, couple, family, and group work. Other than designating the number and relationship of the participants, it should be understood that these modalities do not refer to any particular practice theory or any specific intervention approach. For example, as noted earlier, the term "family therapy" refers to interventions conducted with some or all members of a family. There are many different forms of family therapy, and the skills applied are likely to vary considerably depending on theoretical assumptions and the specific intervention methods used. Group therapy refers to working with the members of a group of persons who are generally not related in a familial way to one another (unless it is a couple's group or family group intervention). Group therapies can be unstructured or structured, directive or non-directive, psycho-educational or therapeutic, psychodynamic, behavioral, gestalt, and so on. Regardless of modality, the interventions utilized are comprised of some combination of essential skills. *Supportive, coping, and case management skills are applied across all modalities, and how those skills are combined determines whether the intervention is likely to be effective.*

Despite differences across major schools of family therapy, they do share a number of common assumptions and intervention methods (Becvar & Becvar, 2009; Nichols & Schwartz, 2006). Family therapies are characterized by recognizing family hierarchies, structure and alliances, patterns of interaction and communication, the role of the identified client (i.e., the member that others in the family identify as the "problem"), and the significance of generational influences. However, these aspects of family therapy apply more to ongoing assessment of family functioning than they do to the intervention skills utilized. With regard to intervention, supportive skills apply to family therapies in the following way:

- Joining with the family (which is another name for engagement and developing a working alliance with some or all family members)
- Developing intervention goals and role expectations of both practitioner and family members
- Utilizing accurate and empathic listening with all members
- Demonstrating respect and positive regard for all members
- Using motivational interviewing methods (e.g., not arguing, rolling with the resistance)

Coping skills include:

- Psycho-education
- Encouraging and modeling constructive communication
- Exploring and gently challenging dysfunctional beliefs family members have about themselves, one another, or other extended family members
- Using stress management techniques with some or all family members
- Helping family members express intense feelings in more constructive ways
- Role modeling, rehearsing, and practicing better communication
- Using problem-solving strategies and planning to carry out specific tasks
- Demonstrating how to apply reinforcement between partners (e.g., increase caring behaviors) as well as between parents and their children (i.e., improved parenting skills)
- Engaging in self-monitoring so family members can anticipate problems, apply what they have learned to interrupt problems, and evaluate their progress over time

More specifically, when helping parents to deal with emotionally and behaviorally troubled children and adolescents, coping skills can be adapted accordingly:

- Teaching basic behavioral parenting skills (e.g., demonstrating nurturance through caring behaviors and play, positive disciplining skills through clear directives, and balancing rewards for prosocial behaviors and mild sanctions for unacceptable behaviors)
- Using modeling and role play to demonstrate to a child how the parent wants things done (e.g., cleaning up the room, getting settled down to study, playing with siblings)

- Demonstrating how to monitor a child's progress and shape their behavior by stringing together a series of rewards and sanctions to reach long-term goals

Social workers should learn to apply therapeutic coping skills at all levels (i.e., individual, couple, and family). Sometimes these skills can be applied one level at a time, other times concurrently. For example, in a case where a child has a serious behavioral disorder that is exacerbated by parental conflict, the intervention may have to address each level in turn. First, the couple may have to learn to communicate better and deal with some of their own interpersonal problems as partners (e.g., money concerns, alcohol abuse, infidelity). Second, the social worker may have to focus on helping them collaborate on improving their parenting skills (e.g., setting limits, rewarding and sanctioning behaviors consistently instead of undermining each other). Third, the social worker may then help the child individually to cope more effectively with some of their emotional distress (e.g., learning to accurately identify feelings, finding more constructive ways to cope with their anger). Last, the social worker may also apply some of these core skills (e.g., communication, psycho-education) when dealing with the larger social system. However, these skills are likely to be combined with case management skills as in the following manner:

- Networking and coordinating interventions with the school administration, school psychologist, and classroom teacher in order to generalize the child's improvements from home to the school
- Helping parents and teachers to work from "the same page" to help the child maintain behavioral and academic improvements
- Advocating for a parent's rights in court-ordered cases
- Helping a family bolster social and instrumental supports to reduce isolation, provide for basic financial needs, and ensure eligibility for other benefits if available (e.g., health insurance for children)

Although essential supportive, therapeutic, and case management skills apply as readily to family interventions as they do individual cases, the application of them can be more challenging when working with a seriously troubled family.

Applying Essential Skills to Group Work

Working with groups in social work practice takes different forms. Perhaps the more common approaches include traditional psychotherapeutic interventions (Yalom, 2005) and behaviorally oriented groups for working with

clients who are experiencing other specific problems or disorders (e.g., Bieling, McCabe, & Antony, 2006). Groups are also used for early intervention
programs, for example, with youth at risk for substance use or other high-
risk behaviors. Traditional psychotherapeutic groups tend to emphasize
personal disclosure, expression of feelings, and address the way group
members interact with the practitioner and each other to engender insight
and improved relationship skills. Although such groups are not well researched, it is reasonable to assume that some clients are likely to benefit
from these experiences. The essential skills applied would include supportive skills (e.g., empathic listening, encouraging expression of feelings), coping skills (e.g., examining conflicted thoughts and feelings regarding
relationship problems, improving communication skills), and, possibly,
case management skills (e.g., referral for medication).

Psycho-education groups are commonly used for a wide range of purposes. Some examples might include: high school students learning to cope
effectively with pressures to have sex and use alcohol and other drugs;
parents learning to cope more effectively with their mentally ill young
adult children; teaching young, single moms how to balance the duties of
motherhood while pursuing their education; and helping the elderly cope
with depression and loneliness. Although psycho-education groups rely primarily on didactic methods, the use of supportive skills is critical. Practitioners still need to connect with and motivate their "audience," listen
carefully to their concerns, and communicate positive regard, respect,
empathy, and genuineness. Psycho-education is also a key therapeutic coping skill. Providing information is a rather direct way to alter cognitions
(i.e., change beliefs, expectations, and attributions). Young adult group
members attending a psycho-educational group regarding sexual behavior
and the use of alcohol and other drugs are often poorly informed about the
risks associated with date rape, transmission of infectious diseases, and
what is required to prevent pregnancy. Prevention studies have shown that
making young people aware of accurate peer drinking "norms" (i.e., how
much their peer group actually drinks) can help participants be more circumspect about their own alcohol consumption. Although providing information alone is often insufficient to dissuade people from engaging in
high-risk behaviors, evidence suggests it is one essential component.

Cognitive-behavioral groups are often used with clients who demonstrate more serious difficulties. These problems include co-occurring mental illness and substance abuse, substance abuse groups with convicts who
have been released from prison, domestic violence (e.g., anger management) groups for offenders, conduct disordered adolescents, young women
diagnosed with eating disorders, or group work with persons diagnosed

with borderline personality disorder. CBT groups also emphasize the application of essential supportive skills to develop a working relationship with the clients, facilitate communication, and enhance motivation. However, CBT groups are also likely to place a heavy emphasis on a wide array of coping skills: challenging dysfunctional cognitions (e.g., regarding the use of substances or use of violence to cope with conflict); practicing self-regulation regarding impulses connected to intense emotions (e.g., self-mutilation, domestic violence, binge-purging by the bulimic client); learning behavioral coping skills through role play and rehearsal (e.g., saying "no thanks" to an offer of alcohol or other drugs, seeking social supports when the impulse to strike out in anger is provoked); using communication and problem-solving skills to improve relationships; and learning stress management skills to enhance an overall healthier lifestyle. In working with clients who experience more serious problems such as these, case management skills are also likely to be utilized extensively for coordinating services among providers, hospitalizing clients in crisis, acting as liaison for court-ordered interventions, advocating for a mentally ill client, and enhancing social and instrumental supports when needed.

Before becoming proficient at using more advanced family and group interventions, practitioners must first master essential supportive, coping, and case management skills. Once these "building blocks" of effective interventions are mastered, practitioners can then learn and effectively implement research-based combinations of these skills in the form of evidence-based practices with individuals, couples, families, and groups.

Evaluation

Evaluating One's Own Practice

Asserting that one claims to use essential skills or implement them in some combination as an evidence-based practice does not guarantee intervention success. The third major component of social work practice is *evaluating one's own practice* (Bloom, Fischer, & Orme, 2009; Siegel, 1984). There are various ways to do this. The most feasible way to evaluate a single case (i.e., individual, couple, or family) is to define and measure one or more key problems during the initial assessment phase, define the actual intervention employed, and monitor changes in those measures periodically over the course of the intervention and, again, at termination. This approach is sometimes referred to as a passive-observational or naturalistic approach to evaluation because no special controls are employed that might otherwise interfere with the usual delivery of services. No artificial baseline periods are planned, no comparison cases are used, and no treatment conditions are altered in a planned manner. This approach can be implemented by using some simple indexes discussed earlier in this chapter or by supplementing them with one or more validated scales. In some agencies, scales now are readily incorporated into the routine clinical documentation required of practitioners (e.g., assessments, treatment plans, and progress notes). Changes over time (e.g., reduced depression in an elderly man, improved school performance in a child, more loving behavior between partners) indicate positive changes in the client. What cannot be readily deduced by this improvement is whether the intervention was responsible for the change. For naturalistic single-subject designs, one simply cannot draw such conclusions with a high degree of confidence since people often get better or worse for reasons other than the effects of treatment. Nevertheless, if the practitioner implemented an evidence-based practice that was familiar, an intervention was used that had a reasonable likelihood of helping the client because it had previously been shown to be effective in controlled research trials with many clients experiencing similar problems.

Other, more complex, single-case designs have been discussed at length in the literature on "evaluating one's own practice," but these approaches have little practical application for everyday social work interventions. These designs involve controlling the implementation of the intervention in stages or making other predetermined changes to the intervention at various intervals to see if variations of the intervention affect client outcomes. They are, in fact, single-subject controlled experiments that lend themselves to clinical research, not routine practice (Kazdin, 1978, 1998; O'Hare, 2015). These approaches are called controlled single case experimental designs, and will be discussed in greater depth in Chapter 4.

It is also possible to use naturalistic evaluation strategies with large numbers of clients in order to evaluate a whole program or a smaller program within a larger agency (e.g., a battered women's group within a mental health agency). Those participating in the program might record their levels of distress using valid scales during the assessment phase (e.g., to measure depression, anxiety, substance use, self-esteem, etc.) and repeat these measures at various intervals during the intervention (e.g., monthly) and at termination. These data can then be used to evaluate the improvement in each client individually and, when data from many clients are aggregated, also provide some measure of improvement for the group or program as a whole. Although, as with the single-subject design, one cannot be certain that the improvements were a result of the program (since no control or comparison group was used), one can place more confidence in the results if large numbers of clients improve and if past research findings indicate strongly that persons with similar problems would probably not have improved or improved as quickly without intervention. Naturalistic program evaluation will also be discussed in more detail in Chapter 4.

Evaluation data from a single client, group of clients, or a whole program do not "prove" that the interventions employed are the best or even that they are primarily responsible for client improvement. However, if done consistently well, evaluation can provide a strong indication that practices are being implemented effectively both at the individual and program level. These data can then be used to identify strong or weaker points in the program and, if analyzed thoughtfully, can provide a basis for program improvement through purposeful supervision and staff training. Many agencies now have quality assurance programs that utilize evaluation methods to improve services to clients.

Monitoring and Evaluating the Use of Essential Intervention Skills: The Psychosocial Intervention Scale (PSIS)

The Psychosocial Intervention Scale (PSIS) (a modified version of the Practice Skills Inventory; O'Hare & Collins, 1997; O'Hare & Geertsma, 2013; O'Hare, Tran, & Collins, 2002) is a self-evaluation practice tool designed to help social workers with the following: (1) become familiar with essential practice skills; (2) evaluate the use of these skills on a case-by-case and session-by-session basis; (3) examine how one might combine various practice skills to form broader intervention strategies; (4) monitor how the use of different practice skills changes over time with an individual client, couple, family, or group; (5) examine how practitioners utilize different combinations of skills depending on the primary problems presented by their client; and (6) compare the combinations of skills used with existing manualized evidence-based practice guidelines. Used in this manner, the PSIS is a self-teaching and evaluation tool designed to help social workers critically examine and better understand how and why they select different combinations of supportive, therapeutic, and case management skills depending on clients' needs.

For example, let's say a social worker is providing an intervention for a seriously mentally ill person with a co-occurring substance abuse problem. The outcome research suggests that developing a good working alliance, using a motivational approach, enhancing coping skills, and encouraging social supports (e.g., a dual diagnosis group) would constitute a promising approach. However, if the practitioner indicates on the PSIS that they are focusing primarily on discussing the client's past relationships and offering interpretations to provide insight into why they abuse alcohol, these data would indicate an approach that is not supported by the current outcome research. The social worker's supervisor might then recommend some readings or additional training for the practitioner, so they can become familiar with state-of-the-art practices.

The PSIS was developed in several research studies to measure supportive, coping, and case management skills. To make the original Practice Skills Inventory more comprehensive and useful for practitioners, new items were added to reflect skills utilized in recently developed EBPs.

The individual items of the PSIS were designed to be somewhat general, so the scale could have broad application to social work service settings and different client problems. For each item, practitioners should specify in their own words (in the lines under each item) how that skill category is being specifically applied to the client's problem, and then rate the emphasis that they place on the use of that particular skill as part of the overall intervention plan. For example, under item #20, a practitioner might specify that they will help a shy adolescent practice (first, through role play with the therapist) how to start up and maintain a friendly conversation with someone they want to get to know in school. That would be a specific and unique application of that particular skill. Key questions to consider when using the PSIS are as follows: Am I using skills that reflect "best practices" for this particular problem area? How am I modifying this particular evidence-based practice to suit this specific client? How is the client responding to the intervention overall? Practitioners and their supervisors can then compare the profile of specific skills used to those recommended in the practice outcome research. A copy of the PSIS is available in Appendix A.

Pulling It All Together: The Comprehensive Service Plan

Together, documenting the completed assessment, describing and justifying the proposed intervention methods to be used, and stipulating the indicators and scales to be used in the evaluation constitute the Comprehensive Service Plan (CSP) (see Appendix B). Most social workers and agencies are required to document their services to clients. This documentation takes many forms and is far from standardized. The format of assessment and intervention plans varies by program, funding source, accreditation guidelines, and by state and federal regulatory requirements. However, some basic assumptions are suggested here. First, documentation is required, necessary, and important for a variety of contractual, legal, risk management, clinical, and ethical reasons. Second, although service documentation is often (and sometimes justifiably) seen as a time-consuming and expensive nuisance, this author maintains that documentation can enhance social work practice in a number of ways: when conceptually well designed, service-plan documentation can improve the validity (i.e., accuracy, thoroughness) and reliability (i.e., consistency) of assessment, clarify intervention objectives, goals, and methods used, and describe the monitoring and evaluation plan. Third, a well-conducted assessment, intervention, and evaluation plan (the CSP) is essential for guiding individual service for clients, and when data from individual service plans are aggregated, they can provide a sound basis for program evaluation. In general, these processes are sometimes referred to as *developing a contract* with the client. This contract is closely tied to the concepts of informed consent and confidentiality, important ethical and legal matters discussed in Chapter 3.

The CSP also includes items from the Psychosocial Well-Being Scale (PSWS) (O'Hare et al. 2003; O'Hare et al. 2002). These items are used to quantitatively rate each area of the MFS assessment. The adjunctive use of quantitative ratings as part of assessment is becoming more common in human-service agencies in response to increasing demands for routine evaluation from both private and public funders. Although qualitative data are critical for evaluating individual client progress, qualitative data cannot be aggregated (summed up and averaged) in any practical way for reporting to private, state, or federal agencies. Quantitative data can be used to monitor individual treatment outcomes and be aggregated for program evaluation. Beginning practitioners should make a thoughtful qualitative assessment first, and then based on all available information about the client, use the PSWS to rate how well or how impaired the client is in that particular area of well-being. Over time, if the client progresses, improvement will be reflected in higher ratings for individual domains and overall psychosocial well-being. Other scales and indexes should be used to supplement the PSWS based on agency needs and the types of problems for which social workers provide interventions. Many reliable and valid instruments are now available in the public domain and can be readily obtained over the Internet. A copy of the PSWS as well as other useful instruments can be examined in *Evidence-Based Practices for Social Workers* (O'Hare, 2005).

After collecting, analyzing, and discussing the information collected from the client, family members, consultants, and others, practitioners often end up with a lot of data. Reducing this information to a concise and useful Comprehensive Service Plan is an essential social work skill, and becoming proficient at it takes practice. After a full assessment, the practitioner must then collaborate with the client on the development of a formal intervention plan. Under the column entitled "Problems" in the CSP summary, the practitioner should very briefly describe those difficulties that are likely to be addressed as part of the intervention. Some efforts should be made to create a problem hierarchy. Under the "Goals" column, practitioners should briefly state what the agreed upon outcomes should be for each problem. "Objectives" are "stepping stones" toward each goal. Objectives are the linchpin of interventions because these are often activities that clients carry out as part of their intervention in order to move closer to their goals (thus, objectives and interventions can sometimes overlap). For example, an objective toward a goal of stopping illegal drug use might be "Attend two Narcotics Anonymous meetings this week." Or an objective for a socially anxious adolescent girl might be "Strike up a conversation with that cute boy in the cafeteria at least once this coming week." Accomplishing this objective might bring the young adolescent a step closer to her goal of being more involved socially, but it is also part of a formal intervention (practicing her social skills). Under the "Intervention" section, the practitioner should describe both the formal title of the intervention (e.g., Interpersonal Psychotherapy) as well as describe specifics (e.g., to meet once weekly). Finally, under "Assessment/Evaluation," practitioners should note any indexes or formal scales they are using to help track client progress and evaluate the effects of the intervention. They should also describe who will collect the data and at what intervals. In Chapters 8 through 12, brief case study illustrations with completed Comprehensive Service Plans will be included to help students learn how to develop their own service plans with the outline in Appendix B.

CHAPTER TWO

The Relationship Between Research and Practice

GENERALLY, SOCIAL WORKERS tend to be compassionate people who want to help others in distress, help them learn to cope better with life's challenges, and help them improve their quality of life. Compassion, curiosity, the capacity to form helping relationships, the ability to help others solve problems and cope, and the initiative to coordinate multiple services are essential characteristics of the effective social worker. However, we also know that compassion and good intentions are not enough to qualify us as professional practitioners. Social workers also need to command up-to-date knowledge regarding the problems they treat, be able to select intervention methods that are supported by a body of research evidence, implement those interventions with good judgment, and, as best we can, evaluate our efforts. In order to utilize the existing professional knowledge base effectively, it is essential that social workers understand how to utilize research findings and employ critical thinking skills to conduct competent assessments, sound intervention planning, and meaningful evaluation. Social workers who think critically use sound reasoning supported by relevant research evidence to make the best judgments they can when assessing client difficulties, planning interventions, and evaluating outcomes.

Based on many years of experience teaching both social work research and practice courses, I have noticed (through my own qualitative research) that students generally see "practice" as quite separate from "research." "Practice courses" are generally sought out with enthusiasm and research courses are taken as a bitter pill only because students are mandated to do so. This impression is a bit disturbing, but reflects the long tradition in social work education of portraying practice knowledge as resulting almost exclusively from "practice wisdom," that is, theory-informed experience dispensed by authoritative practitioners. Although such clinical observations often plant the seed for future developments in theory and practice, it is now understood that theories and interventions have to be tested and supported by a body of research. In order to become knowledgeable about contemporary theories and practices, practitioners must become better consumers of research (not, necessarily, researchers themselves) in order to command up-to-date knowledge of their clients' problems and practices that are likely to obtain optimal results.

Human behavior theories and practice models are now understood to be valuable to the extent that they are based on critically reviewed research findings. Within the context of the helping professions, the contemporary human behavior sciences address two main questions: (1) Why do people develop and behave as they do? and (2) What psychosocial interventions are effective at improving the individual and collective human condition? The first question is predominantly addressed by human behavior research in the form of cross-sectional and longitudinal surveys that are used to test human behavior theories. For example, whether child abuse and neglect are risk factors for future problems is a question that drives hundreds of related research questions and is a major focus of modern research efforts. The second question is addressed primarily through controlled practice research. For example, whether psycho-education and behavioral family therapy with case management can reduce the long-term effects of child abuse and neglect is a question about intervention effectiveness (not the causes or effects of child abuse). Much research continues in this area as well. However, although these two questions are related by theme, they are quite different (i.e., causes of human problems vs. how to ameliorate them), and research efforts regarding these questions follow two separate but related paths. The sequence of developing questions about human problems and interventions is illustrated in Figure 3.

Addressing these two types of questions follows a similar pattern. Practitioners and researchers (and often, practitioner-researchers) pose questions about the nature of a problem or a type of intervention. This new "theory" or "intervention method" then must be well defined and tested in a series of studies. Lastly, whether the evidence resulting from these research processes actually supports the theory or this new form of practice is determined by the findings of these studies and the methodological quality of those studies. Researchers and research-practitioners who engage in this process conduct these studies in the relatively transparent world of blind peer review, and, over time, the collective results of a series of related studies emerge in the published scientific journals. Ultimately, the data tell the story, or as it may also be put: the chips are allowed to fall where they

FIGURE 3. DEVELOPING AND TESTING THEORIES AND PRACTICE MODELS

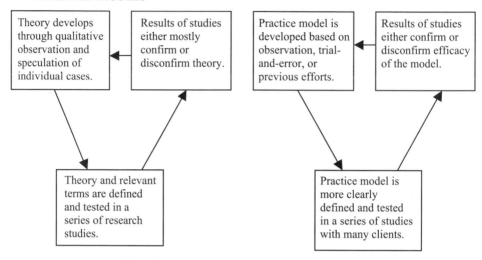

may. Theories and practices should live or die by the quality of the evidence that supports them.

Now, this process is not perfect nor does it happen overnight. Fortunately, there already exists a large body of theory-driven human behavior research findings that supports social work assessment in many areas of practice. Similarly, there is a very large and growing body of controlled research findings on effective practice (i.e., evidence-based practices) to provide solid guidelines for treatment planning. Although there is a long way to go on both fronts (which will keep researchers busy for a long time), the understanding is "you go with what you've got." Translation: practitioners are ethically obliged to use the existing research knowledge base as their guide and fill in the gaps with informed judgment as best they can.

The current chapter has two purposes: (1) to provide a brief overview of how human behavior and practice research can inform our work as practitioners and (2) to discuss how critical thinking skills can help improve our ability to implement the current knowledge base effectively. *Having both a sound knowledge base and knowing how to use it* are two closely linked qualities of competent helping professionals. These processes are illustrated in Figure 4.

The diagram illustrates the iterative process of accessing and using knowledge (i.e., research findings) regarding valid assessment and effective

FIGURE 4. USING RESEARCH FINDINGS TO SUPPORT PRACTICE

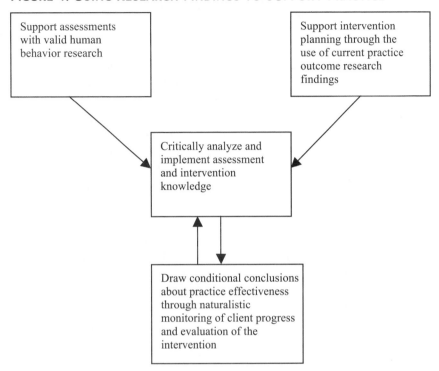

intervention, and critically evaluating the implementation of that knowledge. Information about the client, which we might have acquired directly from the client and others who know the client, is usually not self-explanatory. In other words, these "raw data" do not automatically explain the client's difficulties nor do they readily determine what the best course of intervention may be. In a similar vein, simply being a good "critical thinker" is of little use to the practitioner if he does not have the knowledge or skills to conduct informed assessments or select effective interventions. Thus, both knowledge and clear critical thinking are necessary for effective practice. *This combination of being knowledgeable about people's problems and effective interventions and knowing how to apply that knowledge defines the social worker who is an informed critical thinker.* Lastly, when knowledge is applied in real practice, the feedback from clients will further inform our ongoing assessment and give us some indication as to whether the intervention is working. Thus, information gained by observing and listening to the client and important collaterals in the client's life will further shape the decision-making process during the course of the intervention.

But these "course corrections" will also be guided by expertise, not mere instinct, intuition, or uninformed speculation.

The Foundation of Valid Assessment: Human Behavior in the Social Environment

There are essentially two sources of knowledge regarding client problems: (1) the unique narrative experience of the client and (2) knowledge of human behavior that is derived from theory-driven research. The first approach emphasizes *inductive reasoning.* The second emphasizes *deductive reasoning.* These are complementary forms of critical thinking. Relying solely on the client's narrative to inform the assessment without a grasp of the relevant research (e.g., mental illness, substance abuse, effects of trauma) will not result in an informed and valid assessment. Conversely, relying solely on research without a keen understanding of the client's unique experience will not provide for a sound assessment either. Both sources of information are essential for planning an intervention. Understanding the client's personal narrative provides a partial but essential understanding of cognitive, emotional, behavioral, and situational factors that are unique to that client. Collaterals (e.g., significant others) also provide unique observations from their various points-of-view. (Practitioners who work with couples often get startlingly different accounts of the same event from each partner. One often wonders if they are living in the same house!)

The client's narrative is usually insufficient as a basis for assessment because the meaning and significance of the client's experience might indicate psychosocial dysfunction about which they are unaware, minimize, or do not understand. For example, should a client claim to be an omnipotent superhero who can fly without the aid of aircraft, the practitioner would have to be knowledgeable about serious mental illnesses or mind-altering substances in order to understand the significance of such a claim. If another client is becoming gradually withdrawn, gives up activities they formerly enjoyed, and begins expressing themes of hopelessness, a knowledgeable social worker would not merely empathize and "be in the moment" with the client, but would also understand these behaviors (well documented in the research) as indicators of suicide risk. Understanding the subjective experience of clients requires that practitioners be knowledgeable about human problems such as mental illness, childhood disorders, substance abuse, domestic violence, eating disorders, and other problems, and use this knowledge base to better understand the client's own unique life experience.

Social workers are confronted with a wide array of human behavior theories and practices. How do we, as practitioners, decide which theories of human behavior provide a valid basis for assessment, which interventions are most likely to be effective for a particular client? It is understood in the social and behavioral sciences that no theory is likely to be 100-percent accurate, and no psychosocial intervention is likely to be 100-percent effective. What researchers try to do is to understand what risk and resilience factors cause or mitigate human problems (e.g., causes of mental illness, addictions, eating disorders, etc.) and estimate which practice approach is likely to work best for a given type of problem. For example, although the exact causes of schizophrenia are not known, researchers are fairly certain that biological factors in the limbic system (part of the brain stem) and problems in the regulation of neurotransmitters account for some of the symptoms. Although no specific social stressor has been shown to cause schizophrenia, stress could exacerbate the illness and make it more difficult to treat. These explanations are now considered "more likely" or "less likely" than, say, attributing the cause of schizophrenia to the "schizophrenogenic mother" (i.e., the prevailing view for much of the twentieth century) or demonic possession (which continues to be a prevalent view in some cultures). Although science has yet to fully explain the causes of schizophrenia, practice researchers have demonstrated that some psychosocial interventions can greatly alleviate the suffering of those with major mental illnesses. As in medicine, one need not know everything about the causes of a problem in order to treat it effectively, and practitioners should not presume to know what theories are valid simply because they find them appealing. Thus, a good working definition for "knowledge" in the practice professions is not a guarantee of certainty, but a *measurable reduction in uncertainty*. Although this lack of certainty may be unsatisfying to some, standard social and behavioral science research methods are the best tools we have for testing out our theories and practices. And the better the research methods, the more confidence we can put in our knowledge base. Thus, how the quality of evidence regarding human behavior is judged leads us to this axiom:

The quality of evidence supporting a theory or intervention is only as good as the research methods that produced that evidence.

As noted earlier, many books on social work clinical practice continue to present theories uncritically. Because of this "choose what you like" approach to theory selection, a number of myths have been cultivated regarding the role of theory in social work practice. These myths include the following:

- There is really no way to judge the validity of human behavior theories, so one theory is just as good as any another.
- Theories are really just imaginary constructions of influential and powerful people who want to oppress others.
- Theories are simply metaphors about human behavior, so they do not reflect objective reality,
- Selection of a theory is really just a matter of personal value preferences.

These inaccurate representations of human behavior theory have led many students to adopt substandard approaches to assessment. Theories of human behavior and the attending research regarding serious problems such as major mental illnesses, substance abuse, trauma, anxiety disorders and depression, eating disorders, childhood emotional and behavioral disorders, domestic violence, and so forth are essential in formulating valid assessment procedures. Among behavioral and social scientists, it is well understood that such theories (i.e., models that attempt to explain the factors that cause human problems) *must be supported by a body of research evidence.* Social scientists now largely agree on a number of useful assumptions regarding human behavior theories:

- Human behavior sciences are interdisciplinary, meaning that there are no clear demarcations among anthropology, psychology, evolutionary biology, sociology, and so forth, and the knowledge derived from these various disciplines must be increasingly integrated and synthesized to achieve a more complete understanding of human behavior.
- Human behavior is complex and caused by a wide range of biological, psychological, environmental, cultural, and other social factors that include both risks and resiliencies and limitations and strengths that affect human development and adaptation over time.
- These biopsychosocial processes are moderated by a variety of individual person factors such as age, gender, race, ethnicity, and cultural background.

How Human Behavior Research Supports Assessment

In order for assessment to be valid, it must be informed by contemporary, theory-driven human behavior research. Human behavior research supports valid assessment in the following ways:

- It provides base rate estimates (i.e., incidence and prevalence) of specific disorders and problems in the community: for example, knowing that depression may run 20 percent or higher in the general population, schizophrenia about 1 percent, alcohol dependence 7 percent, and multiple personality perhaps 1 in 10,000 are all useful data and provide practitioners with realistic expectations regarding the prevalence and incidence of serious forms of psychopathology and other behaviors; epidemiology helps practitioners from being overly responsive to the emergence of mental health fads (e.g., a suddenly epidemic of multiple personality disorder).

- It provides rates of co-occurring problems: for example, we now know that children with conduct disorder have a very high likelihood (50% or more) of demonstrating key symptoms of ADHD as well, and that persons with serious mental illness have a 50 percent chance of experiencing a substance abuse problem within their lifetime. Knowledge of co-occurrence helps practitioners avoid the tunnel vision of diagnosis in their assessments or looking for singular causes for complex problems.

- Human behavior research identifies key risk and resiliency factors (both developmental and current) that are likely to contribute to the client's problems or predict recovery. These factors may be cognitive, physiological, familial, social, environmental, and cultural, among others. For example, there are a number of risk factors that increase the likelihood that a client will commit suicide. These include a sense of hopelessness, recent losses, and substance abuse, among others. Dealing with suicidal clients is not infrequent in social work practice. It behooves the astute practitioner to know what researchers know about risks for suicide attempts. Learning these risk factors the hard way (by experience alone) is risky to both client and practitioner (i.e., experience is *not* always the best teacher). We also know that children who are diagnosed as conduct disordered are *more likely* to become antisocial adults, but *most do not* become antisocial adults. Thus, knowing risk factor probabilities helps practitioners to avoid overestimating and underestimating risks and related problems when we conduct assessments.

- Human behavior research also provides estimates of the *relative strength* of risk and resiliency factors. Beyond just knowing *what* risk factors are relevant, research can also provide guidelines to gauge the *relative weight* of those risks compared to others. For example, genetic risk factor for schizophrenia (for a client with one parent with this disorder) is understood to be greater than any known psychosocial risk (e.g., familial stress). On the other hand, environmental stressors may play a relatively stronger role in depression. Practitioners who ignore the relative weight of risk factors are more likely to jump to conclusions about causation and develop incomplete or misinformed assessments and intervention plans.

- Human behavior research explains the multidimensional nature of client problems. Research on eating disorders, for example, helps us understand that young women with binge eating disorders experience distress in several modes: cognitive distortion about the way they see themselves physically, physiological problems (e.g., electrolyte imbalances) from repeated vomiting, and disordered behaviors with regard to eating habits and appetite regulation. Young women with eating disorders also seem to have more difficulties in interpersonal relationships. All these dimensions (among others) need to be addressed in a complete assessment.

- Human behavior research provides support for some theories and invalidates others. Research has dramatically changed the way some problems have been conceptualized. For example, theories regarding the etiology (cause) of panic disorder have moved from assumptions about early parenting habits (e.g., abandonment fears in the infant/toddler) to biological causes that may be triggered and reinforced by environmental stressors or other physiological factors (e.g., substance abuse).

- Human behavior research provides an empirical and theoretical foundation for instrument development. Scales that measure important aspects of human experience (e.g., depression, self-esteem, hope for recovery, self-efficacy in meeting challenges, childhood fears, etc.) must be well researched and validated before they can be used in assessment, evaluation, or research. The knowledge base that informs the development of these scales originates in human behavior research that incorporates the self-report of hundreds or thousands of people from all walks of life.

Human behavior theories evolve through the use of a variety of research designs and methods depending on the question at hand. No design is inherently "better" than another, but each design must be understood in terms of what it can and cannot logically demonstrate within a reasonable degree of confidence. *Qualitative research* typically draws on small samples of clients to obtain in-depth, highly detailed, and nuanced descriptions of client problems and intervention processes. These are good strategies for exploratory research and evaluation. Keeping an open mind to see "what comes of this" can often generate important and interesting questions. Yet qualitative research is not confirmatory, and conclusions from qualitative research are almost always tentative. *Cross-sectional surveys* can be used to obtain data from hundreds or thousands of clients as part of large representative samples in order to estimate the type and nature of human problems including mental illnesses, substance abuse, or general attitudes or opinions toward important social issues. *Longitudinal surveys* are used to look at how risk factors affect people over time. *Small-group experiments* can demonstrate how people behave under different circumstances when some important factor is introduced. Collectively, all research strategies help to fill in the complex picture regarding how biological, psychological, and social factors interact within and between people over time. Theories of human behavior in the social environment are validated by using all these methods to build a sound body of knowledge, but the weight of evidence is applied to designs that provide a stronger basis for making cause-effect inferences (i.e., longitudinal designs) and those that provide a basis for broad generalization of findings (i.e., cross-sectional designs with large samples).

Theory development and testing is critical to the development of valid psychosocial assessment for this reason:

A theory is only as good as the research evidence that supports it.

An accompanying corollary is also critical:

An assessment can only be as valid as the theory and relevant research that support it.

In summary, human behavior research provides the foundation for understanding our client's conditions and conducting valid assessments. All social and behavioral science research methods have their place in the seamless continuum of rational inquiry into human problems and adaptation. To be competent as practitioners, social workers *need not become researchers themselves, but need to cultivate a deep respect for human behavior research, and make every effort to keep up with research developments in their respective area of interest*: serious mental illnesses, substance abuse, child abuse and neglect, and so forth. Figure 5 illustrates the relationships among theory, research, and assessment.

How Practice Research Informs Social Work Interventions

Much of what has been said above regarding research applies equally to practice research and its implications for everyday practice. Interventions

FIGURE 5. THE RELATIONSHIPS AMONG THEORY, RESEARCH, AND ASSESSMENT

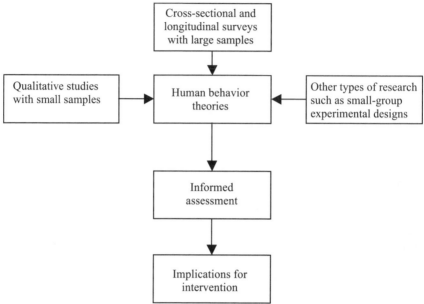

may be somewhat related to or even derived from a human behavior theory, but the actual practice methods employed must be tested in their own right. There are a number of designs utilized to test interventions, and they all have strengths and weaknesses. Some of these designs are "uncontrolled" (do not use comparison groups, participants are not "assigned" to treatment conditions) and are similar to the naturalistic evaluation designs discussed in Chapter 4. However, it is widely accepted by most professional bodies that randomized controlled designs (RCTs) provide the strongest evidence that an intervention will result in substantive positive benefits for the client. RCTs provide the current guidelines for evidence-based practices.

The rationale for using controlled practice designs is quite straightforward: one cannot determine whether an intervention is efficacious (i.e., can work under controlled conditions) unless the intervention is compared to a group that receives "no intervention" or to some alternative intervention under controlled conditions with clients who share similar problems in comparable degree of severity. By controlled conditions is meant that the clients are clearly defined with regard to their personal characteristics (e.g., gender, age, etc.), their problems are defined and measured with one or more valid instruments, the intervention is clearly defined, the practitioners are well trained in the methods to be employed, and meaningful client outcomes are defined. In other words, in a fair comparison, the intervention that results in the best outcomes in repeated trials is considered to be the most efficacious. Controlled trials are the most valid method practitioner-researchers have to determine (1) whether an intervention works at all (when compared with no intervention) and (2) whether one intervention results in better outcomes than another intervention. In short, RCTs are designed to answer the following questions: All things being more or less equal, does the intervention result in substantial improvements for clients compared to clients who receive no treatment? Does the intervention yield better outcomes that some alternative treatment? Although there are many variations of the controlled trial, the basic paradigm is as such:

FIGURE 6. THE RANDOMIZED CONTROLLED TRIAL PARADIGM

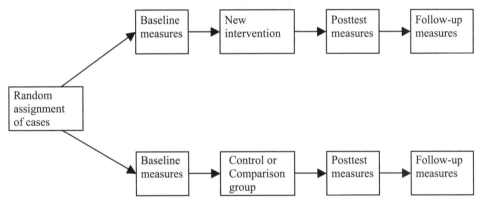

Clients with significant degrees of problems (e.g., depression, alcoholism) are typically recruited from the community or from clinic populations. These study participants should also meet some minimum criteria for the problem to be treated (e.g., usually diagnosis and/or a cut-off score on one or more scales). Random assignment is a key factor in controlled trials because it minimizes the chances that clients improve (or do not improve) based on their own treatment expectations or other characteristics that influence their decision to select one treatment condition over another. Clients in both the new (i.e., experimental) intervention and those in the control or comparison group are assessed by professionals (blind to treatment condition of the client) using the same battery of reliable and valid scales to measure the problems or treatment goals of interest. This method reduces bias. Often, measures are completed directly by clients as well, or some combination of client self-report and clinical judgment is utilized.

The interventions themselves are carried out by persons trained in each respective approach. Strictly speaking, clients in the "control" group initially do not receive any intervention but will receive intervention later on (often after a period of time on a "waiting list.") However, most studies of intervention use "comparison" groups, that is, alternative interventions, often ones that might otherwise be received in everyday community practice settings (i.e., "treatment as usual"). After treatment has been completed (say, after three months), both groups are again assessed utilizing the same (and sometimes additional) measures to see if they improved on several outcomes as a result of the intervention. Ideally, follow-up measures should be taken at six or twelve months (and sometimes up to five or six years) to see if the results of the interventions actually hold up over time.

The overall rationale for the RCT is to conduct as fair a test as possible of the experimental intervention compared with "no treatment" or some alternative intervention. Ethical standards regarding informed consent and confidentiality are very strict and highly scrutinized before and during these types of studies. After two or more replications of such studies demonstrating that an intervention is efficacious with clients who meet valid criteria for specific problems or disorders, the intervention is considered an "evidence-based practice" (EBP). To date, no other research methodology has been offered that provides as rigorous a test of what works, with whom, and under what circumstances. Authors of research reports of controlled trials should provide sufficient detail of all aspects of study design and procedures so that it can be replicated by other researchers.

Now, demonstrating that an intervention is *efficacious* under controlled circumstances such as the RCT is no guarantee that it will be implemented well in everyday social work treatment environments (i.e., be *effective*). Evaluation designs, discussed in Chapter 4, can be used to see that evidence-based practices are implemented effectively. From critical reviews of the outcome research on RCTs for a given problem (e.g., anxiety disorders, drugs, major depression), social workers can learn the following:

- What interventions have the most thorough track record of success for a particular client problem
- Whether there are comparable alternatives
- Whether the intervention is effective with certain groups of clients more so than other groups
- How much impact one should reasonably expect from the intervention

- The average length of time it should take to see substantial results
- Whether the whole intervention or parts of an intervention may be sufficient for most or all clients with a given condition
- How sustainable they should expect the results to be, likelihood of relapse, and whether follow-up "booster" visits might be needed

Of course, before utilizing an EBP, one should become familiar about the approach (there are many good practice texts available that define the methods in detail) and obtain training and supervision in the approach by someone who has the requisite qualifications. Hopefully, before too long, social work curricula will regularly offer EBPs as required coursework for second year practitioner-interns. Room can be readily made in social work curricula by eliminating courses that promote the use of practices that have little or no evidence to support them.

Informed Critical Thinking in Social Work Practice

Critical thinking skills are essential in order for social work practitioners to consistently and accurately apply the knowledge base of human behavior, conduct competent and valid assessments, select and implement effective practices, and evaluate one's own practice. What are critical thinking skills? These are cognitive skills that allow us to draw reasonable inferences and sensible conclusions from, sometimes, ambiguous observations and data (Gambrill, 1990; Nisbett & Ross, 1980; O'Hare, 2015; Tversky and Kahneman, 1974). Although social workers have often been advised to "trust their gut" or "go with their instincts," the hallmark of effective professionals is the judicious application of scientific evidence to inform their assessments and intervention planning. However, applying the social work knowledge base to individual situations is not easy and requires that social workers be aware of some inherent biases in human reasoning.

Cognitive researchers have identified a range of critical thinking errors that we all make from time to time. These critical-thinking errors apply to other professionals as well. There are four main tendencies toward errors in judgment about which practitioners should be aware: (1) the tendency to see explanations for human problems as relatively simple when, in fact, human behavior is generally complex; (2) the tendency to confuse correlation (or, even, coincidence) with causal relationships; (3) drawing firm conclusions from dramatic examples or the experiences of only a small number of people; and (4) the tendency to make arbitrary judgments about the significance of a problem or situation without the aid of valid benchmarks. Although these four biases represent overarching themes, more specific types of thinking errors and relevant examples will be discussed below along with how one can utilize relevant research to reduce these errors when conducting social work assessment, intervention, and evaluation.

Theories that stress one factor as the cause of psychosocial problems tend to be good examples of *oversimplification*. For example, when a practitioner concludes that a young man in his twenties who has a drinking problem, is depressed, and has only transitory relationships with women must have been neglected emotionally as a child (e.g., has "attachment issues"), this conclusion overlooks a host of other possible factors that may contribute to his less-than-happy young adult life. These include genetic and cultural factors that may have increased his tendency to drink excessively and be depressed; an abusive parent or guardian; early losses; having been overindulged by parents who did not care enough to hold him accountable for his actions or provide genuine rewards for real accomplishments; long-term struggles with learning disabilities; traumatic events such as military combat or having been victimized as the result of a crime; having had a head injury as a result of a motorcycle accident; other medical conditions. The list of possibilities is potentially quite long. At a minimum, practitioners should be open to conducting full and complete assessments (including input from other professionals) before drawing simplistic one-factor conclusions.

One of the more seductive thinking errors involves reasoning based on "post hoc" or "after the fact" reasoning. This tendency toward post hoc revisionism is referred to as *hindsight bias*. Let's say that a young woman, age eighteen, is admitted into a community mental health center. There may be some evidence that she has schizophrenia, but given that she is still young, the doctors are not sure. Nevertheless, she has been living on the street for some time and requires the additional psychosocial supports that a community support program can provide. During her intake, there is some evidence to suggest that she may have been involved in some minor crimes such as selling small amounts of marijuana, shoplifting, and occasionally getting into physical fights. One day, a female case manager visits her in a supported housing apartment. During the visit, the client gets angry at the case manager, picks up a kitchen knife, and stabs the worker. The caseworker dies.

The agency administration, lawyer, and practitioners meet the following day. Indeed, this is a tragic event and emotionally upsetting for those employed at the agency. Yet all members of the group have a different view of the situation, and feel the need to place responsibility on someone else since some are concerned about lawsuits or charges of criminal neglect. At one point, the director of the program yells at the person who did the initial intake and admitted the young client into the program: "You should have known that she was going to be dangerous and recommended a more secure setting. It's your fault!" Of course, the intake worker feels angry at being accused, guilty, and resentful about being unfairly singled out. She is erroneously and unfairly blamed for this tragic incident.

"Hindsight is 20-20" is an old expression. However, unless one has a crystal ball and can see into the future, no one would have bet that the young client would ever have murdered anyone. Predicting low frequency events when there is no history of similar behavior is at best a guessing game. If every client in a mental health center who had used illegal drugs or got into an occasional fight as an adolescent was confined on the grounds of being "too dangerous," mental health centers would be empty, and most clients would be locked up in secure facilities. In everyday practice, social workers don't have the luxury of projecting themselves into the future in order to make practice decisions. They have to conduct their assessments and make intervention recommendations based on the best evidence they have at the time. Those who present themselves as experts by reflecting on what "should have, could have" been done are engaging in hindsight bias, an argument that only provides the illusion of expertise. On the other hand, if the young woman had a documented history of violence and it was ignored by a worker who thought, "She seems nice. I don't think she'll do it again," then one would have a case for having ignored invaluable data beforehand (i.e., past violence is a good predictor of future violence).

Practitioners sometimes *confuse correlation with causation*. An elderly man, for example, comes to a clinic for depression. The social worker takes a thorough history and notes that the man has been drinking six to eight beers a day. The social worker concludes, therefore, that the man is drinking too much because he is depressed. Not so fast! All we know is that the man drinks too much *and* that he is depressed. These two things may certainly be correlated, but we would be premature to conclude that his drinking is the result of his depression. That is one possibility. The social worker's more experienced supervisor (who keeps up with the research on "dual diagnosis in the elderly") also considers the possibility that the man is depressed, in part, because he is drinking too much. The client also has a history of depression (even when he had not been drinking), has recently lost his wife, and has recently received troubling results from a medical examination along with other health problems. It is often tempting as a practitioner to infer causality between two co-occurring and temporally proximate behaviors. Although a causal connection is possible, other factors must be considered. How do we avoid jumping to conclusions in this manner? Conduct thorough assessments and use available research to support your assessment hypotheses.

Young practitioners are often told that "practice experience" will eventually guide their careers. This is only partly true. As noted earlier, experience based on unsubstantiated theories does not constitute expertise; experience must be informed by relevant research evidence. However, in the understandable desire to develop a feeling of professional competence, less experienced practitioners are often tempted to develop practice guidelines from exposure to only a few cases. As a result, inexperienced practitioners often cite *dramatic stereotypes* to support their assessments or selection of a treatment approach. The "reasoning" goes something like this: "I once worked with a client who had a certain problem and responded well to this treatment approach. Therefore, I think that this other client, who has a similar problem, will also benefit from the same approach." This "if it worked for him it will work for her" reasoning illustrates the overgeneralization from too small a sample, in this example, a single case. Practitioners should draw from a tested knowledge base regarding the assessment and intervention with a problem to support one's strategy. The client's unique input will also be an essential part of intervention planning. Although considering both the research and the individual client's views are no guarantee of success, this more informed method will yield better results in the long run than relying on one or a few dramatic or available case examples.

A similar problem in reasoning also involves overgeneralizing, not from too few cases, but from *readily accessible information* to inform assessments or select interventions. Experienced practitioners have all met colleagues who seem to consistently use only one theory to inform their assessments (e.g., all clients have either pre-Oedipal or Oedipal conditions) or only employ one form of intervention ("It's all about the relationship!"). These practitioners are relying almost exclusively only on what they know and have failed to broaden their repertoire of assessment and intervention knowledge. They have wedded themselves (and their clients) exclusively to one treatment model and use it on all their clients. This theory or intervention model is, for all intents and purposes, all the information they have readily available to them.

Another example of using only information that is readily available is to conduct assessments by relying exclusively on information provided by the client. Although this may be adequate for minor adjustment concerns for which the client has little reason to withhold or distort information, this approach is generally considered lacking since there are other sources of information that one may need to obtain an accurate and complete picture of what is going on with the client (e.g., other treatment records, family members, law enforcement, etc.). Erroneous assessments that rely on readily available information could also take the form of basing an assessment only on a client's record from another agency, relying on another practitioner's assessment (based on one cursory intake interview), or relying only on one family member's observations about a client's difficulties. Assessments should be grounded in both a relevant knowledge base about the client's problems as well as a careful process of data gathering from the client and other sources to provide a more complete picture of the client and their situation. Relying solely on easily accessible information, particularly when one is overworked in a busy agency, can lead to inaccurate assessments and sub-standard treatment recommendations.

One way to mislead oneself into thinking that one is usually correct in one's assessments, selection of interventions, or evaluations is to only consider information with which one agrees, that is, only consider information that supports one's chosen opinion and avoid observations or evidence that refutes one's beliefs or convictions. This form of reasoning bias is call *selective attention.* Given that new research findings relevant to assessment and intervention with mental illnesses, trauma, childhood disorders, eating disorders, domestic violence, and other serious problems emerge continually, it is surprising that so many experienced practitioners maintain the same assessment and intervention models for very long periods of time, sometimes for decades. If one only selectively attends to those theories and practices that one likes, then one never has to be troubled to examine new ways of engaging in social work practice.

Consider, for example, a female client diagnosed with panic disorder and agoraphobia. If she happens to be referred to a practitioner who believes that all anxiety disorders are caused primarily by childhood trauma (e.g., physical or sexual abuse), the client is likely to spend a lot of time answering questions about her childhood and any traumatic events that occurred. The time they spend together in sessions may be focused almost exclusively on what the client recalls or doesn't recall from early childhood. The practitioner may be so predisposed to the view that anxiety disorders can only be caused by early childhood trauma that, if the client insists that she can't remember these events, the practitioner concludes that this inability to remember is proof positive of child abuse! When thinking critically, practitioners should avoid the tendency to draw conclusions based solely due to familiarity with a theory and review the literature regarding risk factors associated with the particular problem. In the case of this young woman, possible explanations for her troubles include (1) depression and anxiety disorders running in the family, (2) exacerbation by the use/abuse of alcohol or illegal or prescription drugs, (3) panic being triggered by some more recent stressful or traumatic event (e.g., a sexual assault, sudden death of a loved one, an accident, etc.), (4) possible childhood physical or sexual abuse, or (5) some combination of the above or some other explanation. Critical-thinking practitioners keep an open mind regarding theories and stay abreast of the relevant research regarding human behavior theories and effective interventions.

Social work practitioners make judgments regarding the seriousness of human problems all the time. Gauging the severity of a client's problems and strengths is an essential step toward assessment and setting priorities for both programming and intervention planning. *Anchoring* refers to how we gauge the degree of a problem along a continuum (e.g., mild, moderate, severe or low, medium, high). These judgments often involve questions such as: Is spanking a culturally accepted form of discipline in a particular community, or is it a form of child abuse? Is my elderly client just thinking about suicide, or are they really going to try it? Is the consumption of five beers every day considered a moderate drinking problem, or is this client becoming dependent on alcohol? Does a client's witnessing of a fatal accident constitute a traumatic event, or was it just momentarily stressful? Is Johnny's habit of jumping out of his desk in class once a day a sign of ADHD, or is he just a bit rambunctious? Obviously, the way these questions are answered will determine, in part, the assessment and the intervention plan.

Practitioners are constantly making judgments about the seriousness or significance of client's thoughts, feelings, and behaviors. In a general sense, this practice of gauging the importance or severity of client difficulties is a rough form of measurement. The only question is: How consistently and accurately do practitioners measure the frequency, intensity, or duration of a client's behavior in order to judge its relative significance? Judging the relative importance of client problems (or, conversely, how well the client is doing) involves benchmarking frequency, intensity, or duration of a client's thoughts, feelings, or behaviors relative to (1) previous client experiences or (2) the experiences of others in the general population or similar client population. To judge whether a client is having only mild suicidal ideation or is at imminent risk of committing suicide is obviously an important question and involves informed clinical judgment. Anchoring requires base-rate knowledge (i.e., evidence from research as well as a thoughtful assessment of past client experiences) regarding the client's key problem.

One might think that judging suicidal intent is merely a matter of common sense. However, the benchmarking skill for that which constitutes "mild" or "serious" suicidal ideation can vary not only among social work practitioners, but within the same practitioner over time. For example, if one works in an agency that specializes in depression, suicidal ideation may be observed often in many clients. Over time, a practitioner may become somewhat desensitized to signs of suicide. After all, clients say things like "I can't go on anymore" or "I feel hopeless about the future" with a fair degree of frequency, yet most of the clients do not make serious suicide attempts. By contrast, a less experienced practitioner in a broader general out-patient clinic might overreact to every client utterance that suggests suicidal intent. A practitioner's anchoring point regarding what constitutes mild, moderate, or severe suicidal intent may be quite different from other practitioners or may change over time as a result of individual practice experience.

Making sound clinical judgments about the seriousness of a client's problems or their adaptive capabilities is not merely a matter of trusting one's "instincts." There is a considerable amount of research that can help us reduce the effects of anchoring and improve clinical decision making. In the case of suicide risk, a list of known risk factors is widely recognized and includes a client's sense of hopelessness, history of depression, previous suicide attempts by the client or suicide by a parent, heavy drinking or abuse of other drugs, and owning weapons, among others. One way to mitigate the anchoring effect would be for practitioners to consistently use a valid suicide-risk assessment scale. Although no scale can guarantee 100-percent accuracy, using a validated scale can increase both the consistency and accuracy of clinical judgment and reduce "drift" (i.e., over- and under-estimations) for important clinical indicators.

The same principle applies to making clinical judgments about other problems as well. For example, anchoring bias can occur in similar fashion with assessment for child abuse and neglect. After witnessing hundreds of cases of abuse and neglect and feeling pressured to expedite large numbers of cases, a social worker's anchoring point for "serious risk of abuse" may drift gradually toward the severe end of the continuum (in other words, the practitioner's tolerance for what constitutes abuse increases). This phenomenon may account for why overburdened child welfare workers, who may not be equipped with good risk assessment tools, may find themselves underestimating risk of abuse or neglect. Despite the best of intentions, social workers are human, and judgment can drift over time. The more those judgments can be based on sound risk-assessment data, the more accurate they are likely to be.

Somewhat related to the issue of anchoring is the failure to employ *accurate base-rates* of a problem. This can occur in the form of feeling that "everybody has a drug problem" (a conclusion readily arrived at if one works in the substance abuse field) or "every couple I know has relationship issues." Working as a practitioner can lead one to believe that human problems are more common than is actually the case. If anchoring refers to making judgments about severity of problems, accurate base-rate data more specifically refers to the relative frequency with which particular problems occur in the community including the incidence (e.g., how many cases occur in a year in the general population) and prevalence (e.g., what proportion of the population experiences a condition over the course of a lifetime). These data are readily available for many problems including major mental illnesses, substance abuse and addiction, domestic violence, eating disorders, child abuse, and so on.

Nevertheless, because of a tendency of some practitioners to overrepresent the likelihood of rare phenomena or novel diagnoses (e.g., satanic ritual abuse, multiple personality disorder), some less experienced social workers have been influenced to look for more exotic or unusual explanations for people's problems rather than consider more probable explanations. For example, a young man who manifests psychotic symptoms in a hospital emergency room can either be having a first psychotic episode or be experiencing drug-induced hallucinations. Considering the fact that a sizeable proportion of young males use drugs that have hallucinogenic properties, the social worker conducting the screening would be wise to rule out the use of these drugs before committing the young man to a psychiatric facility since only a very small percentage of the population develops serious mental illnesses that involve non-drug-induced psychoses. The likelihood of the symptoms being caused by drugs versus a mental illness are approximately ten to one. Accessing more information about his activities and overall functioning on that day and in the weeks leading up to the crisis would be in order before jumping to the conclusion that he was, in fact, suffering his first psychotic episode. In situations where the facts are ambiguous or in short supply or client self-report is compromised for some reason, practitioners should rule out more likely explanations first before drawing conclusions that lead to inaccurate assessments and, possibly, a less than optimal intervention.

Other similar biases in judgments include engaging in *dichotomous thinking* (e.g., the client is alcohol dependent or not) rather than measuring behavior on a continuum (e.g., the client is not alcohol dependent, but his drinking is negatively affecting his work, home life, and mood). Sometimes using a psychiatric diagnosis (by its very nature) leads to dichotomous thinking (is the client borderline or not?) rather than focusing on the client's distressing thoughts, feelings, or behaviors, and assessing whether they require intervention. Sometimes practitioners deal with the challenges and ambiguity of practice by rationalizing that "social work is more an art than a science." Perhaps a better way to deal with the ambiguity and indeterminacy of working with our clients is to accept the fact that there is much we don't know about client problems and effective interventions. What can we do to increase the accuracy of our judgments? We can make the effort to become as knowledgeable as we can about the problems we deal with and the interventions we provide in our field of practice by keeping up with the latest evidence-based assessment and intervention methods, and practice good reasoning skills to apply that knowledge.

Characteristics of the Social Worker Who Thinks Critically

To accurately evaluate human behavior and practice research, social workers need to be able to think critically; to think critically, they must be knowledgeable about human behavior and practice research relevant to their field. These two essential elements of social work practice are necessary and reciprocal. As a final point, I would like to note some personal observations of critical-thinking colleagues based on over thirty-five years of experience and observation in the helping professions as practitioner, researcher, and instructor.

1. Critical thinkers are not inclined to be dogmatic or rigid in their professional beliefs. They tend to be humble in their professional opinions because they understand the limitations of our knowledge base and what we can achieve with our clients in practice. They generally understand that professional opinions are based primarily on well-considered evidence, not primarily on personal feelings, personal experience, ideology, or one's personal values or political opinions.

2. Critical thinkers are generally curious and open to new advances in the field and are less inclined to cling rigidly to more familiar and comfortable theoretical or practice traditions. Gravitating toward theories and practices with more supporting evidence reveals professional maturity and growth in a social work practitioner.

3. Critical thinkers tend to welcome peer review of their own work and do not shy away from challenges to their opinions.

4. Critical thinkers tend not to take criticism personally but see research and practice efforts as part of a whole enterprise shared with their peers—other critical practitioner-scholars.
5. Critical thinkers share a healthy skepticism toward unsubstantiated claims regarding theories and untested or unproven practices. Put another way, they are not easily taken in by untested theories or practice fads because of professional peer pressure and no matter how attractive they may seem on the surface.
6. Critical thinkers tend to provide measured responses to questions regarding theories and practices such as "some evidence suggests . . ." or "I don't know" or "I'll have to review the research on that."
7. Critical thinkers are not afraid to change their minds when the evidence warrants such a change. Rather, they welcome the opportunity to learn something new.
8. Critical thinkers tend to be specific when providing a professional opinion and understand that one must provide evidence to support one's opinions. They are less likely to become angry or generally resistant when their opinion is challenged.
9. Critical thinkers tend to avoid vague emotional or value-laden arguments to support their methods but refer to theories and practices that are supported by a body of peer-reviewed evidence.
10. Since critical thinkers do not overly personalize their professional opinions, they tend to make enjoyable and productive colleagues. They tend to focus on the important work at hand: thoughtfully providing informed and effective social work services to our clients and keeping up with new research findings to inform practice.

Summary

Social workers must acquire and develop the knowledge and skills to become competent consumers of human behavior and practice research relevant to their chosen field. By keeping up with "the literature" and applying this knowledge critically, social workers can maintain their professional competence, continually hone their expertise, and stay on the cutting edge of their profession over the course of a professional lifetime.

CHAPTER THREE

Essential Ethics in Social Work Practice

THERE IS EVERY REASON to believe that the majority of social workers are caring, committed professionals who strive to behave ethically in all their professional activities. However, occasionally you hear the stories from colleagues, read them in the newspaper, professional newsletters, on the Internet, or see the reports on television. A mental health professional, sometimes a social worker, is accused by a professional body or licensing board of unethical conduct, sued for damages by a client in civil court, or charged with criminally negligent practice. The examples might include charges that a practitioner:

- Inadvertently divulged confidential information to a colleague in the lunchroom
- Showed up for work impaired by alcohol or other drugs once or twice a month
- Had sex with a client as part of providing an "emotionally corrective therapeutic experience"
- Conducted a creative rebirthing therapy by coercing a child to fight her way out of a sack to reexperience the birth trauma (the child dies as a result of the experience)
- Encouraged a client with whom one is uncovering repressed memories to cut off all ties to his presumably abusive family (without sufficient evidence that the abuse occurred)
- Convinced a patient that her problems were caused by trauma that occurred in a past life, during satanic ritual abuse, or as the result of having been abducted by aliens
- Provided treatment for a client after diagnosing him as having more than five hundred distinct personalities

- Got even with restrictive insurance companies by billing them for group therapy conducted in one's backyard hot tub with five of one's closest friends
- Terminated treatment with a client on short notice because they had become overly dependent and troublesome (coincidentally, just as their mental health insurance benefit ran out)
- Ignored a client's homicidal or suicidal threats that were interpreted by the practitioner as passive-aggressive manipulation

These are all examples of unethical, negligent, and criminal activities that have been engaged in by practitioners including some social workers. Some of these are extreme or rare occurrences, yet social workers can be charged with unethical or illegal conduct for less serious and more common transgressions as well. The purpose of this chapter is to help beginning practitioners become aware of key ethical dimensions of social work practice and to teach them how to avoid unethical practices and reduce liability risk by using practice-relevant evidence to inform assessment, intervention, and evaluation.

The NASW Code of Ethics

The "Code" covers many areas related to professional conduct of social workers. These include social workers' ethical responsibilities to their clients and their colleagues, ethical professional behavior in practice settings, and ethical responsibilities to society. Although all areas of ethical responsibilities are important, the emphasis in this chapter will be on those matters that most directly affect their work with clients. Social workers should keep a copy of the Code and related texts available and review these guidelines periodically (NASW.org, 2007; Dolgoff, Loewenberg, & Harrington, 2005; Reamer, 1998, 2006, 2012; Strom-Gottfried, 2007). Since matters of ethics often coincide with legal and liability issues, questions regarding such matters should be referred to qualified attorneys.

Privacy and Confidentiality

Social workers must respect clients' right to privacy and should only solicit information from clients that is germane to providing the service (Houston-Vega & Nuehring, 1997; Reamer, 2003). Social workers cannot disclose information about clients to anyone, including other practitioners or third-party payers, without the expressed written consent of the client.

Even when ordered by the courts, social workers should strive to protect the confidentiality of the client if they deem the disclosure to be potentially harmful to the client. The social worker may request that the court withdraw the order, focus the request as narrowly as possible, or keep the disclosed information under seal and away from public scrutiny. Social workers should take every caution to protect electronic or written information (i.e., written records, computer files, emails, tapes, phone messages, etc.) from being revealed to others by maintaining vigilance regarding secure storage of relevant material. Destruction of client records should follow statutes usually stipulated by state departments of health. Confidentiality is one of the foundation ethical principles for social workers and has been robustly supported by the courts (e.g., see *Jaffee v. Redmond* in Appelbaum, 1996) and by federal legislation, specifically the Health Insurance Portability and Accountability Act of 1996.

Clients also have a right to examine their own records. However, if a practitioner feels that such examination may cause undue distress or psychological harm to the client, they can refrain from letting the client see the entire record or the part of the record they consider potentially harmful. However, the practitioner must record the reason for refusing to let the client see the record. The social worker should also sit with the client and discuss the content revealed in the record to answer questions and clarify the content of the record (e.g., meaning of a diagnosis). If a client is allowed access to the record, the social worker should take steps to protect the confidentiality of others identified in the record.

Social workers may disclose confidential information when appropriate with valid consent from a client or a person legally authorized to consent on behalf of a client.

Disclosure of private information is ethically and legally permissible in order to prevent serious, foreseeable, and *imminent* harm to the client or other identifiable person. Social workers often cite the famous Tarasoff case (*Tarasoff vs. the Board of Regents of the University of California*, 1976) to support their understanding of the "duty to warn" another person should that person be at risk of imminent harm from their client. In that situation, social workers are legally obliged to breach confidentiality and do what they deem prudent and necessary to warn the intended victim. However, even under circumstances in which the client himself or another person is in danger (e.g., suicidal risk), the practitioner should disclose only that information that is necessary to achieve the desired purpose (i.e., protect the person potentially in harm's way). Such situations minimally include known incidents of child abuse, abuse of an elderly person, or imminent threats of violence to anyone.

Generally, whenever feasible, social workers must inform the client about the disclosure of confidential information and the potential consequences of disclosure. This guideline is applicable to situations where the client has given written consent or where the social worker was compelled by law to report information against the client's wishes. Social workers who treat minors should consult legal authorities in their states to explain the limits of confidentiality in order to make informed judgments regarding when to disclose confidential information to parents if they believe it would be important to do so.

Early in the working relationship, social workers should outline the client's rights to confidentiality and also discuss circumstances under which the worker can divulge information to third parties without the client's expressed permission.

When working with multiple individuals (e.g., couples, families, and groups), social workers should seek to honor confidentiality among the members, but the practitioner must make it clear that they cannot prevent clients from revealing confidential matters to one another or to persons outside the group. In short, social workers should keep one rubric firmly in mind at all times regarding confidentiality: practitioners should not release information to anyone unless the practitioner knows that she is on firm ethical and legal grounds to do. If there is any doubt about confidentiality regulations, consultation with an attorney is advised.

Conflicts of Interest

It is paramount that social workers keep the well-being of their clients as the main focus of the intervention. Occasionally, situations arise in which the work with a client competes or potentially "conflicts" with other agendas. For example, a social worker provides psychotherapy for a client whose mother is a real estate agent in town. The social worker happens to be looking for an affordable home, and discussion ensues during one of the sessions about where to find a good deal. The client now becomes a potential ongoing source of valuable information to the practitioner, and the client's "insider" role now becomes a distraction to the treatment process. The social worker begins to schedule meetings more frequently to keep up with emerging prospects for a good deal, or the social worker offers "free sessions" if the client can find her a home.

Or consider the following: a social worker is working with a young woman through a difficult period of her life. The young woman happens to reveal that her uncle, with whom she is close, is on the Board of Trustees of a local university to which the social worker is applying for admission to a doctoral program. The client offers to put in a good word for the practitioner. Although the situation occurs out of pure coincidence, the social worker now begins to reduce the customary fee and continues to work with the client, despite the fact that her psychological state has improved and she is no longer in need of services.

These situations are problematic for one basic reason: the purpose of the original contract between the social worker and the client has been muddled. The purpose of the professional relationship with clients is for social workers to use their knowledge of psychosocial problems and their intervention skills to help clients resolve problems and better cope with their lives. The social worker provides a professional service, and the client pays for that service. Nothing more is relevant to the relationship. Other matters such as potential benefit to the social worker's personal, social, and financial well-being (beyond the satisfaction of helping others and getting paid for the service) go beyond the professional relationship and potentially erode the benefit of the service to the client. The Code properly exhorts social workers to identify and avoid such conflicts of interest whereby the purpose of the professional encounter seems to compete with some other need of the practitioner or where the benefit to the client is somehow compromised (Houston-Vega & Nuehring, 1997; Reamer, 2003, 2006, 2012; Strom-Gottfried, 2007).

Personal Demeanor, Including Sexual Relationships, Physical Contact, and Sexual Harassment

The Code clearly states that social workers should not participate in, condone, or be associated with dishonesty, fraud, or deception. However, social workers have an obligation to maintain professional demeanor that goes beyond merely not breaking the law. These situations include not allowing personal problems such as mental health, substance abuse, and interpersonal or social problems from negatively affecting their ability to perform their professional duties toward their clients. If social workers become aware of these impairments, they should seek whatever professional help is necessary to ameliorate the problem and ensure their ability to carry out their professional responsibilities adequately.

Social workers should not engage in sexual relations with their clients or others close to the client under any circumstances. Social workers, not the clients nor the clients' relatives or close acquaintances, are responsible for maintaining these boundaries. The burden of proof also lies with the social worker to demonstrate that sexual relations with former clients did not cause harm or was the result of manipulation or coercion. Social workers also should not provide services to persons with whom they had a prior sexual relationship. Social workers should never attempt to solicit sexual contact in any form from a client. Any such behaviors should be considered sexual harassment. Clients in those circumstances might be within their rights to sue the practitioner for damages due to psychological and emotional harm.

Social workers should not engage in physical contact with clients where psychological harm may result. Cuddling, caressing, or otherwise physically "nurturing" clients are strongly discouraged. Incidental touching such as handshakes or helping an elderly client from a chair are not ordinarily a problem, but other forms of touching (e.g., supportive hugs, an encouraging pat on the back) should be done with discretion. Clients may interpret even the most well-intentioned contact as a gesture laden with some unintended motive. Interpretation of physical contact may also carry unknown cultural meaning, and practitioners should be aware of these gestures. Clear, professional boundaries should be maintained at all times. Warmth, compassion, and encouragement can be communicated effectively without physically touching clients.

Interruption and Termination of Services

Generally, social workers should provide only those services that clients need. Termination of services should occur when the client can no longer benefit from the service or the service is no longer needed or desired. In doing so, social workers should avoid abrupt termination of services (i.e., abandonment). Social workers can terminate services with a client if the client stops paying for contracted services as long as the client does not pose an imminent danger to himself or another person.

Social workers are obliged to maintain the continuity of services and must make arrangements to continue service for clients should the service be interrupted by the practitioner's unavailability, illness, and even death. Every effort should be made to anticipate termination of services and plan for orderly cessation of services, transfer to another practitioner, or referral in a way that is agreeable to the client.

Informed Consent and Ensuring Competent Practice

Social workers should only claim competence in providing services for which they have had proper training along with associated licensing, certification, supervision, and professional experience. The Code is ambiguous, however, in guiding practitioners in the use of intervention methods for which recognized standards do not exist. Rather, the Code exhorts practitioners to use their judgment and obtain proper training, supervision, and consultation as needed. This injunction, nevertheless, begs the question: *If no such recognized standards exist, then upon what knowledge criteria are the training, supervision, or consultation based?*

Although the Code is somewhat ambiguous regarding the criteria employed to define practice "competence," the authors exhort social workers to:

> accept responsibility or employment only on the basis of existing competence or the intention to acquire the necessary competence . . . [and to] . . . strive to become and remain proficient in professional practice and the performance of professional functions. Social workers should critically examine and keep current with emerging knowledge relevant to social work. Social workers should routinely review the professional literature and participate in continuing education relevant to social work practice and social work ethics. Social workers should base practice on recognized knowledge, including empirically based knowledge, relevant to social work and social work ethics.

Practitioners are guided by the Code to provide clients with informed consent regarding the type of practices they are offering the client and to provide services to clients only in the context of a professional relationship. The problem analysis (assessment and diagnosis) and intervention plan should be discussed with the client in language that is clear and understandable, and clients should also be educated about the nature of the intervention, likely benefits from it, and any possible risks of harm associated with the intervention. Financial matters and associated limitations imposed on the intervention (e.g., cost of treatment, insurance matters, amount of treatment covered, etc.) should also be explained clearly to the client. Key to the matter of informed consent is the obligation of the social worker to *discuss the type of intervention to be used, what benefits are likely to accrue for the client, and what inherent risks may be incurred.* Although there is some ambiguity in the scientific and legal communities as to what knowledge base is adequate for justifying the use of certain forms of social work practice, a sound body of peer-reviewed research provides a much stronger argument than untested therapies or practices supported by anecdotal clinical evidence (e.g., uncontrolled case studies). Courts are making increasing references to evidence-based practices (i.e., interventions shown repeatedly to be effective in randomized controlled trials) as the criteria against which the adequacy of practitioners' interventions will be judged.

Conducting Evaluation and Research

The Code also exhorts social workers to engage in reviews of current practice research and engage in evaluation of their own practice. Keeping up with current knowledge relevant to their clients' problems and effective practices is an essential social work skill that will help maintain professional competence within the current "standards of care." Engaging in evaluation of one's own practice can take a number of forms, from simply monitoring the progress of one's own clients to participating in agency program evaluation initiatives. In any case, practice, evaluation, and research activities share a common ethical rubric:

- Clients should be informed as to the nature of practice, evaluation, and research efforts.
- These activities should be participated in voluntarily whenever possible.
- Confidentiality of all data (e.g., progress notes, quantitative data from scales and indexes, etc.) should be protected.

When practitioners engage in research that goes beyond routine evaluation of agency services, they must obtain permission and follow the guidelines of an institutional review board (IRB) that is commissioned to examine the nature of the evaluation or research, assure the safety of clients, and ensure informed consent and the client's confidentiality. Such participation of clients is voluntary, and they are free to withdraw at any time. Clients are also provided with support should they suffer any undue distress from the evaluation or research activities.

Practitioners and researchers also share the responsibility to provide adequate informed consent to clients by explaining the nature of the intervention or the research-evaluation project and by indicating whether there is any potential for causing psychological distress. Practitioners and researchers are also required to be responsive should clients become distressed in the course of an intervention or research/evaluation procedure. With increasing frequency, practice and evaluation activities are occurring simultaneously (e.g., using clinical scales as part of assessment and clinical review procedures), thus, often rendering the intervention versus evaluation distinction moot for practical and ethical purposes. Whether the activities of social workers are practice, evaluation, or research, they should commit themselves to the core ethical principles of competence, informed consent, and confidentiality (Houston-Vega & Nuehring, 1997; Reamer, 1995, 2006; Strom-Gottfried, 2007).

Malpractice and Liability in Social Work Practice

Although ethical guidelines are important for sound professional practice, social workers must also be familiar with basic legal requirements, usually regulations published by the health authority in states where they practice. "Professional malpractice is generally considered a form of negligence" (Reamer, 2003, p. 3). In general, malpractice means that social workers have provided service in a way that diverges significantly from the "standard of care," that is, the way other competent professionals would act under similar circumstances (Beutler, Clarkin, & Bongar, 2000). Malpractice does not imply that the practitioner necessarily intends to act in an unethical or malevolent manner. It can occur as an innocent mistake (e.g., inadvertently discussing confidential information with someone not authorized to hear it), a mistake in diagnosis or assessment (e.g., not diagnosing a DSM-5 depressive disorder or failing to identify known suicide-risk factors), or can be an egregious breach of proper care (e.g., sleeping with a client to "nurture their inner child"). Malpractice generally occurs when a legal duty has been breached (e.g., confidentiality), practitioners have failed to carry out their duty either through omission or commission of an improper act, or clients have been harmed psychologically, emotionally, or physically by the actions of social workers (Reamer, 2003). Although social work students are often given the misleading impression that practitioners' activities are always benign and researchers' and evaluators' motives are often suspect, it is important to note here that the vast majority of lawsuits are incurred by practitioners, not by those who engage in efforts to test or monitor the outcomes of intervention activities (O'Hare, 2015; Reamer, 2003).

Most malpractice claims that end in settlements for clients have to do with incorrect diagnosis and selection of treatment (Harkness, 2011). These situations are usually related to practitioners who do something improper or fail to do what they should do within the standard of care. Malpractice lawsuits related to improper treatment may be related to failure to provide adequate informed consent, failure to provide adequate diagnosis, assessment, and intervention, or breaching proper practitioner-client boundaries. The literature on liability matters is complex and involves a thorough understanding of legal issues. Reamer's (2003) text *Social Work Malpractice and Liability* (second edition) can serve as an excellent introduction to these and related matters. In addition, his book entitled *The Social Work Ethics Audit: A Risk Management Tool* (2001) is a very useful guide for both private practitioners and agency administrators to review and improve policies that can reduce liability risk, improve the overall ethical climate of practice, and reduce the likelihood of being sued for breaches of confidentiality, divergences from the standard of care, and other unethical actions. However, for our purposes here, basic considerations regarding avoiding malpractice lawsuits by using adequate assessment and intervention methods are the main focus.

Avoiding Breaches of Informed Consent

Informing clients about the nature of the intervention and obtaining voluntary consent (in most cases) is relevant to services with both adults and children. Although in most situations, practitioners must obtain written permission from parents or guardians of minors, these situations vary by state law and apply differently to "emancipated minors," those who have obtained their independence before the usual age of emancipation. As noted earlier, the Code enjoins social workers to explain the interventions to be used in "clear and understandable language." This means, that social workers should be explicit about what type of intervention they intend to use, what the nature of that intervention is, whether there is any risk of harm, what the limitations are of the intervention, and what alternatives are available (Houston-Vega & Nuehring, 1997; Reamer, 2003). Clients should be closely involved in the development of an intervention plan and agree to it. Even in situations where clients are mandated to treatment by the courts, every effort should be made to engage clients in the intervention planning process and provide them with some degree of choice and participation.

Let's say a client presents in a social worker's office with a clearly diagnosed panic disorder. She is understandably terrified by the shortness of breath, fits of trembling, feeling sick to her stomach, and feeling as though she is about to lose her mind. The client recently had to pull off the highway while driving over a suspension bridge because she felt her arms going numb, a feeling that simply increased her terror. Although a combination of antidepressants and antianxiety medication had been prescribed, the client was still experiencing these attacks and was becoming more and more reclusive and afraid to go outside. Her mobility was greatly lessened, and although she had found some alternative ways to get to work and school (e.g., taxis, friends), these options were seen as too expensive or, at best, time-limited. The client was feeling desperate and felt she had no recourse other than to receive mental health care that would alleviate her symptoms and get "back on track."

The social worker met with her supervisor, and they discussed the assessment and diagnosis of the client's condition. The supervisor, eschewed diagnosis, was convinced that the client's panic disorder was caused by a "childhood trauma," advised the social worker to "develop a positive transference" with the client, "identify the root cause of the fear," and help the client "work it through with the help of a proper interpretation."

The social worker left the session with the supervisor with an uneasy feeling. Recently, she had read in a professional journal review article that cognitive-behavioral treatment and graduated exposure combined with medication offered the client the best chance of a speedy and lasting recovery when compared to other known interventions. However, the supervisor had not mentioned this approach. The social worker was new on the job and was reluctant to challenge her supervisor about her recommendations. Her supervisor had a tendency to speak in an authoritative tone, didn't seem to like being questioned about her clinical decisions, and seemed perturbed when any of her colleagues mentioned "evidence-based practices." What should the novice social worker do? Could she give accurate and full information to the client about the type of intervention she was about to provide? Would she incur any liability risk if she failed to point out the availability of this other well-researched approach? Would the chief executive of the for-profit agency be angry with her if she referred the client to another agency where they did provide the current best practices?

Obviously, providing informed consent to clients about effective practices would put this social worker in jeopardy. Nevertheless, providing adequate informed consent requires that social workers be knowledgeable about both the problems they treat as well as the interventions they use. Knowledge of effective interventions must be obtained through social work education, training in field experiences, and ongoing supervision in postgraduate employment. Social workers who become aware of the relative effectiveness of some interventions compared to others should pursue training in those methods if they choose to continue providing interventions for clients with those particular problems.

Consent for treatment should be voluntary (although there are exceptions to this general rule), documented in the client record (although verbal consent is sometimes accepted), and the client must be mentally capable of providing voluntary consent (a matter that sometimes has to be determined by the courts). Clients generally have the right to withdraw consent for services, and social workers should request that the client sign a form that details the risks the social worker feels the client incurs by terminating the intervention prematurely. Generally, in cases where there is an emergency and clients are at risk (i.e., involuntary commitment) or are putting someone else at imminent risk (as in the Tarasoff case, noted earlier), social workers may intervene without the client's informed consent.

Reducing Liability Exposure with Competent Assessments

Although there is considerable ambiguity in the professional literature regarding what constitutes an adequate assessment and ongoing controversies regarding the validity of some DSM-5 diagnoses, social workers should become competent at using methods of assessment and diagnosis that fall within the profession's standard of care. There are a number of schools of thought regarding assessment that are accepted by a substantial number of social workers. Thus, should a social worker be informed by psychodynamic theory, cognitive-behavioral theory, family systems theory, and so on, the courts generally do not pass judgment on which theory or assessment framework is the "right" one. Despite these legal and scientific ambiguities, social workers, at a minimum, should be familiar with the criteria in the DSM-5 since this text is generally accepted and used by most mental health professionals regardless of theoretical orientation. The criteria for diagnoses are descriptive (not theoretically explanatory) and provide helpful guidelines for assessing serious mental illnesses and associated risks (e.g., impulsivity or suicidal intent). Other approaches to assessment may be helpful as well, and social workers should pay attention to key areas of assessment where the client's well-being or the well-being of others may be at risk. Should a client express a good deal of anger at an individual with no apparent threat, this matter needs to be addressed at length and documented. Should a client express suicidal thoughts, these matters should be addressed in further detail, and social workers should become familiar with known risk factors for suicide identified in the research literature. In general, social workers should strive to provide a comprehensive and consistent approach to assessment that includes an assessment of mental status, family and social problems, and substance abuse as well as daily functioning at work, school, and in the community. High-risk behaviors such as substance abuse or impulsive behaviors that endanger the client or others or verbal threats should be duly noted and addressed at length with the client and, if need be, with others. Suicidal ideation should be thoroughly evaluated and be documented in the client record. Assessments that focus on observable or reported facts should be given priority over assessments that are based primarily on a high degree of inference (e.g., interpreting dreams, unconscious motives, drawings, or children's play behavior). If the social workers have serious doubts about the adequacy of an assessment, they should seek expert consultation and document what was discussed. More details about conducting assessments will be addressed in Chapter 4.

Intervention Plans That Reduce Liability Risks

Social workers can also be sued for not providing interventions that meet the standard of care (Harkness, 2011). This situation can occur in any number of ways, including engaging in practices for which the social worker does not have adequate training, performing an intervention poorly with harm resulting to the client, and engaging in practices that are not supported by a significant proportion of the professional community. Because there are a number of therapeutic practices that have not been well researched, but are nevertheless practiced by more than a few therapists, determining what constitutes the standard of care in the eyes of the courts can be an ambiguous matter. However, the courts have awarded judgments to plaintiffs (i.e., clients or relatives who sue their therapists) for having been subjected to "fringe" therapies where harm has resulted. "Rebirthing" therapy, "past life regression," or "recovered memory" approaches have not been shown to be effective in practice research and have resulted in lawsuits against social workers with damages awarded to the clients or their surviving relatives.

Although scientific debate continues regarding the value of some "mainstream" therapies, the courts will generally accept these if they were applied with adequate skill within the standard of care. Nevertheless, social workers would be best advised to employ interventions for which there is a substantive body of peer-reviewed controlled research (i.e., EBPs). Practitioners should be conservative in their choice of interventions and err on the side of restraint by pursuing training and supervision in methods that are well supported in the practice research literature. Practitioners are required to document their intervention plans and provide progress notes in sufficient detail to demonstrate that these interventions were skillfully applied. This strategy reflects the spirit of the Code and, in this writer's opinion, is best for both the client's well-being and for legal protection of the practitioner.

The Code also enjoins practitioners to keep up with emerging practice knowledge. To stay current and fully appreciate the emergence of new practices, social workers must be able to critically read and understand practice evaluation and research reports in such a way that they can distinguish questionable practices from those supported by the preponderance of controlled practice research. Basic guidelines for reviewing practice research are provided in Chapter 2 so that novice practitioners can develop this skill early in their career. Although faculty in schools of social work are professionally responsible for what they teach their students, once students become licensed practitioners, they are fully responsible for the practices that they employ with their clients.

Properly Terminating Services

Informed consent and developing a good working relationship with the client should mark the beginning of intervention, but how interventions end is equally important. Termination of treatment should, under the best of circumstances, be planned, discussed, and proceed with the knowledge that clients achieved some or all of their goals, are satisfied with the service they received, and would know how to return to treatment or seek additional treatment in the future if needed. Social workers will find that such endings do occur regularly and are often satisfying for both the worker and the client. Sometimes, however, things don't end smoothly. If a client, for whatever reason, terminates abruptly or prematurely, the social worker (if given the opportunity) should discuss the client-initiated termination with the client and document their own efforts to understand the client's needs and offer referral services. Should a client pose a danger to the community (e.g., a dangerous client escapes from an in-patient psychiatric hospital) the authorities must be notified.

Additional liability risk occurs when the practitioner fails to be available to the client, extends service beyond what is required, or abruptly terminates services without adequate justification. Once a social worker begins to work with a client, there is an ethical expectation that he will follow through with the intervention until service is completed or until he can no longer provide intervention that will benefit the client. There is also an understanding that the limitations of the initial contract for payment also applies (e.g., insurance covers only ten sessions), but these matters must be discussed at the beginning of the intervention if this information is available. If a social worker feels that he can no longer work with a client for whatever reason, these reasons must be discussed with the client and plans made to terminate and refer the case to someone else if the client is still in need of treatment. A social worker who decides to stop seeing a client because the client can no longer afford to pay the cost or because the client has become uncooperative puts the social worker at risk for a lawsuit. In general, social workers should plan for termination well in advance, should document the discussions, confer with colleagues as needed, and offer referral when the intervention ends (Houston-Vega & Nuehring, 1997; Reamer, 2003).

Informed consent, providing valid and complete assessment, accurate diagnosis, effective intervention, and terminating services properly are core concerns regarding liability risks. However, social workers can be sued for other reasons as well. These include:

- Having sex with clients or former clients
- Providing therapeutic interventions for former sex partners
- Breaching confidentiality
- Failing to report suspected abuse of a child or elderly person (i.e., mandated reporting)
- Reporting abuse in "bad faith," meaning that the social worker did not demonstrate that they had good reason to believe there was evidence of abuse

In all these cases, regularly reviewing the Code, knowing agency policies and relevant state regulations, making every effort to document efforts to provide adequate care that is supported in the practice research literature, and consulting with supervisors and experts can go a long way to prevent violations of ethics or exposure to lawsuits.

Ethical Considerations for Working with Involuntary Clients

Social workers are rightly enjoined by the Code to respect client autonomy and self-determination. At every turn, practitioners should strive to optimize that principle with their clients. However, social workers are often called upon to work with clients who have broken the law, hurt people in their own families and communities, and are at risk to hurt others again. Social work ethical principles, thus, also enjoin practitioners to consider potential harm to the public when making assessment and intervention decisions. The *Tarasoff* decision represents a relatively obvious situation in that the practitioner must respond to an *imminent threat of harm to others* ("I'm going to *kill her* when I get home!").

However, social workers often serve clients where the risk to others does not appear as imminent, but, nevertheless, remains a genuine, albeit, indeterminate concern. Social workers are increasingly being called upon to work with clients who are often described as "involuntary." These are clients who have behavior problems related to mental illnesses, are addicted to illegal drugs, and have been physically or sexually abusive to their partners, children, or others in the community. These and other categories of "committed," "court-ordered," or "involuntary" clients now constitute a large proportion of people served by social workers. The ethical mandate for working with involuntary clients requires a skillful balance between protecting the rights of clients and protecting the public. Knowledge of research regarding known relapse and recidivism rates by involuntary clients in the community is essential when contributing to court decisions as expert witness or as client advocate regarding a client's disposition (e.g., prison, treatment, or some combination of treatment and close monitoring). Working with court-mandated clients requires that social workers balance empathy for their court-mandated clients with compassion for the likely (anonymous) victims of client-recidivists (i.e., protecting the innocent).

Behavior change professionals (including social workers) in the mental health, substance abuse, child welfare, and other fields along with many professionals in law enforcement and the criminal justice system often share common goals of reducing antisocial behaviors in our clients and, simultaneously, protecting the public from their harmful actions. Although public-policy debate often lurches between the extremes of "lock 'em up" and "provide treatment," more thoughtful observers have begun to see some potential for productive accommodation between these two extremes *for selected clients*. Although clients are (except in rare cases such as gross medical impairment) responsible for their actions, society and the criminal courts recognize mitigating circumstances (e.g., mental illness, addiction) and, more importantly, the potential for more effective approaches *by combining the strengths of both effective psychosocial change efforts with the leverage of the criminal justice system* (Nygaard, 2000; O'Hare, 2015; Wexler, 1991). Helping a client become a more prosocial and productive member of society are goals that are commensurate with both the criminal justice system and the human services professions. Although a sound idea in principle, the effectiveness of approaches such as "out-patient civil commitment" and early release "diversionary substance abuse treatment" for convicted offenders must be judged by sound evaluation and outcome research, not ideology, value statements, personal convictions, or political pandering.

The term "involuntary client" is somewhat of a misnomer on at least two levels. First, clients who participate in therapeutic programs and are simultaneously monitored by the courts to see if they participate purposefully and regularly (i.e., comply) are often doing it by choice. The person convicted of a nonviolent drug-related offense may be offered a briefer prison sentence by the judge in a "drug court" if he elects to participate in a therapeutic community for drug addiction and agrees to continue treatment (e.g., half-way house, out-patient) after release. The seriously mentally ill person who repeatedly decides not to take the prescribed anti-psychotic medication may be given a choice of either in-patient hospitalization or commitment to supervised out-patient care (i.e., out-patient civil commitment). Legal guidelines associated with these decisions and other related dilemmas (e.g., estimating risk to others in the community) are complex matters that need to be addressed in court by attorneys, other client advocates, and expert witnesses. One key element in making decisions about "diversionary treatment" in the community versus incarceration involves making scientifically informed (i.e., evidence-based) risk assessments about the probability of recidivism and the nature of the potential criminal act (e.g., a common burglar vs. an aggressive sexual predator). Suffice it to say, these are sometimes difficult matters to resolve, and mistakes will be made by either overly restricting the civil rights of some clients or failing to confine or closely supervise people who pose a high degree of danger to the general public. Nevertheless, social workers must come to grips with their own biases with respect to balancing clients' rights versus public safety.

However, there is a second point to be made about the term "involuntary." Not all clients pressured to accept or comply with treatment are completely resistant to the idea of change. Many "involuntary" clients are quite willing to engage in treatment and (perhaps faced with worse alternatives) give their best effort to make positive changes in their lives. From the social worker's point of view, although such clients may, indeed, be leveraged by the courts with contingencies related to rehospitalization or reincarceration for noncompliance with treatment, practitioners can often offer clients a fair amount of latitude and flexibility with regard to how they participate in treatment and pursue their treatment goals. So, while they may appear to be "coerced," many involuntary clients do have a choice with regard to their type of intervention, and social workers can help these clients develop treatment plans and goals that offer some degree of choice, autonomy, and flexibility within the mandated treatment framework (O'Hare, 1996; Rooney & Bibus, 2001).

Arthur Caplan, the bioethicist, makes, I believe, a reasonable argument for the ethics and morality of coerced treatment for convicted felons addicted to narcotics: although these clients may not be "mentally incompetent" according to law, they are often grossly lacking in autonomy as a result of their protracted addictions, and coerced treatment (provided for a limited time) can help to restore that autonomy (Caplan, 2006). Wynn (2006) notes that mandated treatment is an accepted policy in most countries despite different definitions of psychosis, different rates of coercive treatment, and different laws governing client rights and coercive treatments. According to Wynn, there are two main reasons for using coercive psychiatric treatments: to reduce suffering in patients (e.g., a person with schizophrenia who, as is characteristic of the disease, is very ill but denies the illness and refuses medication) and to protect the public from possible harm. Although the empirical literature is mixed regarding the effectiveness of coercion in the long run, it must be guided by balancing four main principles: respecting client autonomy, acting responsibly in the patient's best interest, being careful to avoid harming the client in any way, and providing quality care for all clients (i.e., justice) (Wynn, 2006).

However, despite the intended beneficence of mandated care, coercing a client to receive mental health treatment might result in further treatment avoidance by clients who would otherwise benefit from voluntary treatment should they be successfully encouraged to accept it. The barriers caused by mandated care are often compounded by other barriers to care that include poverty, drug addiction, and lack of transportation, among other reasons (Van Dorn et al., 2006). Most informed and thoughtful writers on the subject of mandated treatment recognize that arguments for and against it involve a complex interplay of legal, ethical, philosophical, and clinical argument. Overly aggressive use of mandated treatments and categorical refusal to even consider the use of mandated care tend to be seen as fringe positions on the matter. Ultimately, the benefits and costs to both the client and society must be determined by more empirical research on mandated treatments.

Using Research Findings to Avoid Breaching Ethical or Legal Practice Guidelines

Civil and criminal legal actions against social work practitioners are usually related to alleged breaches in the standard of care, and outcome research is beginning to have greater influence in court decisions regarding what constitutes the standard of care. These concerns have increased the anxieties of some clinicians, administrators, evaluators, supervisors, and quality-assurance professionals. Questions arise: Do assessment protocols reliably capture high-risk behaviors? Are we using the best intervention approaches available to help our clients? Are our recently graduated social workers properly trained in evidence-based approaches when they begin their first professional jobs? If their professional education does not include evidence-based practices, what liability exposure do agencies incur, and how much remedial training can agencies afford to provide to bring new practitioners and their supervisors "up to speed"? Are instructors in schools of social work liable if their students employ non-evidence-based practices with adverse consequences resulting? Although these questions involve potentially complex legal arguments, instructors, practitioners, and administrators should, at a minimum, be more circumspect in what approaches are endorsed in the classroom and in agencies. To quote Barbara White, former president of NASW and former Chair of the NASW Insurance Trust: "A social worker's best protection is a solid understanding of the standard of care as it applies to practice . . ." (Houston-Vega & Nuehring, 1997, p. xiv). Since the standard of care is being defined increasingly by competent, critical reviews of the outcome research, one can readily argue that treatments not supported by a substantial body of research are more likely to be considered unethical practices and increase a practitioner's exposure to malpractice lawsuits (Harkness, 2011; Meyers & Thyer, 1997; O'Hare, 2015; Thyer, 2004).

In addition to reviewing the relevant research literature, Reamer (2003) recommends several other steps social workers can take to buttress their decisions and reduce the likelihood of being found negligent in practice: consult expert colleagues and obtain supervision with someone who has the relevant credentials and expertise, review the NASW Code of Ethics, know relevant laws and policies (e.g., confidentiality regulations), document one's decision-making steps, and obtain legal consultation as needed.

What follows are a few basic guidelines to help social workers do their best work and avoid pitfalls that can lead to charges of unethical behavior, charges of criminal malpractice, or civil lawsuits. Although these suggestions are not to be construed as legal advice, making reference to sound assessment and practice guidelines will generally help practitioners do their best work, avoid inadvertent errors in judgment, and provide a rational basis for their practices.

Assessment and Evaluation

- Conduct a thorough assessment using multiple sources and methods (see Chapter 4).
- Conduct a thorough mental status exam, including a thorough assessment of any suicidal ideation.

- Examine all areas of your client's life in addition to the specific target problem. These areas include health status, substance abuse, work or school functioning, and family and community relationships. If you don't query about the client's well-being across multiple domains, they may not volunteer the information, and important assessment data might be overlooked.
- Inquire as to previous mental health and substance abuse treatment and its outcome.
- Examine other conflicted relationships, including history of abuse or violence. Inquire in detail about any evidence of potential harm to children or elderly in the client's life, whether the danger be the result of the client's behavior or another's behavior.
- Conduct a thorough assessment of their immediate relationships (couple, family, children, and extended family members with whom they have regular contact).
- Tactfully inquire about past criminal behavior, arrests, and imprisonment.
- Conduct a thorough functional assessment, that is, ask questions about day-to-day details to identify risk factors associated with the client's problems.
- Document a DSM-5 diagnosis and provide supporting evidence for that diagnosis.
- Use scales and indexes that have a published track record for reliability and validity in the clinical research literature. These measures can provide additional support for the overall qualitative assessment.
- Given the proper informed consent, obtain as much corroborating information as possible about clients and their difficulties. Ask to interview partners and family members. Go beyond that immediate social circle and obtain copies of records with client consent (e.g., legal, mental health, health, etc.) to get a full picture of clients' presenting problems.
- Be thorough, document your observations, and discuss any matters of concern with colleagues, supervisors, and other experts as needed.

Intervention Methods

- After a comprehensive assessment, examine the current research on effective practices and discuss these matters with your client and supervisor.

- Describe to the client what is known about available effective practices, and explain to the client what you believe to be the best choice.
- Encourage the client to collaborate with you in the development of an individualized intervention plan.
- Explain to the client why you think the plan will be helpful, what the benefits are likely to be, what some of the risks might be, and give the client a chance to air any questions or concerns.
- Write the intervention plan with the client, and document the agreement to participate in the plan.
- As the plan is implemented, keep accurate progress notes, and use qualitative and quantitative means to monitor the client's progress.
- Should problems arise, consult supervisors and experts if the client does not seem to be responding well to the intervention.
- If the client does not improve in a reasonable amount of time, discuss options and possible referrals for another opinion if necessary.
- Always keep termination processes in mind, and discuss the client's progress at each visit.
- As the client approaches the end of the intervention, discuss after-care plans and referrals for follow-up should they seem necessary.

In summary, stay abreast of the current research literature regarding valid assessments and effective practices, be open with clients about the interventions you recommend, communicate these opinions in clear and plain language with clients, document essential intervention activities and client responses to them, seek consultation as needed, and always keep the client's well-being foremost in mind.

The profession of social work will face increasing challenges to reconcile clinical practice, research, and evaluation methods with social work ethics as health-care policy continues to evolve. Changes in mental health policy and administration have implications for several areas of the law including: access to managed care treatment in the face of service denials, an increase in the use of involuntary interventions, more attention to defining and measuring psychological and social outcomes, confidentiality issues related to the development and utilization of massive data banks designed for the routine monitoring and evaluation of clinical practice, and other changes in treatment technologies and the health-care structures needed to run them. Social workers will also have to become more involved in developing evidence-based practice guidelines if the profession wants to maintain high ethical standards as well as professional viability and autonomy and compete with the other professions (Howard & Jenson, 1999; O'Hare, 2015).

PART TWO

Essential Practice Skills

CHAPTER FOUR

Conducting the Assessment and Planning the Evaluation

A THOROUGH AND INFORMED ASSESSMENT helps the practitioner and client better understand the client's problems and adaptive capabilities (i.e., strengths), provides an understanding of the role of "personal identity factors" with respect to the individual client or family, serves as a guide to the development of the intervention plan, and provides a foundation for monitoring the client's progress and evaluating the intervention. Valid assessment of clients' difficulties and strengths must be based on a thorough qualitative review of the client's own experiences over time, the observations and concerns of those involved in the client's life, and a solid grasp of human behavior research relevant to the client's specific difficulties (e.g., depression, addictions, domestic violence, etc.). In the current chapter, the essentials of multidimensional/functional/systems (MFS) assessment will be described. MFS assessment is a comprehensive approach to problem analysis that combines a firm grounding in contemporary human behavior theory and research with a respect for each client's unique problem construction within a broader systems context. Many practice traditions across the helping professions have contributed to contemporary social work assessment (Bellack & Hersen, 1998; Franklin & Jordan, 2003; O'Hare, 2015; Sadock & Sadock, 2003). However, one can argue that the best qualities of those approaches can be subsumed under three major concepts: *multidimensionality, functionality, and systemic interaction.*

Before beginning this chapter, one caveat is in order. Competent assessment is closely tied to competent interviewing and engagement skills, that is, the early stages of the intervention process. This chapter focuses on the conceptual content one should master in order to conduct a thorough assessment. In the next chapter, those supportive, interviewing, and engagement skills necessary to carry out the assessment and continue the intervention will be covered.

Key Organizing Concepts of a Valid Assessment: Multidimensionality, Functionality, and Systemic Interaction

There is a range of different approaches to assessment in social work. Traditional psychiatric assessment (i.e., diagnosis) is based on a disease-oriented model and emphasizes disorder within the individual. Cognitive-behavioral assessment emphasizes a functional analysis that combines efforts to understand an individual's thoughts, feelings, and behaviors and how these aspects of the problem are reinforced in their social environment. Systems-oriented assessment emphasizes interactions between and among individuals, family members, and the community. Narrative, constructivist, humanistic, and other phenomenological approaches emphasize the unique experience of each client and the inherent ability of each person to adapt and come to their own solutions. Psychodynamic assessment focuses on the effects of early childhood events and their assumed long-term impact on shaping unconscious motivation and interpersonal relations.

All of these various forms of assessment have positive aspects to them, but each alone can represent an incomplete view of the client's condition. Psychiatric diagnoses are essential when identifying bona fide mental disorders such as schizophrenia and major mood disorders but often do not accurately consider environmental factors that contribute to serious problems and often exacerbate mental illness (e.g., domestic violence). Systems models may highlight interactions between and among individuals within families and communities but often fail to adequately recognize biologically based psychopathology when it does exist (e.g., bipolar disorder). Cognitive-behavioral assessment stresses the role of faulty thinking and reinforcement of dysfunctional behaviors but is enhanced when individual functioning is seen in a broader family and community systems context. Constructivist and other phenomenological practitioners stress the importance of a client's unique experience but are inclined to dismiss real mental illness as a "social construction." Lastly, psychodynamic theoreticians emphasize the importance of early childhood experience and its impact on the development of close relationships but tend to downplay current causal factors that can play a larger role in maintaining client dysfunction. What is needed is an assessment framework that is comprehensive, reflects current scientific knowledge of human behavior, and incorporates the best that these various models have to offer.

As the term "comprehensive" implies, a sound assessment involves a considerable amount of data gathering. This information will generally cover the following areas:

- Individual well-being, including cognitive, emotional, and behavioral functioning
- General health status and ability to attend to activities of daily life
- Family and other proximate interpersonal relationships
- Social functioning and environmental supports including community ties and level of integration with social organizations (e.g., school, social agencies)
- Academic, occupational, and other relevant role functioning

Assessment is a process that includes (1) gathering information about the client's unique experiences relevant to their problems and coping capacities and (2) understanding the significance of that information within the context of contemporary human behavior research that is specifically relevant to the client's presenting concerns. Although a thorough assessment often results in a large amount of information regarding the client and their circumstances, the final assessment summary should be fairly succinct and focus on those problems of greatest significance and potential for positive change.

Assessment is *multidimensional* in two respects: first, the causes of our clients' problems are complex (i.e., multidimensional) and include biological, psychological, and social factors that interact over time. To more fully understand a sexually abused child's fears, a mentally ill person's delusions, an addicted person's anxieties, or an obsessive person's preoccupation with extreme orderliness, practitioners must have a grasp of the relevant research that informs our understanding of these conditions. Secondly, our clients' problems are multidimensional in the sense that their problems and adaptive capacities are usually manifested across multiple interacting areas of every day life: psychological, interpersonal, community, occupational/educational, health, and other domains of daily living. Social work has a long tradition of framing clients' problems within the context of interacting psychosocial systems. However, these broad frameworks lack explanatory power to support assessment with specific problems (e.g., mental illnesses, child abuse and neglect, anxiety disorders, etc.). Thus, "eco-systems" and similar models must be informed by current research findings specific to that problem area (Wakefield, 1996). For example, in order to fully understand the nature of a mentally ill client's thought disorders and interpersonal deficits, the practitioner must have a grasp of the relevant research on mental illness. For a practitioner to more fully understand a battered woman's passivity, depression, and apparent helplessness, a solid familiarity with the research on domestic violence and co-occurring substance abuse would be required. General "frameworks" may outline the perimeter of human behavior problems, but knowledge specific to any given problem is required to more fully understand the significance of each client's unique situation.

Estimating the severity of client problems and adaptive capacities across multiple domains does not in itself result in a complete assessment. Practitioners must also conduct a *functional analysis* of the client's key problems. Knowing *what* the problems are does not mean that we have an understanding about *how* those problems work over time and across situations. What is meant by "how the problems work"? Problem analysis is functional to the extent that it attempts to describe how the various factors related to a client's problems interact in everyday life. For example, although research on substance abuse informs us in a general way about the causes, course, and consequences of addictions, each client will manifest their struggles in a unique way. For one client, daily stressors, problems coping with anxiety, and interpersonal conflict may act as precipitants to binge drinking (and binge drinking, reciprocally, will exacerbate anxiety and relationships). For another person, antecedents to drug use may be associated with otherwise positive social encounters (e.g., parties), even though the consequences may be negative (e.g., mood disturbance, poor school or work performance). A child struggling with symptoms of ADHD and behavior problems at home may have trouble concentrating in the classroom and staying in his seat. At other times, when conditions are more tranquil at home, he may have an easier time getting some of his homework done and respond more readily to praise from his teacher. The functional assessment is important to complement the multidimensional assessment for this reason: although we know much about mental illnesses, addictions, child abuse, ADHD, and other problems, the causes, course, and consequences of those problems will be different for each client.

There are a number of key concepts related to the functional analysis that can help us map out each client's unique experience with their problems and better understand their adaptive capabilities. These include (1) *temporal sequencing and patterning* of thoughts, feelings, behaviors, and social-environmental events related to the client's problem, (2) measurement of the *frequency, severity (intensity), or duration* of specific problems,

(3) identification of *contingencies* (i.e., antecedent events, responses to those events, and resulting consequences, that is, rewards and punishments) that influence the client's behavior, (4) *setting of priorities among different problems*, (5) establishing *progressive hierarchies* to gradually address intervention objectives, (6) understanding the *client's unique construction of the problem and their expectations for change*, (7) focusing on problems that are *amenable to change*, and (8) defining problems in a way that is *sensitive to change over time*.

The third key element of the MFS assessment is an appreciation for systemic interaction, not just among the components of a client's "individual" problem, but those problems as they interact with other people and social systems. Family systems theory has capitalized on this key aspect of assessment to help us better understand how members of a family interact within subsystems (e.g., parents, husband and wife, siblings, parent-child dyads) and how these interactions among individuals and subsystems within a family can continue to reinforce problems of one or more family members (e.g., a conflicted couple focus their anger on an adolescent son or daughter rather than resolving their own differences; a mother-daughter dyad forms an alliance to cope with the husband/father with a serious drinking problem). But an appreciation for systemic interaction can go well beyond the immediate family to include extended family members, friends, neighbors, and other community members as well as school personnel, workmates, law enforcement, and social service workers. Thus, a systems assessment is necessary to obtain a full understanding of factors that cause and maintain an individual or family's difficulties and highlights intersection points for potential intervention (e.g., working with a teacher in schools for a child with behavior problems; coordinating an intervention that includes a child-welfare agency for a mom court-ordered to substance use treatment who wants to regain child custody).

The Five Steps Toward a Complete MFS Assessment

1. Determine the *sources* of data.
2. Decide on the *methods* for obtaining data.
3. Conduct a thorough *multidimensional-functional-systems analysis.*
4. Consider the implications of the data for *intervention planning.*
5. Delineate a plan to *monitor client progress and evaluate the intervention.*

Determine the Sources of Data

Social workers often rely almost exclusively on client self-report when conducting assessments. In some cases, the client's description of their problems may be sufficient as in situations where the client presents mild to moderate stressors or situational problems where there is little reason to hold back or dissemble about important information. But even under these circumstances, clients often provide an incomplete picture of the problem and factors related to it. Individual clients may be quite ambivalent about their reasons for coming to see a social worker, might not fully understand what is troubling them (and are, therefore, unaware of relevant factors affecting them), or might distort or withhold information they deem embarrassing. Court-ordered clients (e.g., substance abuse, child-abuse allegations) may understandably minimize or deny important aspects of their behavior because they fear reprisals (i.e., confidentiality does not come with a 100-percent guarantee). Individual partners may give a very honest yet one-sided view of their relationship problems; children and adolescents are likely to paint a rosy view of their school situation or problems at home; seriously mentally ill persons may simply not be able to give a sensible account of what has been happening to them due to delusional thinking or denial of an illness. Social workers have an obligation to go beyond the client's view of the problem and obtain additional information from other sources to corroborate and complete the psychosocial assessment. Other sources include family members, others in the community such as teachers, other social service professionals, coaches, and medical and legal records, among other sources.

Decide on the Methods for Obtaining Data

Qualitative and quantitative assessment can be conducted in a variety of ways. *Face-to-face interviews* with clients, family members, and other collaterals are the most frequently employed method for obtaining assessment data. The information obtained includes both self-report of individuals as well as their reports about others, including the client. Although client self-report is essential, the information and perspective provided by significant others can also be invaluable with respect to understanding what is going on with the client and those immediately around the client. Face-to-face interviews can be fairly unstructured, semistructured, or highly structured. *Unstructured interviews* are best when there is little predetermined agenda and the interviewer is open to exploring possibilities offered by the client or others who may have important viewpoints on the client's problem. However, social workers usually approach an interview with a client or a collateral source with some assessment framework in mind, and a thorough psychosocial assessment implies some degree of structure that is designed to capture salient psychosocial information. These would be referred to as a *semistructured* approach to assessment. Highly *structured interviews* might be used when there is a specific and specialized reason for an interview such as an investigation of child abuse or a thorough mental status exam for a competency court hearing whereby the practitioner is utilizing a standardized instrument that is well tested for reliability and validity. Structured interviews are also often used in clinical research and evaluation to enhance reliability in data collection and measurement. Any or all of these approaches may be used in an assessment that utilizes face-to-face interviews.

In some cases, the best approach to data gathering may be *observing clients' behavior in their environment* (e.g., home, hospital ward, school, consulting office, or summer camp). Of course, as with all assessments, this approach requires informed consent on the part of the client and/or their parents or guardians. However, unobtrusive observation of a client can be invaluable since clients generally "forget" they are being observed and can demonstrate problem behaviors and adaptive strengths that the prac- titioner can observe live (i.e., in vivo). Live observation has at least one major advantage over client self-report in that the social worker can make a more objective appraisal of some problem behaviors than they could if they had to rely on the client's reported perception of their own behaviors. Consider a social worker trying to understand why a child keeps getting into fights at school. Simply asking that child why he is getting into fights with others at school is likely to yield rather biased results. Simply asking a teacher or school aid might also yield biased results. The social worker may get a more accurate picture if they observed the child at play during lunch and recess. A child who presents himself as a victim in a face-to-face interview may appear to be the bully under in vivo observation.

For younger children, many child therapists attest to the usefulness of drawings, toys, games, and dolls as a method of assessment. Research evi- dence suggests that these methods are an excellent way for practitioners to help engender rapport with children, help children to express themselves, and explore the children's reports of problems or events in their lives. However, research has not supported the view that interpretation of the symbolic nature of children's play or children's drawings is a valid form of assessment or that it adds much to an otherwise competent assessment based on more objective means and should never be used to diagnose a child or confirm child-abuse allegations.

If in vivo observation is not practical, having clients *demonstrate (role play or "act out") a problem situation* can be the next best thing. Clients who are having trouble with social anxiety or communication skills, for example, can demonstrate how they negotiate a social situation either on their own or with the help of a social worker who stands in as a proxy for a client's significant other. Role playing can provide valuable insights not available to the client through self-reflection. Asking parents to role play with their child how they discipline or encourage the child to do a chore or finish homework may be very telling above and beyond the report of the parents. Role playing can serve as both a valuable assessment tool as well as a valuable behavior change method (i.e., a form of rehearsal) as we shall see in subsequent chapters.

Having clients engage in *self-monitoring* their thoughts, feelings, and behaviors across various situations for a week or two (e.g., keeping a diary of their eating-disordered behaviors, having a parent or teacher keep a chart noting a child's homework completion) can contribute to the functional assessment of clients' day-to-day struggles. All of these assessment activities may include the collection of qualitative data, quantitative data, or (preferably) both with the adjunctive use of charts, diaries, indexes, and scales that will be explored in greater depth below.

In general, the more sources of information and methods of data collection in an assessment, the more an accurate picture will emerge about clients' struggles, the severity of those problems, clients' strengths, and other challenges and situational factors they deal with in relation to the problem. However, such a comprehensive strategy is not always feasible, and practitioners must sometimes choose which method seems optimal under the circumstances. Sometimes client self-report is sufficient if there is good reason to believe the client's self-report is accurate. In other circumstances, observation of the client may be best, and in others, corroborating information may provide more accurate data than even the client's own self-report.

Conduct a Thorough Multidimensional Functional Systems Analysis

Given that there are numerous sources and methods for collecting assessment data, we can now move to an examination of the actual content of the MFS assessment.

INFORMATION REGARDING CLIENT IDENTITY

Agencies typically require some basic background information about clients. Often, this information is gathered by an "intake worker" who is not conducting the primary intervention. Other times, the social worker who intends to continue working with the client may collect basic background information as part of the formal assessment. In any case, information such as the client's name, gender, marital status, race, religion, income source, insurance coverage, and so forth, is usually determined by agency policies, and this basic information is usually gathered in the first visit.

Background information can be understood on two levels. Some of it is simply "client identification" data or "demographics," such as age, gender, race, and so on, and can usually be readily determined in the initial interview. However, matters such as sexual orientation, religion, family composition, race, ethnicity, and other "personal identity characteristics" may be very important to the client's identity and are often associated with complex layers of meaning. These matters should be approached in a more thoughtful and informed manner. Matters of sexual orientation, feelings about one's racial identification, subjective ethnicity, or matters of spirituality or religious practices are often of great significance to the client, and can be revisited after the "preliminaries" of the first intake visit are addressed. These matters will be addressed further on in this section.

THE PRESENTING PROBLEM

During the first visit, clients generally expect that they will discuss the reasons that brought them into the agency, that is, the *presenting problem*. Practitioner queries such as "So what brings you in to see us today?" or "What seems to be troubling you?" are acceptable and routine openers. Practitioners should listen carefully to the way clients *describe their problems from their own point of view*. Often, simple prompts such as "uh-huh" or "please go on" are sufficient for encouraging clients who are anxious to talk about their difficulties or distress. Other clients, such as those who are very depressed or have been mandated for treatment, may be less forthcoming and may require a bit more prompting and structuring (basic interviewing techniques will be addressed further in Chapter 5).

Practitioners, however, should feel ready to ask simple follow-up questions to encourage further details in an attempt to more fully understand the client's problems and concerns from the client's point of view. Practitioners should be willing to express genuine curiosity about the client's difficulties and ask questions in a matter-of-fact style. Basic queries should include

WHO: Who did what? Who was there? To whom are you referring? Who else was involved?

WHAT: What happened? What happened before and after? *Then* what happened? What were the consequences?

WHERE: Where did this occur? Where did you go?

WHEN: When did that happen? What time of day? Day of the week, month, year?

WHY: Why do you think they did that? Why did you have to go? Why did you decide to go for help?

In the initial stages of the assessment, it is probably best to avoid openly making judgments or drawing conclusions about clients' difficulties. Only after more data gathering, ideally with input from more sources, can practitioners begin to work with clients to "connect the dots" regarding what factors seem to be related to their presenting complaints.

PSYCHOSOCIAL HISTORY WITH AN EMPHASIS ON PROBLEM TRAJECTORY

History taking is an essential part of a thorough assessment. Most practitioners agree that the client's history is informative with regard to identifying psychosocial risk factors (e.g., abuse, trauma, childhood disorders, etc.) and adaptive strengths and provides a sense of trajectory regarding the onset of difficulties, changes in problems over time, and the client's successful efforts to cope with those problems. Obviously, the relevance of past experiences will vary, in part, by the age of the client as well as how the client personally perceives the importance of past events.

It is also important to obtain a general history of the client's life. This history taking should result in a linear timeline of key normative and problem events. Often, many clients' histories are relatively benign, and most milestones (e.g., starting school, first date, leaving home, marriage, etc.) pass uneventfully. However, within that timeline, events may have occurred that provide important clues to emerging problems. Most notably are those that portend serious mental disorders such as serious withdrawal and bizarre behaviors in high school and early childhood behavior problems such as fire setting, animal mutilation, or use of inhalant chemicals (i.e., "huffing"). Other times, the report of a client's history reveals few notable events only to be suddenly interrupted by a traumatic event "out of the blue," such as the sudden loss of a significant other, being raped, or witnessing a fatality due to a crime or accident. Although some practitioners might place too much emphasis on the minutiae of a client's past, a reasonably well-informed psychosocial history should cover key points in a client's life with special notice given to difficulties in normative psychosocial development or particularly stressful or unpredictable events and the client's attempts to cope with those challenges. Practitioners should note evidence of significant sequencing of important events, evidence of strengths or problems, and obvious patterns related to the client's presenting complaints. The process of helping a client recall past events that appear to have led up to the current problem can provide the client with some distance and perspective on the current situation.

Although retrospective reports can be fraught with distortions, memories of past events are often quite accurate and are usually important for understanding the client's current difficulties. On the other hand, memories can erode with time, and these recollections may have only limited relevance to a client's current difficulties. Both the client's subjective experience of personal history as well as research regarding risk factors can be helpful in determining the salience of historical events. Corroborating data from significant others (particularly when dealing with children and young adolescents) is essential for accurate history taking. The background data for involuntary clients should also be supported through other sources including medical, legal, and other social service records.

Overall, a basic psychosocial history should minimally include the following:

- Place and circumstances of birth and early childhood
- Childhood developmental milestones
- History of family composition and quality of family life
- School experiences
- Relations with peers and others in the community from latency through adolescence
- Reports of abuse, trauma, extreme psychosocial stressors (acute and chronic), or any indications of serious emotional or behavioral disorders
- Work and academic history
- Health history and related treatments
- Emancipation experiences (i.e., leaving home, early adulthood)
- Romantic and sexual relationships
- Early, middle, and late adult life experiences as required

It is also important to understand that assessments with very young children require a solid background in contemporary developmental child psychology. Understanding a young child's behavior at each stage of development assumes some basic knowledge of the child's cognitive abilities and an understanding that these abilities may vary from one child to the next (Bjorklund, 2000). The assessment method employed with the child (e.g., looking at pictures, playing with dolls) should fit the child's level of understanding, although much of the assessment of children can be done by observation in specific contexts (e.g., family, school, peer groups) and by obtaining collateral data from parents, day-care workers, teachers, and others. Early memories of family life (both positive and negative), early school experiences, friendships, community, and later, accomplishments, losses, adolescent experiences with peers, friendships, romantic relationships, and scholastic and work experiences can provide a rich tapestry for better understanding a client's current difficulties and adaptive capacities.

Practitioners should work with clients to develop a timeline of the problem whether it covers days, months, or years as needed. Clients can be helped to remember what happened over time by anchoring their memories with key events (e.g., When did you move to that neighborhood? Is that before or after your father passed away? Was that your freshman year in high school? In what year was your first child born?). Often, key events can trigger a chain of other memories that link to the client's difficulties. Developing a timeline with regard to the problem and linking key people and events to variations in the problem can yield important clues to understanding "how the problem works" (i.e., the functional analysis).

Practitioners can also begin to make some preliminary assessment regarding which factors in the client's life are more *remote* and relatively unrelated to the current difficulties, which are more *proximate* (i.e., more closely related to the client's current distress), which are *acute* (i.e., intense and short-term), and which are *chronic* (of longer duration and either constant or intermittent). Tentatively pointing out those factors that appear more significantly related to the client's current difficulties often helps to engage the client in the process of thinking about the current situation more analytically and helps place the primary complaint into a broader life-span perspective.

As part of history taking, practitioners should also pay attention to *clients' attempts to resolve their problems* either through their own initiative, by seeking help from others, or through professional means. Psychological and social difficulties are often recurrent, sometimes are resistant to change, and people often struggle with them over long periods of time. Practitioners should take careful note of any experiences when clients made an effort to resolve their own difficulties and had some success through those efforts.

THE INDIVIDUAL ASSESSMENT

After collecting basic background data and psychosocial history, the more analytical part of the assessment begins (i.e., What does all this information mean?). Although assessment is best understood within a social context, it is important to focus a considerable part of the overall assessment on the well-being of the individual and gradually broaden the individual assessment to include family and social relationships. This initial focus on the individual should identify thoughts, feelings, and behaviors that are relevant to the client's problems and adaptive capacities. This approach incorporates the *mental status exam*, which includes a possible diagnosis of a mental disorder.

Cognitive disturbances are often a sign of more serious psychiatric disorders. These disturbances may include *hallucinations* (i.e., seeing, hearing, smelling, or feeling stimuli that do not really exist), *delusions* (i.e., having fixed false beliefs that are simply implausible), disorientation, bizarre behavior or speech, memory problems (short- or long-term), serious confusion, or other symptoms of serious cognitive impairment. One or more of these symptoms may indicate any one of a number of serious mental disorders such as schizophrenia or bipolar disorder, organic brain disorders such as Alzheimer's disease, a chemical- or substance-induced condition, or a medical condition such as a brain tumor. Analysis of cognitions should focus on both the *content of thought* (i.e., the nature of clients' beliefs, convictions, and attitudes toward themselves, others, and the world) as well as *thought processes* (i.e., their reasoning abilities, how they arrive at conclusions). Analysis of the content and processes of cognitions is not only relevant for serious mental illnesses, but can also reveal irrational or dysfunctional thinking (e.g., about oneself, others, the world, the future) often at the core of less serious problems related to relationship problems or general functioning in everyday life.

Conducting a thorough and accurate assessment and diagnosis of serious cognitive disturbances requires considerable training in how to conduct a mental status exam and how to use the DSM-5 and is best done in collaboration with a medical specialist in psychiatry and/or neurology. Beginning social workers, however, should achieve some basic understanding of these symptoms and related conditions through a course in psychopathology, develop the ability to identify these symptoms in order to make proper referrals, and be prepared to work with clients who experience symptoms of more serious mental disorders.

Mood and emotional disturbances can be particularly significant when they are acute (i.e., sudden and extreme) or when mood disturbances are chronic and exceed normative expectations given the client's situation or particular circumstances. Mood disturbances usually become problematic when they interfere with a client's close relationships or broader social or occupational functioning and can be associated with depressive and bipolar disorder, substance abuse, and anxiety disorders. Mood disorders and emotional problems are common in both adults and children. Sudden and severe depression may be the result of a sudden tragic or traumatic event such as a sudden loss, life-threatening medical diagnosis, major disappointment, or other stressful event. On the other hand, a serious bout with depression (which often runs in families) can come on gradually, almost imperceptibly, even to those who know the client well, and cause considerable degradation in the person's sleep and overall energy level, loss of optimism and initiative, loss of pleasure in life, withdrawal from loved ones, poor work performance, and even suicidal thoughts and attempts.

Anxiety symptoms can be equally debilitating. The causes of anxiety (as with depression) can be complex in origin and result in symptoms such as chronic worry and dread or obsessive concerns that cause dysfunction in daily life. Serious anxiety can result in sweaty palms, racing heartbeat, and shortness of breath with feelings that one might faint or go "out of control." Anxious clients often begin to avoid situations where they feel afraid, and these situations may multiply to the point that the client begins to avoid work or social gatherings altogether. Anxiety problems may occur "out of the blue" or as a result of extreme stressors or traumatic events. In any event, anxiety problems are often not discrete and may accompany other problems such as depression, substance abuse, and other serious mental illnesses that include other cognitive disturbances.

Behavioral problems refer to more discrete, observable actions on the part of the client that cause the client and/or others distress. Behavior problems can range from the mild to severe and can be related to mental disorders, substance abuse and addictions, deficits in impulse control and poor interpersonal skills, personality disorders, conduct disorder and criminal activities, or other difficulties in self-regulation. Some behaviors may be primarily troublesome for the individual, such as compulsive hand washing for the person with an obsessive-compulsive disorder or avoiding going out of doors for the person suffering from agoraphobia. Behavioral problems may also be troublesome for others, including family members and others in the community. These problems may include violence, drug abuse, or other criminal activities. Practitioners should consider how well clients engage in everyday activities, such as their ability to express themselves effectively, ability to work out problems patiently, and tendencies to verbally or physically lash out at others or communicate constructively, run away from problems, harm themselves, or exhibit a proneness to impulsive, criminal, or drug-abusing behavior.

The assessment should not focus exclusively on behaviors only considered negative or dysfunctional, even though those are the behaviors that usually bring clients into treatment. It is also important to identify and highlight those *coping capacities and adaptive strengths* that clients bring with them as well. These may include a strong work ethic or evidence of even one solid relationship. Clients who have struggled with depression, anxiety, or abusive relationships may have had their share of problems and difficulties coping, but they may also have developed strong survival strategies and the will to persevere. These capacities can be harnessed to help the client address their current crises and ongoing problems.

Social work practitioners are not expected to conduct medical exams or diagnose physical disorders. However, conducting a *general health history* is often a part of a routine psychosocial assessment. Clients often know quite a lot about their health status and are willing to share much of that information including reports of previous and current diagnoses, treatments, and use of any medications. Such information is important because mental health and physical health are closely intertwined. Knowing that a client's medication can make that client depressed or that the client is drinking alcohol against doctor's advice is important. Medical conditions may also affect daily functioning and have a negative impact on a client's ability for self-care (e.g., daily hygiene, going shopping, climbing stairs, driving, etc.). Whether clients can feed, clothe, and otherwise care for themselves are important data to gather as part of the assessment. Lastly, social workers should know that collaboration with the client's physician (with the client's written consent) is a two-way street: social workers need to communicate periodically with physicians to better understand the client's condition as well as to inform the physician of any significant changes in the client's psychosocial condition. The biopsychosocial nature of client problems is often better addressed through interdisciplinary collaboration.

An individual assessment often includes a *DSM-5 diagnosis*. Although psychiatric diagnosis assumes that much of a client's mental illness is caused by factors within the individual, social workers are well aware that many problems are also affected to some degree by familial and broader social factors (e.g., abuse, discrimination, poverty). Nevertheless, it is important to provide a diagnosis for our clients for at least three reasons: (1) mental illness is real, often caused largely by biological factors, and must be identified in order to provide competent mental health treatment; (2) psychiatric diagnosis provides a common nomenclature recognized by other mental health professionals; (3) practitioners are often obliged to provide a diagnosis for administrative, legal, and insurance purposes. Social workers are legally obligated to provide and justify a psychiatric diagnosis.

As client problems are identified, practitioners may also have to utilize more specialized forms of assessment. For example: a social worker may identify depression in an elderly person but may require additional training or consultation with another specialist to identify or confirm an underlying emergence of Alzheimer's disease; a child with behavioral and learning difficulties may need additional specialized testing with a school psychologist to determine if they are suffering from autism or attention deficit hyperactivity disorder; a teenager with an eating disorder and possible drug problem is likely to require a medical exam to determine if they are experiencing other somatic disturbances. In brief, a thorough psychosocial assessment can raise important questions that require further examination by other professionals. These matters may be overlooked in an incomplete assessment. A rule of thumb for social work practitioners should be: when in doubt, refer out (for further assessment and diagnosis).

An Example of the MFS Approach to Assessment

By way of illustrating the individually focused part of the assessment, let's consider a client, Jill, a fourteen-year-old female adolescent who recently started school in a new community (her mother and stepfather just moved).

THE INDIVIDUAL ASSESSMENT

An individual assessment reveals troubled *cognitions* (e.g., "nobody likes me; I don't fit in"), *mood and emotional disturbances* (e.g., fits of anger, chronic worry and depression), and some *behavioral difficulties* (e.g., fighting with other girls, scratching up her arms, and suspected drug use). Jill's *health* is otherwise good. Her *background history* reveals little psychosocial disturbance other than some chronic tension between her and her stepfather that began about four years ago. Although she shows no signs of serious mental disorder, there is cause for concern and probably some linkage among her negative view of herself and others, her emotional upset, and her disturbing behaviors. Diagnoses to be considered after a thorough assessment might include oppositional defiant disorder, substance use disorder, and persistent depressive disorder.

As the model in Figure 7 illustrates, Jill's troubled thoughts, emotional distress, and problematic behaviors are *reciprocally interacting,* meaning that they are mutually self-perpetuating (i.e., reinforcing). Since it is hard to determine where this cycle begins and ends (although cognitive theorists would suggest that cognition is primary), individual assessment does not emphasize a linear analysis but provides a working model of the client's

FIGURE 7. A MODEL ILLUSTRATING ASSESSMENT OF THE INDIVIDUAL CLIENT

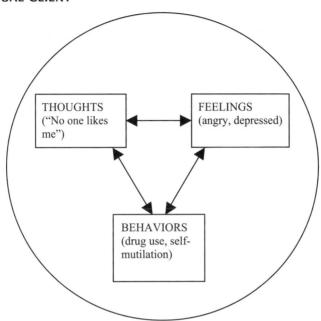

internal experience which can be addressed by interventions on multiple levels: changing thinking, coping with feelings, and modifying behaviors. However, this brief illustration of an individual assessment, although helpful, does not give us the whole picture. To more fully appreciate her difficulties and circumstances, we must place her individual assessment within a broader family and social context.

THE FAMILY ASSESSMENT

Assessing couples and families is also part of a complete MFS assessment. Couples and families must also be assessed on multiple dimensions, and understanding family interactions (i.e., behaviors, communications) is an essential part of the functional assessment (i.e., "how the problem works"). What problems is the family experiencing? How severe are those problems? What adaptive coping skills and strengths does the family have? And, what behavioral patterns, interactions, and sequences define the family's difficulties as well as their efforts to resolve those problems? These are key questions for an MFS approach to family assessment.

Although there is a variety of family therapy "theories," most of them are relatively untested and remain somewhat speculative and abstract. Nevertheless, some generic practical guidelines have emerged from a combination of couples and family research and the "practice wisdom" of family therapists. These key concepts are, more or less, common to most family therapy assessment models (as was noted in Chapter 1) (Minuchin, 1974; Nichols & Schwartz, 2006). These concepts include:

- The family system: the whole of the family is greater than the sum of its individual members.
- Family structure and hierarchy: identifying family roles and who has influence (e.g., power, authority) and who does not.
- Family subsystems: alliances within a family that can be seen as a "system within a system"; these groups may include siblings, parents, or alliances between parents and children; subsystems may be functional or problematic.
- Boundaries (rigid vs. enmeshed) between family members or subsystems: boundaries may be rigid (where family members create nearly impassible blockages between them) or "enmeshed" (where family members may be overly involved with one another in presumably dysfunctional ways).
- Systemic interaction and communication patterns: how members interact, the types and styles of behaviors utilized, the consequences of those behaviors, and the overall "emotional tone" associated with these interactions (e.g., anger, caring, contempt, competition).
- The behavior of individuals in context: individual behavior is better understood within the context of family interactions.
- Triangulation: when a family member becomes a target or vehicle for family conflict (e.g., a couple are angry at each other and fight for their child's allegiance); often causes difficulties for the individual who is deliberately or unwittingly targeted.
- Intergenerational patterns: when family problems are "passed on" from one generation to the next (e.g., a child who grows up in an alcoholic home and takes on a "parental role" by monitoring her own parent's drinking problem; she then develops a drinking problem of her own; and her children subsequently adopt the same parental role toward her). (History taking for one or two generations can provide both the family and practitioner with a better understanding of recurrent generational difficulties. It should be kept in mind, however, that these problems can be transmitted through a combination of both genetic and psychosocial risk factors.)

- Family developmental trajectory: the normative or problematic passage through typical family milestones, including early marriage, young children, the high school years, emancipation of children, "empty nest" years for the parents, the arrival of grandchildren, and so on.

The assessment strategies associated with the more effective family therapies tend to reflect the key aspects of MFS assessment of both individual behaviors and family interactions (Birchler & Spinks, 1980; Duncan & Parks, 1988; Mueser & Glynn, 1999; Northey, Wells, Silverman, & Bailey, 2003; O'Leary, Barrett, & Fjermestad, 2009). The illustration and assessment schematic in Figure 8 owes its influences to both structural and cognitive-behavioral family systems models. In this author's experience, many practitioners use similar approaches when assessing families, and new practitioners should be encouraged to adopt similar assessment strategies. The symbols in the graphic are intuitively straightforward. Key characteristics or problem descriptions can be noted within the circles representing each family member. Single-pointed arrows suggest a positive influence (e.g., support) from one person to another. Double-pointed arrows suggest mutual support or reciprocal influence. Dotted lines suggest a loose or tenuous relationship between persons. Lines with hash marks suggest barriers or conflict between family members; the more hash marks, the more blockage or conflict. Since there are no standardized or well-tested graphic displays of family assessment, practitioners should take what liberties they need to capture family dynamics in a concise but descriptive way. (This author, for instance, likes to use lightning bolts to suggest severe conflict between individuals.)

In this diagram, it appears that there is mild conflict between Rudy and his wife Marsha but severe conflict between Jill and her stepfather. Jeff, Rudy's biological son, is close to his dad, and Jill has a mutually supportive relationship with her sister, Jen. But affection and support toward her mom is not being reciprocated, and Jeff has only tangential relations with his two stepsisters. It is also useful to consider the existence of subsystems within the family. In the above diagram, Jen and Jill seem to be well bonded, as are Jeff and his father. But key alliances that form a wholly supportive family are absent. For example, Rudy and Marsha are really part of two major subsystems: their role as a couple and their shared role as parents. Neither of these two subsystems appears to be operating well at the time of the assessment. Subsystems between parents and children and among the children seem to suggest some fragmentation within this family.

FIGURE 8. MODEL ILLUSTRATING AN APPROACH TO FAMILY ASSESSMENT

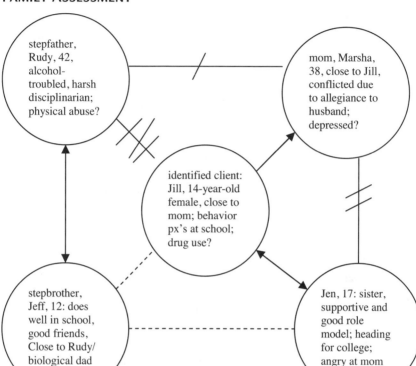

In conducting a family assessment, it is important to recognize that most families these days do not fit the conventional "nuclear" model (e.g., two parents, two kids, and a dog or cat). Many families have one parent present, possibly another biological parent intermittently in the picture, perhaps a stepparent or live-in partner who shares some parenting duties, maybe other extended family members who are involved, and so on. The definition of what constitutes "a family" has become considerably blurred in recent decades, and social workers should be flexible with regard to labeling or defining exactly what constitutes a family. Perhaps a useful definition is as follows: people residing together for a shared purpose of mutual love and support. Although this definition could refer to a well-functioning cult as well as a family, the concept of individual and collective well-being may serve as a useful organizing principle when assessing a family and its members.

The social system assessment

As part of a complete MFS assessment, both the individual and family system assessment should be integrated within a broader social system perspective. This approach to assessment has been well established, for example, as part of evidence-based practices with behaviorally disordered adolescents (e.g., multi-systemic therapy developed by Henggeler, Schoenwald, Borduin, Rowland, & Cunningham, 1998, 2009). This approach links the family assessment to the wider community, including school, workplace, and relationships to other organizations such as human service and health care providers. There is an array of different approaches to graphically displaying these interacting social constructs, and they are all derived from social work's traditional person-in-environment perspective. Nevertheless, a qualitative graphic display of interacting influences in the client's life (using the same symbols as in the illustration of family assessment) can be a useful tool for putting the client's challenges in perspective, identifying important social supports and environmental barriers, and conceptualizing how various social domains of a client's life interact.

A fairly simple qualitative systems model is shown in Figure 9. Practitioners can use it to record how well the client is doing in each of these important domains as well as to identify important persons within the client's various social domains who support or are a liability to the client's well-being.

The diagram provides a somewhat impressionistic overview of Jill's problems within a broader community context. In the center, she is triangulated by family conflict. Although struggling academically, she is receiving some support at school and is cooperating by seeing the social worker. Her stepfather's drinking problem has manifested itself at work and in the community, and he is in conflict with the Department of Child Welfare. Lastly, Jill has a mixed relationship with some peers: they provide emotional support but are a source of problems and conflict due to their mutual involvement with drug abuse.

Summarizing the MFS assessment

Having gathered a lot of information about a client's individual, family, and social functioning from multiple sources using multiple methods, summarizing all these data succinctly can be a daunting task, even for seasoned practitioners. However, the MFS framework can help practitioners do just that if they emphasize three things: (1) focus on those dimensions where the client is experiencing the most problems (e.g., psychological, interpersonal, community, work); (2) describe in sequential fashion those individual, family, or social factors that appear to be closely related to those key

FIGURE 9. MODEL FOR ASSESSING A FAMILY WITHIN THE COMMUNITY CONTEXT

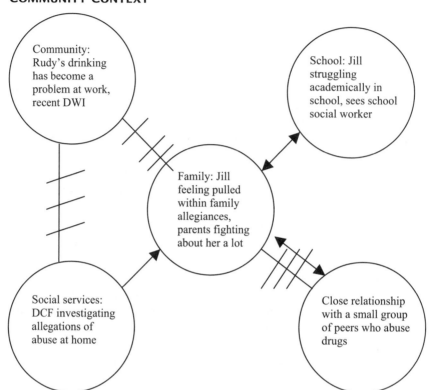

problems (i.e., "How does the problem work on a day-to-day level?"); and (3) make an effort to understand how the individual, family, and social systems interact and contribute to the problems or their solutions.

A succinct summarization of Jill's difficulties may be as follows: Jill is depressed, angry, discouraged about her grades, having behavioral problems at school, and may be exacerbating her problems by using drugs (although the extent of drug use is not clear at this point); and her parents' conflicts are apparently having a negative effect on her, particularly her mother's failure to protect her from Rudy, who has been verbally and physically abusive in the past. Rudy's drinking is causing difficulties for the whole family. Nevertheless, Jill has a close relationship with her sister, who seems somewhat resilient in the face of these family troubles and who has encouraged Jill to continue seeing the social worker. At some point soon, the social worker will have to confer with child welfare. Whether or not

Rudy will seek help for his drinking problem and work on his marriage is currently an open question. Functionally, Jill's emotional and behavioral difficulties seem directly linked to family conflict, abuse from her stepfather, and the negative interactions she has been having with schoolmates and some of her teachers. These problems are not likely to abate until her parents begin to resolve their problems as individuals and as a couple, and collaborate to help Jill with hers.

After having completed the MFS assessment, practitioners may feel that further assessment is warranted if a particular problem requires a more detailed look. For example, if it appears that Jill may be seriously depressed or more extensively involved with drugs, more focused assessment can be targeted at those problems through the use of standardized scales and/or a referral for further consultation. This additional information would be incorporated into the overall assessment when those data become available. Moving forward with an intervention without first further assessing the severity of specific problems would be shortsighted and could lead to the wrong intervention strategy.

There are a large number of brief, reliable, and valid scales practitioners can utilize with their clients to further explore problems such as substance abuse, eating disorders, depression, anxiety disorders, childhood disorders, and marital distress. These scales are not intended to be a substitute for a complete qualitative MFS assessment but can be an important addition to it. Some of these scales are also designed to be used as evaluation tools when administered periodically before, during, and after the intervention to track client progress. Scales and related instruments will be discussed in more detail later in this chapter.

Incorporating Cultural Competence into the Client Assessment

Becoming knowledgeable about your client's cultural beliefs and identity is essential to conducting a sound assessment and establishing a productive working relationship. As with most concepts relevant to the ongoing assessment, this knowledge informs one's judgment continually throughout the intervention process. Both individual and family systems assessments should include an examination of racial, ethnic, religious, and cultural identity and its meaning as defined through the perspective of the client. This "meaning" is likely to vary among individuals and families, and allegiances will vary in quality and intensity across generations. The meaning of ethnic, racial, and cultural identity might also vary by socioeconomic level.

Some of the earlier social work literature on "diversity" had a tendency to oversimplify various characteristics and traits associated with different racial and ethnic groups. The fact is, although there may be some characteristics that appear to be more prominent in some groups, making broad generalizations about various racial or ethnic groups should be avoided. The concept of "ethnic identity" should be considered quite malleable across generations, within and between racial and ethnic subgroups, and within individuals. For one thing, a growing number of people claim multiracial and multiethnic heritage. For another, the extent to which broad characteristics are uniquely attributable to any group is questionable and often borders on stereotyping. For example, some texts have suggested that "family" is more important to one racial or ethnic group than another. To the extent that this might be true, it is probably more a matter of degree, possibly more related to socioeconomic level than culture, and there is likely to be wide variation in the importance placed on family closeness and allegiance from one family to another.

Rather than categorizing, social workers should focus on the *process of engaging clients in conversation during initial sessions about how they subjectively view their own racial, ethnic, and religious affiliations, history, and commitments.* These views can vary considerably, even within the same family across generations, and will often reveal a picture characterized by nuance and subtlety, not ethnic or racial caricature. Guidelines for assessing cultural allegiances might include identifying the birthplace of the client and family members over two or three generations, immigration experiences, differences in assimilation and acculturation experiences across generations, examining clients' use of language (preference for native or English and in what contexts—e.g., work vs. home—they use each), examining the ethnic identity of friends and acquaintances, noting the various types of media they access (TV, newspapers, Internet sites), and exploring clients' participation in cultural and religious events as well as preferences for music, art, entertainment, and food. Practitioners can also gauge the extent to which clients have assimilated into American "norms" and how they feel about those who are not part of their ethnic reference group (Shiraev & Levy, 2007; Uba, 1994). Rather than attempting to become experts in treating a wide array of cultural subgroups (an impractical solution), practitioners should strive to become knowledgeable about the culture of the families with whom they work, avoid their own cultural myopia, and explore each client and family's unique perception of their own cultural background without predetermined assumptions, biases, and prejudices (Sue & Sue, 1999). The "process" versus "categorical" approach to exploring ethnicity, race, and culture readily lends itself to working with a wide variety of clients should one find oneself working in a highly diverse community.

If a practitioner is interested in working with a racial or ethnic subgroup with whom they are largely unfamiliar, they can take some steps to become knowledgeable about the group's history, culture, traditions, and mores. Although some research suggests that clients appreciate seeing "people like us" when they seek social work services, this "demographic matching" is no guarantee of good rapport during the intervention. Beyond having staff who can speak the language of the local nationalities, other factors can impede a good working alliance: generational differences (e.g., a young practitioner is not sufficiently deferential to the family elders; the client's dress and demeanor is too "Anglo"; the practitioner was trained to be "aloof" rather than active, a posture that most clients find cold, if not offensive, etc.). Even practitioners who are two or three generations removed from the "old country" may not be very familiar with many aspects of their own cultural heritage, norms, language, homeland politics, or other topics that clients would expect from "one of our own." Conversely, there is not much evidence that, if the practitioner is not from the client's culture, they cannot successfully engage the client on these issues. Practitioners can compensate for a lack of first-hand knowledge by learning about the client's culture, language, and traditions and inquiring about the client's beliefs in these matters. These efforts can make the work more enriching for the practitioner and also help the client feel respected, more valued, and better understood.

Consider the Implications of the Data for Intervention Planning

A good assessment provides important clues for intervention planning in a number of ways: first, it identifies *what* problems need to be addressed and what *strengths* the client possesses; second, it provides a measure of the *frequency, severity, and duration* of each problem; third, it helps to *set priorities* regarding the relative importance of problems; fourth, it helps us to understand functionally *how the problem works* (thus, providing clues as to how to activate positive change processes); fifth, it describes *systemic interaction* among the people connected to the problem; sixth, it reveals important factors regarding *cultural identity* that might influence engagement and treatment participation; seventh, it lays a foundation for *evaluation* (both qualitatively and quantitatively); and, eighth, it provides some basis for *selection of intervention methods*.

Perhaps the most important implication of a complete assessment is that it provides guidelines for the development of an intervention strategy.

There are two main avenues of information that help practitioners develop the intervention plan. First, there is a large body of clinical outcome research now that provides useful guidelines for selecting interventions that are likely to be effective with a wide range of problems. These interventions are generally some combination of supportive skills used to develop a working relationship, cognitive-behavioral coping skills that help clients learn to deal more effectively with their problems, and case management skills that enhance social and instrumental supports in the community and coordinate complex interventions. The optimal combinations of these skills that have been shown to be effective in controlled clinical research are referred to as *evidence-based practices.*

However, we know that applying these approaches in "cookie-cutter fashion" is neither realistic nor clinically wise and would not be acceptable to many clients. Evidence-based practices need to be applied with some degree of flexibility to accommodate client needs, wishes, and special circumstances. Nevertheless, outcome research provides important guidelines in the selection and adaptation of these approaches to individual clients, but the whole process depends first and foremost on having conducted a thorough and accurate MFS assessment. Beginning with the next chapter, the remainder of this text will be largely devoted to describing the essential skills of social work practice and how these skills can be optimally combined to form evidence-based practices.

Delineate a Plan to Monitor Client Progress and Evaluate the Intervention

A thorough assessment not only provides a framework for *better understanding of the client's problems, strengths, and potential solutions,* but also provides a *baseline for monitoring client change* and, to a more limited degree, *supports the evaluation of the intervention.* Thus, *the assessment and formulation of the evaluation plan happen at the same time* and provide the foundation for intervention planning. It is important that practitioners and clients clearly define the problems qualitatively so that they can be reassessed periodically during the course of the intervention and again at termination of treatment. Examples of qualitative evaluative questions that emerge from the assessment include:

- Does an elderly depressed and withdrawn male client become less depressed and more involved with family and friends over the course of the intervention?

- Does a young woman struggling with binge eating disorder reduce binging and purging, reduce her alcohol consumption, and change the way she thinks about her own body image in a more healthful direction?
- Does a young man with shizophrenia become less thought disordered, begin to interact with others in his social club, and begin to shower and launder his clothes more regularly?
- Does a young conflicted couple become better able to discuss their problems more constructively and make progress toward sharing and compromise?

TYPES OF MEASURES USEFUL FOR ASSESSMENT AND EVALUATION

Although qualitative indicators of client progress are useful and often unique to the client, they can be somewhat vague and often inconsistent. A practitioner's estimate of what constitutes "moderate depression," for example, may vary over time with a client, may vary between different clients, or practitioners on a treatment team may disagree about what "moderately depressed" actually means. *Quantitative measures* can enhance qualitative assessment and evaluation. Scales and simple indexes can provide less ambiguous baseline data (i.e., the initial measurement of key client problems), which provide a benchmark against which future progress is judged. Quantitative measures provide a valuable complement to the qualitative assessment and evaluation plan for several reasons: (1) they are often more reliable than clinical observation alone, (2) they have been shown to be valid with other people experiencing similar problems, (3) they have possibly been shown to be sensitive to client change over time, and (4) the data can be aggregated (pooled with other client data) and used to judge the performance of a whole program (i.e., program evaluation), a process that is now required in many agencies.

Quantitative "instruments" can range from the simple to the complex, but those that are more practical and amenable to daily service delivery are emphasized here. These include simple indexes, unidimensional scales, and multidimensional scales. Single-item indexes measure one specific problem, such as number of drinks consumed per day, number of minutes a child spends doing their homework, severity of depression, number of days homeless, and intensity of intimacy a couple shares with one another. These are important and straightforward indicators that are also sensitive to change and, thus, can provide both a good baseline measure at assessment as well as an important indicator of progress during intervention and at termination. Because of their ease of use, multiple indicators can be used as needed. Simple indicators are generally considered reliable and reasonably valid if the source of data is deemed to be a trustworthy and reasonably objective observer. Other than relying on qualitative impressions, the simple index is, perhaps, the most frequently relied upon indicator of client progress in clinical practice.

When deciding on what to use as an index, practitioners should consider two important points: the *dimension of human experience* to be measured, and the *type of scaling* to be utilized to measure that dimension. There are basically four dimensions or expressions of human behavior that practitioners can observe: a client's *thoughts (cognitions)* (via verbal report); *feelings, affect, and emotions* (via verbal report and observation); *behaviors* (via verbal report and observation); *and physiological indicators* (via verbal report and observation). Although these dimensions interact in complex ways, it is important to distinguish them when considering the design or selection of a specific index. Ideally, one should measure all of them. Consider the person who has a serious anxiety problem. The client may report having very frightening *thoughts* (e.g., "I feel like I am losing my mind"), may report *feeling* overwhelmed (e.g., reports feelings of inability to cope and extreme dread), may indicate *physiological* arousal (e.g., racing heartbeat, light-headedness, stomachaches), and may manifest *behavioral* problems (e.g., avoiding work, driving, and social contact). The practitioner and client may choose to select one or more of these indexes to monitor the client's progress and evaluate the outcome of the intervention. The following changes would suggest improvement: for *cognitions,* lowering the intensity of the client thinking he is losing his mind; for *feelings,* reducing feelings of dread; for *behaviors,* more frequent contact with family or friends and better work attendance; for *physiological* indicators, a general lowering of somatic symptoms.

The second consideration in designing simple indexes is the type of measurement scale to utilize. There are no hard and fast rules in selecting the type of measure, so discussing with the client the best way to measure the specific problem is a good way to give them input into the process. Indexes are typically measured in one of three ways: frequency, severity (intensity), or duration.

Frequency indicates how often the event occurs. How many days per week do you drink alcoholic beverages? How many panic attacks do you have per week? How many times did you yell at your child this week? How many days of school did your son miss in the past month?

If one is concerned with the *severity* (intensity) of a problem, one may use one of the following examples: How severe has your depression been since last week? How close do you feel to your spouse right now? How frightened are you about making that speech in front of your whole class next week? Intensity can be measured with simple scales such as "low, moderate, high" or asking a client to rate the intensity of the problem "on a scale from 0 to 10."

Indexes of *duration* can be simply measured by time intervals (i.e., seconds, minutes, hours, days, weeks, etc.). How long have you been depressed? How long has it been since you've relapsed (or, alternatively, been sober)? How long can your son concentrate on his homework at night without being distracted?

Thus, when selecting a quantitative measure for baseline assessment and monitoring client progress, practitioners should consider three key questions: (1) What is the problem to be measured? (2) What dimension of human behavior will be the focus (i.e., thoughts, feelings, physiological responses, behaviors)? (3) What type of scale will be employed (i.e., frequency, intensity, duration)? The grid below may be a useful guide in determining the best way to construct an index that can be used as part of assessment and ongoing monitoring and evaluation.

	Frequency	Severity	Duration
Thoughts			
Feelings			
Physiological			
Behaviors			

Using the graphic above, practitioner and client could discuss which approach would be most useful. For the person with an anxiety problem, they might decide that *severity* of thoughts of "losing my mind" measured on a scale from 1 to 10 might be most helpful, that *duration* of feelings and physiological symptoms might be best measured in "hours per day," and that *frequency* of contacts with family and friends would be a meaningful indicator of lessening behavioral withdrawal. The strength of using simple indexes is in their apparent validity, ease of use, and the fact that they can be tailored to meet a client's unique problems and treatment goals.

Although simple one-item indexes are quite versatile and intuitively useful, practitioners are increasingly likely to use unidimensional and multidimensional scales in routine practice. Unidimensional scales measure one concept (e.g., depression, self-esteem) but use multiple items to do so. These scales have some advantages over one-item indexes because they are likely to have greater reliability and validity by using ten, twenty, thirty, or more indicators. Different scaling devices are used to measure the items in a unidimensional scale. Three of the more common measuring devices are Likert-style scales (e.g., strongly agree, agree, disagree, strongly disagree), severity scales (e.g., low, moderate, high), and "yes/no" scales (known as dichotomous measures). A brief scale to measure couples' satisfaction in a relationship, for example, might look like this:

I enjoy spending time with my partner.
   Strongly agree (4) Agree (3) Disagree (2) Strongly disagree (1)

I like to share household responsibilities.
   Strongly agree (4) Agree (3) Disagree (2) Strongly disagree (1)

I believe we share a common vision for the future.
   Strongly agree (4) Agree (3) Disagree (2) Strongly disagree (1)

I think we enjoy visiting with each other's families.
   Strongly agree (4) Agree (3) Disagree (2) Strongly disagree (1)

I enjoy making love with my partner.
   Strongly agree (4) Agree (3) Disagree (2) Strongly disagree(1)

Although each item might serve as an important index to gauge improvement in this couple's relationship, the collective strength of five (or more) indicators would provide a better overall measure of progress; the higher the overall score, the greater the progress. Some problems might progress more than others. Many couple satisfaction scales have twenty or more items. Most problems experienced by clients have multiple aspects to them, so it makes sense to measure problems such as the intensity of couple satisfaction by measuring many indicators.

Multidimensional scales are similar to unidimensional scales in that they use multiple indicators. But, as the name indicates, they measure several dimensions of a more complex concept. A more sophisticated couple's satisfaction scale, for example, might have five items for each of the following domains or "subscales": intimacy, parenting, dealing with extended families (in-laws), sharing household duties, money matters, and engaging in recreation together for a total of thirty items (five items for each of six domains). Each subscale or dimension of couple satisfaction would be scored separately, and an overall score would be provided as a "global" satisfaction score for the relationship. The advantage to a multidimensional scale is that it provides a more complex view of the relationship and allows for a more detailed assessment and evaluation of progress in different dimensions of the couple's relationship. For example, the couple may be doing very well with regard to matters of parenting and finances but be having serious conflicts with regard to intimacy and getting along with their respective in-laws.

Overall, using quantitative measures in practice can increase consistency and accuracy in the initial assessment and monitoring of client progress but can only do so if they have been tested for reliability and validity. A scale has good *internal consistency reliability* when respondents complete the individual items of a scale in a way that is consistent with the concept being measured. For example, consider the three items below that are part of a hypothetical thirty-item scale measuring depression:

I think of killing myself.
   a lot (3)   *somewhat (2)*   *a little (1)*   *not at all (0)*

I feel happy.
   a lot (3)   *somewhat (2)*   *a little (1)*   *not at all (0)*

I feel sad.
   a lot (3)   *somewhat (2)*   *a little (1)*   *not at all (0)*

If this scale has good internal consistency, one would expect that, if the client answers "a lot" in response to the item "I think of killing myself," they would also respond at least "somewhat" or " a lot" to the item "I feel sad." One would also expect that they would respond "a little" or "not at all" to the item "I feel happy." If the client answers the same to all three items, this would seem very counterintuitive (since their general mood can't be both very happy and very sad at the same time), and if the client responds in this contradictory way for all the items, one would expect the results to show a low level of internal consistency. However, if they indicated they were very sad, very suicidal, and not at all happy, the scale would likely show high internal consistency (assuming this pattern was consistent for the other twenty-seven items of the scale).

Another form of reliability that is of key importance in everyday practice is *interrater* reliability. Let's say that two practitioners are working with the same client, and both have access to the same assessment data. One practitioner suggests that the client shows only mild suicidal ideation, but the other practitioner insists that the client is very suicidal. One would consider their judgments to be at a poor level of agreement. That is not to say that one is right and the other is wrong. Aside from the issue of accuracy (i.e., validity, to be discussed below), scales need to demonstrate good interrater consistency (interrater reliability). As with the case above, if two practitioners use a "suicidal intent scale" with the same client in two different interviews, the results should be shown to be reasonably consistent. In fact, using scales that have been tested for interrater reliability tend to enhance agreement among practitioners because it puts them "on the same page."

However, just demonstrating that a scale has good reliability does not mean that it is a valid scale. Scales can have good reliability but be inaccurate. Consider a scale that measures all the signs and symptoms of "alien abduction syndrome": high anxiety, a feeling that you've gone on a faraway trip but don't know where you've been; a sense that you have been medically examined against your wishes; a feeling that someone is coming to take you away on another long trip to a faraway place whether you like it or not; and so forth. Practitioners can be trained to consistently rate these "signs" with clients who believe they have been, in fact, abducted by aliens. (Sounds preposterous you say? Thousands of people have claimed to have been abducted by aliens and have sought treatment for the "effects.") In other words, such a scale can be shown to have good reliability, but without hard evidence that people have been abducted by beings from outer space, it would be hard to argue for the validity of this condition.

Validity is a matter of degree and is measured by how well the scale corresponds to more observable and objective measures of the phenomenon. There are four main categories of validity: face validity, content validity, criterion validity, and construct validity. *Face validity* suggests an intuitive confirmation based on expert opinion. Are the three items that measure depression (i.e., degree of suicidal intent, happiness, and sadness) actually indicators of depression? *Content validity* is determined by judging whether a sufficient number of indicators represent the concept (depression). Although three items are illustrated here, they would not be sufficient to measure depression. Presumably, other items would include things like "I feel hopeless," "I have trouble sleeping," "I am pessimistic about the future," and so forth. *Criterion validity* can indicate *concurrent validity* (i.e., the scale correlates with another valid scale or more objective indicator of depression) and *predictive validity* (i.e., the scale will predict treatment outcome in a month or two). Lastly, *construct validity* is, perhaps, the most difficult to demonstrate and requires a variety of statistical techniques to show that a range of indicators accurately correspond to the items of a scale. Scales should also be *sensitive to change,* meaning that, if the client's condition does change, the scale is sufficiently sensitive to measure that change. Although scale development and testing (i.e., psychometrics) requires special research skills, practitioners need not be experts in this area. Many reference books containing reliable and valid scales are now available to social workers for use as aids in conducting more focused assessments and evaluations of practice.

STRATEGIES FOR EVALUATING ONE'S OWN PRACTICE

Evaluation methods used in everyday practice share common characteristics: a clear definition and valid measure of the problem or other area of functioning (e.g., depression, social skills) and a well-defined intervention (so we know *what we are evaluating*). A change in the baseline measure of depression or social skill would indicate change (i.e., the outcome). Qualitative evaluation may be the easiest and most practical to use. Basically, we obtain a detailed accounting of the client's view of the problem, provide some form of intervention, and judge the client's progress (or worsening of a problem) at some point based on their self-report and/or the observations of others (including the practitioner).

Another approach to routine evaluation of individual cases is called *single-subject design*. The simplest approach involves utilizing quantitative indexes (as discussed above) or a valid scale to provide a baseline measure of the problem (represented diagrammatically below as "A"), provide an intervention (represented as "B"), and after some period of time (say, six sessions) repeat the measure ("A") to see if the client has made progress in response to the intervention. This process describes the classic ABA design illustrated below.

A	B	A
take a baseline measurement	provide the intervention	measure the client's problem again

This approach is the most basic, practical, and useful evaluation model and corresponds to what occurs "naturalistically" in daily practice: assessment, intervention, and evaluation.

However, there is a variety of variations on this model in single-subject design literature (Bloom, Fischer, & Orme, 2009), most of which cannot be used in routine care because they constitute *single-subject experimental designs,* and as such, require special permission and approval to utilize them. Single-subject experiments are primarily concerned with *hypothesis testing and knowledge-building,* and not *routine evaluation.* Some approaches involve planned changes in the treatment (i.e., before treatment actually begins, not as a spontaneous change of course) to see if the client responds differently under different treatment conditions.

For example, the practitioner may begin by base-lining the client's problem (alcohol abuse) ("A"); then engage the client with basic relationship and motivational skills for two weeks (intervention "B"); then the practitioner might add specific problem-solving methods (intervention "C"); and, after two weeks or so, measure the problem ("A") again to determine whether the client has increased or reduced their drinking or made no change. The model is short-handed as an "ABCA" design, and there are variations of this approach. The rationale for this design suggests that if the client changes in response to a change in treatment conditions, then they must be responding to some part of the treatment itself (or both parts of the treatment, although it is hard to tell because of "carry-over" effects). Although there are considerable limitations to drawing the conclusion that the client's change was actually the result of the change in treatment, these problems of *internal validity* in research design will not be addressed here. What we can say is that *planned changes* in an intervention made for the sake of testing out the effectiveness of an intervention is far from practical in everyday social service settings, and some might consider it a breach of ethics if done without prior approval of the agency's Institutional Review Board.

What is acceptable and practical in daily practice is the ABA design (initially discussed above) since it does not require any planned change (although agency services might have time limits), and this approach does not test any hypotheses about treatment effectiveness except for the implicit question as to whether the client improved over time. By naturalistic is meant that the practitioner collects assessment and evaluation data as part of routine practice but does not conduct planned changes in treatment conditions as part of that evaluation. Services are provided as they normally would be, but scales can be routinely incorporated into treatment procedures to measure change in the client's condition. *Naturalistic program evaluation* operates in much the same way, except that practitioners would use a common set of measures for all the clients in a specific program (e.g., substance abuse clinic) in order to see if the program as a whole was effective. In addition, for longer-term clients (e.g., severe mental illness) multiple measures might be taken over months or years.

In summary, "evaluating one's own practice" may include the use of qualitative or quantitative judgments (measures) on a routine basis and can inform us as to whether our clients are improving, staying the same, or getting worse. Answering questions about the validity of underlying theories, how clients change, or whether the change was the result of the actual intervention, however, are more difficult and require more rigorous and methodologically sophisticated research and evaluation designs.

Summary

Conducting a thorough MFS assessment and evaluation plan can facilitate the selection and implementation of effective intervention. The assessment is informed by contemporary human behavior research, provides a unique functional analysis of the client's problems and strengths, examines the systemic interaction among those relevant to the problem, and is supported with the use of qualitative assessment and quantitative measures that provide a basis for monitoring client progress. Perhaps the most important reason to conduct a thorough MFS assessment is to provide guidance for the selection of effective interventions. In the next three chapters, the building blocks of interventions (i.e., essential skills) will be examined.

CHAPTER FIVE

Supportive Skills

THE SKILLS OF HELPING that facilitate engagement with the client, put them at ease, establish a trusting and empathic working relationship, provide comfort, understanding, compassion, and encouragement, and further facilitate the implementation of the assessment and intervention are referred to here, for sake of simplicity, as "supportive" skills. As noted earlier, the research on the working relationship and basic counseling skills is voluminous, and the evidence for the importance of a sound working relationship is impressive (e.g., Hill, Nutt, & Jackson, 1994; Hill & O'Brien, 2004; Horvath & Greenberg, 1989; O'Hare, 2015; Orlinsky, Grawe, & Parks, 1994; Orlinsky & Howard, 1986; Rogers, 1951; Truax & Carkhuff, 1967). Implicit in the ability to develop and maintain a good working relationship as well as engage and motivate clients in the change process is the need for practitioners to master basic interviewing skills (Hill & O'Brien, 2004; Shulman, 1999; Sommers-Flannagan & Sommers-Flannagan, 2003). Although practitioners and theoreticians of good will often disagree about the meaning or theoretical significance of the working relationship, most social workers are in agreement that a sound supportive relationship and essential interviewing skills are a critical dimension of effective care.

The Basic Elements of Supportive Skills: Listening and Communication Skills

Interviewing skills are, perhaps, the most elemental of the helping skills. They are not only essential for the effective use of supportive, therapeutic coping and case management skills, but also necessary in order to conduct valid assessments and evaluation. Thus, basic interviewing skills lay the foundation for effectively implementing all social work practice functions. Basic interviewing skills include asking important questions, accurate listening, seeking clarification, accurately identifying feelings, and recounting client experiences. Skillful interviewing creates a level of discourse that encourages a client to be forthcoming about their difficulties, enhances collaboration, and enhances the client's adaptive capabilities. To better understand clients, practitioners must make their best efforts to enter and understand the client's subjective world to better understand who they are, what experiences they have had, how they see themselves and others, how they understand their current difficulties, what they want to achieve, and what they need to do to improve their lives.

At all stages of service provision, from first contact to last, interviewing skills are utilized to: (1) develop and maintain a working relationship with the client; (2) obtain as accurate a picture as possible of what the client thinks, feels, and does; (3) deepen the practitioner's understanding of the role of persons and events that affect the client, both through the client's eyes and by interviewing significant others; (4) encourage the client to engage in the intervention process; and (5) assist the client in monitoring their own progress and evaluating the impact of the intervention as best they can. How interviewing skills are utilized may vary from client to client based on the client's age, presentation style, and psychological and intellectual capacities as well as the practitioner's own personal style. Nevertheless, there are some basic interviewing skills that have been well researched and honed by years of practice experience. They will be briefly reviewed below before considering other supportive and facilitative skills.

Types of Questions Used in the Helping Interview

There are different types of questions one can use to help the client generate their personal narrative and obtain the information necessary for understanding a client's difficulties and adaptive capabilities. A good general approach is to ask questions initially that are somewhat general and then work toward more-specific questions that focus on greater detail. This deductive trajectory from the general to the specific is helpful not only in the first couple of interviews when the practitioner is conducting a thorough assessment, but in later interviews as well when clients are actively engaged in working toward solutions to their problems. Most of what follows regarding basic skills applies to older adolescents and adults. Adapting essential supportive skills to working with children will also be addressed in this chapter.

Open-ended questions are quite general and allow the client wide latitude to talk about themselves and their situation. By using minimal prompts and little structure, open questions provoke the client to take the initiative to discuss what *they* think is important. In the first visit, for example, a practitioner may simply begin with, "So, what brings you into the clinic today?" For some clients, this opener may be more than enough. At some point, the practitioner may have to interject some modest amount of structure in the discussion to obtain necessary information to conduct the formal assessment (see Appendix B). However, for verbally active clients, a little structure and occasional prompts ("So, tell me a little more about when you first felt depressed") may be sufficient.

Closed-ended questions offer a more limited range of answers and encourage the client to provide more definitive answers to specific topics. "So, did you drink alcoholic beverages this weekend?" may be a follow-up to a client's vague report on how they have been coping since being discharged from a detoxification facility. If the client responds in the affirmative, closed-ended follow-up questions might include, "So, how many drinks did you have?" With a court-ordered client, a practitioner might ask, "Have you tried to see your spouse since she had a restraining order taken out on you?" Closed questions are intended to limit the range of possible answers, in this case, to "yes" or "no."

Specific questions are intended to focus the interview in greater detail on important subjects regarding the client's thoughts, feelings, behaviors, or details of a situation or event. These questions are intended to fill in the gaps of a general narrative about especially important events. They may include any of the following as well as others: "When did your husband hit you?" "Was this the first time?" "No? Then, how many times had it happened before?" "How did he hit you? Was it a slap or a punch?" "Did he ever use an object or a weapon?" "What kind of injury did you sustain?" "What happened after the event was over?" "Did you call the police?" "Was anyone else there to witness what happened?" Although in some situations, the interview may sound a bit like an interrogation, this is typically not the case if a sound working relationship has been formed with the client and the practitioner communicates empathic concern. The details of a client's problems and experiences may be critical to understanding exactly what has been going on for them. At times, talking about the events "out loud" may be the first time the client has had a chance to process their thoughts and feelings about a very stressful or traumatic event. The opportunity to discuss the events in detail in the presence of an empathic and trusted listener can be inherently therapeutic.

Detailed querying is also critical when recounting a client's experiences in implementing their intervention outside of the "fifty-minute hour." Most effective interventions involve a client's active participation in the treatment during their everyday lives whether the purpose is working on communication skills with their partner, improving parenting skills with an oppositional child, taking "one day at a time" to stay clean and sober, or trying to master their social anxiety. When client and practitioner meet in session, recounting the client's efforts to implement the intervention in their everyday life usually involves some reconstruction of events to gauge whether they are making progress: "What opportunities did you make to work on your social anxiety this week?" "For how long did you carry on your conversation with that new woman in your office?" "Did you ask her out for a cup of coffee?" "How did your lunch date go?" "Did you ask her about what she likes to do in her free time?" "What did she say?"

Some counseling texts refer to interviewing styles as either directive (structured) or nondirective (unstructured). The fact is, effective interviewing requires a thoughtful use of both. Nondirective interviewing relies more on open-ended questions, creates ambiguity regarding expectations of the practitioner, and gives clients free rein to take the discussion where they want to go. A directive style introduces more structure into the interview, utilizes more closed questions that limit response options, and is more purposeful to the task at hand. As for the client recently discharged from detoxification, mixing closed and open questions might sound like the following: "So, you had about fifteen drinks on Saturday afternoon. Can you tell me what was going on with you emotionally at that time?" (open question); "Did you make any attempt to cut short your relapse?" (closed question); "How did you feel about your slip the next day?" (open question). Utilizing only one interviewing approach or the other makes little sense in social work practice. The exclusive use of a nondirective approach would result in puzzling ambiguity and leave many clients eventually wondering what the purpose of the intervention was. Conversely, an exclusive reliance on a directive style would likely leave some clients wondering if the practitioner were even interested in what they thought or felt, or were simply carrying out some predetermined agenda of his own. Directive and nondirective approaches should be mixed and follow both an inductive (broad information gathering) and deductive (drawing cause-effect conclusions) pattern. The purposes of each interview are guided by the goals of the intervention (previously negotiated between practitioner and client) and the phase of the intervention: completing the assessment, implementing the intervention, or conducting the evaluation. Generally speaking, sessions with clients should probably begin on an open-ended note and move toward a more structured purpose that is linked to treat-ment goals. Imbuing each interview with that kind of rhythm helps to keep the purposes of the intervention at the forefront.

Adopt a Relaxed and Attentive Posture

Helping a client feel at ease is the result of several processes and is closely intertwined with good interviewing skills: careful listening so the client feels that they are being understood accurately; carefully delineating both the practitioner's and client's role; and being relatively nonjudgmental and focusing on an agenda that will solve problems and enhance coping in everyday life. Practitioners must be genuine, authentic, and come across in a way that is congruent with who they are. Clients feel more at ease when the purpose of the meetings is understood, and they feel that they have some input into the treatment agenda. Even court-ordered clients can be given some degree of choice and a sense of control over methods and treatment goals. Clients will also feel more at ease when they feel assured that those aspects of ethical practice (see Chapter 3) known as informed consent and confidentiality will be upheld. Clients feel more at ease when the practitioner communicates that they are knowledgeable, competent, and confident that they have the skills to help the client. Finally, clients feel more at ease when they sense that the purpose of the meetings is to focus exclusively on the agreed-upon goals of the intervention and that there is no other competing agenda insinuated into the meeting. Said another way, the expressed purpose of the meetings is to help the client achieve their goals.

Most clients are at least a little nervous when coming to be interviewed by a social worker, particularly the first time. They may be suffering from a psychiatric disorder, being investigated for alleged abuse, be struggling with a drug problem, or have recently been released from prison. The client may be relieved to have the opportunity to be seen, may be guarded or angry at being coerced into the visit, or may be indifferent. Some clients may be suffering from psychoses and somewhat delusional about the pur-pose of the meeting, and others may be so depressed they are almost unable to respond to questions. In general, it helps to begin by appearing relaxed and attentive. This presentation will communicate to the client that the practitioner is alert, ready and willing to be of assistance to them, and interested in hearing what they have to say. Depending on the cognitive and emotional state of the client, practitioners should be ready to expend the necessary level of energy it takes to engage each client depending on how much initiative the client takes in the interview. The client recently court-ordered to the interview, for example, may be hostile and only give one-word answers, provoking the interviewer to work harder to engage the client in the assessment. A very anxious client may speak very rapidly, obsess over every minute detail of a story, or jump from one subject to the next. Practitioners might need to help these clients structure their presentation and focus on more substantive matters. The depressed client may be almost mute, necessitating that the practitioner work very hard just to excavate even basic background information. Practitioners should consider "relaxed and attentive" a good starting point but be flexible and ready to engage the client according to their needs, abilities, and expectations.

Nonverbal Communication

For the most part, in Western cultures, making *eye contact* is a powerful form of communication in that it demands the other person's attention and also communicates a form of psychological engagement. When you are looking into the client's eyes, it says that you are paying attention to them. Although this may generally be the case, not all clients are comfortable being "stared at" for a lengthy period of time. Clients who are shy or otherwise anxious, are feeling unduly scrutinized, are ashamed, or hiding something they feel uncomfortable about may begin to chafe under a social worker's unwavering gaze. In some cultures, it may be simply impolite or even an affront to make steady eye contact. Practitioners should take notice to determine whether a client is comfortable making consistent eye contact, and if not, perhaps break off the constant gaze by taking occasional notes or looking down or away from the client between questions or points of discussion. Some practitioners have been known to position their chairs in such a way that they need not look directly at the client if they seem uncomfortable. Being flexible about seating arrangements and providing choices for the client can help them be more comfortable during the interview.

If one pays attention to everyday conversation (on line at the check-out counter, at home with family, with friends, or at work) one would readily become aware that much of what passes for conversation is nonverbal. By *nonverbal behaviors* is meant nonword vocalizations and physical gestures that convey fairly specific meaning in everyday discourse. "Nonverbals" are, essentially, powerful shorthand vocalizations and gestures that facilitate communication. The classic "a-huh" encountered in popular media portrayals of therapy is, indeed, a common utterance. It is simple, easily recognized in everyday conversation (although not in all languages), and is infinitely flexible to provide nuanced indication of interest in what the client is saying. "A-huh" can suggest keen interest, boredom, humor, disapproval, concern, or compassion with the slightest inflection. The same can be suggested about "hmmm," "a-hah," or other nonverbal expressions. Practitioners should pay careful attention to these almost automatic utterances and note how clients respond to them since their meaning can be ambiguous.

Other nonverbal utterances, of course, include facial expressions, another powerful form of communication. Generally, social workers do not receive the kind of training that, for example, professional actors do. So they may not be keenly aware of what they are saying (nonverbally) through facial expressions. But, facial expressions can clearly communicate any of the following, often in a more primal and compelling way than words can: concern, compassion, disgust, anger, sarcasm, pity, ridicule, alarm, fear, and so forth. Spending some time in front of the mirror may not be a bad way to examine how one expresses the full range of emotions, and being aware of how one "wears one's feelings on one's face" is critical to becoming aware of how one communicates emotional responses to clients. After several months of this author working with a depressed young woman going through a divorce with an apparently difficult man, she remembered little about what I had said during our sessions but recounted in her last session: "All I had to do while talking about how things were going at home was to look at your face, and I knew that I wasn't the crazy one!" Fortunately, my ingenuous communications of alarm and puzzlement at their encounters validated for her that his behaviors were somewhat extreme, unfair, and sometimes hostile and that the failure of the marriage was not all her fault.

But nonverbal behaviors go well beyond facial expressions. Sitting back, relaxed with one's legs crossed comports with the earlier suggestion to "be relaxed and attentive." At some point, however, such a posture would seem bizarre if, for example, a client is recounting a time when he was sexually assaulted or was contemplating suicide. Physical posture communicates an emotional response, and *practitioners must be aware of what they are trying to say with their physical presentation.* Again, practicing in front of a mirror may help beginning practitioners to define extra concern (e.g., leaning forward in one's chair to listen with extra care, reeling back slightly with a single clap of the hands to express surprise at a fortuitous outcome, or joy at a client's courageous breakthrough). Leaning sideways in one's chair and scratching one's head to communicate a bit of confusion can be an effective way of saying, "Your version of the story seems to contradict what you were telling me last week. Perhaps I'm not getting this right." Although traditional approaches to psychotherapy long extolled the virtues of adopting a somewhat impassive, "blank slate" posture on which clients would project (displace) their deepest feelings about others in their life, this posture can not only seem contrived and artificial to some clients, but can be easily interpreted as apathy. Given that most social work encounters are relatively brief (say, three to twelve visits) there is little benefit in creating such a level of ambiguity and confusion. When it comes to communicating with clients, practitioners should assume that everything they say or do, even silence, is a form of communication. The question is, What is it you are trying to say to your client, and is it in their best interest (i.e., helping them move toward their intervention goals)?

Reflection, Tracking, and Clarifying

Effective communication between two people is generally considered a process of developing mutual understanding of each other's thoughts, feelings, intentions, and behaviors. Most theoretical communication models are represented as feedback loops: one person communicates a message, the other person receives it, analyzes it, and sends back a communication. The first person acknowledges the response and demonstrates that they understood the second person's response, and the cycle continues. Understanding someone you know well or are especially close to can almost seem automatic. At times, you feel that you can anticipate what that other person is about to say. Sometimes friends, family members, or intimate partners can communicate and be fully understood with a gesture. People sometimes talk at one another simultaneously (breaking all the rules of good communication) or finish each other's sentences and, amazingly, can still find mutual understanding at a deep level.

Working with clients is another story, and little should be taken for granted about clear communications. The helping relationship is a professional and somewhat contrived one whereby relative strangers are expected to divulge very personal information in a relatively short amount of time at scheduled intervals. As such, professional helping interviews are a special kind of relationship and require more purposeful communication skills. Understanding what your client is trying to tell you and helping them understand your responses can be much more difficult and these skills must be cultivated with much practice. Helping the client feel understood is a task that often must be accomplished in a relatively short amount of time, not over weeks, months, and years. Communication is facilitated by the practitioner demonstrating that they really comprehend what the client is trying to get them to understand. Practitioners are primarily responsible for seeing that the communication "feedback loop" is completed on a consistent basis. In addition to careful listening, the practitioner can ensure that this communication process is complete by consistently testing the clarity of the signal between practitioner and client.

Reflecting, tracking, and clarifying are related communication skills that are used to focus on one major goal: to gradually string together a clear, accurate, and understandable client narrative and help the client confirm for themselves that you have understood them. Reflecting, tracking, and clarification are three related skills used to continually test the hypothesis that you, as practitioner, are "getting" what the client is saying. Reflecting simply means repeating in a somewhat different way what the client said to see if your meaning is congruent with theirs. This, of course, may take a bit of doing and may require a process of gradual approximation. Clients generally appreciate the fact that you are making the effort to accurately reflect what they are saying before you move the conversation forward. One way to quickly "lose" a client's tenuous commitment to your working alliance is to behave as though you knew what the client meant when, in fact, you didn't. Instinctively, the client might sense that you didn't understand them and failed to make an effort to clarify what they said due to apathy or distraction. Making a concerted effort to understand exactly what the client meant shows respect, empathy, and a real commitment to helping the client. Clients have to feel, first and foremost, that you are willing to try hard to listen and understand what they are saying from *their point of view*. The practitioner may develop their own point of view, and at a later time (after a working relationship has developed) may share their perspective with the client. But, especially early in the helping process, the practitioner must demonstrate that they are willing and able to listen and reflect back to the client a very accurate understanding of what the client is trying to say.

Accurate reflection is more challenging with some clients than others. Young children, for example, might not have the verbal capacity to express their thoughts and feelings or describe others' behaviors or intentions clearly or accurately. Adolescents may use language that is comprehensible only to their immediate social group. Many clients may be struggling with the host country's language. Other clients may have verbal difficulties due to poor education, learning disabilities, or other developmental disabilities. Clients suffering from serious mental illnesses might utilize idiosyncratic language or have difficulty saying what is on their mind due to a thought disorder. Practitioners, whatever the circumstance, should be prepared to be quite flexible and resourceful in finding ways to communicate with their clients. In many circumstances, such as in the case with younger children, persons who primarily rely on a non-native language, or persons with specific problems with verbal expression, practitioners should be prepared to obtain specialized training so they can fully communicate with their clients.

After demonstrating that you can accurately reflect what the client is saying, *tracking* what the client is saying means demonstrating that you can follow their narrative along from one point to the next. For clients who express themselves in clear, organized, linear fashion, tracking the client's narrative may be relatively easy. However, many clients encountered in social work practices are struggling with emotional distress or cognitive impairments as a result of substance abuse, mental disorders, or other learning disabilities. Tracking what the client is saying may involve more than just following along but may take considerable effort on the part of the practitioner to help the client construct their narrative both temporally (i.e., connecting time and dates related to key events) and sequentially (i.e., sequencing cause and effect over time). This process of helping the client track the timeline and causal sequence of events often requires some directive interviewing but must be done with a minimum of interference.

Clarification combines the best of both reflection and tracking. Clarification means accurately communicating to the client not only that you understand specific facts or expressions of feelings, but also that you understand how the client's experiences evolved over time and across situations. When practitioners clarify, they are not simply making sure that they understand each individual fact of the client's narrative, but that they are beginning to get the "big picture" (i.e., put the facts in a broader context) and are beginning to "connect the dots." The "dots," or elements of your client's experiences, are related to all facets of their experience: thoughts, feelings, behaviors, and situations, especially those involving other people in their lives. As a result of clarification and understanding, an intricate picture of a client's experience begins to emerge. To use a more contemporary metaphor, accurate clarification of a client's experiences is similar to the emergence of a picture from a digital camera: the clearer the electronic signal (i.e., the more pixels), the clearer the whole picture. Clarification is, essentially, a descriptive exercise, not an interpretive one. A good test of whether you have achieved clarification is an unambiguous confirmation from the client whereby they will verbally and physically respond with some variation of "Yes, that's exactly what I mean!"

At times, practitioners must confront clients with known facts or the practitioner's professional opinion regarding something that potentially affects the client's well-being or the well-being of others. The term *confrontation* often brings to mind the stern or disapproving admonishments of an authority figure. In the working relationship, confrontation skills are utilized to give clients accurate feedback for two purposes: (1) the practitioner might have information that points out incongruities or apparent falsehoods in what the client has stated and maintained (e.g., evidence of child abuse, drug use, violence toward a partner, or other harmful or unethical behaviors), and (2) the practitioner might feel the need to point out something about the client's behavior that puts her at risk (e.g., repeating behaviors that put the client at risk of harm in a relationship, behaviors that put the client at greater risk of relapse with drugs or psychiatric symptoms). There are many other reasons why practitioners sometimes have to express opinions to clients that the client may be resistant to accepting. For confrontation to be effective, however, a sound working relationship must be in place. For example, if a young woman with a history of dating verbally (and sometimes physically) abusive men says, "I know he's been violent before, but I really think I can change him," the practitioner might respectfully muster the relevant facts of the client's past relationships and present them in a straightforward manner: "Jill, based on our previous discussions, it sounds to me like you're about to make the same mistake you've made several times before. Each time, you thought you could change abusive men by loving them. And, each time, you have ended up being disappointed and, on several occasions, abused again. I think we need to examine more closely why you seem to believe you have this power to change abusive men and why you confuse their efforts to control you with 'love' or 'passion.' Maybe we should talk about this some more before you plunge ahead again. What do you think?"

For a young man struggling to abstain from alcohol and other drugs, confrontation may take the following form: "Joe, you've been in and out of rehab three times now. Each time, you've made an attempt to hang with the same group of guys that like to party a lot. How is this time going to be different?"

Practitioners should develop their own style with regard to confrontation. However, confrontation is a skill to be implemented with a balance of straightforward honesty and sensitivity. Being ambiguous, tentative, or overly sensitive is likely to be both confusing and ineffective. Real compassion requires the ability to be honest and explicit when the practitioner feels that the client is ready to receive accurate feedback. Being sensitive does not mean being ineffectual. Navigating the path toward an effective confrontation takes practice, and confrontations should be used sparingly and, again, only after a sound working alliance is established. Although clients generally expect that they will be given some feedback from their practitioner, it needs to be done in a way that communicates empathy for their ongoing struggle.

Adapting Basic Interviewing Skills to Work with Children

Children, as a function of age and cognitive development see the world differently than do adults. Thus, interviewing children requires special skills and a solid understanding of what cognitive competencies they have at each age. Practitioners who work with young children especially should have a solid grasp of modern child developmental psychology. Young children (younger than age six, more or less), particularly, often have very different ideas about human relationships, the passage of time, and difficulty sorting out the concrete from the abstract. Children may have very good memories of specific events, but retrieving and understanding these memories may be affected significantly by the experience of the interview itself. Children also have many fears and anxieties, some realistic and some not. They are quite susceptible to the vagaries of their imaginations in response to things they are told by others, see on TV, hear in bedtime stories, or see in the movies. The phenomenology of young childhood is quite different than that of older children, adolescents, and adults.

It should also be understood that there are different purposes to interviewing children in social work practice: clinical assessment (to describe the problem and understand those factors related to the problem to prepare an intervention) and forensic assessment (to determine if the child has been abused). Many of the basic principles of interviewing described in relation to adults apply to children as well: careful listening, empathic attunement, putting them at ease, reflecting, tracking, and clarifying are all essential skills for interviewing a child. However, perhaps even more critical information is obtained through observation of children, not only in the consulting room, but in the classroom, at daycare, and during structured after-school activities. Possibly the most critical information is acquired through parents, guardians, and other adults (e.g., teachers, coaches, and other responsible caretakers) who have ample opportunity to observe the child.

Nevertheless, there are some essential data that can be obtained from young children in the traditional one-on-one interview. Focus on their agenda, not yours. Listen with minimal prompts as needed and allow the child to communicate their inner world, their version of events from their point of view. Wilson and Powell (2001) suggest some ground rules for basic listening, tracking, and clarifying with a child. Practitioners should take care to communicate to the child the following: "Let me know if I misunderstand you"; "Tell me everything you can about what happened"; "Let me know if you don't understand something I've said . . . I'll try again using different words"; "Saying 'I don't know' or 'I don't remember' is OK"; "Tell me everything you remember, but don't guess . . . just tell me what you are sure about"; "Even if you think I already know something, tell me anyway"; "Only talk about things that you know really happened"; "You may use whatever words you want to use"; and "I promise I'll not get upset or angry at anything you say to me."

A variety of aids can be enlisted to facilitate interviewing with a child. These include the use of games, toys, and dolls (Morrison & Anders, 1999). When playing with children, use figures or toys that do not overly constrict the child's play or themes that they might elicit. Put children at ease, get down on the floor at the child's level, and participate in a way that encourages the child to play. Be a participant observer. Build rapport with the child, explore general themes, and then delve into promising areas with increasingly greater specificity. Be flexible in the way you approach the interview. Young children are not usually linear in communicating their story.

Research on the validity of using these methods suggests that simple games or activities that put a child at ease and enhance communication with the practitioner are helpful. These activities include playing games or using dolls to recreate or remember events that may be a cause for concern (e.g., physical abuse, sexual abuse). However, practitioners should avoid drawing firm conclusions from children's utterances in response to symbolic play. Young children are suggestible, can be easily led, and often don't understand the significance of what the practitioner is driving at. Making interpretations about a child's unconscious motives or inferring abuse from their symbolic play with toys, games, or from their drawings is very risky, and there is little evidence that such interpretations are valid. Interpreting children's play or artwork is no substitute for more objective evidence when attempting, for example, to determine some external cause of their depression, anxiety, or other behavior problem. As was discussed in Chapter 4, only through the collection of multidimensional data from multiple sources can a practitioner begin to make reasonable yet tentative hypotheses about allegations of abuse, neglect, or other events that may be negatively affecting a child's mood or behavior.

Wilson and Powell (2001) provide some guidelines for the structure of the basic child interview that reflect a similar approach to interviews with adults: establish a basic rapport, introduce the topic for discussion, elicit a free narrative account from the child using open-ended questions, and use prompts minimally to keep the conversation on track. Practitioners should use simply worded specific questions to clarify inconsistencies and obtain sufficient detail. The interviewer should then close with a brief summary and the interviewer should make an effort to provide the child with a chance to correct any mistakes or misunderstandings.

Putting Basic Interviewing Skills to Work: Developing the Working Alliance and Facilitating Change

Communicating Positive Regard and Respect

To successfully engage clients in a working alliance, communicating basic respect for them is essential. Treating a client with positive regard means that the practitioner communicates in words and behavior that they believe the client to have inherent value as a human being. Treating the client with respect means communicating through one's words, intonation, and other nonverbal expression that the client has inherent dignity and is worthy of concern and assistance. This assumption on the part of the practitioner may seem, at face value, to be an obvious prerequisite for practicing social work. However, practitioners, at times, should expect to find this assumption a challenging one to maintain with every client.

It has been commonly observed in the helping professions that some practitioners often find that clients who are more verbal, better educated, and have better incomes seem to be more appealing to work with than clients who are more marginalized or stigmatized in society. Voluntary, educated, and self-sufficient clients tend to be more personally engaging, are better socialized into the purposes and processes of psychotherapy services, are less likely to have serious mental illnesses, tend to place a priority on relationship problems, and are generally less stressful to work with. It is understandable that many practitioners cultivate their practice with clients who appear more amenable to voluntary, private social work services.

Clients who are less economically and educationally advantaged, less sophisticated in the ways of talk therapy, more likely to have serious mental health problems and chronic addictions, and who have run afoul of the law are seen by some practitioners as "less desirable" to work with. Many of these clients are considered to be "involuntary," are less amenable to the role of client, and more likely to be considered "resistant" and "difficult to treat." Some of these clients have been in prison, and some have committed serious crimes including domestic violence, physical and sexual abuse of children, rape, assault and battery, gun-related offenses, and other serious crimes. Some practitioners may find that maintaining a position of positive regard and respect for clients who have engaged in serious antisocial behaviors or are otherwise stigmatized in society is very challenging indeed.

Practitioners, particularly those starting out in their social work careers, should be honest with themselves if they experience a strong degree of ambivalence regarding working with "difficult to treat" or antisocial clients. In order to work with involuntary clients, it is essential that practitioners sort through that ambivalence early on and be willing to distinguish the harmful behaviors of these clients from some of the inherently good qualities they might have. Understanding the contributions of genetic risk factors, the developmental impact of years of physical or sexual abuse, and the enduring effects of other environmental stressors can sometimes promote empathy and help practitioners maintain respect and positive regard for the client. At some point, the client may have been a good son or daughter, a good friend, a good parent, or have contributed to the community in some meaningfully positive way. However, differentiating the person from some of their behaviors (while holding them accountable for their offenses and not treating them as hapless victims) may not be easy for some practitioners. Beginning practitioners who choose to work with clients who have engaged in harmful and antisocial behaviors should honestly explore their feelings about working with these "unattractive" groups and admit any serious reservations they might have about working with them. The social work profession serves many needy populations, and practitioners should work with clients with whom they can establish a commitment and consistently maintain a feeling of respect and positive regard.

Being Genuine, Authentic

Genuineness and authenticity are achieved when one's professional persona is congruent with who one really is as a person. Many clients can instinctively sense when social workers are not being themselves, come across as "playing a role," or present an image that simply doesn't "ring true." Being authentic and being genuine, however, does *not* mean self-confession or self-disclosure with a client. Being honest does *not* mean saying *everything* on one's mind. Such excesses on the part of the practitioner can actually make the client feel quite uncomfortable (e.g., "Who is the client here anyway?"). Every practitioner is somewhat different in the way they present themselves, in their sense of humor, in their comfort level with different clients, and in their style of professional decorum (formal vs. informal). What matters most is that a practitioner maintains good boundaries with the client, communicates a genuine empathy, and keeps the professional purposes of their work together clearly in mind.

Communicating Empathy, Compassion, and Understanding

Communicating empathy means demonstrating verbally and nonverbally that you understand, as best you can, how the client feels. Clients are likely to sense whether what you say and how you say it truly communicates empathy. Empathy should not be confused with agreeing with what the client says or condoning their behavior. Empathy should also be distinguished from compassion. Empathy is an expressed feeling that reflects a sense of shared, often painful, human experience. You may express empathy for a man who has acted violently toward his family ("I can understand your sense of frustration and sense of powerlessness") without communicating compassion. On the other hand, the practitioner is more likely to feel and communicate compassion for a client who has just lost a child to a terminal illness. Compassion goes beyond empathy, beyond merely communicating an understanding of the client's feelings and experience. Expressing compassion lets the client know that, as a person, you can imagine sharing in their disappointment, their loss, or other source of emotional distress.

Engendering Trust Through Consistency and Attending to Client Needs

Many clients have had negative experiences with people in their lives. Many clients have been physically and sexually abused by people they otherwise trusted, betrayed by someone with whom they had an intimate relationship, abandoned by a mother or father, been financially exploited, discriminated against, victimized by crime, rejected by their fellow countrymen after risking their lives for them in combat, or deeply harmed in some other way. Why should they expect a social worker to be any more reliable? Mutual trust is a condition between two people that must be developed, cultivated, and nurtured over time. It is not an assumed condition of the social worker-client relationship. Trust implies constancy and congruency. Clients are more likely to trust their social worker when the social worker does the following: says what they mean clearly and directly; does not hide behind vague answers or use a lot of ambiguous pseudoprofessional language (i.e., psychobabble); does not pretend to know things for which they cannot give a well-informed answer; and consistently focuses on the needs of their client.

Practitioners can engender trust in a client by empathizing with the client's feelings regarding experiences in which they have been betrayed and by being trustworthy as a practitioner. Being worthy of trust means being consistent, reliable, and honest with your client and always keeping their well-being in mind by keeping the main purpose of the intervention contract in the forefront.

Providing Encouragement and Enhancing Motivation

Clients come to receive social work services at different levels of motivation and readiness to make changes. Many clients experiencing personal problems, mental illnesses, substance use disorders, eating disorders, family problems, and the like generally do not feel enthusiastic about asking for help. Some may not feel they have a problem and resent having been "coerced" into social work services either through child welfare, mental health, or the criminal justice system. Some clients may be difficult to engage initially but often participate more when they feel they have some say in how the intervention will progress and they realize that participation may yield some personal benefit.

Other clients are highly motivated: they want to feel better, and they want their situation to improve. These clients are more readily engaged in the beginning, although considerable ambivalence might emerge later as they realize they may have to work hard to make some changes in order to feel better. Seriously depressed clients may have a hard time even getting out of bed in the morning, but they might feel the need to work hard due to obligations to those who depend on them. The person struggling with an addiction wants to stop drinking or using other drugs, but the initial success is often short-lived. The young angry adolescent might be tired of getting into trouble but also does not want to "give in" to the demands of adults around him. The mother being investigated by child welfare struggles with her commitment to give up daily marijuana smoking but does not want to lose custody of her children. All these clients know that they must make an effort to improve their situation, know that change might be hard, and struggle with their commitment to change.

In recent years, practice researchers have focused their efforts on reaching "difficult to engage" clients. Because of an increased emphasis in social work on working with involuntary (e.g., court referred, treatment mandated) clients, practitioners are more likely to deal with clients who don't believe that they have a problem, don't believe that psychosocial interventions are of any value, or simply disagree with practitioners about the nature of the problem or necessity for intervention. They may feel strongly (rightly or wrongly to some degree) that they are being victimized by the "system."

Supportive and facilitative skills that focus on enhancing motivation are now considered essential for engaging clients in the early process of change (Miller & Rollnick, 2013). Perhaps one of the better-known assessment frameworks for identifying a client's readiness to change is that developed by James Prochaska and colleagues at the University of Rhode Island (Prochaska & DiClemente, 1984; Prochaska, DiClemente, & Norcross, 1992). Their research team stipulates five stages of change: *precontemplation,* when clients do not agree that they have a problem, may see others as the cause of their difficulties, or may feel coerced into treatment by the courts or significant others; *contemplation,* when a client is aware of a problem and may want to find out whether therapy can help them; *preparation,* when the client takes some initial steps toward change; *action,* when a client may take more significant steps toward working on the problem and actively seek help in the change process; and, lastly, *maintenance,* when clients have already made changes with regard to a problem and have sought treatment to consolidate previous improvements. Clients may cycle through these stages of change or proceed in a one-step-forward, two-step-back pattern. The stages of change model has been employed with a range of problems including smoking cessation, substance abuse, and other mental health and health-related problems.

As the stages of change imply, clients are usually not clearly in one stage or another and may feel considerable ambivalence in the change process (O'Hare, 1996). If stages of change suggest "when" clients are ready, motivational enhancement methods (designed to help clients move beyond ambivalence and through the stages of change) suggest "how" to help clients engage in the change process (Miller & Rollnick, 2013). Readiness to change is particularly relevant for working with involuntary clients, those more-or-less coerced into receiving social work services and often labeled by practitioners as resistant, hard to reach, hostile, and unmotivated (Rooney & Bibus, 2001). However, the "voluntary versus involuntary" dichotomy is far from absolute and is better seen on a continuum. Strategies designed to help clients move through the stages of change include the following suggestions:

- Accept their initial reluctance: empathize with the client's ambivalence about engaging in treatment or making changes; acknowledge that they may have been treated somewhat unfairly without suggesting that you think they are blameless with regard to their current difficulties; and acknowledge that not everyone benefits from social work intervention. Above all, don't argue and don't try to "sell" the client on the benefits of treatment.

- Avoid premature confrontation: again, don't quarrel. Get the facts from the client and other relevant sources. The practitioner should objectively present their summary to the client and give the client a chance to respond and explain their point of view.

- Clarify one's dual role within the social service/criminal justice system. Be up front with the client. Let them know you empathize with their situation and want to help them with their concerns. However, you are collaborating with the criminal justice system because the client has been convicted of child abuse, drug possession, domestic assault, or some other antisocial act. Communicate the expectation that the client has an obligation to acknowledge the behavior (assuming the accusations are well founded), take responsibility for the behavior, and change the behavior. Not only does the social worker have an ethical obligation to protect society, they also should use the contingencies of the courts as therapeutic leverage to help the client meet the agreed-upon goals of the intervention contract (i.e., therapeutic jurisprudence).

- Explore the client's perspective on the problem, and encourage her to suggest intervention goals and ways to pursue them. Recruiting the client as collaborator this way can provide her with some sense of control and choice in developing the intervention plan.

- List problems by priority, and start with one or two that are more readily resolved; then, break each individual problem and objective down to manageable steps.

- Employ behavioral contracting: collaborate on agreements, keep them specific, and track them to completion.

- Avoid an overemphasis on the client making irrelevant self-disclosures; gauge each client's need to "open up," but don't make it a condition of pursuing intervention goals.

- Anticipate obstacles to treatment compliance: look "down the road" with the client and help them identify scenarios that may interfere with successfully reaching agreed-upon goals.

- Involve significant others when at all possible; encourage clients to recruit people in their life who have a vested interest in the client's compliance with intervention goals.

- Actively enhance motivation: help the client visualize the benefits of working toward intervention goals and consequences of returning to the previous problem behaviors; list the "pros and cons" of changing versus not making progress; empathize with the difficulties of change but communicate optimism about positive change and the benefits that might accrue.

Enhancing the Client's Confidence and Morale

Improving self-confidence, overall morale, or self-efficacy with regard to coping with some specific problem is not something that can be readily imparted to a client. It is a feeling that must be earned by graduated success experiences. Relating positive testimonials of other clients struggling with similar difficulties or reporting relevant outcome research findings might be a little helpful ("You mean I'm not hopeless?"), but there is no substitute for success. For positive success experiences to occur, however, the practitioner must be skilled in clearly identifying the problem and helping clients break it down into manageable objectives. The intervention methods used must be targeted toward achieving modest but substantive objectives, so the client can gradually gain back that true sense of confidence. This linking of client behavior and increased "self-efficacy" (i.e., the belief that one can cope in a given situation) is where the practitioner's ability to cultivate a supportive working relationship facilitates effective therapeutic coping skills. The working relationship, in many cases, makes it possible for clients to take the risks necessary to make real changes and experience success. The practitioner, and the working relationship they cultivate, becomes a catalyst for change.

Clarifying Roles of the Practitioner and the Client

The practitioner has the primary responsibility for being the "expert," that is, the practitioner, not the client, is the one who has the requisite credentials, gets paid for the service, is liable for providing services within established standards of care, and is held accountable for delivering ethical and effective interventions. Clients expect social workers to be knowledgeable about the problems they treat and skilled in the interventions they provide. Thus, in the practitioner-client relationship, the practitioner is responsible for certain roles: to conduct informed assessments, implement interventions that have been shown to be effective in current outcome research, and evaluate the results of those efforts.

Although practitioners bear much of the responsibility for implementing professional services, clients have responsibilities as well. They should

be expected to show up on time, make an effort to participate constructively in treatment, and cooperate with arranging for insurance and out-of-
pocket payments that were initially agreed upon. Clients can forfeit their
confidentiality rights and right of informed consent when they threaten to
harm themselves or other people during the course of the intervention.

Clarifying the role of the practitioner and that of the client, however,
can be confusing at times. For example, for most social work agencies,
maintaining fiscal integrity (i.e., balancing the budget) is critical, so the
agency can continue to serve the public. Sources of income for agencies
can span the continuum from private to public funding and, often, a combination of both these sources. The manner in which practitioners are
influenced by these conditions, however, can influence intervention-
planning decisions. In a busy clinic where service is paid for by a combination of state funding and private insurances, for example, should client
length of stay be determined, in part, by the extent of coverage? As one
can see, assuming even the most ethical of behavior (e.g., avoiding conflicts
of interest) on the part of practitioners and administrators, there are external influences that have subtle but real impact on how social workers
define their role in relation to the client.

Defining the client's role can also be difficult at times. One of the more
challenging situations concerns involuntary referrals. "Voluntary" and
"involuntary" labels are really a matter of degree, perhaps representing a
level of willingness to engage in treatment. If a court-diversionary program, for example, offers a client the choice of drug treatment or jail, who
is the client? The overloaded criminal justice system or the person who
arrives for treatment? If a distraught and depressed middle-aged woman
arrives for her first session, and it becomes clear that she is there because
she does not know what to do about her alcohol-addicted husband, but she
wants to get him to come for treatment, who is the client? If a young
woman is referred for mental health treatment as a condition of having
child custody reinstated by the courts via the approval of child welfare and
mental health professionals, who is the client? The practitioner can help
the client define their role by helping them sort out the reasons why they
sought treatment and how those reasons are contingent on the behavior of
other people in their lives or other institutions. Although many of these
circumstances involve mixed motives in the client, they must be drawn
out. "Is there any reason why you don't want to be here?" "Do you feel that
you are being forced here against your will?" "Is there any reason why you
think this might be helpful to you, despite the fact that you don't really
want to be here?" Helping the client to sort out mixed agenda can go a
long way to helping them define their role as client, a necessary step in

defining mutually agreed-upon intervention goals and engaging in the change process.

Collaborating with the Client on the Assessment, Intervention, and Evaluation Plan

Defining practitioner and client roles also necessitates determining shared responsibilities. One of the most supportive aspects of effective helping is cultivating a shared feeling of collaboration, the sense that "we are in this thing together." True, one does not want to ignore the power differential: the practitioner has the responsibility to implement effective care and has some prerogatives that the client does not (for example, the practitioner can hospitalize the client against their will; the practitioner can breach confidentiality should the client threaten to harm himself or others; the practitioner may be bound to report client information to the courts). However, the practitioner can underscore the importance of collaboration in the following manner: "We both agree that you want to work on _____ and that we will first do that by trying _____ and then see how it goes." To transcend some of the ambivalence about receiving social work services, the client must feel that, on some level, they are voluntarily participating in (and taking responsibility for) the course of the intervention. This collaborative relationship, again, does not obviate the power differences in the relationship, but it does establish a common ground on which practitioner and client can base a productive working relationship.

As part of the intervention, however, the practitioner also "recruits" the client into those activities. Clients provide the information to complete the assessment. Clients might also spend some time on their own completing assessment instruments such as self-report scales, charts, or diaries to help with the assessment and monitor treatment progress. Practitioners might also have clients carry out some of the intervention during the time when they are not "in session." For example, persons struggling with addictions may attend mutual help meetings or psycho-educational classes or they might attend a family gathering (later on in recovery) where they know family members are likely to drink in order to practice relapse prevention coping strategies. A family with a conduct-disordered adolescent may have to spend time in brief family meetings to negotiate guidelines for doing homework and increasing prosocial activities. Clients, in effect, become collaborators with practitioners in order to implement interventions successfully. They are not passive recipients of treatment. The shared feeling that exists between practitioner and client that they are collaborating on the assessment, intervention, and evaluation plan together is the "glue" that holds the working alliance together.

Maintaining Clear Boundaries

Defining clear boundaries and collaborating effectively on the intervention requires that the practitioner take the responsibility for maintaining clear professional boundaries over the course of the intervention. Boundaries are best kept in sight not by maintaining an aloof posture, but by continuing to communicate empathy and respect and by continually focusing on the goals of the intervention contract. To stay on track, a good working question for every practitioner is as follows: Is what I am doing in our meeting with this client today likely to enhance this client's progress? Am I helping them move toward the agreed-upon goals? Practitioners also need to model behavior that reinforces good boundaries, so the client can be reassured about the respective roles of practitioner and client. Clients should be encouraged to express their feelings, participate in the intervention during the session, put what they have learned into action outside of sessions, and help to evaluate whether things are getting better. In other words, for both practitioner and client, their mutual focus should be on getting their work done together.

Clients sometimes have strong feelings about their practitioner. How should practitioners handle these feelings? For a variety of reasons, the helping relationship creates, at times, an ambiguity about the nature of the relationship whereby the client may interject a variety of feelings (e.g., love, hate, anger, envy, jealousy, gratitude, etc.) into the relationship with the practitioner. These ambiguities can lead to a variety of feelings toward the practitioner that may be best understood as *interpersonal misattributions* (O'Hare, 2015) whereby the client distorts the nature of the relationship or how they see the practitioner due to previous experiences in their own lives. The client may communicate these feelings in a variety of ways both directly and indirectly. These feelings may spring from a variety of sources. In the psychodynamic tradition, feelings "displaced" or "projected" onto the practitioner (i.e., transference) were often assumed to be feelings that the client felt about their mother or primary caretaker in the past. Although one's parents may be one source of such feelings, there are many other possible sources as well, including how the person *actually feels* about the relationship with the practitioner (e.g., they may be justified in feeling angry with their practitioner). Other sources of these feelings may stem from experiences the client had with some other person with whom they had or currently have a close relationship (e.g., spouse, friend, employer, etc.). Other legitimate feelings may be evoked from racial, cultural, or socioeconomic differences and tensions. A young African-American man who has had negative experiences with white authority figures may feel suspicious and resentful about his white social worker; a woman who has been abused by men in the past may be predisposed to feel a mixture of anger and shame or other feelings toward her male practitioner; an older client may feel either nurturing or resentful feelings toward a younger social worker; a male client from a culture where women are dissuaded from achieving educational or professional success may feel disdain toward his female social worker. Since a professional helping relationship is not a naturally occurring relationship (e.g., friendship, marriage, parent-child, coworkers, buddies, etc.), ambiguities abound and clients will find a way to fill in those ambiguities, accurately or otherwise. It is the practitioner's job to explore those ambiguities and help clients deal with them realistically and with minimal distortion.

Likewise, practitioners make interpersonal misattributions toward some of their clients. Practitioners can experience a range of feelings that potentially obstruct the helping process. These may include anger, disgust, sexual attraction, a parental need to nurture, and so on. Mild feelings of genuine affection or caring are usually not a matter of concern and may enhance the helping process. However, other feelings toward clients can become a serious obstacle to effective intervention. Anger can lead to punitive behavior toward a client, premature termination, or abandonment; attraction or infatuation can lead to overtures for sexual relations. Practitioners are obliged to identify for themselves what they are feeling, determine whether the way they deal with their feelings helps or hinders the working relationship, and take responsibility for their feelings and subsequent behavior toward the client. Practitioners often sort these matters out for themselves, in discussion with colleagues, or, if the problem is not readily resolved, the practitioner can seek professional consultation. Whatever method practitioners utilize to cope with these matters, keeping the client's well-being in mind should be the foremost priority. Maintaining clear boundaries means continually returning to the key question: Is what I am about to say or do in the client's best interest?

Summary

Supportive and facilitative skills incorporate basic interviewing methods in the service of cultivating a sound working alliance, enhancing motivation, and helping the client engage in a collaborative change process. However, although supportive skills are essential for establishing the working alliance, research on practice processes has clearly shown that they are usually not sufficient for helping clients with more serious and complex problems. To conduct more advanced interventions with moderate to severe psychosocial disorders, expert use of therapeutic coping skills is essential.

CHAPTER SIX

Therapeutic Coping Skills

"THERAPEUTIC COPING SKILLS" is a broad-based term that refers to specific methods used to actively help clients critically examine the content and process of dysfunctional thinking, improve emotion and mood regulation, enhance behavioral coping and self-regulation, improve communication skills, and enhance problem solving. Although coping skills (as they will be referred to here for the sake of brevity) have been contributed to social work practice from different approaches, those that have been shown to be effective in controlled practice research are predominantly derived from cognitive-behavioral interventions for a wide array of problems (Butler, Chapman, Forman, & Beck, 2006; Craighead, Craighead, Kazdin, & Mahoney, 1994; Dobson, 2009; Dobson & Craig, 1996) and have been incorporated into individual, family, and group interventions. However, other approaches such as interpersonal psychotherapy (e.g., Klerman & Weissman, 1993) and emotion-focused therapy (Greenberg, Warwar, & Malcomb, 2010) have made important contributions to coping-skills approaches as well. Although specific coping skills can be used as discrete interventions (e.g., examining dysfunctional thinking, breathing retraining to cope with anxiety, exposure to overcome a specific phobia, improved communication around feelings), they are typically utilized in combinations for treating moderate to severe psychosocial disorders with individuals, couples, families, and groups. Rather than a passive recipient of "treatment," clients are best served when coping skills are implemented within a supportive and collaborative working relationship. The goals for using therapeutic coping skills are not for practitioners to effect "cures," but for clients to learn these skills and incorporate them into their own coping and problem-solving repertoire to ameliorate specific problems and enhance overall adaptive capabilities (i.e., strengths) over time. In subsequent chapters, how these specific skills are combined into intervention approaches for specific problems and disorders will be described in more detail.

Cognitive Change Skills

Understanding the client's experiences, difficulties, and expectations from their perspective is an important starting point, one that has been underscored in basic counseling literature for decades. For some clients, particularly those with mildly stressful and often transitory problems in living, listening to themselves "talk out loud" and helping them to feel understood may even be sufficient for resolving some difficulties. However, for clients with more serious disorders, simply providing accurate listening and reflection is not likely to satisfactorily resolve their situation or enhance their ability to cope. Efforts to inform and educate our clients about their problems and potential solutions often include the use of skills aimed at directly effecting cognitive change.

Psycho-education may be one of the most basic forms of cognitive change techniques in that it is typically used to educate people and correct misperceptions about problems and ways of coping with them. Psycho-education is, essentially, imparting valid information for the purpose of preventing problems (e.g., HIV/AIDS prevention programs), coping with specific situations (e.g., grief counseling), or improving overall lifestyle (e.g., stress-reduction skills). Psycho-education is employed across individual, family, and group modalities. An individual client who has experienced their first panic attack, for example, can benefit substantially by learning about the signs and symptoms of panic disorder in order to alleviate their fear that they are "going crazy." Young and inexperienced couples can benefit from some basic psycho-education regarding communication and problem-solving skills during those often challenging first years of marriage. Small and large groups of adolescents can obtain some benefit from basic lessons regarding safe sex and the risks associated with excessive alcohol use. Imparting information is certainly not a new strategy, but using it for targeted purposes to improve psychosocial well-being and health is often useful and sometimes effective when delivered in a timely manner to a receptive audience.

How does a practitioner provide psycho-education as part of an intervention? Formats are quite flexible and can range from the impromptu and informal to a very carefully planned curriculum that extends over several weeks or months. With an individual, couple, or family, questions

might arise unexpectedly about a variety of issues: the relationship of substance use to depression, what constitutes safe sex, what to do about a
grandparent who is becoming extremely forgetful or appears to be talking
to people who are not actually present, how to relate to a brother who has
schizophrenia, how to help a daughter who has been diagnosed with
ADHD, and so on. Providing psycho-education to a client also requires that
the practitioner be knowledgeable about the given area. If a client's questions are beyond the practitioner's area of expertise, then the client can be
referred to a colleague, an agency, or an organization that can provide that
service.

Psycho-education, because of its didactic nature, is sometimes dismissed
as being less legitimate than other social work services. Often, however,
providing clients with accurate, timely, and complete information is sufficient to meet their needs, prevent additional problems, and can help them
move toward long-term solutions. For larger groups where a more formal
psycho-education curriculum is required, more planning and expertise in
presentation may be necessary. As a complement to practice, many social
workers enjoy providing psycho-education services to larger audiences in
the local schools, hospitals, community centers, and to religious congrega-
tions on today's important topics: coping with Alzheimer's disease, how to
approach a family member with a substance use problem, pros and cons
of transracial adoption, how to cope with and help a family member who
suffers from chronic and severe depression, and so on. Psycho-education
provides a valuable and, sometimes, essential function by itself or as part
of a multifaceted intervention with individuals, families, and small or
larger groups.

Explanation and interpretation are, in a sense, also a teaching function
of social work practice. One might even consider them a form of psycho-
education. Helping a client better understand their depression, an addiction process, their difficulties controlling anger, the dynamics of a relationship problem, or how racial discrimination affects their self-image requires
the social worker to hypothesize aloud about factors that might contribute
to the problem or interfere with their ability to cope. Explanations and
interpretations are usually tentative (i.e., hypothetical) because, on a case-
by-case basis, it is very difficult know with certainty exactly what factors
cause or maintain an individual client's difficulties. In an evidence-based
approach, no assumptions are made concerning "unconscious motivation"
when providing an explanation or proffering an interpretation. The practitioner simply works with the known facts of the client's condition and
considers the available knowledge base that might inform the hypothesis

and help the client better understand his complaint, symptoms, or problems. Nevertheless, some "theorizing" aloud about known factors that might cause and maintain the client's psychosocial difficulties is necessary for ongoing assessment and intervention planning.

To understand, for example, what is behind a schizophrenic young man's incoherent ramblings, an addicted elderly man's reported sensations of "bugs under my skin," a female domestic violence victim's feelings of hopeless defeat, an adolescent's explosive rage, or a child's compulsive ordering of their toy collection, social workers must be knowledgeable about these problems in order to help the client understand their significance and what factors might cause the problem to persist. For example, after one or two visits an assessment reveals that the client is seriously depressed and suicidal. Descriptively, this is important information, but a more complete understanding of the client's depression necessitates more information grounded in current research: What factors seem to contribute to the client's depression? How did things get to this point? Has the client been depressed like this before? Is there a family history of depression? Has the client experienced serious trauma or stressors including sudden losses or disappointments? Has the client been drinking alcohol to excess or been using street drugs or medications? Has the client been physically ill? Have there been any serious interpersonal difficulties in the client's life? Educating the client about factors that potentially contribute to their depression (i.e., explanation and interpretation) assumes that the practitioner is knowledgeable about the problem and can base their assessment and intervention recommendations on a sound knowledge base. Explanation and interpretation does not imply that the practitioner has all the "right" answers, but that they are sufficiently informed about the problems the client is experiencing so that they can at least make educated guesses about what psychological, physical, social, or situational factors might be contributing to the client's current difficulties.

When a client engages in *self-monitoring*, they are collaborating in their treatment in a significant way. Rather than experiencing the intervention as something "done to them," clients who engage in self-monitoring are helping to carry out ongoing assessment and evaluation of the intervention. More specifically, when clients engage in self-monitoring, they:

- Help define problems, goals, and objectives
- Help develop and utilize self-anchored scales to track their progress (e.g., anxiety level on a scale from 0 to 10, days clean and sober, days homework completed)
- Complete the self-report standardized scale for key problems

- Evaluate the apparent effects of the intervention on key presenting problems and have the opportunity to give feedback to the practitioner
- Participate in continued monitoring of long-term progress after termination

Self-monitoring is a highly flexible skill. In addition to having clients utilize standardized scales, practitioners can help clients create self-anchored scales, use qualitative diaries or journals, design quantitative charts (e.g., to track a child's academic and behavioral progress), or develop other creative ways to monitor cognitive, emotional, or behavioral changes over time. As described in Chapter 4, self-monitoring can utilize basic indexes to measure *frequency* (e.g., number of "positive days" for a couple), *duration* (e.g., days without serious suicidal ideation), or *severity* (e.g., level of depression). Clients often appreciate the specific and objective value of demonstrated progress that self-monitoring provides.

Assessing, challenging, and changing dysfunctional thinking have become essential skills for facilitating client change. As discussed earlier, practitioners should initially strive to encourage the expression of the client's personal narrative and understand it with as little interpretation or filtering as possible. For relatively mild forms of distress or transitory life difficulties, the use of basic counseling skills in this way is often sufficient to help the client resolve their dilemma. Clients often need to hear themselves "talk out loud" and come to solutions on their own with little assistance from the practitioner. However, for more serious problems, including substance abuse, major mental illnesses, conduct disorders, antisocial and self-destructive behaviors, personality disorders, and serious interpersonal problems, clients typically require a more robust form of intervention. Assuming the practitioner and client have already formed a solid working alliance, the practitioner can then help the client to question, reevaluate, and challenge some of the more dysfunctional beliefs that appear to maintain their difficulties and prevent them from arriving at more positive ways of coping with their problems.

One can readily assert that practitioners from all schools of thought attempt to influence and change the way their clients think. The practitioner's listening skills, their own nonverbal communications, and how they selectively attend to one topic of conversation or another can influence the client's way of thinking. However, practitioners, depending on their theoretical orientation, may go about the process of influencing their clients differently. Psychodynamic practitioners, for example, might theorize about how a client's early childhood attachments are currently affecting his marriage. Cognitive therapists might challenge a client's feelings of hopelessness by asking her to provide examples of positive things happening in her life right now. A family therapist might ask siblings to engage in a role reversal exercise to help each one see the problem from the other's point of view. A practitioner using narrative or solution-focused therapy might encourage a client to generate alternative constructions of a problem and list three creative solutions to the current dilemma. Suffice it to say, "talking interventions" of all kinds attempt to help clients reflect critically on their difficulties and consider new ways of thinking about their problems and potential solutions.

Challenging clients' beliefs, however, is not premised on the notion that the practitioner is the ultimate "expert," the final arbiter of objective reality, or subscribes to a statistical benchmark for what is "normal." It simply means that, on a practical level, the client's way of viewing himself and others seems to be causing significant problems for him (and perhaps others), and a reappraisal of his views might be necessary in order to at least consider the possibility of change and possibly arrive at meaningful solutions. Since social workers provide services for many involuntary clients, in some cases, the client's views may be seriously immoral or illegal (i.e., harmful to the client or others), and social workers are sometimes ethically obliged to challenge the client's view assertively and intervene even when intervention occasionally requires the breaching of confidentiality as in the case of threats of harm to others.

Cognitive therapy and research has provided the most explicit and well-researched approaches to addressing cognitive change, not just as a way of reducing dysfunctional thinking, but also as a catalyst for improving emotional well-being and changing behavior. Research has demonstrated that a client's difficulties are sometimes grounded in erroneous, distorted, or dysfunctional thinking regarding the client themselves, their relationships, the world around them, and their future. Negative schema (i.e., the cognitive model that a client uses as a template to view herself and others) can promote negative automatic thoughts and subsequently lead to erroneous and illogical thinking and contribute to poor coping skills (Beck, 1976; Beck, 1996; Clark & Beck, 1999). For a woman with very low self-esteem, for example, negative automatic thoughts (say, in response to moderate stressors) might include "Oh, I'm not that interesting. He'll never ask me out" or "I didn't deserve that promotion. I don't think I can do this job." A person with a pessimistic schema may be inclined to think "It doesn't matter how hard we work at this relationship, it will end in divorce just like our parents" or "With the way the world is—the economy, climate change, and terrorism—what's the point of getting my MSW? We're all doomed!"

Cognitive assessment addresses the client's cognitive world on two levels: the *content* of thought (i.e., what a client thinks) and the *process* of thinking (how critically a client thinks) (Clark & Beck, 1999; Gambrill, 1990; Tversky & Kahneman, 1974; Nisbett & Ross, 1980). The content of thought is important because it reveals the client's views regarding themselves, the nature of their relationships, and what they think about the world around them, as well as their expectations about the future. At the more extreme end, some clients suffer from serious mental illnesses, learning disabilities, or suffer cognitive dysfunction from severe substance abuse problems. Cognitive distortions associated with those disorders can be severe and include hallucinations, delusions, and other thought disorders. With more ordinary problems, some clients are simply misinformed about certain matters or have erroneous beliefs or unreasonable expectations regarding relationships, health-risk behaviors, or just coping with daily stress in life.

Enhancing a client's cognitive coping skills also requires an examination of *how* they think, that is, the client's critical thinking processes. These are the same critical thinking skills reviewed in Chapter 2 with regard to using evidence to support professional decision making but applied to the way people see their problems and cope in everyday life. Although the use of critical thinking skills does not guarantee happiness, and engaging in dysfunctional thinking does not necessarily result in serious problems, some key "thinking errors" seem to be associated with problems related to depression, anxiety, and other psychosocial disorders. These are briefly summarized below with accompanying examples.

Some clients use *dramatic stereotypes, emotional testimonials, or draw conclusions from readily available information* to guide their own behavior. A client with a drinking problem, for example, might minimize the negative consequences of his drinking by citing the fact that his father and grandfather were daily heavy drinkers, and "they lived well into their seventies." Although this fact may attest to the family's overall robust health, the client is focusing on an uncharacteristically "good scenario" and might also be overlooking other problems that were related to years of heavy drinking such as depression and domestic violence. Another client may cite the popularity of ultrathin celebrities as justification for routine binge-purging and daily use of diuretics and ignore the risks of potential health problems caused by bulimia nervosa. Practitioners can gently challenge these erroneous beliefs by helping clients access more objective and representative sources of information.

Some clients engage in *dichotomous thinking, all-or-nothing thinking, or good versus bad thinking* rather than seeing most experiences in life on a continuum and people as sometimes motivated by conflicting needs. Clients often apply such thinking to their own mental status (e.g., "Am I crazy or not?"), relapse during substance abuse treatment ("I slipped, therefore, I am a treatment failure."), raising a teenager ("She was a minute late from the dance, so I grounded her for a month!"), work ("I didn't get the promotion—I am such a loser!"), and relationships ("He left me—I'll *never* find anyone who will love me again!"). Practitioners can help clients examine how viewing their situation in such extremes severely limits their options and a wide range of possible outcomes.

In a similar approach to "extreme thinking," many clients *overgeneralize* from limited experiences or draw erroneous conclusions from only a few examples (i.e., small sampling of their own or others' behaviors). Having had a bad experience with a mental health professional, a client may opine, "All you therapist-types are just a bunch of jerks!" A child who experienced teasing at their friend's birthday party might say, "I'm never going to a party again. Kids always make fun of me." An elderly person for whom supervised care is considered the best option might conclude from one visit to such a facility, "I'll never fit in with people like that. These places are all the same—they are just full of a bunch of old folks." A young man from Southeast Asia who recently immigrated to the United States might conclude early on that people here do not like "my kind" and "I'll never be able to survive in this country" as a result of a negative encounter or two. Gently exploring other possibilities and encouraging more experimentation can sometimes help attenuate overgeneralizations based on a limited range of experiences.

Another form of "extreme thinking" is known as *catastrophizing,* that is, always expecting the worst. This form of cognitive distortion lies in a failure to consider accurate base rates for a variety of phenomena. Awful and tragic things do happen to people on a daily basis: people are affected by sudden onsets of terminal illnesses, car accidents, airline disasters, sudden loss of loved ones, and other dreaded events. Nevertheless, on any given day, these events are unlikely to occur in the lives of any single individual. Persons who are inclined toward anxiety and depression (which often co-occur) often spend much of their time ruminating excessively about the "what ifs" rather than enjoying their lives.

Hindsight bias may be among the more common strategies for distorting reality and drawing erroneous conclusions. Many clients suffer from what are colloquially known as the "coulda, woulda, shoulds," a bias caused by the illusion that "hindsight is 20–20." For example, a mother grieving the loss of a child to a rare illness accompanied by common symptoms such as headaches and stomachaches might torment herself with the belief that "if only I had taken her to the doctor sooner, she might have gotten proper treatment and lived," despite the doctor's reassurance that most mothers would have done the same given the seemingly ordinary presentation of the child's symptoms at the time. Sometimes helping clients to recall in detail what they were thinking and feeling at the time of the event and re-create the circumstances in retrospect can help them understand why "I did what I did at the time" and dispel some of the illusion of clarity and accompanying guilt often associated with hindsight bias.

Selective attention occurs when a client focuses disproportionately on details that only support his own point of view. As a result, he might not take into consideration all the representative facts, including those that do not support his opinion. A client with agoraphobia, for example, notes all the "bad things" (e.g., muggings, car accidents, earthquakes, terrorist attacks) that could happen if he starts leaving his apartment and reentering the world but overlooks the potential enjoyment he has deprived himself and the fact that low-frequency negative events are unlikely to happen if one takes reasonable precautions. Selective attention, in this case, appears to be the consequence of a very negative schema influenced by strong feelings of anxiety and the pessimism associated with depression. A depressed, angry spouse may selectively focus on all their partner's failings in the relationship but "forget" to consider other considerate and thought-ful things he does on a regular basis.

Clients often confuse *correlation* with *causation*. As a result, clients often present problems based on their own assessments and see cause-effect relationships in their own and others' lives where there may only be coincidence. For example, a client may come in for treatment for severe depression and report that her grandmother recently died. She might also indicate that she has recently been thinking about her own mother's death ten years ago. She may conclude that she has always been depressed because "you can't count on anyone sticking around for long. They always leave you." The client may feel strongly that this is the cause of her depres-sion and report that she has read many books on "loss issues" and that these experts support her view. The practitioner, upon meeting the wom-an's husband and adolescent son, finds out that the client has been addicted to prescription tranquilizers and alcohol for many years. Although there is little doubt that loss and grief can be related to depression, long-standing and severe depression often has either a genetic or some other physiological base (such as chronic substance abuse). In this case, loss is probably more a "correlated" issue than a "causal" one for depression. Prac-titioners can help their clients identify factors that cause and maintain their problems and distinguish those from other correlated or coincidental events.

Within the context of a sound working alliance, practitioners should strive to (1) explore in detail the content of client's thoughts, (2) examine their cognitive reasoning processes, and (3) hypothesize how those beliefs and thinking processes reflect the client's overall cognitive schema and affect their mood and behavior. Practitioners can then gently challenge dysfunctional thinking through *Socratic questioning*. Socratic questioning is essentially using basic interviewing skills accompanied by empathy and support to encourage the client to justify their problematic thoughts, attitudes, and beliefs. The following dialogue with a depressed adolescent illustrates the practitioner's attempt to coax a rational examination of a client's anxieties regarding meeting new friends:

SOCIAL WORKER: "Jim, you say that you will never fit in at your new school, that you will always be alone. Tell me, what brings you to that conclusion?"

JIM: "I feel like I've always been alone. Nobody likes me. I have no friends."

SOCIAL WORKER: "You have no friends now, but you told me about friends you had last year. What happened in the last year?"

JIM: "You know what happened. My parents moved after my sophomore year. Those f—ing idiots. I told them not to move. I lost all my friends."

SOCIAL WORKER: "So, you're angry at your folks for moving. Now you're in a new school. Most of your classmates are tight with their own groups, and you feel like the outsider, like you don't belong. Do you think things will always be that way?"

JIM: "Seems like that."

SOCIAL WORKER: "Seems like that, but do you really think you will never make new friends again?"

JIM: "I guess SOME-day, I might make some new friends. I've only been here three months. But everyone else is solid with their group."

SOCIAL WORKER: "So, do you think there's no chance of making new friends at this point?"

JIM: "I guess there is a possibility."

SOCIAL WORKER: "If there is a possibility, how might you go about getting to know people a little or having a conversation now and then? That's usually the way it starts."

JIM: "I guess I have to try and talk to people. But I don't think they want to make new friends. I don't think they want me to talk with them."

SOCIAL WORKER: "How do you know that?"

JIM: "They just seem busy."

SOCIAL WORKER: "Busy."

JIM: "Yeah, busy. You know, during class, in the lunch room, in the hall."

SOCIAL WORKER: "So, that means they don't want you to talk to them?"

JIM: "I guess not. But I don't like to interrupt."

SOCIAL WORKER: "So, talking to people means you are interrupting them?"

JIM: "I guess I'm not sure how to start a conversation."

SOCIAL WORKER: "How do other people start conversations?"

JIM: "I guess they just say, 'Excuse me, did you get the homework assignment in the last class?' or something like that."

SOCIAL WORKER: "Seems about right. So, have you tried that?"

JIM: "No, because I don't think they want me to."

SOCIAL WORKER: "Has anyone said they don't want you to? Has anyone objected?"

JIM: "No. I just don't think they'd like it much."

SOCIAL WORKER: "So, there is no real indication that they don't want you to talk with them. You just have this general expectation that they don't want you to try. Right?"

JIM: "I guess so."

SOCIAL WORKER: "So, what evidence do you have that some people would not want you to talk with them?"

JIM: "I guess I really don't have any. I just happen to feel this way."

SOCIAL WORKER: "Sounds like this situation has more to do with the way you feel about yourself and this new situation than how other people feel about you, huh?"

JIM: "Maybe."

SOCIAL WORKER: "Have you had ANY conversations with people since you started at that school?"

JIM: "Sure. Lots of times."

SOCIAL WORKER: "Well, I guess I'm a little confused. So you have had conversations. Did any of them go well?"

JIM: "Yeah. Some."

SOCIAL WORKER: "Good. Did you follow up with those people? Have you tried to talk with them again, you know, say 'Hey, what's up?' Have you asked anyone if they'd like to get together after school?"

JIM: "No. I guess not. I figured if they wanted to, they'd talk to me."

SOCIAL WORKER: "I see. So, because they didn't initiate the conversation, you figured they didn't want to talk to you."

JIM: "I guess. I'm on their turf, you know?"

SOCIAL WORKER: "Have you considered the possibility that maybe they think you don't want to talk with them?"

JIM: "No. I hadn't thought about that. I guess maybe they think I'm the one who isn't too friendly."

SOCIAL WORKER: "Sometimes shy people are seen as aloof or stuck up. Is it possible that some people see you that way?"

JIM: "Hey, I'm not shy. But, yeah, I overheard someone say I was a snob. Maybe I'm the one giving off the bad vibes."

The social worker might continue to use Socratic questioning to help Jim sort out whether his lack of self-confidence is justified by any real shortcomings of his own or whether he is just anxious about being rejected and not "fitting in." At some point, however, questioning and clarifying distortions will have to be used as a springboard to action: by discussing some of his anxiety about being vulnerable and meeting new people (i.e., expressing and identifying his feelings) and by risking a conversation (i.e., behavior change). The key point in implementing cognitive change, however, is identifying the core content of dysfunctional thoughts (e.g., "Nobody likes me."), identifying the thought process that maintains the belief (e.g., expecting the worst: "What if I get told to get lost?"), and sensitively helping the client to examine the belief, evaluate the evidence that supports it, and consider alternative views. Although cognitive change is important, it is usually only a starting point, a potential springboard to further change.

Emotional/Physiological Regulatory Skills

Although challenging dysfunctional thinking can be a helpful place to start, cognitive intervention is often insufficient for engendering lasting change. Often, dysfunctional thinking is related to unresolved emotional difficulties including depression, anxiety, chronic anger, or other forms of emotional distress. Although some cognitive theorists have opined that "cognition is primary" (meaning that thoughts come before feelings and behaviors), others have suggested that it is equally plausible that emotions sometimes precede and influence the content and processes of cognitions. Keeping in mind the graphic in Chapter 1, thinking, acting, and feeling are reciprocally related, and change can be initiated in any of these three modalities of human expression. Most human behavior theoreticians agree that thoughts, feelings, and behaviors are interrelated in a complex way, and emotional distress can strongly affect the way people think and act. Thus, identifying feelings, giving clients an opportunity to express those feelings thoroughly, and connecting distressing emotions to specific behaviors and situations is essential in order for clients to understand better how their emotions play an important role in maintaining problems and preventing resolution of those problems. In some respects, practitioners often need to provide a form of psycho-education about "how feelings work" for both children and adult clients. Practitioners can do this by helping the client develop new ways of accurately recognizing, constructively expressing, and coping with distressing emotions.

Resolving emotional distress and associated physiological changes (e.g., reducing anxiety, coping with depression, regulating anger) often pave the way for lasting change. Historically, most practice theoreticians have agreed that anxiety (aka fear, dread, apprehension) is one of the key impediments to change. Psychodynamic, behavioral, existential-humanistic, and other practitioners agree: *a little anxiety can be healthful and change promoting; too much anxiety reduces the potential for change and growth.* Although these theoreticians often disagree about the roots of anxiety, most agree that anxiety must be brought into manageable limits in order for clients to begin and maintain the change process.

Chronic anger and depression can also exacerbate clients' difficulties and interfere with significant change. Other troubling emotions such as envy and jealousy can be seen as accompaniments to the more basic mood disorders. Researchers who study emotions also assert that they are not synonymous with feelings, cognitive states, physiological responses, or behavior. Emotions seem to encompass all of these modes of expression. When we ask a client, for example, "How do you feel about that?" we are not merely asking about their momentary emotional state, but about a whole cascade of thoughts and feelings related to a range of situations, how they interpret their physiological state, and what behaviors they engaged in as a result. As testament to the complexity of emotions, practitioners should be prepared for a range of responses to the question: "How do you feel about _____?" Clients are likely to respond with answers that cover the range of thoughts, feelings, and behaviors: "I was so angry I thought I was going to hit her!" "I felt awful, like I was going to die." "I was so afraid I just ran." "I was so nervous I just threw up!" Rarely will you receive a simple answer identifying the pure emotional response for this simple reason: feelings are global responses that tie together all modes of human expression—thought, physiological response, and behavior. The responses are also, in part, specific to the situation within which they occur. "Feeling questions" can, indeed, provide important, powerful, and compelling responses about a client's experience. If explored carefully, sensitively and fully, these responses will provide important clues to factors that maintain client problems and suggest potential solutions.

Helping clients initially connect their thoughts, feelings, and behaviors is an essential step before moving on to behavior change. Consider the following brief dialogue between a young woman and her social worker. Melanie has just left home for the first time after a long, conflicted relationship with her parents.

MELANIE: "I'm very upset, very angry about having to leave home. I remember so many good things, but in the last year or so, things have become awful. All we do is argue."

SOCIAL WORKER: "What have you been arguing about?"

MELANIE: "They keep trying to control me. They get angry if I stay out late with my friends. I'm twenty years old, for heaven's sake, why couldn't they cut me some slack?"

SOCIAL WORKER: "That was all they were concerned about?"

MELANIE: "No. They didn't like it if I'd been drinking, and my mom found some pot in my room. I don't smoke much, but she flipped out saying I could get arrested if I got caught with it on me."

SOCIAL WORKER: "So, your parents are objecting to some of the things you want to do, but you don't want to play by their rules anymore. Do you think this situation can be resolved?"

MELANIE: "Not if I stay home. I mean, most of my friends are out of their parents' home, and I could share an apartment. Most of them are taking college classes like me. I guess it's time for me to leave. I'd probably get along with my parents better, and if I'm not doing this stuff under their nose, we'd probably not fight so much."

SOCIAL WORKER: "So, how do you feel about leaving home?

MELANIE: "I guess I'm feeling a lot of things. I'm not really angry at my parents, but at times I am. I guess I'm feeling sad about it. I'm their only kid, so I know it's been hard for them, too. Mom and dad have been very good to me." (She starts to cry.) "I guess I'll miss them a lot."

SOCIAL WORKER: "It must be hard to be angry with them and, at the same time, feel like you're going to miss them. Do you feel anything else going on?"

MELANIE: "I feel so guilty leaving them. They've spent their whole lives focused on me. I'd hate to leave when we're fighting like this. And what are they going to do when I leave home?"

SOCIAL WORKER: "Are you worried that they won't be able to take care of each other?"

MELANIE: (She laughs, wiping her tears away.) "I guess that doesn't make much sense. I know they'll be fine. I mean, I can visit them pretty regularly."

SOCIAL WORKER: "So you can keep an eye on them, right?"

MELANIE: "Yeah, right. It's more like so they can keep an eye on me, I guess."

SOCIAL WORKER: "So, you are feeling angry at them for insisting that you live by their rules, sad about leaving your childhood home with all those great memories, and guilty about leaving your parents 'on their own.' How do you suggest we sort out this jumble of emotions you are struggling with?"

The social worker and Melanie continue to discuss a resolution plan, but before she can move forward, the practitioner focuses on helping the client clarify and sort out the client's "jumble" of feelings and emotions. Helping the client to connect her thoughts and feelings, under this particular circumstance, is an essential part of imparting therapeutic coping skills. Once she has a better grasp of what she is thinking and how she feels about the situation, she can move more freely toward taking some constructive action.

In summary, practitioners of various theoretical backgrounds more or less agree that identifying clients' emotional states (feelings) is of critical importance for a number of reasons: (1) it helps clients give their feelings a name, (2) it helps to increase their understanding about factors that affect the way they feel, (3) it helps clients to understand how their feelings are reciprocally related to the way they think (i.e., how thoughts affect feelings, how feelings affect thoughts), (4) it helps clients to understand better how their feelings affect behavior and how behavior affects feelings, (5) discussing feelings helps clients understand how their physiological state (e.g., anxiety) affects and is affected by their feelings, and (6) it helps clients understand how situations and interpersonal relations can affect and be affected by the way they feel. No doubt, feelings (emotional states), both acute and chronic, can be powerful influences on behavior, and practitioners need to help clients become emotionally more "literate" by examining how emotions tie in with thinking and acting across various situations.

Practitioners can help clients become more "feelings savvy" in a number of ways:

- Have clients identify and express their feelings. Ask clients how they feel about different experiences they report and help them identify those feelings accurately and put them into words, a process that may be surprisingly difficult for some clients.
- Help clients to gauge how intense those feelings are. Some may be related to very stressful or traumatic events. Measuring and tracking emotional changes over time will be important for helping the client self-monitor their own subjective distress over time.
- Teach clients how to analyze their own feelings in relation to their thoughts, behaviors, and interpersonal situations. Many clients simply feel raw emotions and have difficulty thinking about their feelings. This step, however, is important if they are to learn to regulate distressing emotions more effectively.
- Once the client learns to identify, express, and think about their feelings, they will be better prepared to regulate emotional distress rather than simply respond to it. Clients can learn to accept the fact that they can feel intense emotions without having to respond to them by acting on them, sometimes in destructive ways (e.g., drinking, self-mutilation, lashing out at others).
- Over time, clients can learn to anticipate circumstances that may "trigger" intense feelings and be better prepared to deal with that subjective distress in a more constructive way (e.g., talking to someone, taking a walk, distraction with some useful activity).
- Clients can learn to stall, that is, "buy time" to stop, think, and consider alternative ways to cope with distressing feelings.
- Help the client more accurately assess the behaviors and feelings of others in their family and social situations. Often, distressing feelings are triggered in specific social situations when dealing with other people, often people with whom one may have had considerable conflict in the past.
- Help the client visualize situations where troubling emotions might come up, and rehearse alternative responses to diffuse the situation or cope with those feelings directly should the client feel that they are ready (e.g., meeting an ex-spouse at a family gathering).
- Teach anxiety- and stress-reduction skills, including progressive muscle relaxation, breath control, and meditation. These skills directly address an often underestimated component of intense emotions: the physiological mechanisms associated with anxiety,

stress, and anger (e.g., racing heart, sweaty palms, nausea, quivering knees, clenched fists, etc.). An array of videos, audio recordings, and books are widely available on relaxation and stress-reduction methods, and practitioners should learn to use them for their own stress-reduction needs before using them to help their clients learn how to cope with emotional distress and related mood disturbances.

Behavior Change Skills

Identifying dysfunctional thinking and clarifying one's feelings about a given problem or situation are essential steps but are often insufficient for engendering lasting change. Clients must also change their behavior, develop behavioral coping skills, and practice those skills over time (sometimes for life) in order to maintain the lasting benefits of psychosocial interventions. The challenge for social work practitioners is to help clients learn behavioral coping skills, incorporate them into their lifestyle, and generalize those skills to problems that will inevitably surface. There is a range of behavioral coping skills that can be used as individual interventions, but they are often combined as part of more comprehensive intervention plans.

Developing or enhancing behavioral coping skills may be the most robust change agent for lasting improvement. These methods put the client's cognitive and emotional "insights" to the test and result in success experiences that can increase client confidence and sense of being better able to cope with life's challenges (i.e., self-efficacy, empowerment). The reinforcement engendered by gradual success increases the likelihood that clients will improve their coping capacities and adaptive strengths over time. To achieve lasting improvements, the depressed client may have to become more socially involved, the anxious client more daring, the addicted client more confident in saying "no thanks" to alcohol and other drugs, and the conduct disordered child more in control of their anger. All of these changes are difficult to initiate and even more difficult to maintain over time. To achieve lasting change, clients need to learn new ways of behavioral coping, and then practice, practice, practice those new coping skills in a variety of situations. There are no magical insights or easy routes to long-term change.

Modeling can be a powerful inducement to behavior change. Sometimes, showing rather than telling a client how to try something different is a more effective mode of intervention. Most people, particularly children, are readily responsive to the influences of modeling. Research on modeling behavior attests to its negative influence on promoting smoking, heavy drinking, and physical violence. Conversely, modeling can also be used for promoting prosocial and healthful behaviors such as improving:

- Communication skills in a couple
- Parenting skills
- Drinking and other drug-refusal skills
- Social skills in a person with major mental illness
- Conflict-resolution skills in a conduct disordered adolescent
- Anxiety-management skills

Modeling is a very versatile tool and can be utilized as part of an overall intervention package. Modeling can be provided in a number of ways. Practitioners can demonstrate a behavior in the presence of the client and have them try it. Professional videos are available to demonstrate various skills such as how to effectively provide discipline to a behaviorally troubled child or how to overcome problems related to anxiety. Persons suffering from severe social phobia can benefit from watching models demonstrate conversational skills. Often, modeling is used as a prelude to role playing.

In *role playing,* both client and practitioner or clients in couples or family sessions participate in acting out scenarios that facilitate the learning of important coping skills. The practitioner may begin by modeling a parenting skill (for example, giving directives to a child) and then ask the mother to role play the skill with the actual child or the "child" as initially played by the therapist. Thus, the sequence goes accordingly:

- Model the way to give an instruction to a child (e.g., "pick up your toys").
- Role play the behavior by alternately switching roles, with the parent playing both parent and child.
- And, finally, have the parent actually practice the behavior with their child in the consulting office and at home (in both situations, ideally, observed by the practitioner, although this opportunity is not always available).

Practitioners can be quite creative with role play. For example, when working with a client who has been recently discharged from detoxification for alcohol dependence, it might be quite helpful to the practitioner to "play the role" of the client's older brother with whom he has always had a close relationship, but one based largely on drinking together. Should the client be planning a trip home for the holidays (where the family is likely to be imbibing), the practitioner can play the role of the brother and become increasingly insistent with regard to pressing the client to have a drink. In order for the role play to be realistic, the practitioner should become very familiar with the people and circumstances before "setting the scene." What kind of pressure is the brother likely to use? What kind of ploys or inducements to drink? What appeals to filial loyalty and "the good old days" will the brother use? What phrases will the brother likely use to provoke or tempt the client to "just have one"? The more realistic the practitioner can make the action of the role play, the more emotionally compelling it is likely to be. Role playing can be used effectively to activate the client's thoughts, feelings, and behaviors within an at-risk situation that the client needs to master. Modeling and role playing are safe ways to provide the client with an opportunity to practice and fine-tune their coping skills before confronting the real situation, one that can be potentially overwhelming for the client.

At some point, rehearsal ends and clients must deal with their problems in everyday life. *Graduated exposure* is a powerful and effective technique designed to help clients confront their personal challenges in a step-by-step approach. There are essentially two types of exposure: covert and overt. In *covert exposure,* the client gradually confronts their personal challenge in a stepped fashion *in their imagination* while in a relative state of relaxation. In a sense, this is a kind of transitional step between rehearsal and eventually confronting the problem in a real situation (i.e., in vivo). Although clients are best served by approaching their difficulties in real life, this option is not always practical, and clients are not always ready to "jump in." For example, say a social worker is treating a person with severe agoraphobia and panic attacks (i.e., specifically, fear of going into grocery stores for fear of having a severe anxiety attack and fainting). Although graduated exposure (gradually spending more and more time in the store) would be the ideal approach, the client is initially reluctant to try it.

A helpful preliminary step would be to use relaxation exercises and imagery exercises to make the experience as real as possible in the client's "mind's eye" (imagination). This approach is typically done during an intervention session but also needs to be practiced consistently at home (i.e., homework). *Systematic desensitization* is, in effect, the combined use of relaxation techniques and covert graduated exposure. In systematic desensitization, practitioners (1) teach the client basic relaxation exercises (e.g., meditation, breathing retraining, progressive muscle relaxation), (2) teach the client how to measure their subjective units of anxiety (using the Subjective Units of Distress Scale [SUDS]) by gauging and reporting the severity of their anxiety on a scale from 0 to 100 (when prompted by the practitioner), and (3) create a graduated hierarchy (step-by-step approach) of the problem they are going to face. If, for example, the client is a victim of sexual assault who has become housebound and is suffering from PTSD, they would need considerable assistance to learn how to manage and eventually overcome disabling anxiety in order to reenter the world from which they have become seriously withdrawn.

After teaching basic anxiety-management skills and after learning how to measure subjective distress, the client would approach the following hierarchy covertly: (1) go outside to the corner to mail a letter, (2) go to the local supermarket, (3) drive to work, and (4) drive past the town park where they were assaulted six months previously. Although these are the major milestones of increasing difficulty in the hierarchy, the practitioner may find that they have to break down each of these steps into even finer increments. During the covert-exposure process, the client would imagine taking each of these steps, focus on maintaining inner calm by utilizing relaxation exercises (e.g., deep breathing), and periodically report their level of anxiety (0 to 100) when prompted by the practitioner. The technique is relatively easy to learn. Clients generally respond well to it, but it must be conducted with patience, care, and sensitivity. In order to maximize its benefits, practitioners should be prepared to have the client tolerate each anxiety-provoking scene until the client feels that their anxiety has come down to a manageable level before moving on to the next scene. With repetition, clients often find considerable relief and then are better prepared to deal with their challenges in vivo. Other approaches that utilize covert exposure (such as eye movement desensitization and reprocessing, EMDR) are theorized to work on similar principles related to anxiety reduction and cognitive-emotional reprocessing of the troubling events. Aside from preparing the client to gradually face "the real thing," covert exposure can also be used as an effective assessment tool to determine those aspects of the experience that are likely to be the most challenging for the client. A wide range of other problems can be addressed with covert exposure as well, usually as preparation to in vivo exposure.

Although covert exposure and systematic desensitization are effective therapeutic tools for many client difficulties, eventually clients have to confront their problems in real life. The next step is to engage the client in *graduated in vivo exposure,* that is, gradually mastering the problem in an actual situation in an increasingly challenging step-by-step manner. As with covert exposure, a detailed assessment (especially functional analysis) of the problem must precede the intervention. Client and practitioner must work carefully to construct a step-by-step plan to gradually confront the problem at hand while progressively increasing the challenge to the client. After each step in the hierarchy is mastered, the client moves on to the next step. The client suffering from PTSD and agoraphobic symptoms must gradually approach the supermarket door, step inside, spend more and more time, eventually buy one, two, and three items, return to the checkout, stand in line, pack the items, and leave. By taking one step at a time, alone or accompanied by a "coach," and simultaneously utilizing relaxation skills (e.g., breath control, mental distraction), many clients successfully overcome these difficulties. Sometimes the success comes in a "two-steps-forward-one-step-back" fashion, but research on graduated exposure is very positive overall. No other psychosocial intervention has been shown to be as effective for similar anxiety-based difficulties.

Although typically associated with anxiety disorders, graduated exposure is a sound working paradigm for dealing with other difficult problems as well: break the problem down to incremental steps, learn to manage one's internal distress, and deal with problems one step at a time while increasing the challenge after each successful effort. The reinforcement that results from initial successes tends to increase client self-efficacy, reduce anxiety, and lead to further successes and an overall sense of confidence that one can handle similar situations.

The idea that success experiences increase client self-efficacy is based on the well-established principle of positive reinforcement. *Reinforcement and contingency management methods* are the planned use of rewards and sanctions to improve prosocial and other healthful behaviors. Reinforcement and contingency management methods can be used to help an individual improve their own self-regulatory strategies (e.g., control anxiety, improve social skills, maintain abstinence) or help clients influence the behavior of other people in their lives (e.g., improve parenting skills). In practical application, using reinforcement principles usually means rewarding those behaviors that move the client toward positive goals or using sanctions (i.e., negative reinforcement or, to a lesser extent, punishment) to reduce unhealthful or antisocial behaviors.

Although practitioners may provide positive reinforcement through verbal rewards, clients are often taught how to reinforce their own behaviors (i.e., self-regulation skills) or the behaviors of others. Self-regulation skills can be used to help clients improve their own ability to manage anxiety, depression, addictions, eating disorders, anger, and work and study habits, among many other problems. When applied to helping others, contingency management skills can also be greatly effective. Parent-child management skills, for example, are based on the sensitive but straightforward use of rewards and mild sanctions to help a child improve their social behavior or academic performance or reduce unhealthful behaviors (e.g., an autistic child who pulls their own hair or bangs their head repeatedly). The use of sanctions is the planned withholding of rewards (e.g., loss of TV privileges or videogame time for not completing homework).

Generally, punishment (typically the use of verbal rebukes, chastisement, or, as in the case of antisocial behaviors, imprisonment and other forms of social control) is the least preferred type of reinforcement. However, it is sometimes necessary if a child or adult engages in behavior that may have serious consequences to themselves or others (e.g., playing with matches in the home, missing a planned meeting with a parole officer). Extinction (i.e., ignoring a behavior) is often a very effective tool, particularly when the behavior is simply annoying and leads to no serious consequences. Distressed couples and others with relationship difficulties can improve their relationships by learning how to verbally reinforce their partner's constructive behaviors (e.g., reduced argumentativeness, moderated use of alcohol) and ignore small slights and annoying behaviors. Petulant and whiney behavior in children can often be extinguished by simply ignoring it and rewarding them when they take initiative to deal with their own daily stressors and challenges.

The use of positive reinforcement (i.e., rewards), negative reinforcement (i.e., withdrawal of something rewarding), punishment (i.e., mild rebukes, social control, confinement), and extinction (i.e., ignoring certain behaviors) are often associated with applied behavioral analysis (i.e., a functional assessment of antecedents, behaviors, and reinforcement) and behavior modification (i.e., the planned use of reinforcement to improve psychosocial adjustment). Because these approaches have their roots in conditioning theory and research, behavioral approaches have often been misrepresented by self-described "deep and sensitive" practitioners as a cold, technical, and unempathic approach to influencing human behavior.

However, despite these erroneous connotations, the use of rewards and sanctions to influence another's behavior is simply a naturally occurring part of human relationships. The relevant question is as follows: Can basic behavior principles be used in a thoughtful and sensitive way to improve one's own behavior, improve the quality of relationships, and influence the prosocial behavior of others? In everyday life, the planned and thoughtful use of reinforcement is reflected in the following examples: partners saying "thank you" to one another for unsolicited favors and everyday kindnesses; parents saying "good work" to their children after they competently finish their homework or clean up their room; taking a surly adolescent son out for pizza when he decides to say what's on his mind without the usual sarcasm; putting special stickers on a completed assignment for a job well done by a child struggling with ADHD; buying a mentally ill young woman a cup of coffee and telling her how well she's been doing in her new job; ignoring the provocative and annoying behaviors of an antagonistic coworker; revoking the community visiting privileges of a conduct disordered young man in a diversionary addictions halfway house after a relapse. These are all common everyday uses of contingency management and reinforcement methods. What matters is that they are done with sensitivity, consistency, and respect.

When done in a thoughtful, planned, and compassionate manner, the results of properly carried out reinforcement and contingency management techniques (when used in treatment or otherwise) can be quite compelling. What social-cognitive theory and research has demonstrated is that reinforcement must be genuine and salient to the person at whom it is directed. Although reinforcement that immediately follows behavior can be helpful and facilitate positive changes, it is not necessary that it always be immediate. In some respects, reinforcement should be used to help clients move from requiring immediate reinforcement for improvements to working toward long-term, self-generated rewards as the greater goal. Reinforcement may be generated externally (e.g., rewards given to a child for completing homework, an employee for doing good work) or internally (e.g., self-satisfaction of a job well done). Ideally, reinforcement may be best utilized when it becomes part of a person's self-regulatory behaviors: the ability to identify challenges, address them with confidence (i.e., self-efficacy), and feel the resulting personal sense of accomplishment that accrues with persistence. One could suggest that the evolution from requiring external reinforcement to using self-regulatory skills to generate internal reinforcement parallels healthy psychological development from childhood to adulthood.

The use of contingencies (i.e., *contingency management*) is part of the planned use of rewards. The "contingency" is simply an *if-then* statement. "If you take out the garbage every day, then I'll do the dishes." "If you pick up your room, then we'll go out to the movies this Friday." "If you come to my family's reunion, then I'll go to your cousin's wedding." "If you stop mutilating your arms with broken glass, then the staff can increase your community privileges." "If you violate your probation, then you will have to return to prison." Contingency management approaches have been shown to be somewhat effective with clients who have been court-ordered to diversionary addictions treatment, conduct disordered children and adolescents, couples work, and helping children struggling with ADHD. Whether the idea appeals to us or not, life is full of contingencies. Can they be compassionately and purposefully used to enhance client well-being? Absolutely! As with otherwise healthy relationships, the terms of rewards and contingencies in any relationship should be specific, honest, salient, and the reasons for using them transparent.

Coping skills often include efforts to improve *communications*. Implicitly or explicitly, modeling and teaching effective communication skills are often included in interventions with individuals, couples, families, and groups. Social work practitioners, by modeling communication skills, are in an influential position to demonstrate to clients how to (1) listen carefully and attentively, (2) rephrase what the client is saying to ensure that the practitioner understood exactly what the client said, (3) express their own thoughts to the client, (4) have the client rephrase what the practitioner said to demonstrate that they clearly understood the message, and so on. Periodically, if this communication "feedback loop" is interrupted (i.e., if one or the other does not quite understand), the client or practitioner should feel free to stop and request clarification: "Excuse me, let me make sure I understand what you just said."

Teaching and demonstrating empathic communication skills may be one of the more essential aspects of social work practice. Although all couples and families, for example, are likely to encounter problems from time to time, lasting improvement seems to occur when the members of a couple or a family are able to deal with those problems by communicating in a calm and respectful manner. One of the key findings in research with well-functioning couples is not that they never experience problems, but that they have learned how to communicate their differences in a way that does not cause undue anger, hurt, or resentment, and they have learned how to solve problems. Good communications skills are marked by (1) avoiding sarcasm, name calling, or being accusatory; (2) taking personal responsibility for what each partner thinks rather than attempting to interpret their partner's intentions or feelings; (3) listening carefully, taking turns, and not interrupting the other person while they are speaking; (4) staying focused on the subject at hand (i.e., not changing the subject as a diversionary tactic); (5) "agreeing to disagree" and leaving the problem alone at some point should the issue seem unable to be resolved immediately; (6) apologizing with sincerity when it is called for; (7) avoiding unreasonable stubbornness (i.e., stonewalling), a tactic that can readily lead to resentment, contempt for the other person, and a continued downward spiral in the relationship; (8) planning to revisit a contentious issue at an agreed-upon time when both partners are emotionally prepared to discuss it further; and (9) rewarding the other person and letting them know that you appreciate their efforts to communicate honestly and constructively.

In a word, good communication skills demonstrate and foster mutual respect, even if the matter at hand cannot be resolved. Social work practitioners are in a strategic position to use modeling, role play, rehearsal, and homework assignments with clients to promote effective communication skills. Research evidence in couples and family practice demonstrates that communication skills are an effective component of intervention.

Improving communication skills can bring clients one step further to adopting effective *problem-solving skills* as well. Good communications skills should be considered a prerequisite to problem solving (it's tough for a couple or for family members to solve problems if they can't communicate effectively with one another). Problem-solving skills have been well researched over the past few decades and have become a mainstay for work with both adults and children (Bedell & Lennox, 1997; D'Zurilla & Goldfried, 1971; Meichenbaum, 1974). Core skills of various problem-solving models are quite similar: (1) identify what the problems are, (2) brainstorm ideas for solutions, (3) develop a problem-solving plan that is specific and targeted on one problem at a time, and (4) evaluate the results, make modifications to the plan, and try again as needed. This basic approach is quite flexible and can be applied to a wide range of problems. It can also be adapted for work with individuals, couples, and families.

After the client's target problems have improved, therapeutic coping skills can be utilized to generalize those improvements to other problems. Improvement in one area (e.g., depression, addictions) can be a catalyst for changes in other areas (e.g., improving overall health through exercise, improving relationships and family life, improving work performance). To help clients generalize their gains and maintain long-term positive outcomes, it may be worthwhile to discuss *enhancing the client's overall lifestyle*. These changes might include changing diet, exercising, taking a course to improve one's skills, taking up a constructive hobby, joining a mutual support group, and so on. If the changes require the advice of other professionals, social workers can refer their client as needed (e.g., to a physician before beginning an exercise regimen).

Summary

Therapeutic coping skills constitute a wide array of skills that can effectively optimize a client's thinking, feeling, and behavioral capacities. Designing a specific protocol and treatment plan for each client is a highly individual and collaborative affair, and it must be designed to specifically address the unique aspects of the problem from the client's point of view.

Far from being a "cookie cutter" approach, intervention plans using therapeutic coping skills require extraordinary sensitivity, empathy, and a commitment to tailoring the intervention to the client's needs. Coping-skills interventions can be highly variable and often require considerable ingenuity and creativity on the part of the practitioner to tailor the intervention to fit the client's unique challenges. Coping-skills approaches, based predominantly on cognitive-behavioral methods, constitute much of what have now become evidence-based practices. Although treatment manuals are essential for laying out the core principles of evidence-based practices (i.e., tested combinations of essential skills) for specific disorders, no two individual treatment plans are likely to be exactly the same due to the wide range of variations in how cognitive-behavioral coping skills are applied.

CHAPTER SEVEN

Case Management Skills

THE THOUGHTFUL USE of supportive and therapeutic coping skills can successfully alleviate many client difficulties and improve their coping capacities in both the short and long term when they are utilized in combinations defined by evidence-based practices. However, sometimes even those best efforts may not be sufficient for clients with more enduring psychosocial and environmental challenges. Many clients, often those with more complex and severe difficulties, need a broader level of support and coordination for delivering multiple services. These clients can benefit by adding case management skills to the Comprehensive Service Plan. Case management skills include:

- *Enhancing social support,* a skill that goes beyond engendering a sound working relationship with the practitioner but also bolsters ties with family members, mutual support groups, and other community supports
- *Providing instrumental supports,* including arranging for subsidized housing, procurement of health insurance, income supports, and other legislated entitlements and providing supported employment and job coaching
- *Advocating for clients* to ensure that their rights are protected, including assertively inquiring about denied benefits or services, accompanying clients to court to assist their attorneys in defending their legal rights, intervening for clients with landlords, employers, or other community members
- *Networking and coordination* of service providers, brokering services, and making referrals for clients

Despite the often significant impact of applying these skills, case management is many times represented as a less sophisticated approach to intervention than office-based social work practice such as psychotherapy. However, case management skills often enhance the effectiveness of other interventions and are essential for maintaining many clients' well-being in the community. Clients with serious disorders such as severe mental illness (e.g., schizophrenia), chronic addictions, homelessness, developmental disabilities (e.g., mental retardation), and chronic physical disabilities as well as elderly clients with problems and parents charged with child abuse and neglect often require multiple services using a multilevel approach. In such cases, case management can ensure continuity of services and help to maintain positive outcomes over time.

Social workers utilizing case management skills often coordinate a matrix of services involving several professionals: physicians and nurses, bachelor-level case workers, other social service workers (e.g., to ensure entitlements and related financial supports), public defenders, and professionals who provide other contracted psychosocial services (e.g., addictions treatment, psychotherapy). Social workers who provide multilevel case management must be qualified to perform the following functions:

- Conduct multidimensional and functional assessments and, therefore, be knowledgeable about the problems they treat
- Keep up to date on the availability and effectiveness of various services
- Take the initiative and provide leadership for maintaining communication and continuity among various service providers
- Ensure that confidentiality regulations and other ethical standards are followed
- Promote efficiency in service delivery by avoiding redundancy and unnecessary use of services
- Evaluate the results of the overall intervention plan.

To summarize, the effective implementation of case management skills suggests a high degree of knowledge regarding the clients' problems, extensive knowledge of the broader social service arena, and the ability to work at multiple levels with a variety of professionals to bring about successful outcomes for clients with complex needs.

Case management is a term that has been used extensively in the social work practice literature in primarily two distinct ways: (1) to represent the selective use of discrete skills as described above (e.g., enhancing social and instrumental supports, advocacy, networking, etc.) and (2) as a unifying framework for guiding and integrating interventions with multiproblem populations. When used to refer to discrete functions, it is well recognized that case management skills can be combined with other mainstream interventions such as out-patient mental health therapies, medical social work, school social work, and virtually any other social work field of practice. When used as a comprehensive framework, the term *case management* represents more than the use of adjunctive skills secondary to the primary intervention. Case management, as a comprehensive strategy, serves as an organizing structure for coordinating the implementation of multiple services that, collectively, target a common set of goals. Thus, in the current chapter, case management skills will be discussed individually and also presented as a unifying intervention model with two important groups of multiproblem clients: families where there are allegations of child abuse and neglect and with people diagnosed with severe mental illnesses.

Case Management Skills Applied to Child-Abuse and Neglect Cases

It has been estimated that 3.7 million referrals of children allegedly abused or neglected are made annually to state and local child protective services (CPS) in the United States (U. S. Department of Health and Human Services [USDHHS], 2012). These cases, which include overlapping incidents of physical abuse, sexual abuse, and child emotional and physical neglect, result in about 2,000 deaths of children annually (Pecora, Whittaker, Maluccio, & Barth, 2000; Putnam, 2003; USDHHS, 2012). Assessment and intervention with suspected cases of child abuse and neglect require extensive MFS clinical assessment and forensic investigations to determine whether crimes have been committed. Risk factors for child abuse and neglect can include parental psychopathology or other vulnerabilities (e.g., mental illness, addictions, criminality, lack of parenting experience), environmental stressors (e.g., poverty, lack of support services), and, often, multiple interactions of these risk factors. Case management with families where child abuse or neglect have been reported can range from occasional monitoring and psycho-education to multilevel, multiservice interventions that include bolstering social and instrumental supports, ongoing monitoring of the case, couples and family therapies, liaising with criminal justice, and networking with multiple services, including mental health, substance abuse, and other social services. Specialized services for the child and/or other family members (e.g., mental health, substance abuse treatment) and more

intensive home-based multilevel treatment (e.g., intensive family preserva-
tion or family reunification services) may be available as well. Short-term
institutionalization may be used for temporary treatment or respite care.
If the safety of the child is a serious concern, temporary out-of-home placements may be recommended. These placements may include foster and
kinship care, residential care for the child, or termination of parents' rights
and permanent removal of the child. Overall, research evidence suggests
that child welfare interventions show mixed results, in part due to wide
variations in type and quality of service delivery. However, stronger evidence suggests that the inclusion of parenting skills and behavioral family
therapies (to be discussed in Chapters 11 and 12) in a comprehensive case
management model tends to improve outcomes (Kazdin & Weisz, 1998;
Lutzker, Bigelow, Doctor, Gershater, & Greene; 1998; O'Hare, 2015; Smokowski & Wodarski, 1996; Wolfe & Wekerle, 1993).

Essential case management skills utilized in child abuse and neglect
cases include social supports, instrumental supports, and advocacy as well
as networking, coordinating, brokering services, and making referrals.

Social supports, as applied in cases of child abuse and neglect, include
improvements to the family's natural social network, increased links to
other community resources, access to mutual help groups, and assistance
from other family members, among others. Practitioners should also make
efforts to link clients to local social supports such as parent-teacher associations, free parenting skills workshops in local health or mental health agencies, mutual help groups for persons in recovery from alcohol or other
drugs, sexual abuse support groups, and local religious institutions, among
others. Practitioners should also try to connect troubled families with
extended family members who might be willing to provide some assistance, other community networks for sharing child care services, car-
pooling arrangements to lower commuting expenses, and so forth. The
availability of natural and public supports and services will vary greatly by
location, but providers should make every effort to find out what is available and explore their utilization with clients.

Human behavior theory provides a strong rationale for utilizing case
management skills. It has been long recognized in the research that,
although there is considerable variability in the way individuals respond
and cope with stress, chronic social and environmental stressors are
closely associated with poorer psychosocial and health outcomes (Dohrenwend, 1998). Holahan and Moos (1994) identify three main elements
in a model of stress-environment coping: person factors (i.e., inherent
deficits and strengths), stressful events (e.g., trauma, daily stressors), and

physical and social environment (e.g., social and instrumental supports). Psychological stress has been defined as tension between the person and the environment that people perceive as taxing or exceeding their resources and endangering their well-being (Lazarus, 1999; Lazarus & Folkman, 1984), and many families where children are at risk for abuse or neglect suffer from numerous psychosocial and economic stressors (Begel, Dumas, & Hanson, 2010). Coping is defined as the client's cognitive and behavioral efforts to manage internal and external stressors. One factor that has been shown to be critical for mitigating psychosocial distress is social support. It is widely recognized in the child welfare field that the recruitment of informal supports (i.e., family, friends) may be of considerable benefit in some cases (Lyons, Henly, & Schuerman, 2005). Lyons et al. (2005) demonstrated in a large sample of over 800 mothers that informal supports showed some evidence of reducing depression and financial strain as well.

One example of a growing source of social support is what is now referred to as public kinship care. A quarter or more of out-of-home placements in the public child welfare system are now arranged with the child's grandparents (USDHHS, 2003a). Many other children are cared for by grandparents informally, that is, without the intervention of the child welfare system. Whether these arrangements are made publicly or privately, these grandparents not only provide social support, but are in considerable need of social support, too. In a recent study, Goodman, Potts, and Pasztor (2007) found that social supports coupled with financial supports resulted in improved psychological and physical health of caregiving grandmothers.

Instrumental supports are essential to help bolster families where child abuse and neglect has been alleged. Evidence strongly supports the view that poverty is related to the quality of child care and to the psychosocial outcomes of children (e.g., Bagley & Mallick, 2000; Leschied, Chiodo, Whitehead, & Hurley, 2006). Although child abuse and neglect are not the exclusive domain of the poor, children are at greater risk for abuse and neglect when they grow up in poor, single-family households where there is higher stress, violence, mental disorder, substance abuse, and fewer social and instrumental supports. Generally, it is agreed that these risk factors are cumulative, and long-term outcomes for poor, neglected, and abused children are not as positive as they are for children in dual parent households who are higher functioning psychologically, have better social supports, and have stable financial resources. Although the child welfare system cannot be an adequate substitute for adult caretakers who are constant, well-adjusted, and attentive to a child's emotional, physical, academic, and social needs, social workers can make a difference by assertively determining that the clients are aware of their eligibility for available financial supports, including food stamps, state health programs for routine medical care, access to food banks or local charities, and other available resources. Clearly, instrumental supports go hand in hand with social supports. Not only do clients need emotional support to cope with child care burdens, but they require basic financial resources to do so.

Although the debate continues as to the outcomes of welfare reform (Wells, 2006) few doubt the necessity of financial supports for many of those living in poverty, including single mothers and persons with physical and mental disabilities. Single mothers, in particular, are at high risk for involvement with child protective services, and cash assistance appears to lower this risk. Educating clients about financial supports, facilitating access to these benefits, helping clients complete eligibility forms, and advocating for clients turned down for benefits are important case management functions for social workers. Although some social workers do not see the provision of these services as a core function of their practice, having a working knowledge of the laws and eligibility standards is important for social workers in most fields.

Advocacy on behalf of clients includes representing the client's rights with the landlord, the courts, public defenders, other agencies, neighbors, and other community members. Noting the lack of case management coordination in many child abuse and neglect cases, Smith, Witte, and Fricker-Elhai (2006) noted the growing interest in the use of child advocacy centers (CACs) to enhance child protective services by improving coordination of forensic and clinical interventions as well as reducing stress for the victim and other family members. More specifically, CACs use multidisciplinary teams (MDTs) consisting of law-enforcement officers, investigators, prosecutors, mental health and medical personnel, and other professionals to centralize and coordinate the investigation of child abuse allegations with social, medical, mental health, and advocacy services. The use of an MDT is intended to increase inter-agency cooperation, promote accountability, improve tracking of cases, and increase the efficient use of community services and resources (Smith, Witte, & Fricker-Elhai, 2006, p. 355).

Noting the lack of empirical evidence supporting CACs, Smith, Witte, and Fricker-Elhai (2006) conducted a preliminary study comparing CACs with standard child protective services in primarily sexual abuse cases, and found that the addition of formal child advocacy resulted in increased involvement by law enforcement, increased medical exams, and more substantiation of cases than did standard child protection services. One might conclude from this preliminary investigation that CACs illustrate what good case management is supposed to be: centrally coordinated, comprehensive, and accountable provision of multiple services. Clearly, advocacy can provide an important organizing principle when implementing effective case management services.

Networking, coordinating, brokering services, and making referrals are especially critical skills in cases of child abuse and neglect. Such cases often require the well-integrated use of multiple services. Child abuse and neglect cases can conceivably require the coordination of mental health, substance abuse, legal, financial, and other social services. Although referrals to other specialized services can be made for parents who have serious mental health and substance abuse problems, the social worker coordinating the overall intervention for the family can reinforce these efforts or, due to a lack of available services, may also be the main provider of these services. Practitioners can help a parent, for example, who is being treated for bipolar disorder by discussing medication compliance with them, examining whether the client is aware of an increase in depressive or manic symptoms, and discussing with them plans to reach out to either the social worker or their psychiatric professional if they notice a recurrence of symptoms. Clients who have been detoxified from alcohol or other drugs or are recently discharged from rehabilitation are likely to need help with identifying triggers, that is, antecedents to start using substances again. The stresses and strains of daily parenting and maintaining sobriety often lead to relapse in multiproblem families, and parents are likely to need much support from the social worker to anticipate these daily at-risk situations, deal with emotional distress, keep motivated to maintain sobriety, learn and use stress-management techniques to reduce the likelihood of relapse, and even role play scenarios to refuse offers of alcohol or other drugs. Social workers can help their child welfare clients make connections between the quality of parenting skills and their need to maintain good mental health and sobriety. These skills are essential for helping multiproblem families achieve and maintain good outcomes.

As part of case management, practitioners should also be prepared to facilitate contingency management programs with law enforcement/criminal justice to ensure adherence to drug treatment protocol and comply with other court-ordered mandates (e.g., refraining from drug use) as required to maintain custody of children or regain custody of a child in placement. These conditions may also include determining that the parent(s) is/are consistently utilizing contracted mental health or substance abuse services as recommended. Social workers may also have to refer children for brief hospital or residential stays or temporary foster and kinship care.

Comprehensive Approaches to Case Management for Child Abuse and Neglect Cases

Eco-behavioral or systemic approaches are multilevel, multiservice intervention methods built on a case management framework. Variations of these comprehensive models include some or all of the following skills:

- Bolstering of social and instrumental supports for families in crisis where abuse or neglect are of concern
- Making efforts to preserve the family unit rather than placing the child outside the home
- Reunifying families by reintroducing the child to the family after having been temporarily placed outside the home
- Improving the parents' general living skills (e.g., improving safety, cleanliness, providing adequate healthful food, general maintenance of the environment)
- Bolstering other adaptive skills (i.e., enhancing strengths)
- Improving child care (e.g., promoting emotional nurturance and physical care, adequate learning stimulation, safety, improvements in other parenting skills such as positive discipline methods)
- Improving family communication and problem-solving skills
- Enhancing social supports and reducing isolation (e.g., join a parenting group; becoming more involved with parents in the local school)
- Ensuring access to available environmental and financial supports (e.g., free health care for children offered in many states, other financial benefits)
- Referring clients for specialized services such as mental health and substance abuse services for adults or children
- Serving as liaison with schools, health care, and criminal justice to ensure coordination in provision of services
- Conducting ongoing evaluation of services with an emphasis on multidimensional outcomes (e.g., parents' engagement in treatment, children's school attendance, emotional well-being)
- Serving as an advocate for the family for eligible services, benefits, and protection of rights

Variations on eco-systems approaches have a strong conceptual base, and intuitively seem to make a lot of sense. Nevertheless, evidence on the effectiveness of some of these broad-brush programs has been mixed.

Case Management Skills Applied to Clients with Severe Mental Illness

Clients who receive case management services in community mental health services typically meet criteria that include (1) having been diagnosed with a severe and persistent mental illness (i.e., schizophrenia spectrum disorders and major mood disorders including major depression and bipolar disorders) and (2) demonstrating functional deficits that require the client to have ongoing community supports in order to reduce psychiatric crises and avoid unnecessary psychiatric hospitalizations. Many of these clients also have other co-occurring problems, including substance abuse and personality disorders. A growing number of these clients have also been involved with the criminal justice system. When taken together, clients in community mental health case management programs number in the millions nationally.

Assessment with seriously mentally ill clients requires a thorough review of all psychosocial domains, especially with regard to mental status, interpersonal relationships, and community functioning. These clients also have a disproportionate number of serious health problems. Given the multiplicity of problems presented by community mental health clients, intervention requires a comprehensive approach. In addition to psychiatric medication and occasional brief hospitalization, case management models have emerged as the organizing framework for delivering multiple services to clients with severe and persistent mental illnesses, many of whom are the most psychosocially debilitated people cared for by social workers.

Case management models were developed in response to federal initiatives begun in the 1960s (Drake, 1998; Sherrer & O'Hare, 2008) that promoted improved care for the mentally ill and an increased drive toward deinstitutionalization, a policy that has been unfolding since that time. Comprehensive community-based programs were developed to prevent client relapse in the community, avoid re-hospitalization, and enhance psychosocial functioning in seriously mentally ill clients. Case management models were seen as the vehicle for coordinating multiple services within these community-based programs.

Although case management skills with seriously mentally ill persons are often packaged in comprehensive programs like Assertive Community Treatment (ACT), the essential skills employed deserve a closer look. Given that social withdrawal is a common symptom of mental illness and social stigma a common social response, bolstering *social supports* for mentally ill persons has come to be understood as essential for long-term recovery.

Social supports include a wide array of possibilities: improving their natural social network by connecting with family members; linking clients to other community resources, mutual help groups, and client-run social clubs; and enhancing relationships with employers, landlords, and other people in the client's natural social network. Helping clients connect with other mutual help groups in the community can be a challenge, however. For example, clients with co-occurring substance use disorders may feel somewhat alienated from mainstream mutual help groups such as Alcoholics Anonymous, Narcotics Anonymous, or other similar groups. Social stigma against mentally ill people continues to be widespread and exists in many of these mutual support groups as well. Case managers can help clients to work around some of these barriers or promote specialized support groups for those mentally ill clients who cannot make the transition to mainstream organizations. In either case, social workers should attempt to promote acceptance in the community, help clients develop their social skills to transcend some of these barriers, and provide opportunities for more socially debilitated clients to have access to specialized social supports in order to reduce social isolation, recover from addictions, improve medication compliance, and cope with other common difficulties experienced by community clients.

Although facilitating the supportive working relationship is typically discussed in the context of psychotherapeutic or counseling services, many clients with major mental illnesses do not regularly receive such services. However, the case manager, often a bachelor-level social worker or other mental health worker, is in a strategic position to provide such support. Evidence strongly suggests that a case manager's relationship with clients has a positive effect on client well-being (Coffey, 2003; Hopkins & Ramsundar, 2006; Ryan, Sherman, & Judd, 1994). Social supports provided by case managers seem to lessen client symptoms by enhancing participation in treatment and reducing high-risk behaviors that cause other problems. Mueser, Rosenberg, Goodman, and Trumbeta (2002) contend that social supports provided by treatment staff may also reduce PTSD symptoms and improve overall adjustment by further reducing exposure to traumatic events and by providing an opportunity to experience an empathic trusting relationship. Given that professional social support (i.e., the working relationship) has been repeatedly demonstrated to advance therapeutic efforts for clients with other disorders, there is little reason to believe that enhancing social supports through case management efforts would be any less relevant for enhancing both treatment engagement and overall outcomes (O'Hare, 2015).

The benefits of social supports can also be enhanced by teaching clients how to build, maintain, and improve their own social supports. These skills are now incorporated into a comprehensive approach to client skill building known as illness management and recovery, a holistic model of client long-term growth and life enhancement (Mueser et al., 2006).

Instrumental supports for persons with a severe mental illness include income supports, housing assistance, supported employment, medical assistance, and referral to address other basic needs. Persons with severe mental illnesses have substantially higher rates of homelessness and unemployment than non-mentally ill people (Herman, Susser, & Struening, 1998). Unemployment and homelessness exert considerable stress on mentally ill clients, lead to reduced social supports, worsen their symptoms and overall functioning in the community, and put them at higher risk to be victimized by crime. Supported housing has been shown to improve psychosocial functioning, increase medication compliance, reduce stigma, and improve relationships (Browne & Courtney, 2007). Although considerable efforts have been made in the last two decades to develop and maintain residential programs for severely mentally ill persons, homelessness remains a serious problem (Randolph, Ridgway, & Carling, 1991), and mentally ill persons of color appear to be at even greater risk of homelessness (Kuno, Rothbard, Averyt, & Culhane, 2000). Given that homelessness remains a significant national problem, schizophrenia must continue to be assessed and treated within the context of substantial social, environmental, and economic risk factors.

In past years, it was believed that sheltered workshops or extensive preemployment counseling were required in order for clients with severe mental illness to remain employed. However, thinking in this area has changed in recent years. Evidence suggests that *supported employment* (i.e., direct placement into real paying jobs without pretraining), ongoing social support, and respect for client work preferences result in more successful job placement, more time worked, and higher wages earned (Bond et al., 2001; Bond, Drake, & Becker, 2008; Gold et al., 2006). Supported employment is usually provided as a service within a broader case management program. Gold et al. (2006) describe the details of how supported employment is integrated into one successful Assertive Community Treatment (i.e., ACT) program:

Employment specialists assessed each participant's past work experiences, current skills, and tolerance for type and intensity of job demands. Participants chose which jobs to pursue, although specialists strongly urged competitive jobs over work-adjustment experiences in protected settings. Together participants and specialists searched for competitive job openings and/or agreed to placement into new jobs "developed" jointly by specialists and local employers. Specialists provided time unlimited support before, during, and after periods of employment. Like ACT staff, they shared responsibility for meeting every participant's employment goals (Gold et al., 2006; p. 381).

Although helping clients maintain employment over time remains a challenge, significant progress has been made with supported employment programs, and the results continue to demonstrate that this strategy is superior to prior methods such as sheltered workshops.

Social workers *advocate on behalf of clients* in many situations. Difficulties in coping, low socioeconomic status, and social stigma remain serious barriers for persons with severe and persistent mental illnesses. Media portrayals that presumptively characterize a violent person as mentally ill continue to reinforce a public perception that the mentally ill are dangerous. In fact, violent behavior is no more prevalent among the mentally ill than non-mentally ill persons, except for a subgroup of young, aggressive, substance-abusing male offenders with a history of violence (Tehrani, Brennan, Hodgins, & Mednick, 1998). Noncompliance with medication also contributes to aggressive behaviors (Swartz et al., 1998). In addition to better coordination of services among mental health, substance abuse, and the criminal justice systems, social workers often need to advocate for their clients to ensure that they are accorded all rights, benefits, and due process available to them.

In the legal realm, social workers are often called upon to advocate for their clients. Often, this advocacy is conducted in court while accompanying the client's public defender. In making determinations about type of treatment, treatment commitment, or proper placement of clients, judges often want to know how the client has been responding to treatment, how cooperative they have been with treatment, and whether the "least restrictive" intervention is likely to be adequate to ensure proper care for clients and protect public safety. Advocating for clients with mental illnesses requires a keen awareness of the client's rights, a competent grasp of the client's psychosocial status, and the ability to balance the ethical mandate to protect the client's rights with the need to protect the public from harm should a client present evidence of being potentially harmful to others.

Because of some clients' difficulties in reading and comprehension of bureaucratic prose, difficulty concentrating due to intrusive thoughts, low energy resulting from depression, or fears resulting from paranoid ideation, social workers need to advocate assertively for clients to ensure that they are given all due consideration regarding eligibility for public financial supports, subsidized housing, and disability benefits. Many mentally ill clients are eligible for such benefits but would find the application and follow-through processes daunting to say the least. Social workers can guide them through the process, assist them in making follow-up phone calls, and directly challenge and appeal circumstances where clients are undeservedly turned down for applicable benefits. For admission to subsidized housing, clients may require letters of recommendation that clarify the nature of prior offenses (e.g., shoplifting vs. assault and battery) should landlords initially balk at a mentally ill client's application.

Social workers also want to help clients be aware of potentially discriminatory practices and tenant rights. And social workers may intervene to secure some forbearance from landlords should the client not be keeping up their rental property due to a period of decompensation (i.e., return of severe psychiatric symptoms) or is experiencing a personal crisis such as a financial or health problem. Mediating these kinds of day-to-day survival issues is one important dimension of advocacy. Social workers might also advocate with child welfare officials to make recommendations to contribute to deliberations regarding a mentally ill parent's ability to care for their child (i.e., provide adequate emotional nurturance, physical care, and safety). Advocacy may go beyond the individual client and extend to a broader public effort to educate the community about mental illness and, for example, assuage the fears and misconceptions of local townspeople regarding the construction of a new social club for mentally ill persons. Advocacy groups such as the National Alliance for the Mentally Ill, many members of which have children or other relatives with mental illnesses, often invite social workers to make presentations and collaborate with them to advance the rights of persons with mental illnesses.

Although many community mental health centers offer a wide range of services to clients with severe mental illnesses, some services must be contracted with other providers. *Networking, coordinating, brokering services, and making referrals* are essential case management skills for working with severely mentally ill clients. These services include primary medical care, psychiatric hospitalization, detoxification services, legal assistance, job and housing supports, as well as other social services. Because mentally ill persons are arrested more often than non-mentally ill persons, are often held without formal charges being filed, and are not adequately treated for their mental illnesses during incarceration, there have been increasing calls to improve the coordination of services across mental health, substance abuse, and criminal justice systems (Fisher, Packer, Grisso, McDermeit, & Brown, 2000; Lamb & Weinberger, 1998; Lamb &

Weinberger, 2008). Social workers who work with persons who have severe mental illnesses will find that the work is quite challenging and requires a high degree of expertise to adequately coordinate a wide range of different services.

Case Management as a Unifying Framework for Interventions with Persons Who Have Severe Mental Illness

Perhaps the best-known paradigm for community case management models is the Program for Assertive Community Treatment (PACT) model (Drake, 1998; Stein & Test, 1980). Other variations of this program include continuous treatment teams and mobile treatment teams. Although there is considerable variation in how these programs are structured, they generally include:

- The use of social supports to reduce isolation through regular contacts with case managers as well as promoting affiliation with other community groups (e.g., client social clubs)
- Instrumental supports (e.g., arranging for disability benefits, health care coverage, and other income supports as needed)
- Providing ongoing support to obtain and maintain employment in the community
- Advocating for the rights of clients, some of whom may be mandated for treatment by the courts
- Coordinating multiple systems of care (e.g., psychiatric services, primary health care, psychotherapy and counseling services, supported housing services, etc.)

Comprehensive case management programs typically utilize a team approach, offer twenty-four-hour coverage and open-ended treatment, and attempt to keep a relatively low client-to-staff ratio. Although these models appear coherent and intensive on paper, the quality of their implementation varies from state to state (Mechanic, 1996; Mueser, Bond, Drake, & Resnick, 1998; Sherrer & O'Hare, 2008). Nevertheless, evidence suggests that these programs have shown solid gains in reducing hospitalizations and improving the overall psychosocial functioning of these multi-problem clients (Kreyenbuhl, Buchanan, Dickerson, & Dixon, 2010; Mueser, Bond, Drake, & Resnick, 1998; Mueser, Drake, & Bond, 1997; Scott & Dixon,

1995). In addition, programs designed specifically to help mentally ill clients with co-occurring mental health and substance use disorders have shown promising results (Drake et al. 1998; Dumaine, 2003; RachBeisel, Scott, & Dixon, 1999).

In recent years, it has been recognized that case management skills can be enhanced by incorporating what have been traditionally thought of as more "psychotherapeutic" interventions, those treatments provided in consulting offices by social workers and other professionals with advanced degrees. However, as a result of promising research on psychosocial interventions with the mentally ill (e.g., social-skills training, psycho-education with families, coping-skills approaches) an enhanced case management model has been developed that incorporates some of these methods in addition to the more traditional case management methods described above. This more advanced case management approach has come to be termed *clinical case management* (Sherrer & O'Hare, 2008). Clinical case management more explicitly includes those supportive and therapeutic coping-skills approaches previously reserved for more "psychotherapeutic" approaches. Thus, in addition to enhancing social and instrumental supports, advocacy, and coordinating interventions, clinical case management includes the following:

- Comprehensive assessments and monitoring of client progress (e.g., mental status, substance use, family relationships, role functioning in the community and at work)
- Crisis intervention
- Psycho-education and behavioral family therapy with the client and their family
- Stress-management skills
- Social-skills training to help clients better utilize social supports
- Substance abuse counseling including relapse prevention techniques
- Medication monitoring

Clinical case management interventions have great potential for enhancing treatment continuity since the social worker would not only be coordinating much of the treatment, but also be engaged in providing much of the care themselves. In this way, clinical case management represents an ideal model of intervention whereby practitioners can integrate the best of supportive, therapeutic coping and case management skills with clients who present some of the greatest psychosocial challenges in our field.

Summary

Social workers are on the front lines when it comes to working with some of society's most troubled people. Case management strategies used on an "as needed" basis or as an organizing framework for treatment require a high degree of knowledge regarding client's multifaceted problems, assertiveness and initiative on the part of the social worker, and a broad array of skills to address complex problems. Although the application of case management skills with clients accused of child abuse and neglect and those diagnosed with severe mental illnesses were illustrated here, these skills can be applied, when needed, with many other clients who experience significant psychosocial stressors, lack financial resources, and are in need of social and instrumental supports.

PART THREE

Combining Essential Skills with Individuals, Couples, and Children and Their Families

CHAPTER EIGHT

Adult Disorders: Schizophrenia, Mood, and Anxiety Disorders

SCHIZOPHRENIA, major mood disorders, and anxiety disorders cover a broad spectrum of mental health problems from the moderately debilitating to the very severe. Schizophrenia and bipolar disorder are generally considered severe mental illnesses given that they share symptoms of psychosis (i.e., thought disorders such as hallucinations, delusions). Major depression can be equally debilitating but generally is not considered a psychotic disorder (although some very depressed clients may experience transitory psychotic symptoms). Anxiety disorders include specific phobias, panic attacks with agoraphobia, generalized anxiety disorder, post-traumatic stress disorder, and obsessive-compulsive disorder, among others. These disorders often co-occur with substance abuse or dependence and are often accompanied by a wide range of other functional psychosocial problems-in-living. Interventions for these problems are well researched, and clients with these conditions who receive evidence-based practices have a good chance of substantially reducing symptoms and improving overall quality of life.

Schizophrenia

Assessment

There are several subtypes of schizophrenia that share a number of common indicators including positive symptoms: delusions and thought disorders (i.e., implausible beliefs, bizarre logic); hallucinations (i.e., seeing, hearing, feeling, or smelling stimuli that do not really exist); incoherent or disorganized speech (e.g., inability to make any logical sense, construction of odd and novel words); disorganized or bizarre behavior; and negative symptoms, including extreme social withdrawal and flattening of affect (i.e., difficulty with emotional expression). Different subtypes of schizophrenia tend to emphasize some symptoms more than others. For example, persons with schizophrenia who demonstrate severe paranoia are likely to have prominent delusions about being spied on or convinced that they are being watched by aliens or spied on by government officials. Most persons with schizophrenia are diagnosed as disorganized or undifferentiated because they show a mixed presentation of relevant symptoms. To meet DSM-5 criteria, the client must have demonstrated continuous signs and symptoms for six months, which may include a one month "prodromal" or prepsychotic period with active symptoms. During this time, the person, often in their late teens or early twenties, may have become very withdrawn and demonstrated strange behaviors (e.g., muttering to themselves incoherently, engaged in bizarre pre-occupations) but not yet shown a full complement of symptoms to meet the diagnostic criteria. Once the client has demonstrated one month of actively psychotic symptoms, the diagnosis of schizophrenia can be applied (APA, 2013; O'Hare, 2015; Sadock & Sadock, 2003).

Although the onset of the disorder often occurs in the late teens and early twenties, onset for women may be a few years later than for men. Other symptoms and disorders may also co-occur with schizophrenia. Depression and anxiety often accompany the disorder and may be treated concurrently. Many persons diagnosed with schizophrenia also have other neurological disorders such as tics and seizures that can be treated along with the primary disorder. Another common problem associated with schizophrenia is substance abuse. One-third or more of clients in treatment for schizophrenia are also abusing alcohol or other drugs, and about one-half of all persons with severe and persistent mental illnesses will develop a substance use disorder at some time in their life.

Schizophrenia is a chronic disorder that often has a long and deteriorating trajectory. Medications to control psychotic symptoms (i.e., hallucinations primarily) are helpful for many of these clients but are often accompanied with negative side effects on the nervous system. Tardive dyskinesia, for example, is a disorder of the extrapyramidal nervous system indicated by a shuffling gate, involuntary muscle movements, and facial grimacing. Although some progress has been made in recent years with regard to reducing side effects of these drugs, the overall effects of antipsychotic medications on positive and negative symptoms have not improved substantially over decades.

Given that schizophrenia is a biopsychosocial disorder, assessment should go well beyond itemizing the symptoms in DSM-5 criteria. An MFS assessment should examine the following:

- Client's overall mental status: in addition to psychotic symptoms, include an evaluation for depression, suicide risk, problems with anxiety, and substance abuse
- Quality of current relationships: interactions with family; the nature and frequency of those contacts; how much time the client spends alone or with others whom they consider close acquaintances or friends; the nature of those relationships, and whether they are prosocial and healthful connections or whether they increase risk for the client's overall well-being
- Quality of their daily life in the community: document how the client spends their time, where they go, with whom they associate; note any behavior problems that come to the attention of the police or others in the community
- Quality of the client's living circumstances: assess the overall suitability of their housing—the safety, cleanliness, and overall adequacy; query the client about their daily diet, shopping, if they cook or rely on prepared foods (e.g., convenience foods); ask about routine hygiene (i.e., regular showers, laundering clothes); try to determine how they budget their (usually) limited income, how much they spend on cigarettes, alcohol, or other drugs
- General assessment of the client's overall health: obtain relevant medical records; note any physical disabilities and determine the kind of assistance they receive or benefits for which they are eligible

Given that persons with schizophrenia and other severe mental illnesses often suffer from multiple problems, a comprehensive assessment is essential for adequate treatment planning. Practitioners should go beyond taking a one-time snapshot assessment and monitor these different problem areas over time.

A variety of scales are available to enhance routine assessments and provide a foundation for monitoring client's progress over time. Other simple indexes can be helpful as well: Has the client been taking their medication consistently? How often do they miss appointments? Have they been arrested for minor infractions in the community? How often are they admitted to the local emergency room or the regional psychiatric facility? How many days have they worked in the past month? These simple indicators can tell practitioners much about a client's overall well-being and functioning in the community.

Intervention

Treatment of the seriously mentally ill has become more humane in the past few decades as a result of deinstitutionalization, strengthening of civil rights protection, increased advocacy, and better funding for community-based services. Although there have been some negative consequences in the wake of deinstitutionalization (e.g., increased homelessness of mentally ill persons, increased stigma in the community), most observers would agree that these problems pale in comparison to the poor conditions of the past whereby many persons with mental disorders languished in public hospitals for long periods of time with little legal recourse.

Using psychosocial interventions for which there is a body of supporting outcome research has become a major focus of research and responsible treatment policy (Dixon et al., 2010; Lehman, Steinwachs, & the Co-Investigators of the PORT Project, 1998; Mueser & Jeste, 2008). At the forefront has been the widespread adoption of programs for Assertive Community Treatment (ACT) and variations of it (covered in the previous chapter). These models, at their best, coordinate psychiatric care (i.e., medication) with regular contacts with case managers in the community to monitor clients' overall functioning and bolster social and instrumental supports. Often, the agencies become representative payees for the client in order to help them manage their money. Many states also have active programs to provide subsidized housing and assistance in finding employment. However, other interventions that have been shown to be considerably effective have not been disseminated widely. These include cognitive-behavioral coping skills, family psycho-education and behavioral family therapy for people who have a mentally ill family member living with them, and social skills training to help clients become better engaged in daily community life. These interventions have been shown to be reasonably effective in controlled trials, and could be readily integrated by practitioners into a well-coordinated multidisciplinary case management model.

Working with persons diagnosed with schizophrenia can be both challenging and rewarding. The interventions described below are also applied to persons with major mood disorders (major depressive disorders and bipolar disorder) who struggle with recurrent psychotic symptoms and have difficulties functioning independently in the community. Later in this chapter, interventions for nonpsychotic major depression will also be discussed. Clients with severe mental illnesses, both schizophrenia and severe mood disorders, have often experienced considerable trauma in their lives, including physical abuse, sexual abuse, and other forms of violence

(O'Hare, Shen, & Sherrer, 2013). These clients can also be very withdrawn and socially isolated. Given their difficulties in processing information (due to thought disorders), suspicions resulting from delusions, and difficulties relating to other people, persons with schizophrenia may be difficult to engage in treatment. Nevertheless, research supports the view that these clients do respond positively to social supports provided specifically from treatment staff. They can be engaged in treatment, and can learn to connect with others successfully.

Clients with serious mental illnesses including schizophrenia have difficulties relating to and trusting others. Some of this mistrust may be due to the severity of thought disorders, the tranquilizing effects of medication, and learned responses to prior abuse and trauma. For some clients, treatment experiences may have contributed to their distrust of treatment staff either due to negative encounters with mental health professionals or the fact that many entry-level staff members do not remain long in their jobs. Whatever the cause, developing a working alliance with a person who suffers from schizophrenia requires unusual consistency and an incremental approach. However, engagement can vary greatly from client to client and will vary within the same client depending on their mood and mental status over time. A good working principle is to begin with problem-solving efforts that target daily stressors that clients confront at the treatment center or in the community. Over time, as the client becomes more comfortable with the practitioner, he may be willing to reveal some of his more disturbing or bizarre thought disorders and hallucinations. Beyond that, as trust develops, clients might be willing to take on greater challenges such as spending more time in the community, developing relationships further, or taking on a part-time job. Helping a very withdrawn client become more connected to others can be a considerable challenge. For very schizoid or paranoid clients, there may always be severe mistrust of others.

Enhancing motivation can be a challenge, especially for those clients who are depressed and very withdrawn. Medication side effects and substance abuse can also make it difficult to engage many of these clients. It is important for practitioners to start with relatively modest goals and build on small successes over time. Carefully examining goals that the client finds important is essential for successful engagement. Many mentally ill clients have felt somewhat powerless for some time and can benefit from being treated as collaborators in their treatment planning. Keeping goals concrete and achievable is also important. Many of these clients have a hard time accepting the fact that they have a mental illness, and the more practical the goals, the better. Practical goals might include: daily living skills such as doing laundry, grocery shopping, opening a checking account, showing up to appointments on time, and engaging in brief, focused conversations. Practitioners should carefully track these successes and give clear and direct evaluative feedback to clients. As for most clients, motivation is best reinforced by actual successes.

Clients with severe mental illnesses also respond well to practitioners who are authentic in the way they relate to the client. Practitioners should avoid abstract and overly intellectualized approaches and keep their interactions with clients "real." Being "real" means focusing on everyday concerns of the client and keeping one's comments and conversation focused on goals that are essential to the client meeting everyday needs. Clients suffering thought disorders and delusions may be inclined to engage practitioners in apparently "philosophical" discourse such as the meaning of life, whether we have been taken over by aliens, or to what extent we are all controlled by the devil. Practitioners should try to be respectful and reassuring about these matters but focus on concerns that are more immediate to maintaining stability in the community. Over time, sharing these daily concerns will engender a certain degree of trust, and clients may then be more forthcoming about other key concerns (e.g., past trauma, substance abuse).

A range of effective interventions for persons with schizophrenia emphasize the use of therapeutic coping skills. These include cognitive-behavioral therapy and family psycho-education and behavioral family therapy for persons with a mentally ill family member. More recently, illness management and recovery has gained some attention, although the approach is largely comprised of cognitive-behavioral coping skills. In addition, cognitive rehabilitation therapies have shown promise for addressing cognitive deficits (e.g., attention, memory) that are common in people with severe mental illness. Overall, intervention methods for people with severe mental illness share some common essential skills, but have some unique interventions in their own right.

COGNITIVE-BEHAVIORAL THERAPY

Cognitive-behavioral therapy utilizes a combination of skills intended to help clients challenge some of their more disturbing and dysfunctional thinking, regulate anxiety and stress, and improve coping behaviors in the community. Although many clients' problems are accompanied by troubling or dysfunctional beliefs, persons with severe mental illnesses often struggle with beliefs that are very much out of the norm and may be extremely debilitating. Paranoid delusions, fears of persecution, convictions regarding the intervention of alien beings, and auditory hallucinations that command clients to harm themselves or others can create formidable barriers to client improvement. Although hallucinations can be controlled with medication, bizarre beliefs may be less affected by psychotropic drugs.

Nevertheless, recent studies in cognitive therapy with severely mentally ill persons suggest that these clients can derive considerable benefit from this approach (Alford & Correia, 1994; Mueser, Rosenberg, Jankowski, Hamblen, & Descamps, 2004; Mueser et al., 2008) with comparable benefits resulting for white, Hispanic, and African-American clients (Lu et al., 2009). The first step is to help the client identify the problematic belief. This step does not mean verbally convincing the client that the belief is false or unrealistic. It simply means that you both agree that the client's conviction that "we are all controlled by aliens" creates a problem for the client in daily living. If this belief is true, then the client must have little or no control over what they think, feel, or do. Once the belief is identified, the client is then encouraged to keep a log or diary to further examine the belief and rate the strength of this belief daily. The practitioner then encourages the client to examine the false belief for content and discuss the plausibility of the belief ("What evidence supports your belief?"). Although this sounds like an attempt to rationally discredit the belief, it may provide the client with an opportunity to gain some objectivity on the belief and, perhaps, cause some doubts about its plausibility. The practitioner, again, should avoid engaging in debate about the belief but simply introduce some questions that may bring the plausibility of the belief into question in the client's mind. The practitioner may then encourage the client to consider alternative explanations for the belief, and explore these beliefs. Clients should then be encouraged to test out these beliefs and examine evidence that confirms or disconfirms the belief. For example, the client should engage in conversations with persons that they know and (without asserting that *they* believe in aliens) try to determine whether other people appear to be motivated by outside forces controlling them. It may be that a client's delusions may be more pronounced the more withdrawn they get, but as they spend more time with others, the belief in external control by aliens dissipates. Practitioners should stay on task with their client and follow up to see if the client is, in fact, testing out (i.e., behaviorally disconfirming) their hypotheses about alien influences. Thus, monitoring and evaluating client progress is essential.

SOCIAL SKILLS TRAINING

CBT methods can be fairly eclectic, and should be designed to address clients' specific needs. Other methods can be included in an overall CBT plan, such as social skills training, the use of modeling, role playing, and corrective feedback to help clients improve their ability to develop and maintain relationships with others. Rehearsing conversational skills, for example, can be a safe way to help the client identify their strengths and weaknesses relating to others. Results based on over forty years of research have shown that social skills training is moderately effective with people with severe mental illness with good generalization for using those skills in everyday life (Kurtz & Mueser, 2008).

To apply cognitive-behavioral therapy to help clients improve their social skills, practitioners should provide a sound rationale for learning the skills (e.g., making friends, getting a job). Of course, the client is likely to be anxious about initiating a conversation with a stranger, so the practitioner and client should first construct a hierarchy of social encounters that the client can tolerate. For example, the client may begin by making small talk with support staff (e.g., receptionists, administrative assistants, or maintenance personnel) to see if they can become more comfortable having conversations with people they know. To control anxiety, the practitioner can show the client how to calm himself (e.g., deep, slow breathing) before attempting a new conversation. Next, the client might attempt a brief conversation with someone in the community whom they know by sight, such as a friendly cashier in the local convenience store. In short, the hierarchy may gradually increase to initiating a conversation with someone they don't know, again, to discuss everyday things such as the weather or topical news events. Over time (with monitoring and evaluation), clients can become more comfortable, confident, and skilled at conversing with others (Bellack, Mueser, Gingerich, & Agresta, 1997).

Overall, CBT with mentally ill clients is versatile and can be used to address a wide range of problems. In summary, the guiding principles are as follows: define the problem; identify troubling or dysfunctional beliefs; explain the rationale for the intervention; examine and gently question the rationale that supports the belief; set up a series of behavioral tasks to gradually test out the client's belief; and provide modeling, role play, and rehearsal to prepare the client to practice their skills in the community. After the client has shown measurable success, the practitioner can continue to suggest more challenging goals depending on how far the client wants to go.

INTEGRATED TREATMENT FOR CO-OCCURRING SUBSTANCE USE DISORDERS

The skills for working with severely mentally ill clients who have a co-occurring substance use disorder are quite similar to general CBT methods described above. Integrated treatment for co-occurring mental illness and substance use can include a combination of substance use screening, psycho-education, motivational interviewing, relapse prevention skills, coping-skills training, contingency management with a goal of harm reduction (a realistic goal) if not complete abstinence (an ideal goal) (Tenhula, Bennett, & Kinnaman, 2009). Although working with "dual diagnosis" clients remains a challenge, these approaches are strongly recommended by panels of expert reviewers (Dixon et al., 2010). However, the practitioner must be knowledgeable about alcohol and other drugs and the unique risks associated with co-occurring substance abuse and mental illness. Alcohol and other drugs can worsen depression, increase anxiety, interfere with the therapeutic benefits of medication, and lead to impaired judgment and community-related problems. A complete MFS assessment with a mentally ill person requires a thorough substance use assessment: What substances does the client use? How much of each substance do they use? How often? And what seem to be the short- and long-term psychological, social, and physical consequences of their substance use?

Substance abuse can make the development of a good working alliance even more challenging than otherwise. However, practitioners can disarm some of the client's defensiveness regarding the self-report of substance use if the practitioner assures the client that they are not going to be penalized if they are forthcoming about their drug use. The social worker can further impress upon the client that many of the challenges they face in dealing with their mental illness will be only more difficult to deal with if they are using alcohol or other drugs. Thus, the assessment should be marked by a nonjudgmental attitude about the use of substances and one that focuses on the client's healthful self-interest. It is also important to begin linking the client's self-reported problematic thoughts, feelings, and interpersonal difficulties with their use of substances. In addition, identifying key high-risk situations and helping clients to anticipate and cope with those situations (e.g., when depressed or hallucinating) is critical to long-term improvement. Thus, engaging the client in a collaborative monitoring plan to assess their use of alcohol and other drugs is important. The practitioner should help the client *make consistent connections between their psychosocial complaints and their substance use, enhance motivation by collaborating on mutually agreed-upon treatment goals, and emphasize the use of coping skills to target high-risk situations.*

Interventions for dual disorders should also be applied in a staged sequence. Similar to the stages of change discussed in Chapter 4 (e.g., precontemplation, contemplation, preparation, action, and maintenance), a staged approach developed specifically for work with dual disordered clients has been utilized with some success. This approach includes eight stages: preengagement, engagement, early persuasion, late persuasion, early active treatment, late active treatment, relapse prevention, and remission or recovery (Bellack, Bennett, & Gearon, 2007; Mueser, Noordsy, Drake, & Fox, 2003). The purpose of this staged approach is to help clients set goals to their level of readiness to engage in treatment. In early stages, clients are generally not aware they have a problem or are not quite convinced. Helping them test out whether drugs are affecting their mood and behavior might help them "see for myself if it's a problem." A brief period of sobriety can be illuminating for clients. In the middle stages, clients generally begin to cut down and change at-risk behaviors. In later stages, clients focus more on solidifying gains and preventing relapse.

In all stages of improvement, supportive and coping skills are applied as needed. Many at-risk situations threaten to cause clients to back-slide: visiting friends and family, "hanging out" with unemployed acquaintances on the street, dealing with daily stressors, coping with symptoms of their disorders, as well as disappointment and losses. Role play and rehearsal can be used to prepare clients for these likely eventualities and increase their chances of getting through them without serious relapses. Anticipating at-risk situations should be a planned part of intervention. Clients can monitor their progress in coping with at-risk situations and discuss the outcomes with their practitioner, so they can work on improving the client's coping skills. In this way, the intervention is understood as a collaborative work in progress.

PSYCHO-EDUCATIONAL/BEHAVIORAL FAMILY THERAPY

Having a severely mentally ill parent, son, or daughter can be extremely stressful for an entire family's members as well as for the client. The client's bizarre behavior may be upsetting to the family, and family reactions may unwittingly provoke or upset the client. A twenty-year-old man with schizophrenia, for example, living at home may become extremely depressed and suicidal, discontinue his medication (without telling anyone), become very psychotic, respond in a belligerent way to hallucinations telling him that his parents are demons, make matters worse by using alcohol or other drugs, and become enraged when told his hygiene is very poor (as a result of paranoid ideation about someone trying to poison him in the shower). Families with a mentally ill member can benefit greatly from professional care and support in the form of both psycho-education and behavioral family therapy (Dixon et al., 2001; McFarlane, Dixon, Lukens, & Lucksted, 2003). Both of these approaches have been shown to be very helpful, and the elements of both are often combined in an eclectic manner depending on the specific needs of the family. Family psycho-education/behavioral approaches have also been exported to many other countries around the globe where people with mental illnesses are more likely to live with their families, and results have been shown to be equally positive. Studies demonstrating the effectiveness and relatively easy cultural transferability of family approaches have been conducted in Hong Kong with Chinese families (Chien & Wong, 2007), in Canada with Tamil and Chinese families (Chow et al., 2010), in Pakistan (Nasr & Kausar, 2009), and in Iran (Koolaee & Etemadi, 2010).

Psycho-education implies more of a didactic approach that can be done with single or multiple families simultaneously. Curricula usually address the nature of mental illness and general coping strategies within a support group format. Behavioral family therapy, although including a similar educational dimension, is a more formal intervention that focuses directly on enhancing family members' communication, coping, and problem-solving skills. The intervention should also be closely coordinated with psychiatric and case management services. Family psycho-education and behavioral family therapy can vary by modality (single or multiple family groups), should ideally be conducted over longer periods of time (e.g., a year) rather than in the short term, and should be implemented flexibly to accommodate those family members who can attend. The following overview of skills assumes an eclectic psycho-educational/behavioral family therapy approach.

In addition to completing an MFS assessment on the identified client, a thorough assessment of the family system is needed to consider their thoughts and feelings about the client, how they interact with the client, the impact each family member's behavior has on the client, and the effect the client's behavior has on each family member. It is this analysis of the interactions of family members with the client that is essential. A social worker who engages families with a mentally ill member can do quite a bit to instill optimism, provide realistic yet positive expectations, and offer emotional support as a basis for establishing a sound working alliance. The social worker should also be able to make a long-term commitment to resolving crises and stabilize the family's ability to cope with the client's illness. Psycho-education and behavioral family therapy have been shown to provide real relief and improve the overall situation measurably.

Providing accurate and up-to-date information to families about schizophrenia is a very good place to start. For many years, some practitioners promoted untested theories (e.g., the "schizophrenogenic mother," "double bind theory") maintaining that mental illness was caused by the mother or dysfunctional family communication. As with other problems, a stressful family environment can make matters worse, but there is no evidence that the behavior of family members causes schizophrenia or bipolar disorder.

Psycho-education, provided by a knowledgeable social worker, can help families understand that (1) they did not cause the client's mental illness; (2) a mentally ill person can be hard to deal with; (3) if they learned to be calmer and more focused in their dealings with the mentally ill family member, that person is likely to respond in a calmer manner as well; (4) the client's consistent use of medication is very important; (5) the family and the mentally ill member can learn to communicate and solve problems more effectively; and (6) the research on working with families shows that the situation can improve greatly for both the family and the mentally ill person if the family collaborates with the practitioner.

Once the family shows that they understand the importance of medication compliance and "turning down the emotional temperature" in the household by becoming more problem-focused and less reactive to the client's disturbing behaviors, the work on improving communication and problem solving can begin. The social worker should take time to identify positive and problematic interaction patterns between family members and note the effects these behaviors have on both client and family members. It is important to identify both constructive and problem interactions since increasing good interactions can help reduce problematic ones. It is important to hear what everyone has to say and make a special effort to encourage the client to express himself.

The social worker should strive to keep the focus on present problems and avoid excavating past problems (unless absolutely necessary to resolve a current dilemma). An example of a common difficulty may be a client—say, a young man—who stays up late at night watching television and keeps the volume on very loud. His father, who has to get up early for work, becomes enraged and confronts the young man in an aggressive way, leading to a confrontation. This initial outburst leads to much heated argument during which the father expresses disappointment in his son. The son feels provoked and explodes in anger toward his father, attacking him physically.

To prevent a similar outburst, the social worker can ask the father and son to calmly reenact the encounter in the office (or in the home, if the social worker is doing a home visit). Occasionally asking them to stop and talk about what they are thinking and feeling at the moment, the practitioner can help to slow down the action, help them get some perspective on the situation, and remain calm and open to solutions. The family can then brainstorm some solutions and consider ways to express their thoughts and feelings to the client without being overly provocative. After a brief discussion, the immediate solution becomes apparent: the parents decide to buy some headphones so that the young man can watch television at night without disturbing anyone.

Conversation in the next session might then focus on reasons why the young man stays up so late, whether he is having trouble sleeping, if he is taking his medications, using illicit drugs, or simply sleeping too long during the day. What is particularly important about this approach is that it serves as a vehicle to engage the family in a calm problem-solving process, and provides a context for improving communication skills that include a calmer and more measured expression of feelings and needs to one another.

Families should also be encouraged to look for the signs of relapse in the mentally ill family member. These might include excessive withdrawal from contact with others, signs that their son is not taking his medication, or indications that he is using alcohol or other drugs. Early intervention by the social worker can be very helpful at heading off a serious relapse and possible re-hospitalization. Families can also be encouraged to engage in stress-reducing activities that include relaxing activities such as renting a movie and having pizza, going for walks together in the local park, or taking a day trip. Individual family members should also be encouraged to find stress-reducing activities on their own. If one family member carries a disproportionate share of the burden of looking after the client's needs, some arrangements should be made to give that person some planned relief time. When crises do erupt (e.g., should they find their son bleeding as a result of a suicide attempt or overcome by an apparent psychotic episode), the social worker should discuss contingency plans with the family so that they know whom to call and what actions they should take. Of course, long-range planning options should be discussed as well. Although some families may simply choose to be the primary caretakers of a schizophrenic young adult, many families will have great difficulty sustaining that level of care and may decide to help their child make arrangements to live in the community.

ILLNESS MANAGEMENT AND RECOVERY (IMR)

In recent years, the emphasis in treatment of mental illness has gradually shifted from a reactive approach that concentrated mostly on controlling symptoms to a more proactive holistic strategy that emphasizes client initiative, skill building, and enhancing all areas of life, in short, going beyond the "sick role." This comprehensive approach, called Illness Management and Recovery (IMR), utilizes many of the interventions discussed above that emphasize increasing adaptive capacities and life skills. Key evidence-based components of IMR (Mueser et al. 2002; Mueser et al., 2006, p. s33) include:

- Psychoeducation about mental illness and its treatment
- Cognitive-behavioral approaches to medication adherence (e.g., incorporating cues for taking medication into daily routines)
- Developing a relapse prevention plan
- Strengthening social support by social-skills training
- Using coping-skills training for the management of persistent symptoms
- Supported employment to encourage and support independent living

Some have suggested integrating the components and goals of IMR and ACT with an emphasis on client-peer assistants as part of the treatment teams (Salyers et al., 2010). Lastly, these multicomponent approaches to community mental health are now expanding and being adapted to other parts of the world including developing countries where public health efforts have become more of a national priority such as in India (Chatterjee, Pillai, Jain, Cohen, & Patel, 2009; Kulhara et al., 2010).

COGNITIVE REMEDIATION

People with schizophrenia often have cognitive deficits that go beyond the primary symptoms of schizophrenia. These difficulties include attention, memory, tracking inputs, and problem solving. These problems also affect their ability to socialize and maintain employment. Research on cognitive remediation programs has shown that interventions comprised of computerized task modules over several weeks (some programs also include in vivo social skills and relaxation training) can improve cognitive functioning along with social and employment-related skills (Eack, Hogarty, Greenwald, Hogarty, & Keshavan, 2011; McGurk, Mueser, DeRosa, & Wolfe, 2009).

Taken together, there is a range of effective psychosocial interventions for working with people suffering from schizophrenia. In addition to building a strong working alliance and enhancing medication compliance, social workers can make important contributions to community-based care for people with severe mental illnesses by learning and using an array of evidence-based practices.

Mood Disorders

Assessment

Millions of Americans experience moderate to severe mood disorders, conditions that can be acute or chronic, and recur from time to time. Major mood disorders primarily include depressive disorders (major depression and dysthymia) and bipolar disorder. Although estimates of the twelve-month prevalence of major mood disorders range in national surveys due to methodological differences, up to one-fifth of people will develop a depressive disorder and about one percent a bipolar disorder some time in their lives (although some estimates have been over 3%) (Grant et al., 2005; Kessler et al., 1994; Kessler, Rubinow, Holmes, Abelson, & Zhao, 1997). Women are more likely to experience clinical depression, and elderly persons are likely to experience depression when coupled with other medical problems such as memory difficulties including Alzheimer's disease. Depression also co-occurs at high rates with many other disorders including substance abuse, addictions, and anxiety disorders (APA, 2013; Hasin, Goodwin, Stinson, & Grant, 2005).

Major depression is marked by a consistently depressed mood, diminished pleasure in previously enjoyed activities, significant weight loss, substantial changes in appetite, sleep disturbances, marked changes in energy levels, feelings of worthlessness, guilt, difficulty concentrating, or recurrent thoughts of death (APA, 2013). Depression can have a major impact on other areas of the client's life: relationships and job productivity. Depression often coincides with primary health problems. Clients diagnosed with one of the variations of bipolar disorder experience (in addition to periods of severe depression) periods of abnormally elevated mood, irritability, flight of ideas, pressured and rapid speech, distractibility, psychomotor agitation, and sometimes an increase in pleasurable activities that might put the client at risk for negative consequences (i.e., promiscuity, unrestrained shopping sprees). Practitioners who work with clients with major mood disorders should become familiar with differential diagnoses of these disorders as described in more detail in the DSM-5.

Suicide is always a cause for concern for mood disordered clients, and careful assessment of suicide risk should always be conducted (Bolton & Robinson, 2010). Key risk factors for suicide include serious mental disorders (e.g., schizophrenia, alcoholism, or depression); a history of suicide attempts; family history of serious depression, including suicide attempts, expressed suicidal intent, having a plan, and access to means of suicide (e.g., owning a gun, hoarding medications); communicating a sense of hopelessness; having experienced a traumatic or stressful event (e.g., a sudden loss of a loved one); and having recently been diagnosed with a serious physical illness. Practitioners should conduct thorough assessments of suicidal intent in an open, calm, and straightforward manner with clients, consult with supervisors and colleagues, clearly document the client's suicidal ideation, and make a plan to monitor and intervene if necessary. Psychiatric evaluations for medication are strongly recommended.

MFS assessment should go beyond signs and symptoms and examine how mood disorders are manifested across all relevant domains of well-being. In addition to key mental status and diagnostic signs and symptoms, a careful look at any history of impulsivity (e.g., previous suicide attempts) or risky behaviors (e.g., during manic episodes) is warranted along with a detailed history of substance abuse. Unresolved losses and traumatic events are common in clients with recurrent depression and should be carefully reviewed. The quality of relationships with family members, friends, and coworkers may also show indications of problems that are related to depression. Problems in occupational roles (e.g., recent layoff or having been fired) and overall health (e.g., poor prognosis for a serious illness) are often associated with depression as well.

In the functional and systems analysis, reconstructing a two-week diary with a depressed client can provide clues to situational factors that may be exacerbating the symptoms. Depressive symptoms can vary considerably over time. Clients might have good days and bad. Variations in depressive symptoms do not necessarily occur randomly but might occur as a result of work stress, periods of alcohol abuse (e.g., weekends), or as a function of recurrent relationship difficulties. How stressors from different situations are related to depression and suicidal thoughts should be examined carefully. Having clients self-monitor symptoms can help them become readily engaged in the treatment process and help reduce a general feeling of helplessness.

Intervention

Interventions for major mood disorders usually include psychotropic medication. Thus, practitioners should consult with attending physicians to coordinate interventions and keep apprised of the client's consistency in keeping to their prescribed dose. The interventions below were designed and tested primarily with clients diagnosed with depressive disorders, yet these are also applicable in some cases to clients who experience bipolar disorders but who are functioning better in the community.

Interpersonal psychotherapy and cognitive-behavioral interventions have been shown to be comparably effective for depressed clients (e.g., Butler, Chapman, Forman, & Beck, 2006; Hollon & Beck, 1994; Weissman, Markowitz, & Klerman, 2000; Young, Rygh, Weinberger, & Beck, 2008). However, regardless of the formal intervention chosen, effective use of supportive skills and a sound working alliance are essential for helping depressed clients. Depressed clients often present with low energy, and it might take considerable time and patience on the part of the practitioner to help the client begin to express their thoughts and feelings openly. The client's concentration may be impaired to the point where they have difficulty following the conversation. Guilt experienced by a depressed client may be severe, and some depressed clients feel that they are deserving of punishment. Suicide is often considered by the client to be a viable option to ending the emotional misery. A calm and empathic exploration of the client's negative thinking is critical for understanding the client's internal distress, but practitioners should keep an open mind regarding other contributing factors (e.g., depression may run in the family, a serious substance abuse problem, other medical conditions that may cause depression). There is a range of therapeutic coping skills that are helpful for depressed clients. Interpersonal psychotherapy (IPT) and cognitive-behavioral therapy (CBT) for depression share some common skills, but there are distinctions between these two approaches as well. Both are described below.

The practitioner who elects to use CBT for depression should explain the basic cognitive model to the client. The cognitive model of depression focuses on the impact of negative automatic thoughts on the mood of the client, dysfunctional thinking (e.g., "I am a really bad person," "I'll never accomplish much of anything in my life," etc.), and negative cognitive schema. The practitioner initially focuses on negative thought content and dysfunctional thought processes as the primary cause of the client's depression as discussed in Chapter 5 (e.g., dichotomous thinking, absolutistic thinking, hindsight-bias, catastrophic thinking, etc.). Next, the practitioner using CBT should help the client carefully examine the reasonableness of these thoughts, and then, most importantly, test these troubling beliefs out in their daily life. The steps can be summarized as follows:

- Identify negative automatic thoughts.
- Teach client to monitor and record automatic thoughts, associated moods, and situations.
- Actively engage the client in a rational exploration of the presenting problem by examining the client's negative "automatic thoughts" in the hopes of identifying the client's false assumptions and dysfunctional thought processes.
- Follow through in this collaborative exploration to determine whether there is evidence to support these negative and problematic thoughts.

- Encourage the client to consider alternative explanations for their belief.
- Challenge the client to identify the real implications of the belief if it were true.
- Collaboratively design "experiments" to test out whether the client's dysfunctional beliefs or expectations are true.
- Encourage the client to use a journal to document the experiences, and use the data to evaluate the outcome of these experiments. It is likely that the client's dysfunctional beliefs will be disconfirmed.

The client's act of disconfirming his dysfunctional beliefs is, presumably, at the heart of the change process in CBT. Increased self-efficacy is best advanced through behavior change, not interpretation or explanation. As the client improves, the practitioner helps him to solidify what he has learned through self-monitoring and repeated behavioral testing of his dysfunctional beliefs. Since depression can recur, a plan is developed to help the client anticipate relapse of depression and initiate a plan of action.

Consider the example of a late-middle-aged man who retires and becomes depressed. After a thorough examination of his negative automatic thoughts, the practitioner and he conclude that he places an extraordinary value on occupational achievement and being admired by others. He now thinks that "I am worthless . . . I have nothing to do . . . people no longer admire me . . . and there is no hope for me in the future. I am useless. I might as well give up and end it all." After examining these beliefs, the social worker and client agree that they seem a bit extreme, but the social worker empathizes with the client's current feelings and state of mind. After a rational examination of his claims that he is worthless to everyone and has nothing else to offer, the client agrees to test out his beliefs regarding his "worthlessness" within his community, a place to which he recently moved after retirement.

The practitioner then poses the question in contrast to the "I am worthless" belief: "Given your high level of expertise in business, do you really believe there is really nothing for you to do that would help you reclaim your sense of self-worth?" After some discussion, the client agrees to investigate a range of ideas: volunteer work, becoming involved in local politics, doing some limited consulting work with local businesses, and so on. With careful "testing out" of his beliefs over time, the client quickly finds that he is overwhelmed with requests for help from others in the community and that his sense of self-worth gradually returns. It also appears that making new friends and becoming socially more involved has some positive effects on his mood as well.

CBT FOR BIPOLAR DISORDER

The few studies conducted on cognitive-behavioral treatments for bipolar disorder suggest that CBT reduces relapse (Nusslock, Abramson, Harmon-Jones, Alloy, & Coan, 2009). For example, Miklowitz et al. (2000) found that a family psycho-educational program for those with a bipolar member was significantly more effective at reducing relapse and reducing symptoms than standard clinical management. A recent randomized trial of a group-based psychosocial intervention with people diagnosed with bipolar disorder (all taking medication) focused on self-monitoring and coping strategies and showed considerably fewer relapses for the treatment group ($n = 32$) compared with the control group ($n = 40$) over the course of a twelve-week program with nine-month follow up (Castle et al., 2010).

IPT FOR DEPRESSION

Interpersonal psychotherapy (IPT) shares some similarities with CBT. This well-researched approach is also somewhat pragmatic, oriented to the "here and now," goal-focused, and generally short-term in duration. IPT is based on a somewhat different premise than CBT. The main assumption in IPT is that depression has its roots in dysfunctional relationships in the present. Although past relationship problems may have contributed to the client's depression, examination and interpretation of the past is not emphasized in IPT. The essential skills of IPT emphasize that the practitioner do the following:

- Develop a sound working relationship with the client.
- Explore the client's thoughts and feelings relative to depression.
- Encourage expression of feelings.
- Conduct a thorough review of depressive symptoms.
- Refer client for a psychiatric evaluation.
- Conduct a careful analysis of the client's communication patterns and interpersonal behaviors within their relationships and identify significant problems.
- Identify changes the client would like to see in his relationships.
- Use the therapeutic relationship as a laboratory to assess interpersonal behaviors, provide constructive feedback, and suggest changes.
- Encourage the client to experiment with different approaches to relating to others, depending on the problem.
- Monitor and evaluate client efforts to improve his relationships.

IPT is generally used to address three types of interpersonal problems related to depression: unresolved grief, interpersonal role disputes, or role transitions. If the problem is grief, the practitioner facilitates the mourning process, examines the loss and attending symptoms, and helps the client to reconnect with other social supports to help alleviate the depressive symptoms associated with loss. If the focus is an interpersonal role dispute, the conflict should be identified, and problem-solving strategies are reviewed to help ameliorate the conflict. For problems related to role transitions, the practitioner might assist the client in mourning the old role by examining thoughts and facilitating the expression of feelings about the loss. The social worker can then help the client address the new role in a more positive light with an emphasis on attaining mastery and accessing relevant support systems. If the client has interpersonal deficits that impede relationship satisfaction, the practitioner should help the client reduce their isolation, improve social skills, and encourage the formation of new relationships. Termination focuses on helping the client develop a plan to maintain their improvements over time.

How would IPT differ in treatment of the depressed retiree discussed earlier? An IPT practitioner would not focus on examining whether the client's beliefs were dysfunctional or not but focus on helping the client engage other people in his community given that his retirement has left him without his usual social supports. He might also spend some time "mourning" his lost role as an important leader but would be encouraged to rediscover and renew that role by gradually becoming more engaged in the new community. Based on reviews of controlled research, it is likely that either IPT or CBT would be effective interventions in this case. Both approaches emphasize the importance of a strong working alliance and improvement of interpersonal relationships. Perhaps they are two somewhat different roads that end at the same destination.

EFT FOR DEPRESSION

Emotion-focused therapy (EFT) (Greenberg & Watson, 2006) should also be noted here as a very promising approach to depression. Three controlled studies have shown it to be comparable to other evidence-based practices. EFT focuses on enhancing emotional processing and accepting and making sense of distressing emotions. EFT will be discussed in more detail in Chapter 10 as it is applied to addressing couples conflict.

EMERGING RESEARCH ON UNDER-RESEARCHED POPULATIONS

Practice research with underserved populations has increased in recent years. For example, Levy and O'Hara (2010) found that evidence-based practices such as cognitive-behavioral therapy appear to be effective with low-income women struggling with a range of problems associated with poverty including unemployment and other associated stressors. However, these approaches require some modifications to increase engagement in treatment. These methods include the use of psycho-education regarding the nature of depression and its treatment, addressing practical barriers (e.g., transportation problems), and attempting to make treatment more culturally relevant. CBT has also been shown to be efficacious for individuals infected with HIV. One randomized controlled trial (Safren et al., 2009) compared a version of CBT focused on retroviral medication adherence (psycho-education and dealing with barriers to adherence) in a sample of men and women with either major depression or bipolar disorder. Results showed that, over the course of the twelve-month trial, CBT led to superior outcomes in both depressive symptoms and adherence level. When compared with usual care, interpersonal psychotherapy (IPT) also showed a high rate of participation and good response to treatment in a mixed sample of African-Americans and whites both during and after pregnancy for up to six months after (Grote et al., 2009).

Regardless of the method utilized, case management is often an essential part of interventions for depression. Coordinating psychiatric evaluation and medication adherence, bolstering social supports, and encouraging new occupational roles can be essential to achieving successful outcomes for depressed clients.

Anxiety Disorders

Assessment

Anxiety disorders include panic disorder (usually accompanied by agoraphobia), obsessive-compulsive disorder, posttraumatic stress disorder (PTSD), social anxiety, generalized anxiety, and specific phobias. Overall, twelve-month prevalence data for anxiety disorders in adults run in the single-digit percentages but range somewhat depending on the specific disorder: specific phobias (7 to 9%), social anxiety (7%), panic disorder (2 to 3%), agoraphobia (about 2%), generalized anxiety disorders (3%), obsessive-compulsive disorder (1%), and PTSD (3.5%) (APA, 2013). Although there are important differences between these disorders, there is an array of overlapping symptoms and some similarities in the skills that comprise evidence-based practices. In addition, many other conditions co-occur with anxiety disorders (e.g., depression, substance abuse), and clinically significant anxiety can correlate with many of life's challenges: interpersonal problems, occupational stress, financial difficulties, and other problems in living (APA, 2013; Bellack & Hersen, 1998; O'Hare, 2015).

People predisposed to one type of anxiety disorder are at risk of developing others at some time during their lives. Evidence suggests that some people are genetically at-risk to being "nervous," and this increased anxiety sensitivity is likely to manifest itself as one type of disorder or another. For example, a person who is very shy, has night terrors, and is terrified of small animals as a child is at greater risk for agoraphobia or OCD as an adolescent and, later, as an adult. The essential skills needed for treating anxiety disorders will be presented here with the understanding that practitioners need to pursue additional instruction and supervision in the use of evidence-based approaches specifically designed for each disorder.

Panic attacks are accompanied by some combination of accelerated heart rate, sweating, trembling, shortness of breath, feelings of smothering or choking, sometimes chest pain, nausea, feeling faint, or experiencing derealization (feelings of unreality) or depersonalization (being detached from oneself). A client experiencing a panic attack may report that they feel like they are "losing control," "losing my mind," "going crazy," or are afraid that they are dying. Some clients report paresthesias (numbness or tingling sensations) and either chills or hot flushes. *Panic disorder* involves a persistent dread that another attack will occur. If the client begins to consciously avoid being in places or situations where they feel they will experience another panic attack, they may meet the criteria for agoraphobia as well. In severe cases, panic disorder accompanied by agoraphobia can leave a person quite incapacitated, housebound, often depressed, and unable to perform their usual occupational and social functions.

Persons suffering from *obsessive-compulsive disorder* experience recurrent and persistent thoughts, impulses or images that they find distressing, and then engage in a compulsive behavior or mental ritual intended to neutralize the obsession. For example, if a client experiences repeated and intrusive obsessions that they contracted a deadly parasitic disease because they touched another person, then they might engage in a repeated ritualized hand washing to neutralize that thought and the possibility of contagion. For another client, an obsessional thought (e.g., anger at another person) may compel them to engage in compulsive praying to neutralize the thought so that no harm befalls the other person as a result of the obsession. Many people suffering from OCD firmly believe that their thoughts alone can have an actual impact on external events (e.g., "If I think the plane might crash, it will!"). Although most adults realize that their thoughts do not have direct influence on external realities, they still struggle with the obsession. As with panic disorder, OCD can become so debilitating a person cannot function in their normal social or occupational roles because so much mental energy and time is engaged in conducting compulsive rituals. However, the more the client engages in the compulsive rituals to obtain temporary relief, the more they inadvertently reinforce the obsession. A person with a serious "germ phobia," for example, may spend hours each day washing their hands and disinfecting their home to the point of exhaustion.

Most people who experience traumatic events during their lifetime tend to recovery from the incident and go on with their lives. Although they might always recall the trauma with some accompanying anxiety, anger, or sadness, most people who have experienced extreme stressors do not continue to suffer from acute and chronic symptoms of anxiety and depression as a result. *Posttraumatic stress disorder* afflicts people who have experienced extreme stressors or trauma in their lives but do not recover from the impact of these events, even after a few months have passed. PTSD is associated with a range of traumatic events, including near-death experiences such as a severe car accident, witnessing killings in combat or criminal acts, or having been sexually assaulted or otherwise physically abused. The person who develops PTSD in response to these traumas generally develops four categories of symptoms: physiological hyperarousal (e.g., startle, hypervigilance), avoidance (e.g., not thinking about things that remind the person of the experience, avoiding places or doing things that invoke images of the events), numbing (e.g., negative emotional states, selective amnesia about the event, detachment or estrangement), and re-experiencing symptoms (e.g., flashbacks, nightmares, intrusive memories). Depression and substance abuse often co-occur with PTSD, and PTSD symptoms are often seen in people with borderline personality disorder.

Persons suffering from *generalized anxiety disorder* engage in excessive worry for extended periods of time and often feel restless, have difficulty concentrating, are fatigued and irritable, and have trouble sleeping. Persons with *social phobia* experience intense worry and anxiety symptoms when in social situations to the extent that it interferes significantly with their social and occupational functioning. *Specific phobias* are fears of certain objects, animals, or certain situations. When confronted by them, a person with a phobia will experience extreme distress and make every effort to get away from that situation and avoid it in the future. Some might tolerate it only with great discomfort. Common phobias include insects, dogs, and other small animals, flying in commercial airliners, closed spaces, bodies of water, and heights (when one is otherwise safe).

In addition to recognizing key signs and symptoms of anxiety disorder, an MFS assessment requires that the effects of these disorders be gauged across all key domains: overall mental status; emotional well-being, including other forms of emotional distress (e.g., depression); how the disorder is affecting close relationships with family members; and how the anxiety is interfering with social and occupational functioning. Key points in a functional analysis should include identifying antecedents (e.g., situations, thoughts, specific people, use of alcohol or other drugs) that appear to coincide with a worsening of anxiety symptoms. Assessment of anxiety disorder will require the establishment of a hierarchy of fears so the intervention can proceed from a moderately fearful situation to the most fearful. Each target fear will also require a hierarchical breakdown of objectives so that clients can approach the anxiety-inducing situation in manageable incremental steps. This gradual approach helps the client experience anxiety reduction at each successive level and, as a result, reinforces their conviction they can successfully proceed to the next level (i.e., a situation that provokes greater anxiety). This focused functional assessment is a routine prelude to the exposure therapies explained below.

Intervention

Interventions with anxiety disorders require a common set of skills that should be tailored to each client's unique needs and preferences. These skills include psycho-education, cognitive restructuring, self-regulation of physiological anxiety symptoms, imaginal (covert) exposure, and, most importantly, prolonged in vivo exposure to the feared situation whenever feasible. Cognitive-behavioral interventions are well-established evidence-based practices for serious anxiety disorders including obsessive-compulsive disorders (e.g., Abramowitz, Brigidi, & Roche, 2001; Franklin & Foa, 2011; Steketee, 1993), agoraphobia and panic attacks (e.g., Antony & Swinson, 2000; Butler, Chapman, Forman, & Beck, 2006; Sanchez-Meca, Rosa-Alcazar, Marin-Martinez, & Gomez-Conesa, 2010), and posttraumatic stress disorder (e.g., Butler, Chapman, Forman, & Beck, 2006; Resick, Monson, & Rizvi, 2008; Rothbaum, Meadows, Resick, & Foy, 2000) as well as other anxiety disorders described above.

Clients with anxiety disorders can benefit considerably from empathic understanding and the practitioner's motivational support. Most people can relate to the experience of anxiety and fear on some level and have probably experienced intense fear or chronic worry at least one time in their life. Clients may also be embarrassed or ashamed of their fear, despite their common prevalence. By way of support and enhancing motivation, social workers can confidently reassure most clients that, if they commit to an evidence-based approach, conquering their anxiety problems will be well within their grasp.

Practitioners must first become knowledgeable about anxiety disorders, carefully conduct a full MFS assessment to determine whether there are other co-occurring problems that may be causing or worsening the anxiety, and examine the effects of the anxiety disorder on other areas of the client's life. Psycho-education regarding the nature of the disorder is essential and may provide considerable relief to the client.

As part of an extended functional assessment, the practitioner should engage the client in a collaborative effort to monitor anxiety symptoms and use a log, chart, or diary to keep track of the specific patterning of thoughts, anxiety symptoms, behaviors, and specific situational factors associated with the anxiety. Typical questions, depending on the specific disorder, might include "How often do these panic attacks occur?" "Do they occur at some times or in some situations more than others?" "Are your obsessions worse at specific times of the day or certain days of the week more than others?" and "How much time do you spend engaged in rituals to counter the obsession?" Self-monitoring for a couple of weeks can be therapeutic in itself for many clients by helping them feel that they are taking action, collaborating in treatment, gaining some objective understanding of the problem, and feel some beginning sense of mastery and control over their distress.

Dysfunctional thinking associated with anxiety disorders is not necessarily distorted or irrational. Although most adult clients are well aware that their anxiety may be a somewhat exaggerated or an even irrational response to the feared situation (e.g., germs, going into a grocery store), this is not always the case. With PTSD, for example, the client's response to memories of war or having been raped are based on very real and frightening events, and these recollections might continue to evoke acute emotional distress. However, the client knows that the feelings and fears have endured well beyond the situation (i.e., the threat) and are now negatively affecting their life and the well-being of those around them. For persons suffering from severe anxiety, the challenge is not to dispel the reasons for anxiety as "unrealistic," but to accept what has occurred in the past, manage anxiety and associated symptoms successfully, and emphasize coping with life in the present. Cognitive restructuring involves four main steps: (1) teach the client to identify the anxiety-producing belief; (2) generate alternative explanations, predictions, or beliefs; (3) challenge the logic of the original belief and examine the respective evidence for it; and (4) consider a more realistic alternative belief and commit to a more realistic interpretation or prediction.

Before covert or in vivo exposure can begin, however, clients need to learn a critical skill: managing their physiological symptoms of anxiety by learning breath control, progressive muscle relaxation, and meditation.

Anxiety symptoms are self-perpetuating in the sense that physical symptoms of anxiety (e.g., nervousness, quickening heart rate, "butterflies" in the stomach) provoke frightening images in the mind and increase avoidance behavior (which alleviates anxiety only in the short run but further reinforces avoidance behaviors). Taking several deep breaths (slowly exhaling) is an easy and relatively quick way to quell the intensity of some anxiety symptoms. Progressive muscle relaxation involves gradually tensing each muscle group, holding the tension for ten seconds, then releasing the tension and feeling the subsequent relaxation. Practitioners typically guide the client by having them begin with tensioning their toes and working their way up each muscle group to their forehead. Meditation is a practiced discipline of clearing the mind, focusing on something neutral, and relaxing the body. Deep breathing may initially accompany meditation as well. There are many variations on these helpful and well-established methods. Many excellent books and instructional videos are readily available to help practitioners learn these various techniques for their own health and well-being as well as for teaching clients these valuable skills. The approach selected should be the one that the client feels most comfortable with. If nothing else, the anxious client should learn to "think calming thoughts and take long, slow, deep breaths" to reduce anxious feelings. Learning how to reduce physical symptoms of anxiety will also prepare the client to learn and benefit from graduated exposure methods.

Covert or imaginal exposure can be then be used to reduce anxiety related to the object of the client's fears. As with most effective exposure interventions, the practitioner and the client must first build a hierarchy of fears (i.e., make a list of those thoughts or situations from the least to the most frightening). Second, depending on the specific nature of any one of those fears, the practitioner and client may list a step-by-step approach to gradually confronting each fear in turn. Third, the practitioner teaches the client how to use the subjective units of distress scale (SUDS) to indicate to the practitioner how much anxiety they are experiencing at various points during the procedure (0–100 scale, from "no anxiety" to "unbearable anxiety"). As described in Chapter 6, this procedure, which combines relaxation and imaginal exposure, is also known as systematic desensitization.

Let's consider two case illustrations. In the first, a socially phobic woman needs to become a more "public" person in order to advance her career. After a detailed assessment, she may list the following social situations from least anxiety provoking to most anxiety provoking: making a presentation to a small group of familiar colleagues, presenting to a small group of unfamiliar people, having to host an informal business cocktail party for mixed familiar and unfamiliar people, presenting to a large group of familiar colleagues, presenting to a large group of unfamiliar people in a conference hall. In the second case, for a man diagnosed with OCD who obsesses about germs and needs to compulsively wash dozens of times per day, the hierarchy of fears (again, from least fear producing to most) might be as follows: inadvertently touching another person's clothes, touching an exterior door knob or handrail on stairs in their place of business, touching the door knob in a public bathroom, touching the sink, touching the waste basket, touching the toilet. In both cases, the client would be taught to use breath control and muscle relaxation, and then the practitioner would introduce these images into the client's mind beginning with the least fearful (i.e., small group presentation or touching another person's clothes, respectively). As the client considers each step, they are asked to hold the particular image in their imagination for a while and maintain breath control until they feel that their anxiety has been reduced to a minimum. On occasion, the practitioner will query the client to find out how much anxiety they are experiencing. The client can be initially instructed to raise a finger if they are too anxious or simply report their level of anxiety when prompted by the practitioner. An agreed-upon level of, say, "30" on the SUDS can be used for this purpose. At that point, the client and practitioner may either increase the intensity of that particular image (e.g., "You are touching the doorknob now" for 10, 20, 30 seconds, etc.) or, if the client feels that their anxiety about this situation is under better control, they might move onto the next step in the hierarchy (i.e., touching the handrail).

Although covert exposure can be helpful for many clients, there is little substitute in the long run for approaching the feared situation in vivo. Eventually, clients will have to do this if they want to conquer their fear. For some anxiety disorders, covert desensitization is simply not robust enough to resolve the problem, although it may provide an excellent "warm-up" exercise to prepare the client for in vivo exposure. For the socially phobic woman, she will have to prepare presentations for small groups and do this repeatedly until she feels she can take on a larger group, and so forth. For the man with OCD, the exposure intervention will take on a slightly different form. He will not only have to touch "germ-ridden" surfaces (i.e., the exposure), but will also have to refrain from washing his hands right away (i.e., response prevention), and when he does, learn to wash them only once for a minute or so. The approach is called exposure with response prevention (EXRP) and is by far the most successful psychosocial intervention for dealing with this often disabling condition.

Other anxiety disorders such as generalized anxiety or specific phobias can be addressed by utilizing all or some of these cognitive-behavioral skills. For generalized anxiety, just learning and practicing relaxation skills such as meditation and breath control, taking time out three times per week to exercise, and having someone to talk to about one's worries may be sufficient. For specific phobias, graduated exposure is often sufficient. However, anxiety can be a tenacious problem and has a way of insinuating itself into other areas of one's life. It can cause irritability and sleep problems, somatic difficulties (e.g., headaches, nausea), and interpersonal and family problems. Anxiety problems often co-occur with depression and substance use disorders. Many people use alcohol, marijuana, or become dependent on antianxiety and sleep medications rather than learn behavioral methods to cope with anxiety. Lifestyle changes can greatly reduce anxiety and prevent its recurrence. These changes may include vigorous regular exercise (with physician's approval), reduction in the use of alcohol or other drugs, and reducing overall stress (e.g., changing jobs, resolving financial difficulties and relationship conflict). For persons with seriously debilitating anxiety disorders, case management may also be necessary to coordinate multiple services (e.g., psychiatry for medication, primary medicine for a physical examination, treatment for a co-occurring substance abuse problem, and referral to a mutual help group for persons with anxiety disorders).

Summary

Major mental illnesses, mood disorders, and anxiety disorders, collectively, account for a large proportion of clients who receive mental health services. Social workers need to be knowledgeable about these conditions in order to conduct thorough and accurate MFS assessments. In addition, manualized interventions are now readily available for all these conditions to help practitioners learn EBPs and plan effective interventions.

Case Study: José

José Garcia is a seventy-one-year-old man who recently lost his wife to a battle with cancer. He has lived with his son, Hector, and his son's wife, Juanita, for about two years. José and his former wife, Esmeralda, had moved in after it was discovered that she had cancer. The younger couple has two children, Javier and Jesus. Javier is usually away at college, Jesus is in high school and lives at home. After his wife passed away, José became profoundly depressed. Although it appeared to be a severe grief reaction, understandable after fifty-one years of marriage, his depression showed few signs of abating, even one year after her death. Hector and his wife became increasingly concerned and began to inquire about help for José, first from the parish priest, then from a physician who referred José and his family to a social worker at the local community health center.

The Comprehensive Service Plan (Assessment, Intervention, Evaluation)

Use all available information from the client and significant others, your observations, and input from other professionals to conduct both quantitative and qualitative aspects of this multidimensional-functional assessment.

Client identification data: (gender; age; marital status; sexual orientation; family composition; employment; racial, ethnic, cultural, religious/spiritual affiliation and identity; etc.)

José Garcia is a seventy-one-year-old male, recently widowed. He lives with his son and daughter-in-law (Hector and Juanita), has been retired for several years from his job of ten years as an apartment building supervisor and maintenance person. Prior to that job, he had worked for the city supervising building maintenance and engaged in similar work for about thirty years. He remains a devout Roman Catholic, attends church regularly, and defines his cultural background as such: "I came here from Puerto Rico when I was a boy, and I'm proud of being Puerto Rican, but I am, first and foremost, an American. I served my country in the US Army." Mr. G. speaks Spanish fluently, reads a popular local Hispanic newspaper, and enjoys participating in the local Hispanic festivities during holidays.

The presenting problem
Description of problem (client's view)

Mr. G., when asked why he believes he has been referred to this clinic, said the following: "I lost my wife. I don't care whether I live or die. Sometimes I see her. I talk with her. I think she is suffering without me. I want to die so I can be with her and comfort her."

Description of problem (practitioner's view)

Mr. G. is apparently suffering from a profound grief reaction. However, his depressive symptoms have not abated for almost a year since his wife died. It appears that he has reported other signs and symptoms of severe depression. He also appears to be very anxious, wrings his hands constantly, and has a hard time sitting still. He appears to be quite agitated at times, especially when he reported that he "talks with his wife and feels that she is suffering" in the afterlife.

Psychosocial history with an emphasis on problem trajectory

Mr. G. was born and raised in Puerto Rico. He came to this country with his parents when he was six years old. He grew up in New York City, joined the army after high school, and moved to this area after he was honorably discharged. As the United States was not at war at that time, he did not engage in combat. He grew up locally, worked for the parks department and other city maintenance jobs, and worked his way up to become a supervisor. He and his wife, Esmeralda, were married in their early twenties (after Mr. G. was discharged from the army), and they had two children, Hector and his sister Margarita, who is married and moved to the Midwest a few years ago. He reports having always been on good terms with both his children.

Mr. G. recalls drinking alcohol heavily in his youth, and although he drank during his years in the service, he reports that he moderated his alcohol use after he married. He says he stopped drinking for a while because he had recalled his father's heavy drinking when growing up and remembers some physical fighting between his parents. When his wife became pregnant with Hector, he resolved not to let the same thing happen. He recalls his father often being absent and wonders aloud if his dad was depressed. He also recalls himself becoming depressed off and on over the years and once spent three weeks in a psychiatric facility after having tried to hang himself. He reports now that he felt discouraged in the early days about not being able to make a living and support his wife and children adequately. At that time, Mr. G.'s father was still alive and would often criticize his son's willingness to "be a man and make something of himself." Mr. G. reported that, after his suicide attempt, his wife took him to see the local priest and made him promise that, if he ever became depressed again, he would not try to hurt himself. The priest impressed upon Mr. G. that he would not be admitted into heaven if he died by suicide and could not be buried in a Catholic service. Since then, Mr. G. recalled that he had fewer problems with depression, especially as his children got older and his life became more financially stable, but always suffered from chronic worries. His wife was able to take in sewing work in addition to outside jobs to help with the bills, and he reported he and his wife felt a great sense of pride as they gradually became better able to maintain good standing in their neighborhood.

However, about ten years ago, Mr. G. had another episode of serious depression after he retired from working for the city. He reports that he did see a mental health counselor at that time with his wife and began to feel better after he took on a part-time job as an apartment building maintenance man, a job that later became a full-time job. Since then, Mr. G. reports that he has felt fine. And although he was concerned during his wife's illness, he did not experience a return of serious depressive symptoms until she became seriously ill and, even more so, after she passed away.

Attempts to resolve the problems, previous treatment, and relevant outcomes

Over the past year, Mr. G. has become almost incapacited by his depression. His son and daughter-in-law have been very supportive, but Mr. G. has shown little sign of rebounding. Although previous interventions for depression were noted earlier, no efforts to provide treatment for this latest recurrence have been attempted. The family has assumed that this response was a normal grief reaction and has hoped that he would come around on his own. The couple became particularly alarmed when he said he no longer wanted to attend mass and that he no longer had faith in God. They felt that he was feeling hopeless. They are also concerned because he has been talking to himself loudly at night and recently has seemed very forgetful. They became nervous as, more than once, he forgot to turn off the stove and, one cold night, wandered outside on his own. When they found him sitting under a tree in the nearby park in only his shirt and pants, he was talking aloud and did not seem to know where he was.

The individual assessment

Mental status—cognitive disturbances: Describe the client's level of hallucinations, delusions, disorientation, bizarre behavior or speech, memory problems, serious confusion, or other symptoms of serious cognitive impairment. Include other troubling or dysfunctional beliefs or convictions.

Beyond the normative indicators of a grief reaction, Mr. G. appears to be severely depressed, a problem he has had off and on during his adult life. He also expresses clear suicidal ideation. In addition, although details are limited at this time, he appears to be showing signs of memory problems. He also speaks with conviction about seeing his deceased wife and talking with her (she, apparently, converses with him). Whether these experiences are the result of extreme grief reactions or are indications of delusions associated with severe depression or are related to some other cognitive disturbance that might be influenced by cultural/religious beliefs is not determined at this time. Mr. G. also seems to be very restless, often agitated, and his son and daughter-in-law seem concerned about his excessive worry, wringing of his hands, talking to himself at night, and wandering the house at all hours. They are worried about his leaving the house unannounced again and are concerned for his safety. The existence of an anxiety disorder should be examined further.

How would you rate the client's overall mental status during the past month?

POOR [0]   IMPAIRED [1]   MARGINAL [2]   GOOD [3]   EXCELLENT [4]

Mental status—emotional distress: Describe the client's level of depression, anxiety, and overall ability to regulate her/his emotions.

Mr. G.'s depression appears profound; he suffers from feelings of hopelessness, helplessness, despair; he reports somatic distress, trouble sleeping, and loss of appetite. There have never been signs of mania or hypomania. His anxiety may also account for some appetite and sleep problems, and his constant hand wringing is accompanied by an acute worry that his wife continues to suffer in the afterlife. He seems inconsolable that he can't be with her to comfort her.

How would you rate your client's emotional well-being over the past thirty days?

POOR [0]   IMPAIRED [1]   MARGINAL [2]   GOOD [3]   EXCELLENT [4]

Behavioral problems: Describe your client's overall ability to regulate her/his behavior. Consider things such as their ability to express her/himself effectively, ability to work at things patiently, tendencies to verbally or physically lash out at others, run away, harm her/himself, or proneness to impulsive, criminal, or substance-abusing behavior. How would you describe the client's overall impulse control?

Mr. G. has demonstrated some troublesome and unpredictable behaviors. He has walked out of the house, unannounced; otherwise, he is generally inactive, and he has shown little interest in his usual sources of pleasure—working around the house or in the yard, doing minor repairs, seeing some of his acquaintances in the local park. He has attempted to kill himself in the past, although he has made no suicide gestures in recent years despite his expressed desire to die. His risk of suicide should be considered moderate at this time.

> How would you rate your client's behavioral control generally over the past thirty days?
>
> POOR [0]   IMPAIRED [1]   MARGINAL [2]   GOOD [3]   EXCELLENT [4]

Adaptive strengths and coping abilities: Describe your client's ability to cope with problems and everyday stressors. How would you describe the client's ability to assess problem situations, deal with "triggers," cope with stress, solve problems, and perhaps reach out to others for help in order to deal effectively with her/his difficulties?

Until this past year, Mr. G. was very active, outgoing in a number of ways. As noted above, he was active around the home. He has friends in town, mostly retired men his age, and he would spend time with them playing cards or just visiting. He took an active interest in his grandchildren and seemed to be on good relations with them. His coping abilities and usual adaptive strengths are quite impaired at this time.

> How would you rate your client's overall adaptive strengths and coping abilities over the past thirty days?
>
> POOR [0]   IMPAIRED [1]   MARGINAL [2]   GOOD [3]   EXCELLENT [4]

Health problems: Describe the client's overall health. Aside from normal, transient illnesses, think about the client's general health habits (e.g., smoking, heavy drinking, exercise, weight), chronic primary health disorders, the client's opinion of her/his own health, ability to engage in her/his usual activities relatively free from discomfort, overall energy level, hospitalizations and treatments for illness other than psychiatric ones. Consider her/his documented medical history and any ongoing treatments.

Mr. G. is in very good physical health, has not been taking medication in recent months, although he does suffer from arthritis in his knees. Occasionally, he has been known to take some analgesics for the pain.

How would you rate your client's health over the past thirty days?

POOR [0]   IMPAIRED [1]   MARGINAL [2]   GOOD [3]   EXCELLENT [4]

Use of alcohol and other drugs: Describe the client's use of alcohol, illicit substances (cocaine, heroin, marijuana, hallucinogens, etc.), and abuse of prescription medication. How often does the client use them, in what quantity, and how serious are the psychological, physical, or social consequences associated with their use?

Although he reported a history of alcohol abuse when he was young, Mr. G. reports no problems with alcohol and has never used illicit substances or abused prescription medication. He drinks sherry now and then but usually confines his consumption to a glass or two according to his son's report.

How would you rate the client's functioning in the past month with regard to substance use?

POOR [0]   IMPAIRED [1]   MARGINAL [2]   GOOD [3]   EXCELLENT [4]

Recreational activities: Consider what the client does for fun (alone or with others), hobbies, relaxation (reading, TV, video games, playing cards, etc.), and physical exercise (walking, jogging, biking, etc.). How would you describe the client's overall involvement in positive recreational activities?

Although active physically and socially in recent years, Mr. G.'s recreational outlets have been seriously limited over the past year (noted above).

How would you rate the adequacy of the client's participation in healthy recreational activities over the past thirty days?

POOR [0]   IMPAIRED [1]   MARGINAL [2]   GOOD [3]   EXCELLENT [4]

Material resources: Describe your client's current or (if client is institutionalized) most recent living situation overall. Consider such things as adequacy of food, clothing, shelter, and safety.

Mr. G. is well cared for. He contributes to his son and daughter's household with his retirement income and all his physical needs are adequately met.

How would you rate the overall adequacy of the client's material resources over the past month?

POOR [0]   IMPAIRED [1]   MARGINAL [2]   GOOD [3]   EXCELLENT [4]

Independent living/self-care: Describe how well your client manages her/his household, takes care of personal hygiene, eats, sleeps, and otherwise cares for her/his own basic needs.

Although his physical needs are met, Mr. G. would not currently be able to care for himself since he has been suffering from this acute grief reaction/recurrent depression. Sometimes he needs encouragement to take care of daily hygienic needs, and his son and grandson have assisted him in this manner. He would also go without eating on occasion without some coaxing.

How would you rate the client's ability to live independently and take care of her/his basic needs over the past thirty days?

POOR [0]   IMPAIRED [1]   MARGINAL [2]   GOOD [3]   EXCELLENT [4]

Work (role) satisfaction: Describe the client's current work-related or other important role-related activities (e.g., employed, student, homemaker, volunteer, retired person, disabled, etc.). Describe those activities and responsibilities that occupy the client in a productive manner.

Although retired, Mr. G. remained active before his wife became seriously ill, helping neighbors, keeping up maintenance on his son's house, and visiting friends and neighbors whom he thought needed company. Generally, those activities have fallen by the wayside.

> How would you rate the client's work or role satisfaction over the past thirty days?
>
> POOR [0]   <u>IMPAIRED [1]</u>   MARGINAL [2]   GOOD [3]   EXCELLENT [4]

Legal problems: Describe any legal problems the client has had or continues to have. These include minor infractions (e.g., public drunkenness, shoplifting inexpensive items, minor traffic violations, public disturbances) and more serious crimes (e.g., assault and battery, rape, burglary, driving under the influence, etc.). Consider the client's status (probation, awaiting imprisonment, parole). Also, consider any civil suits leveled at the client, pending financial judgments against her/him, and so on. Overall, how would you describe the client's current legal situation?

Mr. G. has never had any legal difficulties of note.

> How would you rate the client's legal situation over the past thirty days?
>
> POOR [0]   IMPAIRED [1]   MARGINAL [2]   GOOD [3]   <u>EXCELLENT [4]</u>

DSM-5 Diagnosis

Major depressive disorder, recurrent severe, 296.33
Generalized anxiety disorder, 300.02

Family relations: Describe the client's current family structure, including authority, hierarchy, alliances, roles, rules, boundaries, subsystems (e.g., couple, siblings, parent-child alliances); patterns of interactions and quality of communications; specific problems within the family; specific adaptive strengths within the family; and how the family members describe their own racial, ethnic, cultural, and religious identities.

Mr. G., based on his report and that of his son and daughter-in-law, has always been close to them, and they have consistently provided support to him and their mother over the years. After moving into Hector and Juanita's home, there was a period during the first year or so of tension and some verbal conflict. Mr. G., as reported by Hector and Juanita, often "intruded" on the parents' efforts to counsel and, occasionally, discipline their son Javier, who was sometimes in trouble during his high school years. The couple was making efforts to resolve this dispute with Mr. G. when Hector's mother took a turn for the worse and Mr. G. became more preoccupied with his wife's difficulties. In addition, with Javier out of the home much of the time, there is no occasion to provoke these disputes. The couple reports no problems with Jesus, who appears to be doing well in school and reports a good network of friends. The parents report no problems with him at home. Overall, this appears to be a supportive household of three generations.

How would you rate the quality of the client's immediate family relationships over the past thirty days?

POOR [0]   IMPAIRED [1]   MARGINAL [2]   GOOD [3]   EXCELLENT [4]

Immediate social relationships (close friends and acquaintances): Describe the quality of your client's relationships with those available friends and acquaintances, as applicable. Over the past month, how would you describe the quality of the interaction overall between your client and them with respect to closeness, intimacy, general interpersonal satisfaction, effective communications, degree of conflict, level of hostility, aggression, and evidence of any emotional or physical abuse?

As for Mr. G., his relationships with friends and acquaintances have suffered a lot since his wife died and his depression set in. Although some of his friends have called or stopped by to see him, he has told Hector and Juanita that he does not want to see anyone or have any company. He continues to isolate himself from those who seem to care about him.

How would you rate the quality of the client's immediate social relationships over the past thirty days?

POOR [0]   IMPAIRED [1]   MARGINAL [2]   GOOD [3]   EXCELLENT [4]

Extended social relationships: Describe the type and quality of relationships between your client and others in the client's community (other than close friends and family). These people might include other families, law enforcement, human service agencies, school personnel, coworkers, and others from whom the client receives support or with whom the client is having serious conflict.

According to Hector, Mr. G. is well respected and liked in his community. As noted earlier, he is on good relations with his neighbors, is known by local law enforcement for his work on the community watch committee, and has been active for years on committees that organize local Puerto Rican Day festivities. Even local school personnel are acquainted with him through these efforts. Since his wife's illness and death, however, he has been noticeably absent from these activities.

> How would you rate the quality of the client's social relationships over the past thirty days?
>
> **POOR** [0]   **IMPAIRED** [1]   **MARGINAL** [2]   **GOOD** [3]   **EXCELLENT** [4]

A concise summary of the MFS assessment: Highlight the client's areas of distress and adaptive strengths. Emphasize those areas that are most likely to be emphasized in the intervention plan.

Mr. G. appears to be suffering from an acute grief reaction and a concurrent major depressive episode. In addition, he may be experiencing an exacerbation of a preexisting anxiety disorder. Mr. G. should be considered a suicide risk as well. His depressive symptoms include hopelessness, sleep and appetite disturbance, loss of pleasure in daily activities, social isolation, and lowered activity and energy level. Of additional concerns are Mr. G.'s unusual behavior, apparent memory problems, and reports of having conversations with his deceased wife. Although the nature of these reports is not clear, further examination for cognitive disorder should be pursued. Mr. G.'s symptoms appear to be affecting most domains of well-being, and, on a functional level, he has been quite debilitated since his wife's death. Nevertheless, he is being well supported by an attentive son and daughter-in-law, who are in a good position to monitor his behavior and provide emotional support.

Recommendations for further focused assessment (note recommended referrals to consultants or additional instruments to be used)

Referral to psychiatric evaluation is strongly recommended.

THE COMPREHENSIVE SERVICE PLAN SUMMARY

Assessment/Problems	Goals	Objectives	Interventions	Evaluation plan
(Briefly describe key problems to be addressed.)	(State desired outcome for each problem.)	(Describe specific "stepping stones" toward each GOAL. Update as client progresses.)	(Describe specific interventions to be used.)	(Describe indexes to be used for tracking progress.)
Acute grief reaction/recurrent depressive symptoms including hopelessness, suicidal ideation, poor sleep and appetite, lowered energy and activity level, and social isolation/withdrawal	Resolve grief and alleviate all symptoms of depression	Initial objectives would include helping client to acknowledge wife's death and begin verbalizing his feelings of despair and loneliness	*Supportive skills:* Develop a working relationship with Mr. G., and join with his closest support system—his son and daughter-in-law—as collaborators	Monitor Mr. G.'s suicidal ideation closely; coach Hector and Juanita regarding signs of increased suicidal risk
	Reduce frequency and intensity of suicidal thoughts	Discuss any specifics regarding plans to hurt himself if he is feeling suicidal	*Therapeutic coping skills:* Carefully examine Mr. G.'s beliefs regarding his concerns about his wife's well-being in the afterlife, his sense of hopelessness, that his life cannot go on	Have H. and J. keep a chart regarding Mr. G.'s sleeping and eating habits
	Improve appetite and sleep	Begin developing a more consistent routine around sleeping and eating habits; monitor changes		
Chronic anxiety	Increase activity level and return client to socialization level prior to wife's death	Plan at least one brief home visit from a close friend within the next week or two		Monitor frequency of visitors and how long they stay (i.e., how long Mr. G. socializes with them)
	Reduce/alleviate stress and anxiety level	Reduce stress through supervised walks, moderate exercise	Conduct a review of his life with Esmeralda, and explore his openness to reviewing pictures, other memorabilia, and, perhaps, creating some kind of memorial to her in his garden or in some other way	Later, note increases in Mr. G.'s activity level around the house and any other increases in social activities
Memory problems; question of delusional beliefs?	Further assess apparent cognitive dysfunction			

The Comprehensive Service Plan Summary (Continued)

Assessment/Problems	Goals	Objectives	Interventions	Evaluation plan
(Briefly describe key problems to be addressed.)	(State desired outcome for each problem.)	(Describe specific "stepping stones" toward each GOAL. Update as client progresses.)	(Describe specific interventions to be used.)	(Describe indexes to be used for tracking progress.)
			Encourage his expression of feelings about his grief and fears about his wife's well-being	
			As he slowly improves, increase social contacts in his home	
			Case management skills: Later, bolster social supports by encouraging visitors and gradually returning client to former level of social activity	
			Consider referring him for spiritual counseling when he seems open to discussing his wife and his anger at God	
			Refer client for psychiatric services for specialized mental status exam and consideration of medication for his depression	

CHAPTER NINE

Adult Disorders: Substance Use and Personality Disorders

Substance Abuse

Assessment

TENS OF MILLIONS OF AMERICANS meet the criteria for substance use disorders due to problematic or habitual abuse of alcohol, illicit, and prescription drugs. Substance use disorders cost the nation hundreds of billions of dollars in general health care costs, treatment for addictions, lost productivity, criminal activity and adjudication, and other related social problems (Bouchery, Harwood, Sacks, Simon, & Brewer, 2011; Hasin, Stinson, Ogburn, & Grant, 2007). Estimates for twelve-month "alcohol use disorder" (based on DSM-5 criteria) is about 8.5 percent (APA, 2013; Grant et al., 2004). Hasin, Stinson, Ogburn, and Grant (2007) estimated lifetime prevalence for alcohol abuse to be 17.8 percent and lifetime dependence to be 12.5 percent. Most people with alcohol use disorders never seek or receive treatment. Compton, Thomas, Stinson, and Grant (2007) revealed that 2 percent (2.8% male; 1.2% female) of the US population had been diagnosed with a drug use disorder within the twelve months prior to the survey, and 10.3 percent (13.8% male; 7.1% female) met lifetime criteria for a drug use disorder.

Although previous editions of the DSM distinguished substance abuse (failures in fulfilling major role obligations such as work, school, and home) from substance dependence (e.g., physical tolerance, withdrawal symptoms, difficulty cutting down), the DSM-5 now recognizes what addiction science has shown for some time: substance use disorders occur on a continuum of severity with no clear demarcation between abuse and dependence.

Scientific research strongly suggests that substance use and addictions are caused by a variety of interacting biopsychosocial factors: genetic predisposition, family learning history, cultural influences, and social-environmental influences. Substance abuse and addiction also co-occur with a range of other psychiatric and psychosocial disorders: schizophrenia, mood disorders, anxiety disorders, eating disorders, personality disorders, domestic violence, and child abuse and neglect. Regardless of field of practice, social workers will encounter many clients who abuse and are addicted to substances. It is of utmost importance that all social workers have a working knowledge of the pharmacological properties of the most common drugs of abuse (e.g., alcohol, narcotics, amphetamines, tranquilizers) and, at a minimum, know how to conduct screening and assessment of substance abuse and refer clients for subsequent intervention. Ideally, all social workers should be trained to provide some level of intervention for substance use disorders given its high co-occurrence rate with other disorders and psychosocial conditions.

There is a wide range of instruments available to assist in an MFS assessment of substance abuse and addiction (USDHHS, 2003b). However, scales should be used within the context of a multidimensional qualitative assessment whereby the practitioner explores these core essential questions (O'Hare, 2015): (1) What substances does the client use? (2) How much of each substance do they use? (3) How often does the client use them? (4) Under what circumstances do they use? (5) What are the short- and long-term consequences of drug use with regard to psychological, emotional, behavioral, interpersonal, and community functioning?

Will clients who abuse substances answer such questions accurately or truthfully? The answer is, it depends on the circumstances. Many clients are quite forthcoming about their use and abuse of alcohol, illegal drugs, and prescription medication. Other clients are more withholding because there is stigma associated with substance abuse and addiction and because clients are understandably concerned about admitting to illegal behavior. However, some clients might minimize their use or deny the importance of consequences of use largely because they truly believe that they do not have a problem. Sorting out use patterns, severity of the consequences of use, and to what extent the client's concerns are congruent with the actual magnitude of the problem can be quite challenging.

With experience, practitioners can become adept at facilitating client disclosure of their substance use and abuse. Linking together psychological, behavioral, legal, and medical indicators of substance abuse in a straightforward and nonjudgmental way can often help the client be more forthcoming. Employing information from multiple sources and confronting contradictory information in a straightforward manner can be illuminating. However, research on motivational interviewing and intervention (Miller & Rollnick, 2013) suggests that arguing with clients does little good and simply invites resistance. Collaborating with clients to sort through the pros and cons of using substances is less coercive and places the responsibility on the client to decide whether they want to do something about the problem. Focusing on careful listening, rolling with resistance, and respecting the client's personal autonomy will encourage treatment engagement.

Functional analysis is critical to a complete substance abuse assessment. Most clients follow somewhat of a pattern in their abuse of alcohol and other drugs. A two-week monitoring period can be helpful if the client is ready to engage in treatment. Keeping a log and having the client document what substances they used, how much, how often, and under what circumstances can be productive and help practitioners to identify key cognitive, emotional, or situational factors that increase the client's likelihood of using alcohol or other drugs. This analysis will be particularly valuable for setting goals and implementing therapeutic coping skills targeting "at risk" situations.

A person with a substance use disorder often manifests the problem in different areas of their life, although not always to the same degree. A systems assessment should focus on locating not only which domain of life (e.g., home, work, in the community) the problem is localized, but how these various dimensions of the problem interact to either provide incentives to cut down or reinforce the problem. Substance use disorders often play out as a personal, interpersonal, and social problem simultaneously.

Intervention

Although treatment of substance use disorders remains challenging, those interventions shown to be most effective in controlled trials use variations of behavioral and cognitive-behavioral techniques. These include brief motivational treatment, cognitive-behavioral therapy, behavioral couples therapy, community reinforcement, and contingency management approaches (Alessi, Rash, & Petry, 2011; Carroll & Onken, 2005; Gryczynski et al., 2011; Higgins et al. 2003; Magill & Ray, 2009; McCrady, Epstein, Cook, Jensen, & Hildebrandt, 2009; Miller, Meyers, & Hiller-Sturmhofel, 1999; Monti & Rohsenow, 1999; O'Farrell & Falls-Stewart, 2003). These approaches utilize an array of therapeutic coping-skills methods including motivational interviewing, cognitive appraisal of the pros and cons of using, coping with emotional distress that can trigger relapse, improving social skills, practicing drink and drug refusal skills, seeking out sober social supports, and reducing risks associated with use (i.e., harm reduction) to support sobriety, reduce relapse, and prevent recidivism. These strategies are well researched (although more needs to be done) and have been increasingly incorporated into traditional approaches to addictions treatment as well. In addition to out-patient settings, behavioral methods are often utilized in in-patient treatment, halfway houses, therapeutic communities, and traditional recovery services. Practitioners help the client conduct an accurate functional analysis of their behavior regarding substance use by recognizing how specific thoughts, feelings, behaviors, and situations put them at risk to relapse. Once the client becomes skilled at recognizing these antecedents (i.e., "triggers") they can utilize an array of standard cognitive behavioral self-regulatory skills to moderate or abstain from use and possible relapse.

Many clients seek help from mutual support groups with or without ever having sought formal treatment. These include Alcoholics Anonymous, Narcotics Anonymous, and other similar groups. Although studies of mutual help groups for substance abuse have shown mixed results, there is reason to believe that clients who "stick with it" have a better chance of achieving and maintaining sobriety. Practitioners can actively facilitate client participation in traditional twelve-step approaches (e.g., Humphreys, 1999; USDHHS, 2000). However, one review concluded that professional interventions "infused" with twelve-step beliefs were no more effective than approaches that did not incorporate those beliefs (Miller, 2008). Nevertheless, given that twelve-step and similar programs are voluntary, widely and freely available, and are not considered professional interventions, they should not be judged with the same standards as treatment provided by licensed professionals.

Clients with substance abuse problems arrive in treatment for many reasons and at many levels of readiness to change. However, many clients who seek social work services, despite having a substance abuse problem, do not present it as their primary reason for seeking help. Clients are more likely to present mental health concerns (e.g., depression, anxiety), family problems (e.g., couples conflict, parent-child problems), health-related concerns, or legal problems (e.g., court-ordered domestic violence, other crimes) as their presenting complaint. Depending on the client's referral circumstances and their readiness to change, practitioners should be flexible in how they initially approach the matter of substance abuse and be ready for a range of responses from the client when the issue is broached.

Evidence has demonstrated that the therapeutic alliance is as important to clients with substance abuse problems as it is with other clients. Substance abuse still carries with it a degree of stigma, and emphasizing a nonjudgmental approach is important. Despite the fact that many prescription drugs of abuse are pharmacologically more dangerous than some street drugs, those who use "illicit" substances tend to be seen in a more negative light. Providing effective care for the client requires a solid working alliance that communicates to the client that you are not there to judge but to help the client recognize the personal psychosocial and health costs associated with substance abuse, motivate them to take action, and improve the client's overall quality of life.

Engaging clients with a substance abuse problem depends, initially, on where they are in the change process. Prochaska, DiClemente, and Norcross's (1992) stages of change model (described in Chapter 6) provides a helpful descriptive rubric for determining a client's readiness to engage in the change process. Clients who are in the *precontemplation* stage generally do not think they have a substance use problem. These clients are often court-ordered or otherwise involuntary clients and generally are not interested in treatment. Clients in the *contemplation stage* are thinking, "Yeah, maybe I drink (or use other drugs) too much sometimes . . ." and tend to be more willing to explore the possibility that they do have a problem. Clients in the *preparation* stage have made up their mind that they have a problem and are on the verge of doing something to deal with the problem. Those in the *action* stage have accepted that they have a substance use problem and are fully engaged in treatment. Clients in the *maintenance* stage have been through a period of treatment and are now trying to solidify their gains and prevent relapse. Meeting the client "where they are" is essential for successfully engaging the client and increasing the chances that they will make a commitment to substance abuse treatment.

Research on motivational interviewing (Miller & Rollnick, 2013), noted earlier in this section, has also demonstrated that, when clients are treated respectfully, allowed to come the formulation of a problem on their own, and are given a choice of treatment goals in a spirit of collaboration, they are more likely to engage in treatment. Flexibility in setting those initial treatment goals is important so the client feels that they are not being coerced by the practitioner's agenda. Practitioners should "roll with the client's resistance." Many clients attempt to cut down or eliminate the use of one drug or another. This approach may work for some, and at a later date, they might be more willing to consider abstinence if they fail to moderate their use. A "two steps forward, one step back" pattern of change is not uncommon when working with clients who abuse or are dependent on substances. Practitioners should avoid ideological approaches to substance abuse treatment based on personal or anecdotal experience (e.g., always insisting on abstinence despite the client's age or problem severity) and focus on using well-researched methods that allow for partial successes early in treatment as well as a range of intervention goals (e.g., harm reduction, moderation, and abstinence).

Clients experiencing substance abuse and addiction have developed patterns of using alcohol and other drugs in response to an array of psychological, emotional, behavioral, and situational vulnerabilities and risk factors. Some clients are more likely to drink as a result of depression or anxiety, others as a way of coping with social situations or loneliness, and others, who might be more physiologically dependent, as an attempt to neutralize withdrawal symptoms. Using substances to cope with psychosocial or physical cues does, in fact, provide some temporary relief and pleasure. For the person with a substance use disorder, this reward, however, might increasingly come at a price should use of substances increase. Due to the habit-forming nature of substances (as a result of both psychological and physiological factors), changing one's use patterns through situational adjustments (e.g., not drinking before driving) or cutting down or abstaining can become increasingly difficult. When the costs of use override the benefits, people who abuse alcohol or other drugs are more likely to seek help, often under pressure from others (e.g., family members, doctors, or the courts).

There is a range of coping-skills approaches that, alone or in some combination, have been shown to be moderately effective with persons who abuse alcohol or other drugs. *Psycho-education* is certainly an important part of an overall approach but is typically not sufficient by itself to cause lasting change. Psycho-education is often an initial step in *brief treatment*. In brief treatment, practitioners might tailor a psycho-educational approach to provide individualized feedback to a client after having conducted a full assessment, possibly with collaborative input from a physician as well. After having examined the type and amount of substances used over time and having made some estimates about how much impact there has been on the client's psychological, social, and physical well-being, a social worker would sum up their assessment about negative consequences and make treatment recommendations. Many clients, particularly those who are abusing substances but are not dependent (e.g., youthful substance abuse, excessive social drinking in adults), often respond positively to this feedback and make positive efforts to cut down and moderate their consumption level. It is also important that practitioners help clients to link reduction in substance use with other improvements in their life, such as feeling more energy, being more productive at work, improving important relationships in their life, and improving overall health.

This initial progress can also serve as an extended assessment (in the form of client *self-monitoring*) to determine if the client has an abuse problem or if they are dependent on alcohol or other drugs. It also provides an opportunity to examine other co-occurring problems (e.g., depression, anxiety) to see if there is any change in these areas as well and further assess potentially co-occurring disorders. Extended self-monitoring can be a powerful therapeutic tool that engages clients in determining for themselves how serious their substance use difficulties actually are. The practitioner can facilitate an analysis of the pros and cons of their substance use and help the client come to their own determination about the seriousness of the problem. The practitioner and client can then collaborate on determining what goals seem realistic and feasible. In this way, a judgment about the seriousness of the problem is not imposed on the client—they come to that determination on their own with the support and informed guidance of the social work practitioner.

Self-monitoring thoughts, emotional states, behaviors, and situations that precipitate drinking or drug use might be the most important survival skill for the client who is struggling to control abuse or overcome dependence. Distorted or negative thoughts (e.g., "I'll never get another good job," "My kids will never want to see me again," "I'll never feel better physically") can be very discouraging and a good excuse to say, "Oh, the heck with it," and yield to the urge to drink or take drugs to block out negative thoughts. Alcohol and other drugs are also an effective short-term way to anesthetize oneself against anxiety, depression, grief, anger, disappointment, and other negative feelings. Clients who learn to identify negative mood states as a potential antecedent to substance use can prepare for those situations and have alternatives available to them: calling a nonabusing friend, calling an AA or NA sponsor, going for a walk, or other healthful distractions. Early in the recovery process, cravings may have a strong physiological component; later on, psychological cues can be just as compelling. (Just ask a former cigarette smoker about situational cravings, even ten years after quitting.) Clients' routine behaviors and circumstances associated with substance use can also be powerful triggers. A middle-aged man in early recovery (who for years met his friends at the local tavern four or five times per week) will have a hard time abstaining if "I just stop by the local tavern to say 'hi' to my buddies." Over time, engaging in self-monitoring provides a client with a cognitive "map" that helps them anticipate where the trouble spots will be on the road to recovery and how to avoid them or deal with them when they can not be avoided.

An examination of dysfunctional thinking regarding substance use may also be an important part of the initial stage of treatment. Over time, people who abuse alcohol and other drugs develop rather specific but erroneous beliefs about the effects that substances will provide for them. These beliefs are referred to as *alcohol expectancies* (Brown, Goldman, Inn, & Andersen, 1980). These include expectancies of increased social assertiveness, tension reduction, and sexual enhancement, among others. Expectancies are also associated with substance use *motives,* more immediate antecedents to using drugs or alcohol, and include using substances to cope with negative emotions or to enhance a sense of well-being or enhance social encounters (Cooper, 1994). Although alcohol and other drugs do provide some positive effects in the short run and in moderate doses (e.g., enhance socializing, reduce tension), negative consequences tend to compete with these positive effects after years of abuse. Expectancies and motives can reinforce continued abuse (Hasking & Oei, 2007). Despite the negative consequences of abuse, clients often continue to deny, minimize, or rationalize their substance abuse, regardless of the negative consequences (e.g., arrests for drunk driving, loss of job, divorce, and health problems). Respectfully presenting the evidence to the client and having them consider the discrepancies between their expectancies, motivations, and the actual consequences can be helpful for reducing denial and minimization.

Other cognitive distortions regarding substance abuse may occur as well. As a result of depression (secondary to heavy chronic drinking) the client may think that they are hopeless, they will never be able to stop their use of alcohol or other drugs, and their lives will never get any better. Practitioners can offer evidence that many people feel despondent initially and that their thinking may be distorted by feelings of hopelessness caused by depression that is substance-related. The practitioner can help the client focus on incremental gains "one day at a time" to stimulate some initial reinforcing progress, increase the client's feelings of self-efficacy, and boost optimism about making further progress. Behavioral successes can "debunk" the dysfunctional belief that they are "hopeless," and encourage them to achieve incremental successes. As clients begin to feel better (e.g., reduced depression, less negative feedback from loved ones), cutting down and sobriety can become positively reinforcing.

Many clients with addictions have had serious relationship difficulties, in part, as a result of their substance abuse. Some of these problems might also have been related to inadequate social skills, made worse by the effects of intoxication. Modeling, role playing, and rehearsing assertiveness and better communication skills can be of great assistance for clients when they encounter interpersonal emotional "triggers." For example, a woman engaged in substance abuse treatment following a divorce may have to deal with a formerly abusive husband with whom she shares child-care arrangements. These situations trigger raw and difficult emotions about problems not yet resolved and may put the client seriously at risk for relapse. Role playing such a scenario can be a good way to prepare for an encounter. Rehearsing how the client may feel in such a circumstance and helping her plan to cope with those feelings can help her get through the encounter without resorting to drinking ("forewarned is forearmed"). Success experiences in situations that are likely to provoke relapse can increase self-efficacy and help her maintain sobriety.

The same stress-management skills described for dealing with anxiety problems (see Chapter 8) can also help maintain moderation or sobriety. When overly stressed, a client in recovery can stop, take a deep breath, think, endure the immediate feeling, and learn to accept passing emotional upsets without resorting to drinking or using other drugs. This thoughtful pause can give the client time to initiate a previously discussed action plan (e.g., go home, call a friend, take a long walk, and wait for the feeling to pass). In the long run, many people struggling with abuse or addictions turn to exercise to reduce anxiety and depression and the emotional distress that can precede relapse. Before recommending any exercise regimen, practitioners should encourage clients to be examined by a physician.

Despite deciding to cut down or stop drinking and eliminate illegal drug use, clients are still likely to find themselves in social circumstances where others are drinking or using drugs. Role playing and rehearsing *drink-refusal skills* and practicing them in vivo can be beneficial for the person who may feel uncomfortable in the early stages of recovery. Practicing easy-to-remember phrases such as "no thanks," "I'm all set," "I've got my drink" (seltzer with a twist), "I'm taking medication," or "I'm not feeling well today" can be just enough to ward off the temptation to say, "OK, why not?"

Cognitive-behavioral coping skills for helping substance use disordered clients are currently at the forefront of contemporary approaches for early intervention, treatment, and recovery. Practitioners who learn these approaches can help clients cope with cognitive and emotional triggers, and prepare clients to cope successfully with situations that put themselves at risk for relapse. However, clients often need more than improved coping skills. Successful interventions for substance abuse and dependence often require the cooperation of two or more service providers as well as improvements in social and instrumental supports.

A case management framework is often used to augment some of the more effective intervention programs for persons with addictions. These are multifaceted approaches that emphasize coordinating treatment efforts among various agencies, facilitating access to other social and health services, and following through with the provision of social and concrete supports. Community reinforcement and contingency management approaches have been shown to be among the most effective interventions for seriously addicted clients (Abbott, Weller, Delaney, & Moore, 1998; Azrin, Sisson, Meyers, & Godley, 1982; Carroll & Onken, 2005; Higgins et al. 1993). Community reinforcement approach (CRA) is a multifaceted strategy designed to help seriously addicted persons by using multiple layers of social and instrumental supports to help clients stay clean and sober. These supports are likely to include some combination of job or housing assistance, financial benefits, mutual help groups, and substance abuse counseling. For many clients who have been court-ordered to continue treatment, contingency management (CM) may be added to CRA to balance rewards with possible sanctions if the client is caught using illegal drugs again. The emphasis in CM is on the "if-then" (i.e., the contingency) condition: if the client remains abstinent from drugs (e.g., clean urine screens) and does not otherwise violate probation, then they can continue to receive treatment and other forms of assistance in the community; if they use drugs or commit a violation, then they might have to return to prison (depending on the specifics of the contract or court-ordered conditions). CRA and CM programs vary from state to state and their implementation depends largely on the levels of coordination among the criminal justice system, mental health, and substance abuse treatment agencies. These programs are very promising as noted above but require more research, evaluation, and closely supervised and coordinated implementation. The growing use of "drug courts" suggests increased interest in finding alternatives for nonviolent drug offenders, but outcomes with these studies are hard to interpret given a range of methodological weaknesses.

There has also been a growing interest in Internet-based interventions, some linked to personalized professional feedback. One randomized controlled trial compared three approaches with a large sample (about half women): an online CBT-based Internet therapy (self-monitoring, self-regulatory skills, motivational enhancement, and social support), an online chat forum, and a no-treatment waitlist group. They found superior outcomes for the CBT approach at six months compared with the online chat forum and the waitlist group (Blankers, Koeter, & Schippers, 2011). It is likely that similar online approaches will be forthcoming.

Case management skills are often essential in providing substance abuse interventions. Coordinating medical referrals, linking clients to social supports such as twelve-step and other mutual help groups, and communicating with employers, probation officers, and the courts are essential skills for implementing complex and effective substance abuse services for seriously substance dependent clients.

Personality Disorders

A personality disorder is defined as "an enduring pattern of inner experience and behavior that deviates markedly from the expectations of the individual's culture, is pervasive and inflexible, has an onset in adolescence or early adulthood, is stable over time, and leads to distress or impairment" (APA, 2013, p. 645). Personality disorders remain a somewhat controversial area in psychiatry (Skodol, Bender, Morey, & Oldham, 2013). However, there is little doubt that social workers encounter clients in mental health, forensic, and other social service settings that do display some of the cognitive, affective, and behavioral features described below. In this section, two of the more commonly diagnosed personality disorders will be addressed: antisocial and borderline personality disorders.

Assessment of Antisocial Personality Disorder (APD)

Persons diagnosed with APD often demonstrate a pervasive pattern of disregard and violation of the rights and safety of others (e.g., criminality, deceitfulness, violence, and impulsivity), a record of irresponsibility with regard to relationships, work, or financial commitments, and a lack of remorse regarding the violation of others' rights (APA, 2013). This last quality is often associated with psychopathy, a quality manifested by a subset of antisocial persons (Hare & Neumann, 2009). Population estimates for APD run at about less than 1 percent to 3 percent of the population. Although many persons, mostly male, engage in criminal acts in their youth (e.g., stealing, selling small amounts of drugs), many mature out of these activities and grow into responsible adults and contribute to society. The antisocial person who demonstrates psychopathic personality traits, however, tends to be a more chronic and inflexible person who shows little remorse for his behavior and seems to lack an awareness of others' feelings and needs altogether (Hare et al., 1990). Many antisocial and psychopathic persons also have substance use disorders and are at very high risk to perpetrate domestic violence against their partners and any children living with them.

In addition to a complete mental status exam, MFS assessment with antisocial personalities should carefully examine interpersonal and occupational history, substance abuse, and other impulsive high-risk behaviors. Functional assessment should examine patterns of impulsive, substance abusing, or other socially offending behaviors for significant patterns and high-risk situations. Access to relevant medical and legal records as well as previous mental health and substance abuse treatment information is very important. Antisocial clients can be engaging and charming and often are very good at "covering their tracks." Assessment should also include expert consultation for a violence risk assessment as well as standardized testing for psychopathy (Hare & Neumann, 2009).

Intervention

Antisocial and, particularly, psychopathic persons are potentially dangerous and very hard to treat. Occasionally, one hears reports of social workers having been seriously harmed or killed by their antisocial clients. These reports serve as a stark reminder that, if one chooses to work with antisocial clients, one should be working as part of an expert team where comprehensive assessments (including risk for violence) are conducted and there is close supervision at hand. Despite the best of intentions, traditional psychotherapeutic interventions (e.g., insight-oriented) have been shown to be ineffective with antisocial clients. Only external contingencies (e.g., balancing rewards and sanctions) and close structured supervision (e.g., collaboration with probation or parole officials) provide a reasonable chance of keeping some of these clients' behaviors in check and improving overall psychosocial functioning. Thus, working with antisocial and psychopathic persons is best done as a collaborative effort that includes some combination of mental health and often substance abuse services in collaboration with court-ordered supervision. In addition, because many of these clients are prone to violence, the likely effectiveness of psychosocial interventions has to be morally weighed against the danger some of these clients pose to the community at large. Criminal justice and mental health collaborations have yet to arrive at reliable criteria balancing "when to treat" and "when to incarcerate." Thus, much work remains to be done in advancing more coordinated interventions efforts for working with criminally involved clients.

However, a number of structured cognitive-behavioral interventions have been shown to be effective with clients diagnosed with antisocial personality disorder, many of whom are court-mandated to treatment and abuse alcohol and other drugs (Gendreau, 1996; McGuire & Hatcher, 2001).

Often, these approaches include the use of community reinforcement and contingency management approaches described earlier. Thus, in the most effective programs, cognitive-behavioral interventions are initiated while the client is serving time in prison and then are continued when they are paroled and released into the community. Such treatments may include a halfway house, therapeutic community, or other supervised arrangement (often including the services of a parole officer). Due to the high rate of co-occurring substance use disorders, preventing drug relapse postrelease is also a major component of these multifaceted programs. Currently, the policy debate regarding "what to do" with antisocial persons has moved beyond the "prison" versus "treatment" dichotomy. A third way suggests an integration of law enforcement efforts and psychosocial intervention services. The difficulty in determining the effectiveness of "drug courts" was noted earlier in this chapter.

Working with APD clients (we'll assume for the sake of simplicity that some, but not all, are also psychopathic) is often challenging. To increase the chances for good outcomes, practitioners must make an effort to culti-vate a respectful and sensitive relationship with each client. Because these clients can sometimes be charming, well spoken, humorous, and engaging, they can also be quite manipulative, seductive, and exploitive if given the opportunity. Inexperienced social workers might begin with rather ideal-ized expectations about working with antisocial clients. Before long, some become disillusioned when they realize that, despite the client's apparent sincerity, the practitioner was being used for other purposes (e.g., engaging in pseudotreatment to improve chances of early release). With close super-vision and experience, however, practitioners can learn to detect when a client is being candid and when they are engaging in manipulation for some other gain.

There are methods to enhance engagement with antisocial clients. These include being realistic with the client about meeting court requirements; being clear about the limits of informed consent and confidentiality (e.g., the practitioner must report on treatment progress, lack of compliance to the treatment contract, illegal behaviors); reviewing a treatment contract that provides unambiguous guidelines regarding their responsibilities (e.g., showing up on time, following through on tasks such as attendance at Narcotics Anonymous meetings, etc.); giving the client some flexibility regarding treatment goals; assessing for readiness to change; and advocat-ing for the client's rights when necessary (Rooney & Bibus, 2001). Despite the justified caution, some antisocial involuntary clients genuinely do want to change and do want to improve their lives (O'Hare, 1996), and these

clients should be accorded every opportunity to demonstrate their commitment to change, but by adhering to standards that demonstrate measurable
and consistent improvements.

Antisocial clients often have a particularly negative and dysfunctional
view of their relationships with others (e.g., "The whole world is a
battlefield—it's dog eat dog," "You gotta take what you can get, any way
you can get it"). No doubt, given the abuse histories of many of these
clients (as victims), it may be understandable that they see interpersonal
relations in exploitive terms. But even the most hardened criminal knows
that not everyone is out to harm other people; these characteristics may
simply describe the kind of people *they* are used to spending time with.
These beliefs, at a minimum, can be challenged respectfully to help the
client at least consider the fact that there are trustworthy people in the
world (some of whom they may have known at one time), that not everyone in the world is out to harm or exploit others, and that they might
also be able to develop more worthwhile and genuine relationships in the
future.

It may also be helpful to associate this distorted thinking and negative
view of the world with an increased likelihood of reoffending and going
back to jail. Some of these clients may not be able to imagine positive
alternatives. Nevertheless, it is worth trying to help antisocial clients at
least consider more positive outcomes while, at the same time, being realistic about their willingness to make positive changes and engage in more
prosocial behaviors.

For the court-ordered client who seems to genuinely engage in treatment, self-monitoring can be a useful and concrete way of identifying "at
risk" situations in their daily life. By at risk here is meant being in situations that increase the likelihood of reoffending, such as reestablishing
relationships with their old street buddies, drinking or using illegal drugs
(which puts them at risk to reoffend), committing a crime (even a petty
crime such as shoplifting), and engaging in violence, among other offenses. In order for these clients to change, they must become more adept
at using foresight to see where the "at risk" situations are ahead of time.
Helping antisocial and impulsive clients "connect the dots" ahead of time
through self-monitoring might forestall relapse in recovery or commitment of another crime. This might be a difficult cognitive skill to develop
since many antisocial adults started out early on as conduct disordered
children and adolescents, and many of them with learning difficulties
(e.g., ADHD).

This deficit in foresight on the part of many antisocial clients is often accompanied by an unwillingness to accept responsibility for one's behavior. For example, a client might say, "I had no intention of using drugs, but they put it right in front of my face. How could I resist? It wasn't my fault!" Whereas, with a little planning, the client might have surmised that going to a party with former associates would expose the client to alcohol, drug use, gambling, consorting with prostitutes, and so on. Self-monitoring can be learned by otherwise impulsive clients, but it takes considerable practice and rehearsal with the social worker who should focus not only on the potential positive outcomes of avoiding high-risk situations, but also the likelihood of punishment if the client slips. High relapse and reincarceration rates among criminally involved antisocial clients underscore the challenges social workers face when working with these challenging clients.

But what does the client do if they, in fact, encounter a high-risk situation? Having engaged in self-monitoring and identifying high-risk circumstances, the practitioner can also help the client improve their coping skills. For example, the social worker can role play and rehearse with the client some ready excuses for removing himself from a high-risk situation (e.g., "I can't stay—I have to go to work," "I'm on my way to see my probation officer and I'm late," "I've got a doctor's appointment"). As the client makes more progress, they might get to the point where they can actually tell the truth ("I'm not staying—I don't feel like going back to prison," "I don't drink and don't use drugs anymore," "I'm in recovery," "I'm trying to stay clean").

Other coping skills that may be of help include stress management and brief meditation to help impulsive clients pause before acting on sudden urges that may put him or another person in jeopardy. Learning not to give in to snap decisions can be very hard for impulsive antisocial clients. The use of imagery during meditation can be helpful, for example, by contrasting images of staying on the "outside" versus "inside" (returning to prison).

Antisocial clients are also likely to demonstrate deficits in interpersonal skills. Role playing and rehearsing how to engage a prospective employer or how to communicate constructively with a potential friend or romantic partner can be challenging. But these skills must be practiced in vivo. Including the spouses or family members of antisocial persons should be considered when possible. Social workers can incorporate skills for working with couples and families as needed. Communication training, problem solving, and enhancing social supports can go a long way to helping antisocial clients establish a behavioral repertoire that goes beyond just avoiding high-risk situations but also makes their life more rewarding on multiple levels.

But it is unlikely that therapeutic coping-skills methods alone will be sufficient to keep antisocial clients from relapsing. More comprehensive approaches require the coordinated efforts of a professional team: social workers, psychiatrists, and probation officers all working within a well-run, court-mandated program. The approaches noted above, community reinforcement approach (CRA) and contingency management (CM), are best implemented within the context of a case management model. Successful utilization of these programs usually involves networking with mental health, substance abuse, and health and criminal justice professionals as well as arranging and facilitating the provision of social and instrumental supports. However, methods used to test and evaluate "drug courts" and other forms of *therapeutic jurisprudence* (i.e., combined use of mental health and the justice system to increase prosocial behavior) must improve before they can be generally endorsed.

Because of the difficult and sometimes intractable nature of antisocial, criminal, and psychopathic behavior, programs that include a sound working alliance, coping skills, community reinforcement, and contingency management methods require a long-term commitment if they are to be successful. Case management services are essential to ensure coordination and clear communication among various services, maintenance of benefits to which clients may be entitled, and ensuring consistent follow-through by clients enrolled in these programs.

Assessment of Borderline Personality Disorder (BPD)

Population estimates for the lifetime prevalence of BPD run anywhere from 1 to 6 percent (APA, 2013; Leischenring, Leibing, Kruse, New, & Leweke, 2011; Pagura et al., 2010), and about one-third of those also meet criteria for PTSD. People diagnosed with BDP demonstrate a combination of characteristic behaviors that often include severe mood swings, short-lived psychotic episodes, unpredictable and often impulsive behaviors, suicidal or pseudosuicidal gestures, and other high-risk or dangerous behaviors. Often, these problems are worked out within the context of tumultuous relationships where clients seem to vacillate between emotional extremes. Clients diagnosed with BPD are often very depressed, and substance abuse should also be considered as a co-occurring condition that may exacerbate many of their cognitive, emotional, and behavioral difficulties. Helping clients diagnosed with BPD is a challenge given the client's highly disordered thinking, emotional outbursts, and impulsive and some-times dangerous and unpredictable behaviors. Although researchers have debated the reliability of the disorder (i.e., the consistency with which it is identified by trained diagnosticians), interventions that focus on problems related to deficits in regulating extreme emotional outbursts and impulsive behaviors have been shown to be effective.

A thorough MFS assessment is likely to show problems across most domains of psychosocial well-being. Mental status symptoms are likely to include distorted thinking, depression, suicidal thoughts, and anxiety prob-lems, among other difficulties. Impulsivity is often accompanied by high-risk behaviors that might include harmful acts directed at the self or at others. Self-harming behaviors are particularly troublesome and can por-tend suicidal risk. Interpersonal conflict is often evident in both close rela-tionships as well as with antisocial problems in the community. Substance abuse frequently co-occurs with BPD, and very depressed clients often show serious deficits in basic self-care. Health problems should be re-viewed and clients referred for medical exams given the higher risk for transmittable diseases associated with unprotected sex and drug abuse (e.g., sharing needles).

Functional assessment is crucial with clients who manifest symptoms of BPD. Often, these clients will go through periods of relative calm, but tracking behavior over time (especially if the client is willing to cooperate with keeping a log or diary early on in treatment) will reveal important data regarding interpersonal or situational antecedents associated with impulsive outbursts, self-mutilation, substance use, or bouts of depression. As with many clients, self-monitoring is a good way to help the client become a collaborator in the intervention and help them to "intellectualize" their problems, a step that might help the client to better cope with intense surges of emotion and gain some perspective on their distress.

Intervention

Dialectical behavior therapy (DBT) (a modified form of CBT) is currently the treatment of choice for borderline personality disorder (e.g., Davidson et al. 2006; Geisen-bloo et al. 2006; Leischenring, Leibing, Kruse, New, & Leweke, 2011; Linehan, 1993; Linehan et al. 2006; Simpson et al. 1998). DBT is particularly effective for reducing self-harming behaviors (McMain et al., 2009; Verheul et al., 2003), has also shown good results with comor-bid substance use disorders (Harned et al., 2008), and transfers well to "real world" settings (Kroger et al., 2006). Other approaches, including variations of psychodynamic therapies (e.g., Clarkin, Levy, Lenzenweger, & Kernberg,

2007; Gregory et al., 2008) and mentalization therapy (Bateman & Fonagy, 2009), a combination of CBT and psychodynamic therapy, have been much less studied but have shown some promising results as well.

Clients diagnosed with BPD are likely to respond positively to a practitioner who provides a mature, calm, reliable, and empathic working relationship. The working alliance can serve as a "laboratory" to help clients learn to identify dysfunctional thinking, better regulate emotional distress and mood disturbances, and learn to engage in more adaptive and healthful approaches to coping and problem solving. Successful incorporation of coping skills can also lead to a greater ability to regulate intense emotions, control impulsive behaviors, cultivate less conflicted relationships, and lead to a more satisfying life in general.

DBT practitioners utilize a range of modified CBT skills to help clients develop more effective ways of dealing with dysfunctional thinking, intense feelings, and impulsive behaviors. In that respect, DBT is like other cognitive-behavioral treatments, but these skills are often tested to the extreme when dealing with very troubled and often unpredictable clients. DBT practitioners are also flexible in that they utilize a flexible range of modalities, sometimes in combination, including individual therapy, supportive and skills-based group therapies, and, sometimes, brief hospitalization when needed in response to suicidal threats or attempts. Because of the high probability that BPD will co-occur with other disorders such as substance abuse, PTSD, or depression, concurrent interventions may be utilized (e.g., detoxification, substance abuse counseling, antidepressant medication). In addition, it is often the case that clients diagnosed with BPD also find themselves in high-risk circumstances such as being involved in criminal activities (e.g., dealing drugs) or are sometimes victims of violence (e.g., physical or sexual assault). High-risk and sometimes traumatic events precede the client's involvement in treatment and often occur during the intervention. Thus, flexibility and resourcefulness are required of the practitioner who takes on the challenge of working with these multi-problem clients. Although flexibility may be the watchword, there are essential skills that have, as a treatment "package," been shown to be helpful for persons diagnosed with BPD. A brief description of these skills follows.

Practitioners who choose to work with clients who manifest symptoms of BPD require considerable confidence in their skills, inner calm when dealing with clients who express extreme emotions, a clear focus on guiding the intervention plan, well-defined personal boundaries regarding where one's responsibilities to the client begin and end, and a high tolerance for clients who engage in high-risk behaviors. Clients diagnosed with

BPD have often been known to threaten suicide, cut, burn, and otherwise mutilate themselves privately or in the presence of others, engage in dramatic and attention-seeking behavior that puts them at considerable risk, and often vacillate between extremes of false self-confidence and protracted periods of self-described helplessness, worthlessness, and dependency. Clients with BPD may go through periods where they are hospitalized for suicide attempts, engage in illegal behaviors, are sexually promiscuous, or make multiple and frequent phone calls demanding the practitioner's undivided attention. Episodes of screaming rage and child-like sobbing may occur within the same hour-long session.

Practitioners should strive to maintain a balance between empathic attunement to the client's pain and maintaining a matter-of-fact, problem-oriented approach to helping the client articulate their emotions and improve daily coping skills. Practitioners should avoid the inclination to be overly nurturing. Although generalizations should be taken with caution, clients who present themselves as chronically unable to cope with their emotions or take responsibility for their day-to-day behavior are likely to become less functional when practitioners reinforce their sense of helplessness or the feeling that the client is out of control. However, if the client expresses strong suicidal ideation, practitioners should err on the side of caution and intervene as needed, despite the fact that such ideation is often a "false alarm" and is not followed up by genuine suicide attempts.

CBT skills have been shown to be readily adapted to the struggles of clients diagnosed with BPD and can be used to address the often extreme distress these clients experience in their thinking, dealing with emotions, and in their problem behaviors. However, Linehan and colleagues have adapted CBT skills specifically for these clients. Clients diagnosed with BPD need help in identifying dysfunctional thinking, challenging these thoughts, and understanding how they are linked to extreme emotions and emotionally upsetting situations. These clients often have highly distorted thinking that provokes or is activated in response to extreme emotions. Extreme and distorted kinds of thinking can range widely from "I am worthless and deserve to die," "I want to kill my boyfriend (girlfriend)," and "I am evil and need to be punished severely," to "I have genius intelligence and can't learn anything from you therapists," "No one can possibly understand me," "I am clairvoyant, and I can read minds," "I can heal people's cancer through therapeutic touch," and "I am a warrior princess and was present at the battle at Avignon. I want you to conduct a past life regression on me." Although some of the distortions of the client diagnosed with BPD might sound delusional and suggest psychosis (i.e., on the "borderline" between psychosis and neurosis, according to earlier theories about BPD), these beliefs are often ephemeral and come and go in response to external stressors or perceived threats to the client's self-worth. True delusions, as in clients diagnosed with severe mental illnesses, tend to be more consistent and accompanied by other serious symptoms (e.g., hallucinations, prolonged social withdrawal).

Dealing with dysfunctional thoughts initially requires some standard Socratic questioning as one might engage in when using CBT with a depressed client. If a client diagnosed with BPD reports that she feels overwhelmed with shame and rage and can barely control her behavior when she sees a former abusive boyfriend at work, a close examination of automatic negative thoughts might identify a core problem—for example, if the client says, "When I see him, I get really embarrassed. I know he's been talking about me to everyone, telling them lies. I wish I could kill him—I'd like to see him burned alive for what he did to me." Of course, after establishing that the client is just being characteristically intense, is *feeling* this way and *has no intention* of actually harming him (or having someone else do it for her), these thoughts need to be isolated, identified, and explored to determine their level of reasonableness. Helping the client cognitively examine the situation can help her identify those feelings, bring those feelings into some perspective, and help the client gain some inner sense of calm and control.

The practitioner might empathize with the client about how difficult it must be to feel this intensely when she sees him at work but suggest the following: "Let's see if we can work together to help you learn how to cope with these upsetting feelings, so you are not feeling so overwhelmed." The practitioner might guide the client in analyzing the details of what she experiences and feels when she sees her boyfriend. Consider the following illustration:

PRACTITIONER: "What is the first thought that comes to mind when you see him walk through your work area at the office?"

CLIENT: "I feel humiliated, and I want to run away."

PRACTITIONER: "It must be terrible to feel that kind of embarrassment, but I really want you to tell me what you are *thinking* when you see him. What is going through your mind?"

CLIENT: "Well, I guess what I am thinking when I see him is that he's probably telling everyone about our sex life and how we did drugs together. I know he wouldn't be saying nice things about me—he hates me. I think people are laughing at me behind my back. He's probably having sex with another woman in the office. It's so humiliating."

PRACTITIONER: "So you are concerned that he is presenting you in a bad light to other people and discussing personal things, stuff you may not feel too good about?"

CLIENT: "Yeah, that's about it, I guess."

PRACTITIONER: "So what is the worst thing that he might say about you?"

CLIENT: "You know, what guys say—that I'm a slut, a crack whore, or something like that."

PRACTITIONER: "It sounds to me that you think everyone will believe him. I thought you told me he had been suspended for being drunk on the job a couple months back. What makes you think everyone will believe him if he says awful things about you?"

CLIENT: "I guess I just assume that people will believe him, that they will think the worst of me."

The ensuing conversation then stimulates a broader discussion about why she has such a low opinion of herself and how her lack of self-confidence and self-worth affects her behavior in relationships. By identifying and discussing her automatic negative thoughts about herself the client might also begin to challenge her extreme negative self-statements. It may also help her to understand and cope with the intense feelings that are provoked by similar situations.

However, disconfirming her low opinion of herself will take time. For a client struggling to control her more extreme emotions, coping skills are needed to help deal with them in the present, regardless of whether she can change her negative thinking about herself in the short run. Borrowing from Zen philosophy, Linehan and colleagues teach *core mindfulness skills* to help clients reduce overreactions to emotionally provocative situations. Core mindfulness skills focus on helping clients to "take perspective," that is, step back and observe themselves in the moment with some psychological distance, reflect on the provocative situation calmly, and fully experience the "here and now" of events. The practitioner might suggest the following: "Look, when you see your ex-boyfriend, you feel intense shame and rage, and you have a hard time keeping your cool. Next time you see him at work, I want you to try this: pretend that you are in a play. I want you to watch what is happening to you. Take notes after the incident—write down what you were thinking, feeling, doing, and, generally, what is going on around you. In this way, you can see yourself in the situation and not let the situation control you. Do you think you can try that?"

No doubt, for a client having a tough time keeping a grip on her intense feelings, such a task would be a challenge. The practitioner might suggest rehearsing the scenario in the session. After getting some details about similar situations that have happened, role playing the scene with the client can be a helpful way of preparing her to deal with a similar circumstance. As troubling thoughts and feelings (and, possibly, behaviors) emerge during the role play, the practitioner can ask the client to note them, stop the role play, and explore exactly what is going on with the client cognitively and emotionally. In this way, role play can prepare the client to stay calm during the next actual encounter. Being able to "survive" the next encounter without succumbing to an "emotional meltdown" can boost the client's self-confidence so that she may be able to control these feelings, instead of having them control her.

Practicing and achieving core mindfulness can be hard work. The client diagnosed with BPD often engages in dysfunctional or even self-destructive behaviors (e.g., cutting, drug abuse) to avoid having to deal with distressful emotions. The DBT practitioner teaches *distress tolerance skills* to help the client learn how to accept emotional distress as a part of life. *Emotion regulation skills* are taught to help clients be more in command of their emotions. These skills include accurately identifying feelings and determining what purpose a particular emotion serves. Practitioners can help clients reduce their vulnerability to what Linehan refers to as the "emotion mind" through problem solving, taking action to increase positive emotional events, taking a paradoxical stance by acting in ways that are contrary to an emotion evoked in a situation (e.g., being polite and civil to someone who is being sarcastic at your expense), and by increasing awareness and acceptance of one's emotions. Clients diagnosed with BPD (or any client trying to better regulate emotional distress) need to learn that experiencing strong emotions is not a calamity but simply an uncomfortable experience that can be remedied through calm reflection, taking action that ameliorates the situation, and by engaging in activities (e.g., talking to a friend, going for a walk, taking a hot bath) that can provide comfort and relief from the "slings and arrows" of everyday life. Clients are encouraged to stop overreacting, not make the situation worse, take a deep breath, experience the intense feelings but let them pass, seek solace and relief in concrete and healthful ways, and keep focusing on long-term solutions.

Many problems experienced by clients diagnosed with BPD concern the distress they experience within the context of relationships—with parents, siblings, children, friends, lovers, coworkers, and neighbors. Thus, in order to help clients learn to clarify their thinking and better regulate their emotional reactions, they must develop behavioral skills to defuse and prevent the small fires from turning into major conflagrations. This goal can be achieved through modeling, role playing, rehearsing, and practicing *inter-personal effectiveness skills.* Learning how to cope better in interpersonal and other social situations requires learning better communication skills and assertiveness skills. Essential components of these approaches include the following: (1) teaching the client how to actually listen to what the other person is saying, (2) coaching the client to communicate their thoughts and feelings clearly and calmly to the other party, (3) encouraging the client to take action as needed, and (4) having the client commit to following through on their intentions.

There may be no better way for the practitioner to teach good listening skills than to model them for the client. Good listening is a cultivated and practiced skill. Even experienced practitioners get distracted and lose focus now and then when a client is speaking to them. Practitioners can also role play an upsetting scenario with a client and instruct the client to pay attention to what is being said and not to allow their emotional distress to distract them from careful listening. After the brief exchange, the practitioner can ask the client "So, what was it that I was trying to say to you?" and "Were you really listening to me, or were you thinking about something else, like, what to say next?" Role playing in this way can help the client prepare for an upsetting encounter with a boss, an ex-husband, family members, or another emotionally evocative situation. The practitioner can suggest that the client write down their reflections in a diary after the actual encounter to integrate their practice of "core mindfulness." Through success experiences in everyday life, the client's self-confidence is likely to increase along with their long-term ability to achieve self-control over emotional and behavioral responses.

Self-regulation skills also include improvements in problem-solving skills (i.e., brainstorming, coming up with possible solutions, experimentation, and evaluation), utilizing self-reinforcement methods (e.g., "If I finish this project, I'll take myself out to dinner with a friend"), and learning to cope with minor setbacks and relapses without becoming overly despondent (e.g., a mistake is not the end of the world). Reminding clients to avoid "catastrophizing" and interpret problems as temporary setbacks can be reassuring for clients who tend to see things in extremes of success versus failure rather than their efforts as a work in progress.

Over time, as the client diagnosed with BPD begins to feel more confident as a result of some successes, practitioners can help them formulate an overall long-term plan to maintain their progress. Good health habits, maintaining positive relationships, moderating or abstaining from alcohol and other drugs, and maintaining financial stability can help avoid crises and maintain long-term satisfaction in life. Clients should also be reassured that seeking help in the future during times of stress is a sign of strength and good judgment, not weakness or failure.

Clients diagnosed with BPD or those who demonstrate similar problems can also be helped through the coordinating efforts of case management. Given the nature of these clients' difficulties with emotional regulation and impulse control, crises do occur, and many of these clients also exhibit co-occurring problems and disorders. Practitioners should be prepared to access and coordinate a range of services including psychiatric emergency rooms, detoxification facilities, as well as other treatment services as needed. Clients with BPD who also struggle with maintaining stability in the community may also need help with additional social and instrumental supports. Lastly, it is important to keep in mind that the problems associated with BPD are not *unique* to BPD. Many people experience various degrees of emotional and interpersonal upheaval in their lives and difficulties regulating their behaviors. The skills employed with clients diagnosed with BPD are applicable to other disorders marked by problems in emotional and behavioral coping.

Summary of Essential Skills for Substance Abuse and Personality Disorders

There is a range of common essential supportive, coping, and case management skills that, when offered in optimal combinations, can provide effective care for clients with substance use and personality disorders, conditions that often co-occur. Although many of these clients are also considered "resistant" or "hard to treat," they provide a potentially gratifying challenge for the practitioner who has strong personal boundaries, a deep reservoir of empathy and patience, and a strong commitment to help these clients lead more useful and satisfying lives. Variations of cognitive-behavioral coping skills implemented within a well-coordinated case management framework have been shown to be the most promising approaches for many of these clients.

Case Study: Nikki

Nikki is a nineteen-year-old white woman who was recently referred to an out-patient mental health clinic after having been admitted involuntarily (via the hospital's emergency room) to an in-patient psychiatric facility for two weeks. She had been found unconscious on the street by police responding to an anonymous phone call. They found her on the sidewalk in front of an abandoned building in the industrial end of the city. Apparently, Nikki was highly intoxicated on alcohol and also had other drugs, including hallucinogens, amphetamines, and marijuana, in her bloodstream. After a few days of detoxification on the in-patient unit, she became more forthcoming about her difficulties over the previous few years.

The Comprehensive Service Plan (Assessment, Intervention, Evaluation)

Use all available information from the client and significant others, your observations, and input from other professionals to conduct both quantitative and qualitative aspects of this multidimensional-functional assessment.

Client identification data: (gender; age; marital status; sexual orientation; family composition; employment; racial, ethnic, cultural, religious/spiritual affiliation and identity, etc.)

Nikki is a nineteen-year-old white single female. Aside from occasional contact with her estranged mother, she has no other family. She has never obtained regular employment, and she claims to be a member of a satanic religion (she maintains it is not a cult). She was not raised in any formal religious denomination and is of mixed northern-European ancestry.

The presenting problem

Description of problem (client's view)

Nikki maintains that, aside from being "down" once in a while, she doesn't really have any problems. She feels she was "having a bad day" when the police found her and that she does not need psychological or psychiatric care. She feels that she needs to recommit to her satanic beliefs and, perhaps, be more careful about the amount and mix of drugs she uses.

Description of problem (practitioner's view)

This practitioner believes that Nikki has had a long-standing problem with depression, very poor self-esteem, has engaged in much self-loathing, and appears to engage in many high-risk behaviors, including self-mutilation, high-risk sexual behaviors, and uncontrolled drug abuse. The social network with whom she associates is engaged in criminal behavior, and she has been sexually assaulted on numerous occasions by members of this group. She also appears to maintain a range of implausible beliefs, notwithstanding the fact that she claims they are religious in nature. She also claims to be able to foretell the future, read people's minds, and sometimes control others' behavior through the intercession of Satan. Thus, Nikki maintains a number of implausible and dysfunctional beliefs, has extreme difficulties maintaining her mood and regulating her emotions, engages in a number of high-risk behaviors that are potentially very harmful to herself (in addition to direct self-mutilation), has very poor interpersonal relationships, often with people who are clearly exploiting her. She has no employment history, educational deficits, and no social supports.

Psychosocial history with an emphasis on problem trajectory

Nikki reports that, since she dropped out of her junior year in high school, she had been living on the street with a "group of people like me." Apparently, the group is reported to be a self-styled group of satanists who practice black masses and similar rituals. These "meetings" usually involve getting together in known abandoned buildings on the outskirts of the city, using large amounts of alcohol, drugs, and "anything else we feel like using," engaging in various "anti-god" rituals, and having indiscriminate sex. Upon describing these events, it soon became apparent that some of the sexual encounters amounted to sexual assault. Nikki reports that the members often pool their money in order to survive, and members engage in a variety of part-time occupations, some legal and some not. Illegal activities include selling drugs, prostitution, and doing errands (e.g., delivering or selling drugs) for local criminal gangs. Nikki claims that she attempted suicide because she felt that she no longer wanted to belong to this group, and there did not seem to be any way out.

Nikki was raised by both her parents until she was about twelve years old. The parents considered themselves to be members of a group of self-described "pagan witches." Her father, Ted, worked odd jobs, was a heavy drinker, used drugs, and was often verbally abusive to Nikki. He and her mother, Lucy, who claimed to be a pagan "faith healer" and expert in reading "Tarot," would often have sex in the home without making any effort to shield Nikki from these encounters. Often, other friends and associates of theirs would participate in group sexual encounters. Nikki often witnessed these, and when she was eleven, she was raped by one of the male participants, an acquaintance of her father. This act was, apparently, beyond even her mother's tolerance, and she told her husband to leave or she would call the police and report the rape. He left and has not been heard from since.

Nikki and her mother continued in a rather tumultuous relationship. Nikki reported having little or no limits. Her mother continued to have friends and lovers in, although she was more discrete about her relationships and sexual activities after Ted was gone. Nikki began using alcohol and marijuana at age twelve, began missing school, and somehow remained enrolled in classes until she was sixteen. She dropped out of school after the first week of her junior year.

After dropping out of school, her mother told her she could no longer live with her, and Nikki joined a group of acquaintances who lived primarily on the streets of the nearby city. Homeless youths in that locale have been caught sleeping in some of the local abandoned buildings and are suspected of being responsible for a number of crimes including slashing people on the street with box cutters as a form of initiation. Youth workers have identified a number of them as heavy drug users, peripherally involved with some criminal gangs, and are known to be at higher risk of contracting sexually transmitted diseases. Nikki was diagnosed with an STD but negative for the AIDS virus.

Although she has had various tattoos for three years now as well as having adorned herself with metal objects (pierced tongue, ears, eyebrows, and other body parts), over the past year she has taken to using a box cutter to carve satanic designs in her skin. She claims that one particular design has to be recarved weekly to "keep it fresh for Satan, my lover." She believes that through this bodily portal, she receives his strength. Thus, the place where she maintains the design is particularly mutilated and is often bleeding. She claims that when the police found her, she had slit her wrist, not really meaning to do it, but felt hopeless and that even Satan had abandoned her.

Attempts to resolve the problems, previous treatment, and relevant outcomes

Nikki, despite her problems, has managed to survive for three years on the street, occasionally using homeless shelters, has contacted the homeless youth workers, has managed through some legal means to obtain temporary work (usually "off the books"), and is (despite her high-risk behaviors) in good health overall. She has never had formal treatment to quell her high-risk behaviors, possible mood disorder, or substance abuse.

The individual assessment

Mental status—cognitive disturbances: Describe the client's level of hallucinations, delusions, disorientation, bizarre behavior or speech, memory problems, serious confusion, or other symptoms of serious cognitive impairment. Include other troubling or dysfunctional beliefs or convictions.

Although client manifests no clear thought disorders on the level of hallucinations, at a minimum, the client may entertain some delusional beliefs about her abilities to predict the future, read people's minds, and affect their behaviors through mind control (with the devil's help). However, since people of various other religions claim as much, a conservative view would suggest that the client maintains some odd or implausible beliefs outside the boundaries of ordinary religious practices. Despite these apparently grandiose ideas, she does seem to have a very low opinion of herself and routinely puts herself in circumstances where she is likely to encounter risk of harm. She expresses some degree of hopelessness about her situation and is not particularly oriented toward the future (i.e., she does not discuss plans beyond daily survival).

How would you rate the client's overall mental status during the past month?

POOR [0]   IMPAIRED [1]   MARGINAL [2]   GOOD [3]   EXCELLENT [4]

Mental status—emotional distress: Describe the client's level of depression, anxiety, and overall ability to regulate her/his emotions.

Client appears to be extremely depressed, although Nikki maintains that she is usually "OK." Her affect is almost flat, she expresses extreme pessimism about herself, the world, her future, and reports little pleasure in life aside from drug-related experiences. It is hard, because of her lifestyle, to get a baseline on her sleeping and eating habits since they are so irregular anyway. She does report angry outbursts, occasional physical fights, and expresses an enormous amount of rage toward her parents, other people she has kept company with on the street, and society in general. Her mood swings are likely to be related to her drug use, but it is hard to determine at this point what her moods are generally like since she has had only two weeks of sobriety since detoxification.

> How would you rate your client's emotional well-being over the past thirty days?
>
> POOR [0]   IMPAIRED [1]   MARGINAL [2]   GOOD [3]   EXCELLENT [4]

Behavioral problems: Describe your client's overall ability to regulate her/his behavior. Consider things such as their ability to express her/himself effectively, ability to work at things patiently, tendencies to verbally or physically lash out at others, run away, harm her/himself, or proneness to impulsive, criminal, or substance-abusing behavior. How would you describe the client's overall impulse control?

Nikki's high-risk behaviors and impulsivity in general are a major concern. She appears to manifest little judgment or concern about the risks associated with the people with whom she consorts, sexual behaviors, and her drug use. Her emotional outbursts have often been associated with fighting, although she tends to describe these incidents as primarily justified by self-defense.

> How would you rate your client's behavioral control generally over the past thirty days?
>
> POOR [0]   IMPAIRED [1]   MARGINAL [2]   GOOD [3]   EXCELLENT [4]

Adaptive strengths and coping abilities: Describe your client's ability to cope with problems and everyday stressors. How would you describe the client's ability to assess problem situations, deal with "triggers," cope with stress, solve problems, and perhaps reach out to others for help in order to deal effectively with her/his difficulties?

As noted above, Nikki does demonstrate quite a bit of resourcefulness and "street smarts." She has survived on the streets with little external financial support for about three years. She is articulate and has written some interesting poetry, although the subject matter is disturbing. She has published two pieces in the local homeless persons' newspaper.

> How would you rate your client's overall adaptive strengths and coping abilities over the past thirty days?
>
> POOR [0]   IMPAIRED [1]   MARGINAL [2]   GOOD [3]   EXCELLENT [4]

Health problems: Describe the client's overall health. Aside from normal, transient illnesses, think about the client's general health habits (e.g., smoking, heavy drinking, exercise, weight), chronic primary health disorders, the client's opinion of her/his own health, ability to engage in her/his usual activities relatively free from discomfort, overall energy level, hospitalizations and treatments for illness other than psychiatric ones. Consider her/his documented medical history and any ongoing treatments.

Aside from her diagnosed STD (now being treated), her being somewhat malnourished, and some superficial wounds, the client is in relatively good health. Long-term concerns include the fact that she may continue to use illicit substances and the fact that she has smoked cigarettes since she was fifteen years old.

How would you rate your client's health over the past thirty days?

POOR [0]   IMPAIRED [1]   MARGINAL [2]   <u>GOOD [3]</u>   EXCELLENT [4]

Use of alcohol and other drugs: Describe the client's use of alcohol, illicit substances (cocaine, heroin, marijuana, hallucinogens, etc.) and abuse of prescription medication. How often does the client use them, in what quantity, and how serious are the psychological, physical, or social consequences associated with their use?

As best as can be determined, at this point, the client has been a regular user of alcohol since she was thirteen years old and began using marijuana about that time as well. In more recent years she has also used hallucinogenic drugs including psilocybin, mescaline, and a variety of MDMA-type drugs that also typically include amphetamines. Although she has also used crack cocaine in the past year or so, she has never injected drugs, never used narcotics (e.g., heroin), and has never abused pharmaceuticals claiming that the drug companies are not to be trusted in any way. Much of the use of hallucinogens appears to be associated with the "satanic" rituals engaged in by her with her associates, but her usual (often daily) drugs of abuse seem to be alcohol (inexpensive vodka or wine) and marijuana. When the police found her unconscious, she was primarily intoxicated on alcohol and marijuana. When she was detoxified during hospitalization there was no evidence of delirium tremens, and she was not sedated during that time.

How would you rate the client's functioning in the past month with regard to substance use?

POOR [o]   IMPAIRED [1]   MARGINAL [2]   GOOD [3]   EXCELLENT [4]

Recreational activities: Consider what the client does for fun (alone or with others), hobbies, relaxation (reading, TV, video games, playing cards, etc.) and physical exercise (walking, jogging, biking, etc.). How would you describe the client's overall involvement in positive recreational activities?

Other than occasional TV watching, the client reports few recreational activities. Although she has occasionally written and published poems as noted above, she spends most of her daily activities procuring small amounts of money and looking for supplies of food, alcohol, and places to spend the night.

How would you rate the adequacy of the client's participation in healthy recreational activities over the past thirty days?

POOR [o]   IMPAIRED [1]   MARGINAL [2]   GOOD [3]   EXCELLENT [4]

Material resources: Describe your client's current or (if client is institutionalized) most recent living situation overall. Consider such things as adequacy of food, clothing, shelter, and safety.

Although client has managed to survive on the streets, in a conventional sense her access to material resources is quite impaired.

How would you rate the overall adequacy of the client's material resources over the past month?

POOR [o]   IMPAIRED [1]   MARGINAL [2]   GOOD [3]   EXCELLENT [4]

Independent living/self-care: Describe how well your client manages her/his household, takes care of personal hygiene, eats, sleeps, and otherwise cares for her/his own basic needs.

Similar to comment above: client is surviving minimally.

How would you rate the client's ability to live independently and take care of their basic needs over the past thirty days?

POOR [0]　IMPAIRED [1]　MARGINAL [2]　GOOD [3]　EXCELLENT [4]

Work (role) satisfaction: Describe the client's current work-related or other important role-related activities (e.g., employed, student, homemaker, volunteer, retired person, disabled, etc.). Describe those activities and responsibilities that occupy the client in a productive manner.

Other than surviving, the client has serious educational deficits and has little record of employment. Other than surviving on the streets, she has embraced little by way of a productive role.

How would you rate the client's work or role satisfaction over the past thirty days?

POOR [0]　IMPAIRED [1]　MARGINAL [2]　GOOD [3]　EXCELLENT [4]

Legal problems: Describe any legal problems the client has had or continues to have. These include minor infractions (e.g., public drunkenness, shoplifting inexpensive items, minor traffic violations, public disturbances) and more serious crimes (e.g., assault and battery, rape, burglary, driving under the influence, etc.). Consider his/her status (probation, awaiting imprisonment, parole). Also, consider any civil suits leveled at the client, pending financial judgments against her/him, and so on. Overall, how would you describe the client's current legal situation?

Surprisingly, despite her activities, the client has no outstanding legal charges or judgments against her. She has never been charged with a crime. Although confronted by the police on a number of occasions, they have only referred her to the homeless shelters and encouraged her to seek mental health or substance abuse treatment.

How would you rate the client's legal situation over the past thirty days?

POOR [0]　IMPAIRED [1]　MARGINAL [2]　GOOD [3]　EXCELLENT [4]

DSM-5 Diagnosis

Alcohol use disorder, moderate, 303.90
Cannabis use disorder, 304.30
Persistent depressive disorder, 300.4
Borderline personality disorder, 301.83

Family relations: Describe the client's current family structure, including authority, hierarchy, alliances, roles, rules, boundaries, subsystems (e.g., couple, siblings, parent-child alliances); patterns of interactions and quality of communications; specific problems within the family; specific adaptive strengths within the family; and how the family members describe their own racial, ethnic, cultural, and religious identities.

Although she has had occasional phone conversations with her mother, Nikki has seen little of her over the past two years. Her mother did visit her in the hospital during the two weeks she was in-patient. They tentatively agreed to meet, perhaps during out-patient sessions. Other than this connection, Nikki has no family relations to speak of.

How would you rate the quality of the client's immediate family relationships over the past thirty days?

POOR [o]   IMPAIRED [1]   MARGINAL [2]   GOOD [3]   EXCELLENT [4]

Immediate Social Relationships (close friends and acquaintances): Describe the quality of your client's relationships with those available friends and acquaintances, as applicable. Over the past month, how would you describe the quality of the interaction overall between your client and them with respect to closeness, intimacy, general interpersonal satisfaction, effective communications, degree of conflict, level of hostility, aggression, and evidence of any emotional or physical abuse?

Despite the risky and dysfunctional nature of her peer group, they are the only social supports that she has, and they do provide some level of companionship and material support. Some of her relationships within the group do not appear to be abusive. Although these would not generally be considered "healthy" associations, in light of the lack of any other supports, they do assist her in daily survival.

How would you rate the quality of the client's immediate social relation-ships over the past thirty days?

POOR [0]   IMPAIRED [1]   MARGINAL [2]   GOOD [3]   EXCELLENT [4]

Extended social relationships: Describe the type and quality of relation-ships between your client and others in the client's community (other than close friends and family). These people might include other families, law enforcement, human service agencies, school personnel, coworkers, and others from whom the client receives support or with whom the client is having serious conflict.

The police, workers in the homeless shelters, members of voluntary organi-zations, and a variety of other informal contacts in the community (some store owners, restaurant workers, etc.) have provided a tangible level of social and material support for Nikki. She seems to know a lot of people and some appear to be motivated by good will.

How would you rate the quality of the client's social relationships over the past thirty days?

POOR [0]   IMPAIRED [1]   MARGINAL [2]   GOOD [3]   EXCELLENT [4]

A concise summary of the MFS assessment: Highlight the client's areas of distress and adaptive strengths. Emphasize those areas that are most likely to be emphasized in the intervention plan.

Nikki is a homeless, drug- and alcohol-dependent, depressed, and otherwise interpersonally impoverished young woman who engages in a range of behaviors that carry a high risk of self-harm. Her views of herself, others, and the future are quite negative and pessimistic. She appears to be chroni-cally depressed and chronically abuses drugs, engages in self-mutilation, and has maintained only marginal relationships with people also addicted to drugs. She maintains some unusual beliefs associated with an unconven-tional type of religion but otherwise demonstrates no clear mental illness (i.e., psychosis). Her lack of long-term family nurturance, healthful role modeling, and normative disciplining appear to have left her interperson-ally and emotionally impoverished. Although she has developed some impressive survival skills, she is likely to deteriorate on the streets in coming years without psychological intervention and long-term social and material rehabilitative supports.

Recommendations for further focused assessment (note recommended referrals to consultants or additional instruments to be used)

More intensive substance use assessment and psychiatric assessment for possible use of medication.

THE COMPREHENSIVE SERVICE PLAN SUMMARY

Assessment/Problems	Goals	Objectives	Interventions	Evaluation plan
(Briefly describe key problems to be addressed.)	(State desired outcome for each problem.)	(Describe specific "stepping stones" toward each GOAL. Update as client progresses)	(Describe specific interventions to be used.)	(Describe indexes to be used for tracking progress.)
Severe, chronic depression; suicidal ideation	Reduce depression, suicidal ideation to minimal levels	Begin examining cognitions regarding sense of hopelessness about herself and her situation; have her monitor weekly	*Supportive skills:* Develop collaborative working relationship with client and focus on initial motivation; acknowledge initial distrust, suspicion	Monitor and report level of hopelessness weekly: o ("hopeless") through 10 ("very optimistic")
Hopelessness, negative appraisal of self/others	Improve self-image	Begin to identify emotional responses and link to negative thoughts and problem behaviors; monitor as above	*Therapeutic coping skills:* Examine and review client's negative beliefs about self; explore nature of relationships with others (including effects of family upbringing); later, explore and challenge unusual religious convictions and beliefs in her own paranormal powers	Have her note any occasion of self-mutilation and her cognitions, mood, and circumstances prior to it
Difficulties regulating emotions, impulsivity, self-mutilation, and other impulsive behaviors	Develop better controls over emotional regulation and impulsive behaviors	Identify "triggers" that potentiate relapse		Have her self-report type, frequency, and quantity of drug abuse and antecedent mood or events
Drug abuse	Reduce/eliminate abuse of alcohol and other drugs	Examine nature of relationships; identify best mutually supportive relationship she has had recently; consider scheduling a meeting with her mother at a future date to discuss tentative ongoing relationship	Help client identify disturbing thoughts and upsetting feelings; help client learn to accept and tolerate distress without responding impulsively (including both self-harming behaviors as well as responding by using alcohol and other drugs, etc.)	
Lack of meaningful interpersonal relationships including estrangement from her mother (only available family member)	Examine potential for more satisfying relationships/explore potential for reconciliation with mother			
Educational and employment deficits and related lack of instrumental supports	Assess employment potential and completing high school equivalency	Consider residence in halfway house for at least six months; participate in skills review for possible part-time employment		

Teach basic stress management (e.g., breathing, meditation) to cope with stress, emotional distress, and upset; role model and practice drug-refusal skills

Coach clients in conversational and other interpersonal skills that she may practice during her stay in halfway house residence

Coach conversations in sessions with mother (later in treatment) focused on potential reconciliation

Case management skills:
Facilitate psychiatric referral and follow-up as needed

Review social supports and link client to mutual help groups

Review potential instrumental supports and other available financial benefits

Explore opportunities to complete G.E.D., and/or obtain skills training or supported employment

CHAPTER TEN

Couples in Conflict

ONE WOULD BE HARD PRESSED to find a committed couple where the partners did not experience some degree of conflict and relationship distress. Partners who are very much in love and highly committed to one another will disagree about any or all matters covering a wide range of topics: how to raise their children, how to spend their money, how to balance domestic responsibilities, what types of relationships each partner can have outside the marriage, how to best cope with in-laws and other relatives, where to go on vacation, and so on. The difference between marriages that fail and marriages that thrive is reflected in the research findings on good marriages: partners who maintain longstanding and loving relationships treat each other with respect, are willing to compromise, and are effective communicators and problem solvers, that is, they reconcile differences constructively and without doing harm to one another. In a word, committed couples also have problems, but they learn to cope with them more effectively (Gottman, 1993a,b, 1998).

One should be mindful of the fact, however, that much of what is now considered the "good marriage" in middle-class America is somewhat tied to the idea of the "egalitarian" relationship. Although many heterosexual and same-sex couples willingly embrace the idea of equality and "power sharing" in marriage, couples from some religious and cultural traditions do not share the same view that marriage is a collaboration of equal partners. Instead, men and women must subscribe to specific roles in marriage that are not "equal." Thus, before applying the essential skills of assessment and intervention with a couple, one should ask the couple to help the practitioner understand their beliefs and expectations regarding what they consider to be the "good marriage" before commencing to improve their relationship skills. In addition, with many couples not marrying and with divorce rates ranging from 40 to 50 percent (Birditt, Brown, Orbuch, & McIlvane, 2010), most families in the United States do not have two adult parents or guardians in the home. The conventional "nuclear family" is now a statistical minority. One should also be open to a broader definition of what constitutes the "family unit" and work with available adults whether they are partners "just living together," relatives from different generations, family kinship relationships, and so forth. Family assessments based on conventional views of the family are less relevant than they were a few decades ago.

Couple conflicts are sometimes associated with a wide range of problems, many of them potentially quite serious. These problems include: domestic violence, child abuse and neglect, substance abuse, isolation from the wider community (e.g., neighbors, schools), and other co-occurring disorders such as anxiety disorders, depression, and other forms of mental illness (Caetano, Vaeth, & Ramisetty-Mikler, 2008; Joutsenniemi, Moustgaard, Koskinen, Ripatti, & Martikainen, 2011; Kolves, Ide, & de Leo, 2010; Schonbrun & Whisman, 2010). Couple conflicts and divorce can have short- and long-term effects on children: poor modeling for conflict resolution, shame, anger, guilt, depression, and negative outlook on intimacy and long-term commitments (Clavarino et al., 2011; Stutzman et al., 2011). Thus, assessment and intervention with couples often provide a foundation for additional work with children and the family as a whole. Interventions applied within the context of family therapy to address emotional and behavioral disturbances in children and adolescents will be addressed in the following two chapters.

Assessment

It is helpful to conceptualize couple problems in terms of both content and process. Clearly identifying *what* (content) couples are conflicted about and *how* (process) they attempt to cope (e.g., communication patterns) provides two important avenues for completing the assessment and developing the intervention plan. As with an individual assessment, it is important to assess couples across multiple domains. One should begin by simply asking the couple to take turns describing what they see as the problem from their point of view. However, relying exclusively only on what each partner presents in an unstructured narrative will result in an inadequate assessment for at least these three reasons: (1) the couple may simply not be aware of how one problem in their relationship affects another (e.g., couple problems causing emotional or behavioral problems in their children, effects of depression or substance abuse on the other partner); (2) they may not be aware of how problems with their children may be straining the marriage as well (e.g., differences in child-rearing practices may be rooted in personal history or cultural differences); and (3) they may have reason to lie in order to cover up embarrassing or even criminal behavior (e.g., child abuse, illicit drug deal use). Thus, a multidimensional assessment of both the couple and each individual client is necessary.

As noted earlier, couples tend to engage in conflict over a number of relatively common concerns: relationship commitment and sex, personal finances, child rearing, relationships with extended families, sharing household responsibilities. Certainly, there are others. It is important to allow each partner to explain, from his/her point of view, what each sees as the problem. Listening carefully, patiently, and respectfully provides effective modeling for the other partner (who should be discouraged from interrupting). It demonstrates to each partner, in turn, how to listen attentively, acknowledge that the message is understood, and accept what their partner is saying (even as they disagree) in both content and feeling. One does the same as the other partner takes the opportunity to explain his side of the story. The very act of each partner saying what they feel as the other partner listens can be a compelling experience for both—possibly the first time they have engaged in respectful listening for weeks or months. Such an experience can set a new tone for further discussion, a feeling of "starting fresh."

After both partners have had a chance to express their views, the practitioner should explore the experience further: "Frank, what were you thinking and feeling as you listened to Sharon tell her side of the story?" And then offer Sharon the same opportunity. Again, this experience provides them with another chance to engage in active listening as their spouse responds. At this point, it is likely that the "listening" partner will interrupt since the other partner is reacting, perhaps emotionally, to what their partner was saying. Again, the practitioner should gently discourage the partner from reacting and ask them to listen quietly and patiently. Orchestrating an experience where couples have to contain their emotional responses while listening to the other partner can be a rewarding experience for them—one that reinforces the belief that they can discuss emotionally upsetting content with one another without the discussion erupting into a destructive quarrel. Planned exchanges such as this during the office visit must be repeated at home during the week at mutually convenient and relaxing times. The couple should agree to a particular topic they want to discuss while with the practitioner during each visit.

Subjects should initially be chosen from the bottom of the problem hierarchy (start with easy problems first, then gradually work toward the tougher ones). But the couple must commit to respectful listening without interruption and accept that, even if they can't resolve the issue at hand, they can "agree to disagree" for the time being. This process might take a few weeks of practice, but it lays the foundation for successful couple intervention.

Although this listening exercise might sound more like an active part of the intervention (in fact, they are working on communication skills, to be discussed further below), it is actually an essential part of the assessment as well. The practitioner has the opportunity to observe closely how each partner acts in the presence of the other: what they say, how they say it, facial expressions, body language, and other behaviors. These behaviors can indicate how the couple behaves at home and, especially, how they treat one another. This "process" analysis is often at least as important as the actual content of their presenting complaints.

Once the partners are able to speak and listen to one another successfully without interruption, the assessment can continue. Practitioners should explore the details of their marital complaints in depth, again, giving each partner the chance to explain their side without interruption. An exhaustive list of problems and questions would fill a large volume, so a few examples are offered here.

- *Intimacy and commitment:* Do you spend time together? What do you like to do with each other? Do you both enjoy that? Do you actively make plans to spend time together? Do you avoid spending time together? Are you affectionate with one another? How do you express your affection for each other? What kind of personal friendships or other relationships do you maintain outside your marriage? Are any of them exclusive to one of you or the other? Are you both OK with those relationships? Do you share any friends in common?
- *Extended family:* Whose family do you see around the holidays? How did you come to that arrangement? How do you get along with one another's family members? Do any family members visit your home? How long do they usually stay? Are their any financial ties or obligations with any extended family members? Are there any conflicts with one another's family that cause either of you distress?
- *Work and home finances:* Do you both work outside the home? How many hours per week do you work, including your commuting time? Are your jobs stressful? How does your work affect your

mood when you are at home? Who pays the bills? Do you share responsibilities for paying the bills? Do you have separate checkbooks or credit card accounts? Do you maintain separate budgets? How is that working out? Do you fight about money? Are you having financial problems, such as excessive debt? Have you ever declared bankruptcy or have collection agencies come after you for unpaid obligations? Have you ever worked on a budget together? Do you discuss major purchases together?

- *Parenting:* Do you have a shared parenting philosophy, or do you often disagree about how you reward or discipline your child(ren)? What day-to-day expectations do you have of your child(ren) regarding their behavior and responsibilities in the home, school performance, social activities, and so on? What do you do if your children don't meet them or disobey you? How much fun time do you spend with your kids playing, reading, watching movies, and so forth? Do you do this together as parents or do you take turns depending on your schedule? What activities do your kids enjoy the most with you? Do these occasions often end in conflict? How does that come about usually?

- *Household obligations:* What routine chores need to be done around the house? Do you share in some or all of these activities, or delegate different jobs to one another? Do either of you feel that the distribution of domestic duties is unfair given the amount you work outside the home? Do your children participate in routine household duties? How does that work out?

Questions such as those above make very good openers for matter-of-fact discussions about the mundane aspects of everyday life. However, asking only one or two questions often opens a Pandora's box of conflict in other areas as well. Again, discussing the content of these problems is important in order to understand the couple's type and severity of difficulties, but it is equally important to observe their communication style, emotion, and body language as they discuss these matters. The level of affect (e.g., anger, distress, anxiety, sadness) and body language expressed during these discussions can often recreate the couple's distressing experiences quite realistically. With minimal coaching (and occasional refereeing), practitioners can obtain a relatively accurate re-creation of how the couple is struggling—their thoughts, feelings, behaviors, and the situations that precipitate conflict. The content of the couple's problems and strengths (both as individuals and as a couple) should cover all domains of psychosocial well-being, and an analysis of how the couple relates to one another will likely provide a firm foundation for detailed functional assessment.

Although most sessions should include both partners together, there are at least two reasons to interview each partner alone at least once: (1) they may have problems that are not the result of couple's conflict, but may contribute to the couple's problems; and (2) each partner may have a private agenda that they do not wish to discuss with the other partner. The purpose of conducting an individual assessment (in the presence of the other partner, if both agree to it) is to determine if each partner has any significant problems that may be affecting their relationship. These problems can be relatively common such as depression, anxiety and stress, substance abuse, criminal behavior, or other problems. History taking on these matters can certainly help to determine to some degree the age of onset and trajectory of these problems and to what extent couples problems are exacerbating the problem or, reciprocally, whether a long-standing problem with depression or substance abuse has been straining the couple's relationship. Disorders that are clearly longstanding and precede their relationship may require individual intervention and, possibly, referral (e.g., out-patient detoxification, medication, etc.) before couples work can resume. Conducting an individual assessment was covered in Chapter 4, and practitioners should follow the protocol with each partner individually.

As for this second point, practitioners need to know if there are problems that one partner has kept from the other (e.g., one partner is having a romantic affair, has huge gambling debts, or has a drug problem about which their partner is unaware, etc.). If a partner does have a secret, the practitioner needs to discuss with that person whether they are willing to reveal the secret at some point and, if so, what the consequences might be. If the client chooses not to reveal the secret, the practitioner needs to discuss with that individual whether couples work can realistically continue. These problems are sometimes difficult to resolve, and there are no solid guidelines for these types of dilemmas.

In addition to focusing on multiple problem domains (e.g., psychological, social, health, substance abuse, etc.) with each partner and as a couple, practitioners should also complete a detailed functional assessment building on the initial analysis of their communication style. How do these couples interact during times when things are going well in addition to when they are in conflict? What is the couple's typical week like? What situations or problems seem to trigger animosity or outright conflict? How does the couple fight? Do they simply avoid each other and "not talk about it," or do they fight openly? How long does the conflict and animosity last? What attempts do they make to short circuit the conflict or reconcile afterward? What additional problems seem to be related to the conflict?

What factors (e.g., external stressors at work, substance abuse, money problems, etc.) seem to precipitate conflict? Are these problems also the results of conflict?

Having the couple work together on a self-monitoring diary can be a helpful way to carry out a functional assessment of their life together, get the couple more engaged as participants in treatment, and give them an opportunity to collaborate as a couple on an important task. Practitioners can instruct the couple to construct the diary over the course of two weeks. The partners should keep this task simple by having the couple take brief notes about their daily schedule, key behaviors, important events, what they did, and how they felt about what was happening. By working closely with the couple to recreate their typical weekly scenario, one can obtain a relatively accurate and intimate view of their daily lives. Although this approach may sound a bit pedestrian for some practitioners, recreating the details of everyday life is an excellent way to illuminate the highlights of when and why things go well or go poorly for the couple. As a young and inexperienced practitioner, the author was having a difficult time sorting out why a couple was routinely arguing, until I had them conduct a similar exercise and realized that they only fought intensely on Friday nights: after the husband came home from the local tavern having spent a good portion of his weekly pay. This oversight underscores a key point about conducting a thorough MFS assessment: if you don't ask, the client may not tell you! Knowing what risk factors are associated with couple's problems and knowing how clients' thoughts, feelings, behaviors, and situations interact over time provides an invaluable assessment template for understanding the couple's strengths and vulnerabilities. One can then collaborate on setting intervention priorities.

Intervention

A fair amount of controlled research has been conducted on interventions for couples' problems. In addition, other research has shown that couples therapy can be helpful for clients where one partner is suffering from a specific disorder such as depression, an anxiety disorder, or substance abuse (Shadish & Baldwin, 2005). Couples' interventions that have garnered the most evidence for effectiveness include emotion-focused therapy (EFT) (Greenberg, Warwar, & Malcomb, 2010; Johnson, 2007; Johnson & Greenberg, 1995; Snyder, Castellani, & Whisman, 2006) and behavioral couples therapy (BCT) (Fals-Stewart, Lam, & Kelly, 2009; Jacobson & Addis, 1993; Jacobson & Margolin, 1979; Lebow, 2000; O'Farrell & Fals-Stewart,

2003; O'Farrell & Schein, 2011; Shadish & Baldwin, 2005; Snyder, Castellani, & Whisman, 2006; Thomas & Corcoran, 2001). A meta-analysis of twelve selected studies covering 754 study participants generally confirmed the prior positive reviews of BCT (Powers, Vedel, & Emmelkamp, 2008), underscoring its effectiveness with substance abusing couples as well as gay and lesbian couples (Fals-Stewart, O'Farrell, & Lam, 2009). Although EFT and BCT are two distinct approaches, the essential skills of both models will be presented here in an eclectic framework highlighting what seem to be complementary aspects: the importance of both partners learning to communicate empathically to better understand the sources of one another's emotional distress as well as engage in mutually reinforcing behaviors and effective problem solving.

Accurate listening and empathic responses are central to the helping relationship, regardless of the presenting problem, and working with couples provides the practitioner with the opportunity to model these skills. As each partner, in turn, addresses the practitioner at various points in an interview, the other partner has the opportunity to watch closely as the practitioner listens, subtly encourages further expression, and then responds in a way that helps the speaking partner feel respected and understood. This experience can be invaluable for each partner and provides them both with a template they can reference when they are practicing these critical skills at home. The practitioner teaches this skill through modeling. The practitioner demonstrates that listening requires giving the "other" your undivided attention and respecting and accepting what is being said, even when the other partner is communicating emotionally charged material that might be critical and hurtful to the listener.

Supportive skills also facilitate the setting of intervention goals. Helping couples build a problem hierarchy can help them feel less hopeless or out of control. In this way, supportive skills also help bolster the couple's morale. Many couples are quite pessimistic when they begin couples work after having been demoralized after months or years of conflict. In addition, one or both partners may not be ready to make any changes, or may be at different stages of readiness to change. Supportive skills can be used to encourage clients to weigh the pros and cons of change, even after having been in a troubled relationship for many years.

Supportive skills lay the groundwork for implementing the key skills of EFT. A cornerstone of EFT is to help (through modeling, rehearsal, and practice) each partner attend to the other's emotional responses. This approach involves the use of basic supportive skills including attentive, empathic, and active listening discussed earlier. It also includes having partners demonstrate through clear empathic communication that each really understands what the other is saying and feeling. The recognition and mutual understanding of each other's emotional responses is central to maintaining feelings of trust and intimacy. It also lays the groundwork for helping the partners recognize the "re-cycling" of dysfunctional relationship patterns that may have been learned in one's family of origin or in a previous intimate relationship.

Of course, getting to the point where partners can communicate empathically with one another and demonstrate a willingness to communicate on a deep emotional level often requires wading through some emotional conflict. As common sense suggests, relationships do not develop independently from the effects of our interpersonal history. Everyone has a relationship history of some kind, usually beginning with our parents. The effects and consequences of relationships over the years cumulatively influence the strengths and deficits we bring to an intimate relationship as well as our selection of partners. For some, being in an intimate relationship is easy, exciting, and relatively conflict free; for others, intimacy is anxiety provoking, disappointing, and fraught with frustration, anger, ambivalence, and conflict. Some people have had close, caring relationships with their parents and siblings as children, and these lessons carried over to the formation of close friendships and close intimate romantic relationships. Others who grew up with chronic conflict with adults who provided poor modeling in respectful communication and effective problem solving have more difficulty maintaining satisfying intimate relationships as adults. Regardless of history, however, adults who succeed in successfully cultivating deep intimacy seem to have the ability to communicate feelings accurately and show a deliberate willingness to attend to the feeling states of their partner in an authentic way. These behaviors are more likely to result in satisfying long-term relationships. It is the acquisition of these skills that the practitioner attempts to impart to troubled couples in EFT.

The core skills of EFT can help conflicted and emotionally troubled partners cultivate emotional attunement if the practitioner provides sufficient support and helps each partner gradually take the necessary risks to be vulnerable with their partner. For individuals who have suffered emotional rejection, harsh criticism, trauma, or other forms of emotional and physical abuse by important people in their lives, the process of opening up to one's partner can be difficult. Practitioners need to establish a hierarchy of topics or problems to be addressed and, based on client level of emotional response, start with problems that evoke moderate levels of emotion before gradually moving up the hierarchy to matters that evoke more intense feelings. Gradual exposure to highly affect-laden material will work better than "diving right in," an approach that is likely to cause some clients to close up and even discontinue therapy.

Although learning to listen and empathize with one's partner lays the foundation for better communication and increased intimacy, these improvements might not be sufficient to resolve serious problems and maintain a healthy relationship over time. Learning to recognize and deal with emotional conflict is a coping skill, a skill that practitioners can facilitate and have partners practice with one another. Once underlying feelings are expressed and acknowledged by each partner, the practitioner can then help them link their feelings to past experiences. How did they come to feel this way? What prior experiences might account for some of these feelings? Are these feelings the result of a prior relationship in one's family of origin, a previous romantic relationship, or are they the result of harm incurred in the current relationship?

Practitioners who employ EFT endeavor to help couples reenact the core emotional conflicts in the here and now, that is, to bring the past into the present by discussing conflicted themes that seem to echo from prior relationships. Once such a conflict presents itself in the present, practitioners and clients can name it and attempt to understand how it affects their current relationship. This interpretation or explanation linking previous and current conflicts can be instructive for partners, help them to better understand one another, engender mutual empathy, and help them to resolve their own conflicts in a more realistic light. As a result of improved understanding, the partners can be more accepting of each other and address their mutual needs in a more realistic and less distorted light. With practice, partners can help each other interrupt these negative interactive cycles.

It is also widely recognized that interpretation and improved understanding of "why we do what we do," although sometimes helpful, is not sufficient for lasting change. For partners to improve and maintain an intimate, stable relationship over time, they must maintain clear communication, become effective problem solvers, and improve the way they consistently behave toward each other. Insight means little if partners merely understand better why they have problems but fail to change the way they communicate, solve problems, and treat one another. Behavioral couples therapy has been shown to be effective because it emphasizes the need for partners to take responsibility for their own behavior and sustain mutually rewarding behaviors over time.

There are two major areas where partners can improve: better communication and more successful problem solving. If increased empathic understanding is achieved initially (as described earlier), then improved communication skills can help sustain it over time. As mutual good will is built up, communication becomes easier, partners become more tolerant of minor infractions, and each is better prepared to take on problem solving when more serious conflicts arise. Again, practitioners must take the lead in modeling good communication skills. Careful and respectful listening, reflecting what one has heard, and allowing the other person to respond in order to verify that the message was understood accurately are essential skills that the couple need to practice throughout the course of couples therapy and their relationship. The process is repeated until each partner feels that they have gotten their message across and they have been adequately understood. Although the practitioner takes the initiative in modeling this process, clients should be encouraged to practice their skills in the session and during the week at home.

In addition to empathic listening and "taking turns" in the communication process, the practitioner can also help clients apply basic cognitive skills to help them avoid some of the communication pitfalls that often provoke conflict. These are the same critical thinking skills that were discussed in Chapter 2. During emotional encounters, partners may lapse into dysfunctional ways of making their points such as extreme exaggeration (i.e., catastrophizing), all-or-nothing thinking (dichotomizing), engaging in hindsight bias ("Monday morning quarter-backing"), and overgeneralizing. Other unhelpful and provocative habits can also destroy good will, including name calling, cursing, deliberately not listening to the other partner, interrupting the other partner while they are speaking, turning away and leaving the room in a fit of anger, or running out of the house (i.e., leaving in a huff). Of course, these behaviors, while not conducive to effective communication and problem solving, at least stop short of more extreme behaviors, such as shoving, spitting, kicking, hitting, and other more dangerous forms of aggression often associated with domestic violence. Nevertheless, learning to "keep the temperature down" by using effective communication skills and not resorting to more emotionally provocative methods can reduce the likelihood that verbal arguments will escalate into physical violence, a problem for which younger couples are at greater risk.

If the couple can begin mastering effective communication skills, they will then be prepared for addressing some of those "content" problems: money matters, parenting, extended family conflict, collaborating on household tasks, and so on. Problem-solving skills involve identifying the problem, expressing each other's views clearly and calmly, brainstorming a hierarchy of possible solutions together, putting the plan in motion, and honestly evaluating the results. If, for example, a couple disagrees on how to handle an adolescent son's disobedience (e.g., staying out after their allotted time, smoking marijuana, hanging out with known gang members), they can consider a hierarchy of potential solutions that consists of having the family discuss house rules, initiating mild sanctions (no TV or video games), revoking other privileges, or resorting to restrictions on the youth's freedom (i.e., grounding). The couple may disagree about how to proceed. One partner may want to be more lenient, while the other may want to consider a more aggressive approach. The practitioner can help them come to a consensus such as beginning with lighter restrictions first and then moving up the hierarchy to more-restrictive methods as needed. If the couple sticks together on the plan and evaluates each step honestly, they will either succeed or have to resort to more assertive methods. The fact that they work collaboratively on the project might, in itself, have positive effects on their son's behavior as well. Children and adolescents often feel a profound sense of disappointment and anger when their parents engage in conflict over parenting practices and can't "get it together."

BCT works on the assumption that the quality of a relationship depends on the couple's ability to engage in mutually pleasing (i.e., reciprocally and positively reinforcing) behavior. Although it would seem ideal if a sense of mutual caring could be enacted through empathic listening alone, often "actions speak louder than words," and behavior changes more readily increase a sense of mutual good will. To get things started, the practitioner needs to carefully interview the partners in the presence of one another to find out what behaviors each finds pleasing and rewarding. This discussion alone can be an epiphany for some couples since they have engaged in years of "mind reading" rather than asking each other what the other likes. This phenomenon can cover a host of areas, from preferences for food, entertainment, sex, and social engagements to housework, vacation plans, getting together with extended family, and money matters. After taking a thorough inventory of preferences, the couple can then develop a hierarchy of intervention goals. Assuming there are no emerging crises to address, gradually moving up the hierarchy from easier challenges (e.g., sharing housework) to the more difficult (e.g., having extended family members as houseguests) is recommended. As couples therapy evolves from demonstrating good listening skills, empathy, and mutual understanding to following through consistently with behaviors that demonstrate love and commitment to the other partner, couples stand a real chance of maintaining a constant and loving relationship over time.

Adapting Couples Work for Specific Problems:
The Example of a Substance Use Disorder

Most clinical research on couples work with substance use disorders has been conducted with behavioral couples therapy (e.g., Epstein et al., 2007; O'Farrell & Fals-Stewart, 2003; O'Farrell & Schein, 2011). Substance use disorders are both common and difficult to treat, and special considerations need to be met prior to undertaking couples intervention for this specific problem. As indicated in Chapter 9, understanding different drug effects and recognizing the psychosocial and health consequences of substance abuse is necessary in order to conduct a thorough assessment in couples where the abuse of alcohol or other drugs is a factor. Substance abuse problems can be highly variable, often do not follow the expected trajectory of "stage" theories, and can be addressed with a number of different goals in mind depending on the client: reduction in use, changing the context of use (i.e., harm reduction), or abstinence. Partial successes toward any of these goals should be rewarded, and constant monitoring and evaluation is required over long periods of time to maintain successful outcomes. Often, one partner seeks treatment initially and the other joins later. However, practitioners should be prepared to engage in "couples work" with only one partner (unilateral therapy), a topic that will be addressed briefly at the end of this section.

Practitioners should be prepared, especially early on in treatment, to intervene in crises as needed. Binge drinking, drug overdoses, domestic violence, child welfare interventions, hospitalizations, police interventions, and so forth, are all potential occurrences that accompany work with substance abusing clients. Medical consultation is also very likely with the prescribing of psychiatric medications (e.g., antidepressants, antianxiety drugs) as well as drugs that help some clients initially stay clean and sober (e.g., naltrexone, disulfiram). In BCT, the nonaddicted spouse participates in the medication regimen by monitoring the addicted client's cooperation in taking their medication. After a period of initial stability, BCT practitioners emphasize implementing homework assignments and engaging in behavioral rehearsal. These may include practicing basic communication and problem-solving skills for, initially, smaller problems and gradually taking on the more difficult ones as success experiences accumulate. It is important early in treatment to increase a sense of "good will" through improved empathic communication in order to take on the difficult work of helping the substance abusing partner remain clean and sober or continue cutting down, as the case may be. Helping the abusing partner deal with urges to drink by finding alternative behaviors (e.g., taking walks together, going to the movies) or reducing other "at risk situations" (e.g., planning grocery shopping together rather than stopping off at the bar, skipping what was formerly "cocktail hour" at home) are structural changes that can help the drinking or drug using spouse stretch out that important initial period of sobriety. Other coping skills, such as those discussed in Chapter 9, can be facilitated by one partner and rehearsed in couples work as well. Stress management, improved social skills, engaging in "drink refusal" skills when in social situations can be practiced together at home.

The initial period of sobriety can be difficult for both partners. But, if they are successful in avoiding a serious relapse, couples can move to the next step of improving their relationship, a step that can also be challenging if their mutual problems have been long standing. But, if they succeed, the improvement in the quality of that relationship can provide a bulwark of support for the addicted partner and help them reduce the chances of relapse. One step couples can take is to plan special days when they simply devote much of their time to something that is mutually pleasing—taking a short trip together, going for a hike, working in the garden, taking in a ball game, and so on. These activities should be opportunities to engage in non-drinking events that both can enjoy. After a period of sobriety and after "good will" has improved, the same skills can be applied to other problems as well. However, couples and practitioners should be prepared to continue working on relapse prevention strategies simultaneously. Identifying potential "triggers" of drinking and drug use, having ready alternatives, knowing what to do if there is a "slip," and having a contingency plan to recover from it quickly should continue for as long as necessary.

A Unilateral Strategy for Helping the Spouse of a Substance Abuser

Should the substance abusing partner simply refuse to engage in treatment, "couples" work can continue with the nonabusing spouse. Although there are variations of this approach, they share common skills. Practitioners should conduct an extensive assessment of the substance user's history (based on the attending partner's report) and of the couple's current difficulties. Nonabusing partners often unwittingly engage in behaviors that indirectly reinforce the spouse's substance abuse (e.g., nagging, calling into work "sick" for the abuser, drinking with the abuser, making hollow threats and pointless ultimatums, etc.). The nonabusing spouse needs to be "coached" to help them better understand the nature of the other partner's addiction, avoid taking responsibility for the abuser's drinking or other behaviors, and learn ways of enhancing the relationship during times when the drinking partner is sober. An "intervention" may be useful at some point if the nonabusing partner can recruit mutual friends and respected family members to gently but firmly confront the abusing partner. Although this approach carries risks, it can sometimes motivate an addicted person to seek help. The nonabusing spouse may also benefit from counseling regarding the effects of substance abuse on their children or the risks for domestic violence. At some point, however, treatment should focus on helping the nonabusing spouse learn to cope with the problem or assisting them in ultimately leaving the relationship if they choose to do so.

A couple that experiences severe or multiple problems might also benefit from case management skills. Partner violence, child abuse or neglect, substance abuse, other co-occurring mental illnesses, or other difficulties may require coordination of services with law enforcement, the courts, child welfare, primary health, and mental health agencies. Clients may also be referred to other mutual help and similar support groups such as Alcoholics Anonymous, Narcotics Anonymous, anger management groups, support groups for depression, and so on. Keeping in close contact with physicians after the client has been detoxified is also an important way to link psychosocial and health-related intervention goals. Other case management activities might include employment counseling, advocating for full access to benefits, and referral for further assessment for psychiatric disorders.

Summary of Essential Skills for Couples Work

Couples work can be both challenging and satisfying. Balancing the needs of both partners, maintaining a "neutral" posture, and facilitating improvements in empathic listening and effective problem solving often yield good results. Couples work also lays a foundation for effective work with children and adolescents through family interventions.

Case Study: Anita and Bashir
The Comprehensive Service Plan (Assessment, Intervention, Evaluation)

Use all available information from the client and significant others, your observations, and input from other professionals to conduct both quantitative and qualitative aspects of this multidimensional-functional assessment.

Client identification data: (gender; age; marital status; sexual orientation; family composition; employment; racial, ethnic, cultural, religious/spiritual affiliation and identity; etc.)

Anita is a twenty-year-old married woman of mixed Iranian and Italian background. Her parents live about one hour away, and she has a brother in high school. She works as a waitress but wants to enroll in the local community college to pursue studies in human services. She was born and grew up in the United States. Her father, an engineer, had moved to the United States in the late 1970s, prior to the Iranian Revolution, and met Anita's mother at work. Her mother became a full-time homemaker after she married Anita's father.

Anita is married to Bashir, a twenty-four-year-old man who immigrated as a teenager with his parents from Lebanon in the late 1990s. He is an only child. His parents run a bakery, and Bashir drives the delivery truck for their large and growing business. Neither Anita nor Bashir are devout in their religious beliefs (both identify themselves as non-practicing Muslims), but they are both proud of their cultural heritage and celebrate all relevant holidays together and with extended family. Anita and Bashir have been married for three years, and they have a three-year-old son (Anita was pregnant with Habib at the time of the marriage).

The presenting problem

Description of problem (client's view)

The couple has been fighting off and on since they were married, and things escalated soon after the birth of Habib. Bashir complains that he works very hard and that Anita expects too much from him around the house. Anita complains that she is too home bound and that she wants to pursue her education, so she can have a career in human services and increase their income in the future. She complains that Bashir is too authoritarian, does not listen to her, and spends too much time away from the home when he is not working. Bashir complains that he expected his wife to show more commitment to their home and raising his son, wants more children in the future, and that she should put off her education for now. He says he can make enough money to meet their needs.

Description of problem (practitioner's view)

The couple appears to have fundamental differences about their respective roles and expectations for their future life together. Anita made reference to the fact that her mother was a full-time homemaker, had given up a good job at the request of her father, and has always resented that decision to some degree. Anita feels strongly that she does not want to make the same mistake and feels that, with more education, she could contribute financially as an "equal" in the relationship. In order to achieve this, she wants Bashir to assume more of the domestic duties. Bashir, on the other hand, feels that they had an implicit arrangement when Habib was born—Anita would raise his son, and he would be the full-time provider. Bashir claims that he has the support of both his parents and his father-in-law and that, aside from Anita's mother, she has little support from both families regarding her desire to pursue a human services career. Thus, there is some tension between Anita and Bashir regarding extended family alliances. As for communication, the couple appears to be committed to one another but show poor communication skills. They tend to shout a lot and interrupt often. They feel very strongly about their respective positions, and there seems to be little room for compromise at this point. There does not appear to be any history of physical violence, and they both adore their son Habib.

Psychosocial history with an emphasis on problem trajectory

Bashir grew up in Lebanon and moved to the United States with his parents. He reports a generally uneventful childhood, although he was well aware of political tensions and violence in his own country. His father had relatives in the United States who helped him immigrate and set up a bakery business. Bashir admires both his parents very much. After completing high school, he went to work full time for his father driving a delivery truck. The business was growing, and Bashir believes that he will take over the business some day as his father decides to slow down and retire. Bashir reports no history of mental health or substance abuse problems but feels that he has been under a lot of stress in the past few years. He has no regrets about the unplanned pregnancy and birth of his son Habib but feels that it has placed a great strain on him financially and has caused a lot of tension with Anita.

Anita grew up in a middle-class neighborhood and considered her father to be very "old world" and somewhat strict. Her mother, as noted above, stayed at home, but was somewhat resentful of not having pursued her career. Nevertheless, she and Anita's father seemed to have a solid marriage. Anita recalls that her father particularly set very strict limits regarding her dress, make-up, where, when, and with whom she could socialize, and so on, and felt a bit "out of it" socially compared with her friends, whose parents seems to be more permissive. Although she does not outwardly resent her father for his strictness, she seems to bristle at Bashir's injunctions that she "commit herself to motherhood full time."

Anita claims to have "rebelled" somewhat in high school and started smoking cigarettes, drinking alcohol, and smoking pot. When her father found out, she recalls that she was restricted to the home for three months during her junior year in high school, a time that disrupted her social life with long-lasting effects. She had been seeing a young man with whom she felt she was, at the time, in love and resented her father for disrupting that relationship. It ended soon after Anita's "confinement." Although she stopped using alcohol and marijuana when she found out she was pregnant (Bashir also disapproved of her drug use, although he occasionally smoked pot as well), Anita continues to smoke cigarettes when Bashir is not around (she revealed this as a "secret" during our individual assessment interview).

Anita and Bashir were married in a civil ceremony and, since then, have been mainly preoccupied with the daily stresses and strains of raising their young son, paying their mounting bills, and surviving financially. Anita says she is bored, resents being housebound, and wants more freedom to socialize with friends as well as pursue her education. Bashir is resisting her wishes.

Attempts to resolve the problems, previous treatment, and relevant outcomes

The couple has only discussed their concerns with each other's parents, a strategy that only made Anita resentful. Both Bashir's father and father-in-law are more sympathetic to his case, disapproving of Anita's desires, but Anita's mother provides her with some support. These discussions were causing some tension between the families, so the couple decided not to discuss the matter with them anymore for the sake of keeping the peace. Neither partner has any mental health or substance abuse treatment history.

The individual assessment[1]

Mental status—cognitive disturbances: Describe the client's level of hallucinations, delusions, disorientation, bizarre behavior or speech, memory problems, serious confusion, or other symptoms of serious cognitive impairment. Include other troubling or dysfunctional beliefs or convictions.

---

[1] For illustration purposes, both individual assessments are combined here. Under usual circumstances, individual assessments would be documented separately.

Anita: no indications of cognitive disturbances; some indications of guilt regarding her desire to pursue her education further.

> How would you rate the client's overall mental status during the past month?
>
> POOR [o]   IMPAIRED [1]   MARGINAL [2]   GOOD [3]   EXCELLENT [4]

Bashir: similarly, no serious indications of cognitive disturbance; expresses some resentment regarding Anita's desire to pursue a profession.

> How would you rate the client's overall mental status during the past month?
>
> POOR [o]   IMPAIRED [1]   MARGINAL [2]   GOOD [3]   EXCELLENT [4]

Mental status—emotional distress: Describe the client's level of depression, anxiety, and overall ability to regulate her/his emotions.

Anita appears to be somewhat depressed, expresses some guilt about her unplanned pregnancy, the circumstances of her marriage, and feeling that she is "letting down" Bashir and her father by not conforming with their expectations of her. She does report some difficulties sleeping, and has been smoking more, which she also feels guilty about since she is carefully hiding this behavior from Bashir who she knows would disapprove. She feels that sometimes "I am just dragging myself throughout the day." It is possible she suffered from postpartum depression, but she was not treated, and her symptoms do not appear to be severe. When asked, she reports no suicidal ideation at this time or recently.

> How would you rate your client's emotional well-being over the past thirty days?
>
> POOR [o]   IMPAIRED [1]   MARGINAL [2]   GOOD [3]   EXCELLENT [4]

Bashir reports a fair amount of stress. Although his presentation is generally upbeat and he shows no signs of depression or related somatic complaints, he does talk about losing his temper often. He reported an incident recently where he almost became involved in an altercation during a traffic jam. Another driver accused him of "cutting in" at a tollbooth and yelled a racial epithet at him (the name of the business on the truck clearly suggests Middle-Eastern culture). Bashir jumped out of the truck, but was dissuaded from taking further action when a state trooper emerged from a patrol car parked on the nearby grass median. Bashir just smiled and waved, glared at the other driver, and got back in the truck. But he was upset with himself for almost going too far and fuming over the incident for the next couple of hours. "I wouldn't normally let an incident like that bother me, but I've been pretty on edge lately. I really need some time to relax, but things are pretty tight right now at home, and my dad depends on me. The holidays are coming up, too, so orders are off the charts, which is good for business but not my blood pressure." He also reports trouble sleeping and regrets occasionally losing his temper at home—yelling at Anita and pounding his fist on the kitchen table.

How would you rate your client's emotional well-being over the past thirty days?

POOR [0]   IMPAIRED [1]   MARGINAL [2]   GOOD [3]   EXCELLENT [4]

Behavioral problems: Describe your client's overall ability to regulate her/his behavior. Consider things such as their ability to express her/himself effectively, ability to work at things patiently, tendencies to verbally or physically lash out at others, run away, harm her/himself, or proneness to impulsive, criminal, or substance-abusing behavior. How would you describe the client's overall impulse control?

Anita: As suggested above, her energy level appears to be down, and although three-year-old Habib keeps her busy, she feels that she no longer has time or wants to do some of the things she used to enjoy—reading in particular.

How would you rate your client's behavioral control generally over the past thirty days?

POOR [0]   IMPAIRED [1]   MARGINAL [2]   GOOD [3]   EXCELLENT [4]

Bashir: Has considerable amount of stress, has been losing his temper, having difficulty relaxing and feeling at ease.

> How would you rate your client's behavioral control generally over the past 30 days?
>
> POOR [0]   IMPAIRED [1]   <u>MARGINAL [2]</u>   GOOD [3]   EXCELLENT [4]

Adaptive strengths and coping abilities: Describe your client's ability to cope with problems and everyday stressors. How would you describe the client's ability to assess problem situations, deal with "triggers," cope with stress, solve problems, and perhaps reach out to others for help in order to deal effectively with her/his difficulties?

Anita: Despite the mild-to-moderate depression, Anita is holding up well. She reports being quite active with her child, spends a lot of time playing with him, cuddling, and otherwise caring for him. She clearly enjoys being a mother but seems exhausted much of the time, possibly as a result of the depression.

> How would you rate your client's overall adaptive strengths and coping abilities over the past thirty days?
>
> POOR [0]   IMPAIRED [1]   MARGINAL [2]   <u>GOOD [3]</u>   EXCELLENT [4]

Bashir: He is a hard worker, responsible, and determined to make things work out at work and at home.

> How would you rate your client's overall adaptive strengths and coping abilities over the past thirty days?
>
> POOR [0]   IMPAIRED [1]   MARGINAL [2]   <u>GOOD [3]</u>   EXCELLENT [4]

Health problems: Describe the client's overall health. Aside from normal, transient illnesses, think about the client's general health habits (e.g., smoking, heavy drinking, exercise, weight), chronic primary health disorders, the client's opinion of her/his own health, ability to engage in her/his usual activities relatively free from discomfort, overall energy level, hospitalizations and treatments for illness other than psychiatric ones. Consider her/his documented medical history and any ongoing treatments.

Anita: Aside from some depressive symptoms, she reports being in very good health. Smoking is a concern that she acknowledges.

How would you rate your client's health over the past thirty days?

POOR [0]   IMPAIRED [1]   MARGINAL [2]   GOOD [3]   EXCELLENT [4]

Bashir: Also in good health, but he, as does his father, has high blood pressure. He does not take medication but is aware of the need to relax, reduce stress, and exercise.

How would you rate your client's health over the past thirty days?

POOR [0]   IMPAIRED [1]   MARGINAL [2]   GOOD [3]   EXCELLENT [4]

Use of alcohol and other drugs: Describe the client's use of alcohol, illicit substances (cocaine, heroin, marijuana, hallucinogens, etc.) and abuse of prescription medication. How often does the client use them, in what quantity, and how serious are the psychological, physical, or social consequences associated with their use?

Anita: Has reported occasional marijuana smoking on the few occasions where she has been able to "get away" and visit her women friends. Otherwise, she is not drinking or using other drugs.

How would you rate the client's functioning in the past month with regard to substance use?

POOR [0]   IMPAIRED [1]   MARGINAL [2]   GOOD [3]   EXCELLENT [4]

Bashir: Reports occasionally drinking beer or wine with his male friends. Other than occasional intoxication, he reports no problems with alcohol and does not use illicit drugs or any nonprescribed pharmaceuticals.

How would you rate the client's functioning in the past month with regard to substance use?

POOR [0]   IMPAIRED [1]   MARGINAL [2]   <u>GOOD [3]</u>   EXCELLENT [4]

Recreational activities: Consider what the client does for fun (alone or with others), hobbies, relaxation (reading, TV, video games, playing cards, etc.) and physical exercise (walking, jogging, biking, etc.). How would you describe the client's overall involvement in positive recreational activities?

Anita: In the last couple of years, reports very little by way of enjoyable recreational activities. Bemoans feeling "overweight and out of shape." She used to be more active, jogged, and enjoyed other activities such as reading, noted earlier. Reports she has not been out to a movie or similar activity in two years.

How would you rate the adequacy of the client's participation in healthy recreational activities over the past thirty days?

POOR [0]   <u>IMPAIRED [1]</u>   MARGINAL [2]   GOOD [3]   EXCELLENT [4]

Bashir: Also reports less time "for fun" but does go out once a week with his male friends. They sometimes play cards or backgammon, have a few drinks, tell stories (most are of Middle-Eastern descent and met through business dealings), and he looks forward to this time each week. He also complains about lack of exercise, although he's "on and off the truck all day—it can be a work out, just not much fun."

How would you rate the adequacy of the client's participation in healthy recreational activities over the past thirty days?

POOR [0]   IMPAIRED [1]   <u>MARGINAL [2]</u>   GOOD [3]   EXCELLENT [4]

Material resources: Describe your client's current or (if client is institutionalized) most recent living situation overall. Consider such things as adequacy of food, clothing, shelter, and safety.

Anita: Material resources are good. Although they are struggling financially, their basic needs are adequately met.

> How would you rate the overall adequacy of the client's material resources over the past month?
>
> POOR [0]   IMPAIRED [1]   MARGINAL [2]   <u>GOOD [3]</u>   EXCELLENT [4]

Bashir: Same as above.

> How would you rate the overall adequacy of the client's material resources over the past month?
>
> POOR [0]   IMPAIRED [1]   MARGINAL [2]   <u>GOOD [3]</u>   EXCELLENT [4]

Independent living/self-care: Describe how well your client manages her/his household, takes care of personal hygiene, eats, sleeps, and otherwise cares for her/his own basic needs.

Anita: Has been somewhat neglectful of daily self-care; appears a bit disheveled at times; possibly related to depression and constant child care.

> How would you rate the client's ability to live independently and take care of her/his basic needs over the past thirty days?
>
> POOR [0]   IMPAIRED [1]   <u>MARGINAL [2]</u>   GOOD [3]   EXCELLENT [4]

Bashir: Does not appear to have any significant problems in this area.

> How would you rate the client's ability to live independently and take care of her/his basic needs over the past thirty days?
>
> POOR [0]   IMPAIRED [1]   MARGINAL [2]   <u>GOOD [3]</u>   EXCELLENT [4]

Work (role) satisfaction: Describe the client's current work-related or other important role-related activities (e.g., employed, student, homemaker, volunteer, retired person, disabled, etc.). Describe those activities and responsibilities that occupy the client in a productive manner.

Anita: Although more than adequately filling her current role as mother and full-time homemaker, she is despondent and frustrated over her perceived lack of opportunity to pursue her education further.

How would you rate the client's work or role satisfaction over the past thirty days?

POOR [0]   IMPAIRED [1]   <u>MARGINAL [2]</u>   GOOD [3]   EXCELLENT [4]

Bashir: Seems satisfied with his role as primary breadwinner and likes his role in the family business despite daily stress and strain.

How would you rate the client's work or role satisfaction over the past thirty days?

POOR [0]   IMPAIRED [1]   MARGINAL [2]   <u>GOOD [3]</u>   EXCELLENT [4]

Legal problems: Describe any legal problems the client has had or continues to have. These include minor infractions (e.g., public drunkenness, shoplifting inexpensive items, minor traffic violations, public disturbances) and more serious crimes (e.g., assault and battery, rape, burglary, driving under the influence, etc.). Consider her/his status (probation, awaiting imprisonment, parole). Also, consider any civil suits leveled at the client, pending financial judgments against her/him, and so on. Overall, how would you describe the client's current legal situation?

Neither partner has any legal problems to report.

Anita:

How would you rate the client's legal situation over the past thirty days?

POOR [0]   IMPAIRED [1]   MARGINAL [2]   GOOD [3]   <u>EXCELLENT [4]</u>

Bashir:

How would you rate the client's legal situation over the past thirty days?

POOR [0]   IMPAIRED [1]   MARGINAL [2]   GOOD [3]   <u>EXCELLENT [4]</u>

DSM-5 diagnoses

Anita: Persistent depressive disorder, 300.4
         Relationship distress with spouse or intimate partner, V61.10

Bashir: Relationship distress with spouse or intimate partner, V61.10

Family relations: Describe the client's current family structure, including authority, hierarchy, alliances, roles, rules, boundaries, subsystems (e.g., couple, siblings, parent-child alliances); patterns of interactions and quality of communications; specific problems within the family; specific adaptive strengths within the family; and how the family members describe their own racial, ethnic, cultural, and religious identities.

As indicated, there is some tension between these partners that is inadvertently provoked by their respective parents. Although the couple's parents have not interfered, with the exception of Anita's mother, they have let their feelings known that they think Anita should stay home and give up her plans to return to school. This has provided Bashir with some degree of support for his views but has increased tension between him and Anita. Other than that, there has been no overt conflict among these respective family members.

How would you rate the quality of the client's immediate family relationships over the past thirty days?

POOR [0]   IMPAIRED [1]   MARGINAL [2]   GOOD [3]   EXCELLENT [4]

Immediate social relationships (close friends and acquaintances): Describe the quality of your client's relationships with those available friends and acquaintances, as applicable. Over the past month, how would you describe the quality of the interaction overall between your client and them with respect to closeness, intimacy, general interpersonal satisfaction, effective communications, degree of conflict, level of hostility, aggression, and evidence of any emotional or physical abuse?

As a couple, Anita and Bashir have no friends in common. They both have separate friends that they see, with Bashir seeing his much more frequently than does Anita. The couple married soon after Anita discovered she was pregnant, and the couple has had little time or opportunity to meet other young couples with children.

How would you rate the quality of the client's immediate social relation-ships over the past thirty days?

POOR [0]   IMPAIRED [1]   MARGINAL [2]   GOOD [3]   EXCELLENT [4]

Extended social relationships: Describe the type and quality of relation-ships between your client and others in the client's community (other than close friends and family). These people might include other families, law enforcement, human service agencies, school personnel, coworkers, and others from whom the client receives support or with whom the client is having serious conflict.

The couple has little involvement in the community. Outside of work, Bashir has a few friends, but the couple is somewhat cut off from their community, is not involved with the school as of yet, and has no other ties with community or religious organizations. They appear to be somewhat isolated.

How would you rate the quality of the client's immediate social relation-ships over the past thirty days?

POOR [0]   IMPAIRED [1]   MARGINAL [2]   GOOD [3]   EXCELLENT [4]

A concise summary of the MFS assessment: Highlight the client's areas of distress and adaptive strengths. Emphasize those areas that are most likely to be emphasized in the intervention plan.

Anita and Bashir are a young couple who genuinely care for one another and are attentive parents to their young son Habib. As with many young couples, they are under considerable stress financially, have some tension over extended family relations, do not have a mutual support group of friends or acquaintances, and are somewhat cut off from their community in general. Bashir shows signs of stress and can be angry and argumenta-tive during discussions at home, and Anita is frustrated with him and her "stay-at-home" status and appears moderately depressed. Attempts to discuss their respective concerns often end in heated arguments usually without any resolution.

Recommendations for further focused assessment: Note recommended referrals to consultants or additional instruments to be used.

Continue to monitor Anita's symptoms of depression. Refer for psychiatric evaluation if they do not abate after a few couples sessions.

The Comprehensive Service Plan Summary

Assessment/Problems	Goals	Objectives	Interventions	Evaluation plan
(Briefly describe key problems to be addressed.)	(State desired outcome for each problem.)	(Describe specific "stepping stones" toward each GOAL. Update as client progresses.)	(Describe specific interventions to be used.)	(Describe indexes to be used for tracking progress.)
Great difficulty communicating constructively regarding differences about each other's respective roles	Come to a mutually satisfactory resolution about short- and long-term roles for both partners in marriage	Identify those areas regarding roles that are open for discussion by either partner and those that both are willing to discuss; list in a hierarchy from least difficult (e.g., child care) to most difficult (e.g., Anita returning to school)	*Supportive skills:* Focus on joining the couple, and modeling empathic listening skills	Develop self-anchored scale for each couple to rate how well they felt their partner listened and demonstrated understanding (e.g., 0 "not at all," 1 "a little," 2 "some," 3 "a good amount," 4 "very well"); report results weekly
Mild-to-moderate depression and stress symptoms in Anita and Bashir, respectively	Reduce symptoms of depression and stress; enhance opportunities for healthy relaxation	Identify and list potential opportunities for physical and social recreation for them as a couple;	*Therapeutic coping skills:* Teach and coach emotion-focused communication skills (i.e., empathic listening to emotional content without interrupting); demonstrate mutual understanding verbally and nonverbally	Use same scaling device above to have each partner rate how well the other partner made efforts to help or soothe the other during the week; have them report weekly and provide specific examples
Social isolation; lack of mutual friends and similar social supports	Expand social supports; reduce isolation	Identify local community organizations of mutual interest	Have couple practice in the office and (initially) twice weekly at home after Habib is asleep; start with easier items on the "objectives" list	
			Have couple review perceptions of their own respective parents' marriages; consider what they believe worked for them and what didn't; examine how goals for their life together may be similar/different	

Identify those mutually reinforcing activities that each
partner can do for the other at
home; these may include
household and child-care
duties; also include activities
that are mutually soothing to
reduce depression and stress;
emphasize mutual gain over
competition

Demonstrate basic stress
management to Bashir; have
him practice as needed and
report results weekly

Case management skills:
Explore participation in local
Muslim-American organiza-
tions, particularly those geared
toward younger couples; these
may include mosque-related
activities; enlist in-laws to
provide 1x weekly baby-sitting,
if possible

Explore Anita's return to
school (part-time, initially)
within six months if mutual
social supports become
available

Consider referring Anita for
medication evaluation if
depression worsens

CHAPTER ELEVEN

Internalizing Disorders of Childhood and Adolescence

INTERNALIZING DISORDERS, the focus of this chapter, refer primarily to depression and anxiety disorders in children and adolescents. Although sadness, disappointments, and a variety of fears and worries are common during childhood, internalizing disorders are more chronic and generally more severe than transitory problems of mood that may be a function of family problems, general distress, or problems in school. Internalizing disorders refer, more specifically, to depression and a range of anxiety disorders including: school phobia (i.e., school refusal), specific phobias (e.g., bugs, dogs), obsessive-compulsive disorders, posttraumatic stress disorder, and social phobia (i.e., extreme shyness), among other disorders. Although epidemiological data are lacking and estimates vary widely, recent data suggest that twelve-month prevalence for any particular anxiety disorder in children is about 1 percent, with mood disorders more common at 3.7 percent (Merikangas et al., 2009).

The biopsychosocial framework provides a sound underpinning for understanding children's internalizing disorders. Many children inherit a predisposition to anxiety or depression (or both), and this tendency may be exacerbated by real stressors in their lives. Often, these stressors have their origins in the child's family: domestic violence, physical and sexual abuse, neglect, high conflict in the household, unemployment, substance abuse, divorce, and so forth (Beedso, Knappe, & Pine, 2009; Tandon, Cardeli, & Luby, 2009). Children often have good reasons to be sad and anxious. Nevertheless, depression and anxiety can be debilitating and portend a lifetime of struggle with anxiety and mood disorders and associated behavioral problems.

There is good reason, however, to be hopeful in working with children given that there are effective interventions available. If the family is relatively intact and supportive, child-focused interventions can be readily implemented. If the family is highly conflicted or exhibits evidence of child neglect, abuse, or other forms of domestic violence, the focus must first be on the family as a whole with the emphasis on stabilizing the parent/couple subsystem or intervening with a single parent as needed. Without the cooperation of the parents or guardians, interventions with younger children, in particular, are less likely to be successful. Thus, the current trend in the outcome research is to implement interventions for children and adolescents in the context of a family therapy strategy when possible.

Externalizing disorders, the focus of Chapter 12, refer to childhood and adolescent problems marked primarily by behavior disorders including oppositional defiant, conduct disorders, and to some extent, attention deficit disorders. Anxiety and depression sometimes co-occur with externalizing disorders. Thus, these two categories should be considered frequently overlapping conditions. In adolescents, for example, depression often co-occurs with conduct disorder and substance abuse.

One might find it helpful to think of interventions with children and their families as a kind of transfer of learning across several levels. First, the social worker might conduct an assessment with the child alone and also with a parent or both parents present. In this way, the practitioner obtains their own perspective on the child, can observe the parents' behavior with the child, and can also provide modeling for the parents regarding how to connect with and relate to the child more effectively. Parents frustrated with their child's behavior may be inadvertently overwhelming or shaming to a child in their effort to motivate them to be less fearful, do better in school, or change some other behavior. Should assessment proceed to intervention, the skills the practitioner demonstrates with the child in the presence of the parents can provide effective modeling to improve parenting skills (e.g., empathic listening, nurturing, positive disciplining), improve communications among family members, and demonstrate a calm and rational approach to problem solving. Thus, through modeling the practitioner is transferring their skills in relating with the child to the parents, an essential goal for long-term maintenance of gains for the child.

Lastly, one cannot overlook the importance of connecting with community resources outside the family: teachers and school administration, law enforcement, medical professionals, coaches, and so on, depending on the problems the child or adolescent is experiencing. These important participants in the child's life can serve as responsible monitors and reporters of the child or adolescent's progress and are in key positions to help reinforce important changes. If, for example, a child is severely phobic in social situations, it makes little sense to focus on the child's well-being exclusively within the context of the family. Although there may be dynamics within the family that discourage the child from becoming more involved socially (e.g., the child's mother suffers from agoraphobia, parents are socially disconnected due to domestic violence or child abuse in the home), it would be helpful for the child if the practitioner coordinated services with some interested party (e.g., a teacher, sports coach) outside the home to monitor progress. In keeping with the generic social work ecosystem assessment model, monitoring the problem and intervening on several levels is, again, the hallmark of effective social work practice with children and adolescents. Working exclusively with a child alone in a consulting room, insulated from the inputs of family, teachers, and other collaborators is no longer considered competent practice with children and adolescents.

Assessment

"Internalizing disorders" is a term that is somewhat of a misnomer since some problems associated with anxiety and depression are externally observable. Very anxious children may suffer from debilitating shyness, compulsive rituals to ward off the anxiety related to frightening or disturbing obsessions, or traumatic distress associated with child physical or sexual abuse. Depressed children may generally appear to be withdrawn socially, chronically angry, or despondent.

Assessment with children, generally, should be conducted on several levels: (1) alone with the child to observe their behavior and to get a "feel" for how they relate to the practitioner without the family members present, (2) in the presence of the family to observe how the child reacts to family members and how they relate to the child, and (3) through consultation with persons outside the family (teachers, coaches, etc.)—in short, anyone (with consent of the parent/guardian) who is in a strategic position to observe the child in another social context.

An MFS assessment for internalizing disorders should include an analysis of how the child's difficulties developed over time, how the problem has varied in intensity within the context of family and other social contexts, and how the problem currently manifests itself across various domains including mental status, family and social well-being, recreational activities, and school performance (Beidel & Turner, 2005; Chorpita & Southam-Gerow, 2015; O'Hare, 2015; Stark et al., 2006). Children suffering from anxiety and depression may have vague notions about what is bothering them or may be very specific about why they are sad or afraid. These reasons should be listened to carefully. Depending on the child's age and abilities, a variety of methods can be employed to help children discuss the potential sources of sadness or fears: drawing, playing games, using dolls or other figures, using story books that depict other children dealing with fears or sadness, or through the use of other creative outlets. Children, depending on their age, may have difficulty articulating what troubles them through ordinary interviewing methods. There is also the possibility that the child does not want to reveal certain facts because they feel threatened by a parent, guardian, or other person or because they are worried about the consequences of reporting certain events. The causes of these concerns may involve problems at school, child abuse, domestic violence, drug use, or other potentially criminal behavior. Children learn at a young age to censor themselves if they have been taught not to talk about their problems with "strangers" or "outsiders."

Other children may reveal their troubles indirectly. A child who fears going to school might talk about a child abduction case reported on television. The depressed child may focus on unhappy themes such as loneliness, loss, or disappointment expressed by characters in a storybook. Accepting a child's reasons for their fears or sadness at face value, initially, can help the child to express their feelings and expand upon the specific theme. But it may take some sleuthing and more in-depth analysis of family interactions and reports from others to identify what the actual sources of fears or sadness really are. There is also the possibility that the child may have very supportive parents and an otherwise supportive social environment and may be struggling with emotional difficulties for which there is a family history (e.g., depression or anxiety disorders) and no obvious environmental cause. Nevertheless, it is important to try and rule out possible environmental factors that may be contributing to the child's distress.

Keeping in mind that the causes of depression and anxiety disorders in children, adolescents, and adults can have multiple biopsychosocial sources, practitioners should keep a balanced approach in mind and avoid premature conclusions during an assessment. In some cases, there may indeed be one prominent factor that overwhelmingly seems to account for a child's emotional distress: consider the impact of sexual or physical abuse, traumatic losses, or witnessing deadly violence. However, most cases will not yield to simple explanations. One way to avoid premature formulations is to examine the changes in a child's life over time, that is, develop a detailed trajectory of when the child began to demonstrate difficulties (e.g., the family moved, the child started school, a sudden loss in the family, etc.) and follow that trajectory to the present. Examining changes in the family, particularly the parents, over time can help provide a cause-effect analysis that will yield useful clues as to what social or environmental factors may be negatively affecting the child.

Depression and anxiety are problems that often run in families due to both genetic and transgenerational family behavioral problems (e.g., alcoholism, criminality). Taking a careful family history can be helpful in this regard. Many young children are shy and fearful at times, but most mature out of this phase. Some do not. An analysis of family interactions sometimes suggests reasons why children are afraid or depressed. Other times, however, children who are well cared for and loved at home experience most of their difficulties outside the family system. Children and younger adolescents may have problems with anxiety and depression related to school (e.g., learning difficulties) or other broader social activities (e.g., bullying). When the child appears well nurtured in the home, yet is having emotional difficulties in other social venues, assessment from objective observers in those situations can be revealing.

Anxiety and depression can also be associated with more severe forms of child psychopathology such as serious mental illnesses, developmental disabilities, or neurological problems. Referral to specialists who can provide testing and diagnosis for these disorders is necessary. Should these more serious causes be ruled out, practitioners should consider how the child's emotional distress manifests itself in other areas of their life: How does their distress affect other family members, including their parents? Are the child's difficulties affecting their ability to relate to their peers at school and inhibiting their social development? Is the child's emotional distress interfering with their school performance? How does the teacher respond to a child who is fidgety, anxious, or listless and disengaged in the classroom? One should also consider the possibility of substance abuse, especially as children approach middle-school age. The use of alcohol, marijuana, inhalants, or other drugs is a real possibility and would readily contribute to symptoms of internalizing disorders including social withdrawal and depression.

Practitioners should also be attuned to the cultural context and level of assimilation to American child-rearing "norms" and expectations when assessing internalizing disorders in children. Although one should avoid overgeneralizations about any ethnic, racial, or religious group, asking the parents to help you understand how their cultural traditions influence their child-rearing practices (e.g., rewards, discipline, social expectations, etc.) is important. In cases where parenting practices diverge somewhat from the practitioner's cultural expectations, practitioners should strive to find common ground or explain in a non-judgmental way how the family's norms may be somewhat different from those of other families, the school, or broader community. Children will often use other parents' behavior as a benchmark to challenge their own parents, particularly as the children get older. The child's parents should at least be aware of what other parents consider ordinary, so the client can better judge their own estimations of what is "too strict" or "too permissive" in parenting practices. Above all, parents need to agree on norms, so they can use sanctions or provide rewards to the child with a unified voice.

There may also be occasions when the parent's ideas of what is acceptable behavior or what constitutes reasonable discipline may be too much out of the norm. For example, in some religions and other subcultures, corporal punishment is acceptable and even considered a positive form of punishment. Of course, the term "corporal punishment" can mean a lot of things, and the practitioner (in keeping with their own beliefs and local laws and customs) has to decide where to draw the line (e.g., three "whacks" on the behind with an open hand vs. hitting a child with a paddle, belt, or kitchen utensil). The practitioner should also be transparent about their beliefs regarding acceptable forms of disciplining and communicate them to the parents. However, if a social worker considers that a parent's disciplining practices go "over the line" and constitute neglect or abuse, the practitioner then has to report the incident to the local child welfare authorities. This may sever any working relationship with that family, but that is a risk that the social worker is legally obligated to take.

The functional assessment is critical for determining factors that may be causing or exacerbating the child's depression or anxieties. Tracking the details of a child's behavior over the course of a "typical week" at home, school, and elsewhere can be very telling in terms of sequencing factors that affect the child's well-being over time. When is the child doing well? Under which circumstances? When and where are they manifesting problems and emotional distress? How frequent and severe are the problems? Do the problems vary a lot in terms of frequency and severity, and do they vary as a function of specific circumstances? How do the parents, siblings, teachers, friends, acquaintances, coaches, and anyone else in the child's life respond to the child's fears or withdrawal behaviors? How do these responses affect the child? What responses seem to improve the child's mood or help them become more involved socially?

Once the social worker has a solid grasp of the patterns and sequencing of factors that affect the child's mood and behavior, working with the family to create a hierarchy of problems is the next step. Starting with a problem of moderate difficulty and working toward the more challenging problems is, generally, a sound way to proceed. For example, for a very shy child, setting up a play date for an hour with one child whom they seem to like would be a safe start. Gradually increasing the amount of time and adding another playmate or two over time is likely to be a winning strategy. At the same time, if the child's parents are having serious marital problems (possibly one source of anxiety for the child), couples work should be initiated concurrently. Making therapeutic progress with a child or adolescent's social phobia will be considerably undermined if the child lives in constant fear of witnessing violence between their parents anytime they go home from school. Consulting with key school personnel would also be helpful if teachers and playground monitors are recruited to encourage the child to engage socially rather than withdraw.

Detailing the day-to-day life of a child struggling with depression or anxiety will generally reveal those key psychosocial factors that contribute to their difficulties. Practitioners should also note situations where the child appears to be functioning better. A balanced assessment that highlights both the child's vulnerabilities as well as strengths provides a good working template for intervention planning.

Intervention

A large and growing body of research supports a range of cognitive-behavioral therapies for internalizing childhood and adolescent disorders (e.g., Beidel & Turner, 2005; Brown et al., 2008; Chorpita & Southam-Gerow, 2006; Compton, Burns, Egger, & Robertson, 2002; Kazdin & Weisz, 1998; Ollendick & King, 1998; Saavedra, Silverman, Morgan-Lopez, & Kurtines, 2010; Silverman & Berman; 2001; Stark et al. 2006). What is also becoming increasingly apparent is that, although these approaches can be implemented in individual and group modalities with success, CBT approaches with children are being implemented with increasing regularity and effectiveness within the context of behavioral family therapies (e.g., Compton, Burns, Egger, & Robertson, 2002; Makely & Falcone, 2010; Northey, Wells, Silverman, & Bailey, 2003). CBT and behaviorally oriented family therapies have been shown to be the treatment of choice for a range of internalizing disorders including: social anxiety, panic disorder, obsessive-compulsive disorder, and posttraumatic stress disorder, among others. These approaches have also been shown to be helpful for children and adolescents with depressive disorders. Some have noted, however, that outcomes and research for depression lag behind those for anxiety disorders (Tandon, Cardeli, & Luby, 2009).

EBPs and Culturally Competent Practice with Children

Can evidence-based practices be used effectively with children and adolescents from racial minorities and other cultures? The answer to this question appears to be a resounding "yes!" Evidence increasingly reveals that CBT and behaviorally oriented family therapies work comparably well for children from racial minorities in the United States, including African-Americans, Hispanic-Americans, and Native Americans as well as for children in other countries (Brown et al., 2008; Morsette et al., 2008; Saavedra, Silverman, Morgan-Lopez, & Kurtines, 2010). For example, Cognitive Behavior Interventions for Trauma in Schools (CBITS) is a community-based approach to treating trauma and has been carried out in several minority communities in the United States and elsewhere. Rolfsnes and Idsoe (2011) conducted a meta-analysis of nineteen studies across nine countries and found that CBT-based school interventions can be quite effective for traumatized children. Based on their experiences in implementing CBITS, Ngo et al. (2008) concluded the following: "What seems to be important is to strike a balance between fidelity to evidence-based treatment and culturally informed care" (p. 858). They recommend maintaining the core elements of CBITS (i.e., psycho-education, cognitive-behavioral coping, relaxation, social problem-solving, and the use of narrative exercises to process the traumatic event) while working with stakeholders and making common-sense adjustments to increase cultural congruency (e.g., language, symbols, references to cultural role models). In the first successful testing of CBITS with a Native American school, Morsette et al. (2008) noted the following:

> Overall, the group facilitators were pleased with how well CBITS worked within their schools. They also reported that the psycho-educational nature of the intervention fit well within their schools, noting how initial concerns about students' transitioning from a possibly intense treatment group to classroom after trauma work did not materialize. Of particular significance was the increase in the facilitators' sense of professional efficacy in working with children who had experienced trauma. Prior to implementation, group facilitators registered doubts about their abilities to work with such intense difficulties [and they concluded that] [t]he data suggest that CBITS was an effective method of treatment for American Indian children suffering from symptoms of PTSD and depression. (pp. 176–177)

Despite dire warnings from some (Aisenberg, 2008; Roysircar, 2009) that evidence-based practices cannot be effectively utilized with people from other racial, cultural, or economic backgrounds, evidence continues to mount that, with common-sense cultural tailoring, evidence-based practices transfer quite well across cultures. Perhaps these findings result from the fact that, despite cultural and socioeconomic differences, the essential skills of evidence-based practices activate a range of common human change processes in people from many walks of life: feeling comforted and understood in response to an empathic and supportive helper; learning new ways of coping with frightening or depressing thoughts and physical symptoms of anxiety and depression; learning to develop new behavioral coping skills; and benefitting from mutual support from peers and local community groups organized through the advocacy and networking of good case management. If seriously traumatized children and adolescents from different cultures and countries can benefit from CBT and other evidence-based practices, social work practitioners should be open to and positively disposed toward utilizing these approaches with a wide range of clients with confidence.

Essential Skills of Working with Children and Adolescents Who Have Internalizing Disorders

Although many of the "essential skills" of working with children are fairly easy to learn and implement, the real art of applying evidence-based practices with children is demonstrated when practitioners learn to apply these skills concurrently on several levels: with the child, with the parents and family as a whole, and, often, in conjunction with other key persons in the child's life. Although we present some basic skills here, they are applied somewhat differently depending on the specific disorder. Further description of these more specific applications can be reviewed in O'Hare (2015) and other relevant texts on evidence-based practices for young people.

General considerations regarding the application of supportive skills with children and adolescents certainly apply when dealing with the anxious or depressed child. However, the depressed or anxious child or adolescent may require a slower pace and bit more patience to draw them out, help them to talk about what is troubling them, and then motivate them to try new ways of dealing with their problems. Children, particularly younger children (age six and younger) may have a hard time articulating what is troubling them, and the practitioner may have to work with the child's own metaphors and adult reporters around them to link their internal experience with what is going on in their daily life. As noted above, play, drawing, story telling, and the use of dolls or other figures can be useful vehicles for facilitating communication with a child (Makely &

Falcone, 2010). However, verifying one's clinical hunches with verifiable indicators should accompany these techniques. Developing a rapport with a child on a one-on-one basis is important, but should not be the exclusive form of engagement. Seeing the child alone and with their family will result in a more accurate assessment of the child's psychological, emotional, and behavioral well-being.

Developing trust with a depressed or anxious child or adolescent will depend in part on how adults (primarily parents) have treated them. It stands to reason that young people will come with predisposed expectations about their social worker based on past experiences with other adults. The working relationship with a child provides an ideal opportunity to determine what those expectations are (e.g., adults are trustworthy, adults are scary, adults want to hurt me, adults make me feel bad about myself, etc.). Again, rather than guessing at interpretations based on the child's self-report, body language, or symbolic communications in play, practitioners should test out their clinical hypotheses through data gathering: multiple types of information from multiple sources, including observations of the child during the one-on-one interview.

The younger anxious or depressed child might be hard to motivate. By working with the child alone and with the family, it is important to find out what they enjoy, what makes them feel good about themselves, and what helps them to feel safe. Younger children are less likely to respond to explanations, psycho-education, or interpretations, so it is important for interventions to be more action-oriented early on to help them achieve small but significant successes and reduce their feelings of helplessness and despair. Planning helpful tasks early on can be beneficial for the child and also provides an opportunity to see how committed to the intervention the other family members are. Observations of family members along with their self-report can help answer ongoing questions: Is the child suffering from emotional neglect? Is there psychological or physical abuse going on? Asking the family to try new things may help bring out some of these matters into the open. Keeping a close eye on family interactions will also provide many clues regarding the overall level of care, cooperation, and emotional well-being in the family. Developing a relationship with the other family members is as important as developing a rapport with the child. After all, the long-term goal is usually to help the family function better and learn coping skills that will sustain the child's psychological and physical well-being over time. Such a goal requires that family members change as well.

The younger adolescent client presents a somewhat different situation with regard to developing a working relationship. They have had more experience with adults in their life, and they can benefit substantially from the one-on-one relationship they develop with the practitioner, even if their parents are only marginally supportive. How they relate to their social worker may tell a fair amount about the relationships they have had with other adults in their lives. Are they withdrawn from the practitioner and show little interest in engaging in treatment? Are they hostile, cynical, and generally negative in their initial dealings with the social worker? Careful listening and gentle reflection can help remove some of these barriers. Simply asking a young client to tell you about the people in their lives (e.g., parents, friends, teachers) can be illuminating. Unlike younger children, older (latency) children and younger adolescents often have a greater capacity to articulate what troubles them. Being authentic and showing genuine concern for his distress (without being too maternal or paternal) can help the younger adolescent feel that he has an ally in whom he can confide.

Finally, joining the family (i.e., developing a working alliance) is critical in order to cultivate and maintain their cooperation in helping the child or adolescent client. This often involves a balancing act, particularly when there is evidence of emotional or physical abuse. Maintaining this alliance can be a challenge if the parents or guardians feel that they are being blamed for the child's emotional difficulties. It is important to identify both strengths and areas that require improvement when working with families. Emphasis, however, should not focus on laying blame, but on solving problems and maintaining those improvements over time. Including all family members when possible can help to forge a feeling that helping the identified child requires everyone's contributions. The working alliance must also be extended to other important adults in the child's life such as teachers and others who can contribute to supporting and maintaining the child's improvements over time.

Educating the child about how their thoughts, feelings, and behaviors work together in different situations can be especially helpful for them. Although younger children may have difficulty dealing with these abstract concepts, older children and adolescents can benefit from some help in identifying and articulating thoughts and beliefs that affect their mood positively or negatively. The depressed or anxious child may secretly harbor dysfunctional ideas about themselves, other people, and the world around them. These beliefs, expectations, and attributions may be closely associated with despair, feelings of hopelessness, vague anxieties about life, outright fears of very specific things, current situations, or their future. Anxious children may be worried about their parents (e.g., "Will they leave me?" "What if they get sick or die?"), other children at school (e.g., "Why don't they like me or want to play with me?" "I'm afraid of getting hurt by other kids."), or circumstances in their neighborhood (e.g., "Some bad men live on my street." "I know a kid who got shot and died."). Children's fears range from imaginary monsters to specific fears such as bugs or dogs. At the severe end of the spectrum, other children have experienced horrific trauma (e.g., repeated physical abuse, sexual assault), and, for others, violence is a factor in everyday life. Many children have suffered losses early in their lives and may be suffering from feelings of despair that they may not understand and cannot articulate. Other children may simply have inherited an anxious temperament or proneness to depression that colors their everyday life. Identifying what these troubling thoughts are and stating them in the open can help a child open a door to better understanding regarding what their fears or sadness are all about. Often, parents may simply not know what is troubling their children or are too preoccupied themselves with daily stressors to attend to their children's emotional well-being. In other circumstances, the parents may be a primary cause of their child's emotional distress, and thus, may be even less likely to recognize and validate the child's experience.

Practitioners can teach children to evaluate their own thinking processes and feelings by educating them about their own emotional processes. These skills include helping children to identify, differentiate, and understand their feelings, identify frightening thoughts, and develop a more keen awareness of how physical sensations can provoke anxiety. Children can learn to assess and gauge their own anxiety level and track their progress over time. One common method for helping children identify their feelings is by using picture books that illustrate different emotional expressions and helping them accurately identify those feelings and think about times "when you have felt like that." Linking the child's anxiety to specific circumstances can help them better anticipate problems and understand the effects of anxiety in everyday life. This step helps to prepare them to learn anxiety management and problem-solving skills to cope better with their fears.

Practitioners can help the child to follow through on self-monitoring their thoughts, feelings, and behaviors by teaching them to recognize and evaluate their own covert (inner) self-talk and discover ways to cope with depressive and frightening thoughts. When children feel anxious or sad, practitioners can encourage them to "talk to themselves" in an analytical way about what they are feeling at the moment so that they can examine emotionally charged thoughts in a realistic light and gain some perspective. Thoughts that provoke anxiety or depression need to be assessed realistically before coping strategies can be considered. For example, a child who is fearful of a bully in school can use self-talk as follows: "I know that Billy is mean and likes to frighten people, but I can ignore him and stay close to my friends. There's nothing wrong with being afraid of someone who likes to hurt other people. The school social worker also told me that it's not wrong if I tell the teacher or playground monitor because it would help others who might be afraid of Billy too."

A child who is depressed may think that her divorcing parents don't really love her, otherwise they would do everything possible to stay together as a family. The practitioner might help her engage in a different kind of self-talk: "I know a lot of kids whose parents got divorced. They don't say their parents don't love them. They say they have two parents and two homes to go to. Just because my parents got divorced and don't want to live with each other doesn't mean that they don't love me." Although many problems cannot be resolved merely by helping the child reframe the problem, helping them to link their thoughts and feelings together can help them understand that they can exercise some control over their own negative feelings. Identifying, monitoring, and engaging in some "cognitive coping" can provide a solid foundation for behavior change methods and improve the child's ability to cope with depression and anxiety in the long run.

Behavioral coping skills for children and adolescents are used in a variety of combinations depending on the client's needs. These include teaching relaxation-training skills and using imagery, behavioral rehearsal, role play, modeling, and practice. Problem-solving and self-regulatory skills (i.e., self-assessment, evaluation, reinforcement) can help maintain their gains over time. These skills can be applied in treating both depression and anxiety.

Ideally, therapeutic coping skills should be implemented in a graduated sequence: first, engage in cognitive coping exercises (as described above); second, use relaxation techniques (i.e., simple breathing exercises) to help the child gain some control over anxiety; third, prepare the child to start taking action by using covert (e.g., imaginal) change techniques to rehearse changes in their mind's eye; fourth, rehearse the planned changes through role play and practice; and, fifth, begin making the actual changes in vivo, that is, in their everyday life. A key point in the change process is to make these changes gradually by working up the hierarchy from moderately challenging situations to more difficult problems.

Although this sequence may define the ideal approach to planning and implementing change, there is a place for initially taking more active steps early on with some young clients. Young people who are depressed, for example, often benefit from being coaxed into action. These can be relatively straightforward tasks that may help motivate the client and provide him with a sense of accomplishment. If the child is poorly motivated as a result of depression, has become somewhat inactive, and is also avoidant due to fears and anxieties, developing a step-by-step plan to increase their activity level can be very helpful initially and also serve as a catalyst for further change. Identifying activities that they used to enjoy or ones that they would like to try can take some discussion, but once identified, the plan should be implemented gradually with short-term goals linking up to overall significant gains. These activities might include cleaning and organizing one's room, helping mom with housework or cooking a simple meal, or helping dad clean out the car. Or they might be more ambitious tasks: writing a story for a school contest, starting a small garden, or starting a part-time job (for older adolescents). For the child or adolescent who is more socially withdrawn or even socially phobic, joining a club, structured group activity, or community project can be helpful since the activities are planned out for them and carried out in an interactive environment. These more action-oriented approaches can reduce isolation and provide a sense of accomplishment and self-worth. However, with very anxious clients, one should not move too quickly. Encouraging young clients to take more active steps initially should be decided on a case-by-case basis. Overall, a good rule of thumb is to have young clients consider doing just a little more than they think they are capable of accomplishing.

Taking some initial action steps can help many young clients become more readily engaged in the change process and provide them with some initial feeling of genuine success. Success leads to increased self-confidence and optimism. However, lasting change, especially for clients with more serious depression or anxiety disorders, depends in large part on achieving incremental success while working up a hierarchy of increasingly challenging objectives. *Not only does this involve listing problems in order of difficulty, but it also means breaking each individual problem down into manageable steps in a logical sequence so the child or adolescent can achieve success one small step at a time.*

Teaching a phobic child to control their anxiety symptoms is a key step before moving toward a more action-oriented phase of the intervention. Relaxation skills for children and young adults can be readily taught and easily learned by children and adolescents alike. They should be kept relatively simple. By now, the child should have learned that what they think, how they feel, and what they are doing are all interconnected. Anxious thoughts create anxious feelings, and what the child does next can either worsen or lessen the anxiety they feel. Practitioners who have successfully taught the client how to identify when and why they are feeling anxious can introduce relaxation training by teaching the young client to simply take a few moments and take a few slow deep breaths, hold it for a few moments, and exhale slowly. As with watching a suspenseful movie, people will almost stop breathing when they are anxious, afraid, and waiting to see what happens next. Practitioners should model and instruct the young client as follows: "Stop, pause, take a deep breath, and let it out slowly. Do this exercise two or three times, and tell yourself, 'I can cope with this situation.'" When childdren are overly anxious, they will tend to lose their focus and be less likely to cope successfully with an anxiety-provoking situation, a setback that tends to makes matters worse and can leave them feeling less confident, more anxious, and more discouraged than before. Other forms of relaxation exercises include progressive muscle relaxation and guided imagery. Meditation may be more appealing to older adolescents and involves a bit more education and practice. It has become a core skill for many persons who have learned to cope with daily stress, anxiety disorders, and depression.

Once children have learned to calm themselves and control their anxiety, they can incorporate the next essential therapeutic coping skill: covertly rehearsing what they want to accomplish next. This approach appeals to children and adolescents. Children understand what daydreaming is, and the practitioner can put that ability to good use. Through the use of imagery, the young client can begin to master fears or overcome depression by practicing what they want to achieve, step by step, in their imaginations. Systematic desensitization was described in Chapter 6 and is essentially the same technique. The use of the SUDS scale can be a big help during these exercises since it provides the young person with a tool to measure how anxious they feel during the imaginal exposure exercise and can be reinforcing when they employ it as a form of self-evaluation.

Say, for example, a child is afraid to leave home and go to school and also appears to be depressed due, in part, to being isolated from peers. Having completed an MFS assessment, results reveal no compelling family problems that would account for the child's distress. A good starting point is to help the client imagine confronting their difficulties a little bit at a time. For younger children, the practitioner can help them imagine themselves leaving the house with a new backpack, getting on the school bus with the other kids in the neighborhood, riding to school, sitting in the classroom engaged in their studies, having lunch in the cafeteria, making new friends on the playground, and coming home at the end of the day—activities that might initially be scary for him to think about. The practitioner can begin by having the child do some simple breathing exercises and then proceed through this sequence of events in his imagination. The practitioner should closely observe the child's body language (e.g., tensioning, squirming in their seat, not breathing fully) should he begin to become anxious. As the client proceeds from one step to the next, the practitioner can help the child remain calm by reminding him to breathe fully and maintain the image in his mind until he feels comfortable with it. Then, he can move on to the next step in the hierarchy.

If the child is not comfortable with this type of exercise, the practitioner can use other activities such as play figures and blocks (e.g., build a model of the school with blocks, invent and play out scenarios with other children, etc.) or use a blank coloring book to create images at each step along the hierarchy (e.g., the school bus, sitting at the lunch table, etc.). Over time, the child is likely to become calmer discussing each scene in the hierarchy.

Covert exposure and using coping skills in the relative safety of the practitioner's office is a good start but is usually not sufficient for helping the child master their fear or overcome depression. Children and adolescents (and adults, for that matter) generally don't achieve their intervention goals until they successfully use their new skills in everyday life. The next step is to help the client begin engaging in graduated exposure, that is, practicing the behavior a little at a time while gradually increasing the challenge. Planning the first action steps is critical to ensure initial success. Assuming a supportive parent is in the picture, planning that first day of school for the phobic child should begin by making the day as positive as possible. For the first few days, it might be helpful for a parent to accompany the child to school, if that is possible, spend a few minutes with the child before the school day begins, and gradually reduce the amount of time to a quick hug and goodbye as the child becomes more readily engaged with the other students. At that point, perhaps, taking the bus may be the next challenge, and the child (having had some initial success) may take to this goal more readily. Graduated exposure may take a few days to a couple of weeks, but most anxious children will become readily engaged once they attain some mastery over the anticipatory anxiety and make it through the first few days of school.

For the socially anxious child, the practitioner and parents might arrange an opportunity for the child to practice a brief presentation in front of people the child knows—a couple friends from an after-school program or some neighborhood children. Although presenting to a friendly audience might not be as compelling as the real classroom experience, it might be enough of a confidence booster to help the client feel more able to take on the real experience. Whatever the source of fear (as long as it presents no real danger), graduated exposure treatments remain the most effective form of intervention for anxiety disorders in children.

Kendall (1992, 1994) developed and tested a sixteen-week program focused on teaching children how to better cope with emotional disorders. This program incorporates, in a more formal way, the skills discussed above. The skill package developed by Kendall and associates is quite similar to a range of other eclectic CBT models, including those targeting depression in children and adolescents. These approaches also combine psycho-education, emotional regulation, problem solving, social skills, and efforts to increase the young person's activity level in social contexts (Stark et al., 2006). A brief summary of these essential skills follows:

- Session 1: The practitioner develops a rapport with the child, creates a nonpressured environment to put the child at ease, assesses the child's understanding of the problem, and gauges readiness for treatment.
- Sessions 2 and 3: The practitioner helps the child to accurately identify and better understand their own feelings and emotional responses. Methods often include looking at pictures of people and identifying what each might be feeling, role-playing scenarios to demonstrate how a person might act when they are sad, anxious, or angry, for example. The practitioner moves at the child's pace.
- Session 4: When the child has learned to identify anxiety accurately, the practitioner helps them to use tension as a cue for using relaxation skills (e.g., muscle relaxation, breathing exercises).
- Session 5: The practitioner helps the child identify and articulate the content of their cognitive processes through "self-talk," covertly challenging these cognitions, and replacing them with coping "self-talk" to reduce anxiety.
- Session 6: The child then learns and starts using problem-solving strategies. The method focuses on helping the child identify distressing situations, feelings, and thoughts and then explore coping and problem-solving responses to ameliorate the situation.
- Session 7: In this session, the child learns to engage in self-evaluation of their own performance without judging themselves too harshly. This includes self-reinforcement for good efforts and partial successes.
- Session 8: The child reviews their progress, summarizes what they have learned, and records these coping skills for future reference.
- Sessions 9 through 16: The child then builds on their self-assessment and coping skills by implementing them with real

anxiety-provoking problems—covertly and in vivo in a graduated manner using their anxiety self-rating scale (0–100).

- The termination process emphasizes evaluation, reward for successes, anticipating future challenges, and requesting occasional booster sessions as needed. Parents (who should be coached in these techniques along the way) need to "take over" at this point and help keep the child on track with encouragement, reminders, and reinforcement.

When working with children, case management skills are often a key part of the intervention plan and may include any and all of the following:

- Making referrals for psychological testing, medical examinations, other specialized assessments (e.g., childhood sexual abuse);
- Interviewing key informants in the child's life (e.g., teachers, coaches, other significant adults);
- Coordinating services with other providers (e.g., school social worker, juvenile justice officer, "big brother" or "big sister," etc.)

Depending on the service mission of the agency, social workers should think well beyond the consulting room (having obtained informed consent) and work with the larger community system, those key persons who can observe, influence, and reward psychosocial improvements in the young client's life.

Incorporating Essential Coping Skills into Family Therapy for the Depressed and Anxious Child

There are three major reasons for utilizing family therapy in the context of helping the depressed or anxious child and adolescent: (1) to resolve other problems within the family—which may include mental disorders, couples conflict, domestic violence, child abuse and neglect, substance abuse, or other behavioral problems in the parents or siblings—that appear to have a negative impact on the identified client; (2) to have at least one parent and, possibly, other family members learn how to help the identified child or adolescent practice these new coping skills and reinforce the child's use of these new skills; and (3) to improve communication and problem-solving skills in the family for the benefit of the identified client and to improve family functioning as a whole. Practitioners and researchers increasingly agree on this point: interventions with children or adolescents will be hampered considerably if problems in the family that contribute to that child's difficulties are not addressed in a constructive manner. Children and adolescents are more likely to succeed if other family problems are addressed concurrently and if other family members support the child's efforts to improve.

Summary

Multiple factors often contribute to the cause and maintenance of childhood and adolescent anxiety and depressive disorders. If the family is relatively intact and well functioning, children and adolescents might respond well to a combination of individual and family interventions, with other family members serving as important allies in helping the child overcome their difficulties. If an MFS assessment strongly suggests that the child's emotional difficulties are, at least in part, a result of family dysfunction, then improvements in the child or adolescent's condition are likely to require direct intervention through the use of family therapy to improve family communications and resolve specific problems that may be negatively affecting the child directly. These problems might include substance abuse, domestic violence, or other forms of psychopathology. Contemporary evidence-based approaches to child and adolescent emotional disorders flexibly combine individual and family interventions to optimally address the child's distress and factors that maintain it. Case management approaches are also often necessary to recruit other collaborators in the community to help the child or adolescent generalize their progress to other settings such as the school environment. Case management efforts are also necessary to coordinate care with other providers such as school psychologists, child psychiatrists, and other professionals.

Case Study: Lyla

The Comprehensive Service Plan (Assessment, Intervention, Evaluation)

Use all available information from the client and significant others, your observations, and input from other professionals to conduct both quantitative and qualitative aspects of this multidimensional-functional assessment.

Client identification data: (gender; age; marital status; sexual orientation; family composition; employment; racial, ethnic, cultural, religious/spiritual affiliation and identity, etc.)

Lyla is a seven-year-old African-American girl who lives with her mother. Philippa, Lyla's mother, is twenty-seven years old and works as a nurse's aide in a local general hospital. Her father, Antwon, is thirty-four. Philippa and Antwon are not married and do not live together, but in the last two years, Antwon has visited Philippa and his daughter at least once weekly. Antwon works during the day as a manager of a small grocery store in town and works three nights per week as a security guard. For the past three years, he has also been a secular deacon in his church. Philippa and Antwon both trace their heritage to the rural southern United States.

The presenting problem

Description of problem (client's view)

In response to this practitioner's query as to why she came with her mom, Lyla responds (while hiding behind the chair in which her mother is sitting), "I don't know." Her mother reports that Lyla "has a lot of fears," that she "does everything she can to stay away from school," and that she "wakes up crying sometimes at night." She adds that when she is in school, she tends to keep to herself, does her work, and likes to color a lot. She sometimes plays with one other girl in her class.

Description of problem (practitioner's view)

In addition to Philippa's description, it also appears (based on a private interview with Philippa) that there has been a lot of conflict since Lyla's dad come back on the scene. These heated encounters apparently are very upsetting for Lyla, and she tends to have more night terrors after these incidents. This increased anxiety may also contribute to Lyla's school phobias and clinging to her mother.

Psychosocial history with an emphasis on problem trajectory

Philippa reports that Lyla was a difficult child from the beginning, that she was very difficult to soothe, cried excessively, and "always seemed to be real sensitive." Early on, she was diagnosed with a congenital immune deficiency for which she has been treated on and off for many years. Lyla has had a series of serious infections and has spent a lot of time in the hospital for one so young, often weeks or months at a time. She missed a fair amount of school, was never in day-care or preschool programs, and is a bit behind in her education. Despite being almost eight years old, she is just starting the first grade. Philippa, with the urging of a friend who is an elementary school teacher, did a fair amount of remedial work with Lyla, especially with regard to teaching her how to read. Lyla reads at a fourth-grade level but needs to catch up in other areas.

During those early years, Antwon was actively in the picture but was struggling with a drug problem according to Philippa. She finally insisted that he not come around anymore because his presence was too upsetting for Philippa and possibly for Lyla as well. There was some evidence of physical abuse directed at Philippa, although she characterized it as "not that bad. I could handle him OK."

Philippa grew up with both parents, two sisters, and a brother in a working-class home. Her dad worked on the local commuter railroad, and her mother, who stayed at home when the children were young, would later take part-time work cleaning offices downtown after business hours. During that time, the children would be on their own to do their homework and take care of some of the domestic duties. Philippa recalls her own trouble with anxiety as she became a teenager and had (what she later found out by reading a popular woman's magazine) a "panic attack." Despite the attack, Philippa pressed on, told no one about it, and over time, found that she was able to "work through it" and, eventually, "got over it." She still occasionally feels a "little panicky" but has learned to slow down, breathe deeply, and "let it pass." She also reports that she finds prayer to be helpful in times of stress.

After Lyla was born, Philippa was supported, in part, by her own mother and father, who helped her out financially for a time while she was finishing her associate's degree and, then, training as a nurse's aide. Once working, she was able to afford her own apartment, and moved out of her parent's home. She has been working steadily since then, enjoys being a mom, and has good friends she can reach out to in time of need. Antwon, having been out of touch for a while, returned a couple of years ago and wanted to "reconnect." Although Philippa does not want to marry him (and he hasn't broached the subject), she feels that it is important for her daughter to know her dad. Despite some heated arguments over parenting and other personal matters, Philippa continues to let Antwon visit. When they are not arguing, Lyla seems to enjoy her father's company. Antwon entered drug rehab about four years ago and joined a local congregation. Over the past year, he was appointed a deacon and participates in various church activities.

Attempts to resolve the problems, previous treatment, and relevant outcomes

Because she spent so much time away from formal classes, it has only been recently that Philippa has sought help to cope with Lyla's clinging behavior, her refusal to go to school, and her disturbing night terrors. She was hoping Lyla would "grow out of these problems" as things became more stable at home.

The individual assessment

Mental status—cognitive disturbances: Describe the client's level of hallucinations, delusions, disorientation, bizarre behavior or speech, memory problems, serious confusion, or other symptoms of serious cognitive impairment. Include other troubling or dysfunctional beliefs or convictions.

Lyla reports being afraid of the other kids in school; she says, "they can be loud and tease me sometimes." She talks about being afraid that her mom won't come and pick her up after school (her mom works the 7-to-3 shift) or that something will happen to her mom while she's away. She has also drawn colored pictures of some of the images she recalls from her night terrors: images of witches carrying her away from home to some dark faraway place. She says she sleeps with her mom a lot of the time and is afraid that these witches will come into the house and take her away. The fears and anxieties, based on both mom's observational reports and those of Lyla's, seem very intense and quite debilitating. These are more than transitory childhood fears.

How would you rate the client's overall mental status during the past month?

POOR [0]   IMPAIRED [1]   MARGINAL [2]   GOOD [3]   EXCELLENT [4]

Mental status—emotional distress: Describe the client's level of depression, anxiety, and overall ability to regulate her/his emotions.

In addition to her reported fears, Lyla appears to be depressed, does not smile, and seems to be under a fair amount of emotional distress. Her mother reports that when she wakes up from night terrors, she sometimes cries uncontrollably.

> How would you rate your client's emotional well-being over the past thirty days?
>
> POOR [0]   IMPAIRED [1]   <u>MARGINAL [2]</u>   GOOD [3]   EXCELLENT [4]

Behavioral problems: Describe your client's overall ability to regulate her/his behavior. Consider things such as their ability to express her/himself effectively, ability to work at things patiently, tendencies to verbally or physically lash out at others, run away, harm her/himself, or proneness to impulsive, criminal, or substance-abusing behavior. How would you describe the client's overall impulse control?

Aside from her refusal to go to school, Lyla is very obedient and compliant. She will do most of what her mother asks her to do. Philippa reports that she seems to be so cooperative so that Philippa will not get angry at her for any particular reason. She is able to play by herself when she knows her mother is nearby and will color or read for hours at a time.

> How would you rate your client's behavioral control generally over the past thirty days?
>
> POOR [0]   IMPAIRED [1]   MARGINAL [2]   <u>GOOD [3]</u>   EXCELLENT [4]

Adaptive strengths and coping abilities: Describe your client's ability to cope with problems and everyday stressors. How would you describe the client's ability to assess problem situations, deal with "triggers," cope with stress, solve problems, and perhaps reach out to others for help in order to deal effectively with her/his difficulties?

Aside from her fears and depression, Lyla appears to be a very intelligent and well-behaved girl. She shows potential to do very well in school once she becomes more comfortable there and less socially isolated. At this point, however, she is not coping well with the normal transition from home to school.

> How would you rate your client's overall adaptive strengths and coping abilities over the past thirty days?
>
> POOR [0]   IMPAIRED [1]   <u>MARGINAL [2]</u>   GOOD [3]   EXCELLENT [4]

Health problems: Describe the client's overall health. Aside from normal, transient illnesses, think about the client's general health habits (e.g., smoking, heavy drinking, exercise, weight), chronic primary health disorders, the client's opinion of her/his own health, ability to engage in her/his usual activities relatively free from discomfort, overall energy level, hospitalizations and treatments for illness other than psychiatric ones. Consider her/his documented medical history and any ongoing treatments.

Lyla's chronic immune system disorder appears to be improving. She is not taking antibiotic treatments at the time, although doctors are monitoring her condition regularly. Other than this condition, she is in good health.

> How would you rate your client's health over the past thirty days?
>
> **POOR** [0]   **IMPAIRED** [1]   **MARGINAL** [2]   **GOOD** [3]   **EXCELLENT** [4]

Use of alcohol and other drugs: Describe the client's use of alcohol, illicit substances (cocaine, heroin, marijuana, hallucinogens, etc.) and abuse of prescription medication. How often does the client use them, in what quantity, and how serious are the psychological, physical, or social consequences associated with their use?

There is no current evidence of the abuse of alcohol or other drugs by the client or her parents.

> How would you rate the client's functioning in the past month with regard to substance use?
>
> **POOR** [0]   **IMPAIRED** [1]   **MARGINAL** [2]   **GOOD** [3]   **EXCELLENT** [4]

Recreational activities: Consider what the client does for fun (alone or with others), hobbies, relaxation (reading, TV, video games, playing cards, etc.), and physical exercise (walking, jogging, biking, etc.). How would you describe the client's overall involvement in positive recreational activities?

Aside from her interests in coloring and reading, Lyla's recreational outlets are very circumscribed. She gets little exercise, and is used to staying indoors, perhaps as a consequence of past long convalescences.

> How would you rate the adequacy of the client's participation in healthy recreational activities over the past thirty days?
>
> POOR [0]   IMPAIRED [1]   MARGINAL [2]   GOOD [3]   EXCELLENT [4]

Material resources: Describe your client's current or (if client is institutionalized) most recent living situation overall. Consider such things as adequacy of food, clothing, shelter, and safety.

Lyla's material needs are well cared for.

> How would you rate the overall adequacy of the client's material resources over the past month?
>
> POOR [0]   IMPAIRED [1]   MARGINAL [2]   GOOD [3]   EXCELLENT [4]

Independent living/self-care: Describe how well your client manages her/his household, takes care of personal hygiene, eats, sleeps, and otherwise cares for her/his own basic needs.

Not applicable to Lyla. Mother's abilities as homemaker and parent are exceptional.

> How would you rate the client's ability to live independently and take care of her/his basic needs over the past thirty days?
>
> POOR [0]   IMPAIRED [1]   MARGINAL [2]   GOOD [3]   EXCELLENT [4]

Work (role) satisfaction: Describe the client's current work-related or other important role-related activities (e.g., employed, student, homemaker, volunteer, retired person, disabled, etc.). Describe those activities and responsibilities that occupy the client in a productive manner.

Lyla's role as a student is somewhat limited at this time. When she is in school, she works well independently, but she is socially isolated because of her fears and anxieties.

How would you rate the client's work or role satisfaction over the past thirty days?

POOR [0]   IMPAIRED [1]   MARGINAL [2]   GOOD [3]   EXCELLENT [4]

Legal problems: Describe any legal problems the client has had or continues to have. These include minor infractions (e.g., public drunkenness, shoplifting inexpensive items, minor traffic violations, public disturbances) and more serious crimes (e.g., assault and battery, rape, burglary, driving under the influence, etc.). Consider her/his status (probation, awaiting imprisonment, parole). Also, consider any civil suits leveled at the client, pending financial judgments against her/him, and so on. Overall, how would you describe the client's current legal situation?

The client and her parents are having no legal problems at this time.

How would you rate the client's legal situation over the past thirty days?

POOR [0]   IMPAIRED [1]   MARGINAL [2]   GOOD [3]   EXCELLENT [4]

DSM-5 Diagnosis

Separation anxiety disorder 309.21

Family relations: Describe the client's current family structure, including authority, hierarchy, alliances, roles, rules, boundaries, subsystems (e.g., couple, siblings, parent-child alliances); patterns of interactions and quality of communications; specific problems within the family; specific adaptive strengths within the family; and how the family members describe their own racial, ethnic, cultural, and religious identities.

Current conflict between Philippa and Antwon, although not the main cause of the child's fears, certainly does not help the situation. The conflicts they have are of long standing, although in the past year or so they have made progress agreeing on when Antwon can visit and talking about their own tenuous relationship together. At this point, Philippa's parents express concern about Antwon but have become more accepting of his return to the picture since his standing in the community has improved as a result of his steady appearance as deacon. Their future together is currently uncertain. Philippa continues to feel a strong bond of support from her parents. Antwon's parents are both deceased.

How would you rate the quality of the client's immediate family relationships over the past thirty days?

POOR [0]   IMPAIRED [1]   MARGINAL [2]   <u>GOOD [3]</u>   EXCELLENT [4]

Immediate social relationships (close friends and acquaintances): Describe the quality of your client's relationships with those available friends and acquaintances, as applicable. Over the past month, how would you describe the quality of the interaction overall between your client and them with respect to closeness, intimacy, general interpersonal satisfaction, effective communications, degree of conflict, level of hostility, aggression, and evidence of any emotional or physical abuse?

Lyla's social adjustment is somewhat limited for her age. Whereas most children in her age group are more actively engaged socially, she keeps to herself, and only interacts with other adults or children when encouraged.

How would you rate the quality of the client's immediate social relationships over the past thirty days?

POOR [0]   <u>IMPAIRED [1]</u>   MARGINAL [2]   GOOD [3]   EXCELLENT [4]

Extended social relationships: Describe the type and quality of relationships between your client and others in the client's community (other than close friends and family). These people might include other families, law enforcement, human service agencies, school personnel, coworkers, and others from whom the client receives support or with whom the client is having serious conflict.

When considering Lyla and her mother as a family unit, they are not well integrated into the community. Although Philippa has friends at work, she has been somewhat isolated herself over the past couple of years given that most of her nonworking time is spent caring for Lyla and taking care of related responsibilities. Philippa has been somewhat cut off from former friends, her church attendance, and other social connections.

How would you rate the quality of the client's social relationships over the past thirty days?

POOR [0]   IMPAIRED [1]   MARGINAL [2]   GOOD [3]   EXCELLENT [4]

A concise summary of the MFS assessment: Highlight the client's areas of distress and adaptive strengths. Emphasize those areas that are most likely to be emphasized in the intervention plan.

Lyla's anxiety problems are likely the consequence of a number of contributing factors: an inherited anxious temperament (her mom struggled with anxiety problems for years), early and prolonged separations due to medical problems, and disruption in family life with accompanying conflict. Although her mother has provided a comfortable, nurturing, and enriching upbringing for Lyla, she has been working as a single mom and has often lacked the supports she needed to help Lyla spend more time away from her. These activities include after-school events, weekend "day camp" activities sponsored by the church, and similar opportunities where Lyla could socialize and become more engaged with other children.

Recommendations for further focused assessment (note recommended referrals to consultants or additional instruments to be used)

None at this time.

THE COMPREHENSIVE SERVICE PLAN SUMMARY

Assessment/Problems	Goals	Objectives	Interventions	Evaluation plan
(Briefly describe key problems to be addressed.)	(State desired outcome for each problem.)	(Describe specific "stepping stones" toward each GOAL. Update as client progresses.)	(Describe specific interventions to be used.)	(Describe indexes to be used for tracking progress.)
Fears and night terrors	Reduce anxieties and night terrors	Develop an evening ritual with fun stories; set up schedule for gradually having Lyla sleep in her own bed consistently	*Supportive skills:* Develop a working relationship with mom; include dad when it seems necessary to quell couple's tensions; develop a fun and relaxed rapport with the child, first with mom, then alone	Develop a chart, so Lyla can record how many hours per night she sleeps in her own bed (based on mom's observations); also, document incidents of night terrors
Lyla's separation anxiety and school refusal	Have child attend school regularly; increase other social activities	Develop a clear morning ritual and schedule for getting ready for school; discuss reward system with mom to facilitate this plan	*Therapeutic coping skills:* Help Lyla identify her feelings and fears, learn what anxiety is, and help her understand how it affects the way she thinks and behaves; use drawings, pictures, and other "fun" media to help her better understand that her fears can't harm her or her mom	Use a similar chart to record how much time it takes Lyla to get ready for school; set reasonable goals for a special weekend reward
Need for more social networking and supports for mom	Increase social activities for mother without Lyla		Role play some of the situations at school that she might find scary; help her learn to breathe deeply, exhale, and quell her anxiety when she feels scared	

Help Lyla practice "self-talk" to covertly challenge her fears when her mom drops her off at school and reassure herself that her mom will be there every day to pick her up;

Develop an exposure hierarchy with mom; start by planning time together at the school a few minutes early (before school begins); during this time, she and her mom can read part of a story about brave princesses and daring little girls; this time should be gradually reduced by a minute a week and Lyla encouraged to play with other children before class begins

Improve communication and problem solving between mom and dad to make visits more fun for Lyla and less anxiety provoking; visits should be extended, so Antwon can spend more time with Lyla without mom present

THE COMPREHENSIVE SERVICE PLAN SUMMARY (CONTINUED)

Assessment/Problems	Goals	Objectives	Interventions	Evaluation plan
(Briefly describe key problems to be addressed.)	(State desired outcome for each problem.)	(Describe specific "stepping stones" toward each GOAL. Update as client progresses.)	(Describe specific interventions to be used.)	(Describe indexes to be used for tracking progress.)
			Broaden Philippa's social network and supports, so she spends at least one weekly event without her daughter; participate in more parent-teacher and similar school and church activities where children are supervised in activities separate from parents	

CHAPTER TWELVE

Externalizing Disorders of Childhood and Adolescence

EXTERNALIZING DISORDERS refer to observable behavioral problems including oppositional defiant disorder (e.g., chronically disruptive, disobedient) and conduct disorder (e.g., fire-setting, theft, animal cruelty, sexual promiscuity, interpersonal aggression, drug use, and other high-risk behaviors). Oppositional defiant disorder (ODD) is usually associated with younger children whereas conduct disorder (CD) tends to be identified with adolescents. Externalizing disorders have been shown to be associated with family risk factors, including substance abuse and criminality (particularly in fathers), other forms of mental illness in the family, highly disruptive family conflict, domestic violence, and child abuse and neglect. CD may also be somewhat predictive of joining gangs and development of adult antisocial personality. Adolescents who show a pronounced lack of concern for others' welfare and a virtual absence of remorse or guilt concerning the harmful consequences of their behaviors are more likely to meet criteria for adult psychopathy. Practitioners should also be prepared to assess for attention deficit/hyperactivity disorder (ADHD), a problem that co-occurs often with conduct disorder. This level of assessment may also require the assistance of a professional trained in specific diagnostic testing for ADHD and associated learning disabilities (e.g., reading, math).

Assessment

DSM-5 criteria for ODD and CD reflect the basic description above and should be reviewed in detail (APA, 2013). However, assessment should go beyond basic description and practitioners should conduct a thorough MFS assessment that minimally includes an examination of how the child or adolescent's disruptive behavior is associated with key mental status indicators (e.g., thought disorders), emotional well-being (e.g., depression), level of impulsivity (e.g., aggression), interpersonal relations at home and in the community, school performance, substance abuse, and overall health. Any and all of these problems can exacerbate behavioral problems, and, reciprocally, conduct disorder can aggravate other psychosocial difficulties and co-occur with other childhood and adolescent disorders (Chen, Thrane, Whitbeck, Johnson, & Hoyt, 2007; Connor & Lochman, 2010; McMahon & Frick, 2005; McMahon, Wells, & Kotler, 2006; O'Hare, 2015; Smith, Barkley, & Shapiro, 2006). For example, mental status and mood should be reviewed carefully to identify more serious distortions such as delusional thinking and the possibility of major mood disorder or onset of schizophrenia in older adolescents. Impulsive behaviors including violence and substance abuse should be carefully examined to identify more immediate dangers of harming others, becoming involved in criminality (e.g., drug dealing, gang affiliation), or the risk of the child or adolescent putting themselves in harm's way. Family relationships should be assessed carefully to determine if the child or adolescent is being physically abused and to determine the competence of parental supervision. Older adolescents may also be putting others in the home in danger (e.g., physically or sexually abusing a sibling, threatening adults for drug money). Associations in the community with gang members, street criminals, and drug dealers should be explored. Some effort to determine the client's general health should be made to determine if the adolescent is at risk for sexually transmitted diseases or other risks (HIV) via intravenous drug use.

A functional assessment of a child or adolescent's behavior over time is essential. Disruptive behavior in children and more serious conduct disordered behavior in adolescents does not happen at random but will reveal specific patterns that highlight important antecedents associated with conduct disordered behaviors. Is violent behavior, for example, more likely to occur at home or in the community? Where, with whom, and how often is the abuse of alcohol or other drugs occurring? Does the adolescent associate with anyone who appears to have a more prosocial effect on their behavior (e.g., older adults who act as unofficial mentors)? How structured is the child or adolescent's behavior during the week? Does he leave home and return at regular hours? Does he attend school regularly if at all? What other strengths and positive adaptive capacities does the adolescent have? Is he using them to his potential? At what times during the week does he seem more likely to get into trouble? How often does he have encounters with law enforcement or school administration? Although implicit in the above, practitioners should take care to utilize a systems perspective as they collate their assessment data. Positive and problematic behaviors in the context of family, school, peers, and community should be seen as interacting and somewhat reciprocal in their effects.

Given the nature of some of these behaviors, it is unlikely that adolescent clients will provide a fully transparent picture of their daily routines, particularly those activities that they don't want you to know about. Interviewing adults in the family is essential whenever possible. It is also important to acquire informed consent from parents and guardians to talk with juvenile officers, teachers, coaches, and others who may have regular opportunities to observe the child. Laying down the expectation early that you want all the adults in the child or adolescent's world to be in contact with you (the practitioner) gives a clear signal that you will not be able to help your young client unless you know what is really going on in his life. Relying solely on the client's self-report, or even his parents, is likely to lead to a skewed or incomplete representation of the facts.

For obvious reasons, the social worker should expect that parents or guardians might not be forthcoming in their support for the child or adolescent. In the case of younger children, they may be either more defensive about the child's "bad" behavior or more willing to blame the child exclusively, especially if there has been abuse in the home. If abuse is suspected as one contributing factor that might account for their disruptive behavior, a more thorough abuse assessment will have to be conducted. If cooperation is more readily provided, practitioners will have an easier time identifying the antecedents to the child's behavioral difficulties. As a result, the practitioner will be better poised to help the parents improve their nurturing and disciplining skills. For the more troubled adolescent, there may be a longer history of domestic conflict, ineffective parenting, and greater difficulty in helping the parents to employ effective disciplinary measures. For the older adolescent who is getting involved in criminal activities, the emphasis may have to shift to engaging external authorities to rein in the client's behavior. Only after having completed a thorough MFS assessment based on multiple informants can the practitioner design an intervention plan at the proper level of care. Can this problem be managed within the family unit alone? Should school personnel become involved? Is it necessary to coordinate efforts with the criminal justice system? In more serious cases, practitioners should be prepared to intervene at all levels.

Co-occurring ADHD

Many behaviorally disordered children also struggle with the signs and symptoms of ADHD (McMahon & Frick, 2005). These children and adolescents struggle with being able to pay sustained attention to academic and other tasks, become easily frustrated and bored, can be easily distracted, tend to be disorganized and forgetful, are often fidgety, and react impulsively to frustration. Many of these symptoms overlap considerably with the "behaviorally disordered" child or adolescent, and the casual observer will not be able to distinguish the causes of their impulsivity, difficulty following directions, or staying "on task." These behaviors, frustrating for teachers, parents, and other adults, tend to be disruptive to the daily routines of others. Sorting out ADHD from other behavioral disorders can be difficult, but one can determine if the signs of ADHD are situational or not. Some children may do well in the relatively quiet structure of a well-run classroom but not at home. For other children, home life may be conducive to completing their work but they may have difficulty functioning well in school. When contextual disparities such as this become apparent, practitioners should consider the possibility of situational problems before applying a diagnosis of ADHD.

Intervention

A large and growing body of research supports a range of cognitive-behavioral and contingency-management therapies for externalizing childhood and adolescent disorders (e.g., Alexander, Waldron, Newberry, & Liddle, 1988; Corcoran, 2008; Farmer, Compton, Burns, & Robertson, 2002; Foster, 1994; Kazdin & Weisz, 1998; McMahon & Forehand, 1984; McMahon, Wells, & Kotler, 2006; Ollendick & King, 1998; Silverman & Berman; 2001; Smith, Barkley, & Shapiro, 2006; Thyer, 1995; Webster-Stratton & Herbert, 1994). Cognitive-behavioral approaches for children's disorders are now increasingly implemented within the context of behaviorally oriented family therapies (e.g., Brown et al., 2008; Compton, Burns, Egger, & Robertson, 2002; Northey, Wells, Siverman, & Bailey, 2003; Sexton, 2011) and are often incorporated into ecological and multisystemic frameworks to deal with complex and serious behavior problems such as youthful delinquency (e.g., Henggeler, Schoenwald, Borduin, Rowland, & Cunningham, 1998; Henggeler, Schoenwald, Borduin, Rowland, & Cunningham, 2009). Treatment for co-occurring ADHD is likely to include stimulant medications. Although serious debate continues with regard to overprescribing, well over one hundred studies including controlled trials attest to their effectiveness in improving concentration, enhancing school performance, and reducing disruptive behaviors. These medications have been shown to work particularly well when combined with well-run contingency management programs in the classroom and in the home (Fabiano et al., 2009;

Farmer, Compton, Burns, & Robertson, 2002; Smith, Barkley, & Shapiro, 2006).

Developing and maintaining a supportive, collaborative, and empathic relationship with behaviorally disordered children, adolescents, and their families can be challenging. Children with "internalizing disorders" (e.g., depression, anxiety) tend to be a bit quieter and more compliant and, perhaps, evoke greater sympathy. They tend to suffer in silence and incur less social disapproval from the adults around them. Parents, teachers, school officials, juvenile officers in the community, and social workers, however, are more likely to have their attention drawn to behaviorally disordered children and adolescents and become increasingly frustrated in attempting to deal with them. Often, overly punitive measures or, conversely, the lack of constructive disciplinary measures further reinforce much of this "bad" behavior.

To maintain an empathic link with conduct disordered children and adolescents, it is important for practitioners to keep in mind that these children are generally not happy with their circumstances. Their goal in life is not to incur the wrath of adults around them, although the opposite may seem to be the case. Impulsivity, learning difficulties, trouble regulating emotional responses, and failure to get along with others reveals a picture of young persons who are quite distressed. Their frustrations are palpable, and their readiness to disobey or associate themselves primarily with others who are often in trouble seems, at times, almost beyond their control.

Developing a working relationship with behaviorally disordered children, adolescents, and their families is a challenge. Often, both parents are not currently in the picture, so practitioners should be prepared to deal with a single parent, often one who is feeling overwhelmed. If both parents (or guardians) are in the picture, there is a good chance that it is a second marriage, and the stepfather or stepmother is probably not too happy being burdened with what they see as their spouse's "baggage." Constant complaints from the school and others in the community only increase the parent's frustration, often leading to ineffective punitive methods, hollow threats, and occasional contempt and despair about ever having a normal family life again.

Practitioners must connect with the identified child or adolescent as well as the parents/guardians in a way that does not communicate blame. Although taking history and a conducting a thorough analysis of the problem over time is essential, practitioners must take pains to be empathic and emphasize a forward-looking, problem-solving approach. Depending on the severity of the problem, practitioners should communicate optimism that many behavior disorders in children and adolescents can be brought under control, but everyone will have to consider making adjustments. Communicating a sense of "we'll have to work on this together" is a helpful and positive stance.

Each family member must be carefully listened to. When everyone feels that their concerns, frustrations, and desires have been "heard," practitioners can then underscore the common ground they all share: we all have expectations, and we all have to give something to get what we want and live together as a family. Unless there is outright abuse and criminality (e.g., sexual or physical abuse, domestic violence), practitioners should avoid the victim-villain characterization many troubled families bring into the consulting room. If there is abuse or violence, social workers then have to confront the challenge of balancing their roles as both mandated reporter with maintenance of a viable working alliance. If that is not feasible, then therapeutic work may have to be continued by another practitioner after the case has been adjudicated.

The child or adolescent and their family are often very discouraged and feel that there is little likelihood for improvement. It is important to do two things to help bolster the family's morale: (1) help to motivate them by focusing on problems that can be improved, and (2) set reasonable goals. Although it may be temporarily heartening to tell parents and the child that you know (based on your experience and expertise) that matters can improve, this will do little to convince your clients over the long run. In order for them to feel "in their gut" that things can get better, they must experience some initial successes. These immediate goals can be any one of the following examples: a time-out from fighting; a temporary "truce" or contract to abide by certain house rules; eliminating yelling and name calling, those behaviors that are unnecessarily provocative and create a contentious atmosphere; an agreement on the part of the parents not to make any decisions about their child or adolescent until they agree upon a basic policy (this is an important step since much dysfunctional parenting results from a lack of parental consistency and cooperation); and an agreement on the part of the child/adolescent that they share in some part of the solution, so their cooperation is important. If these basic guidelines can be honored for even a week or two, it can create an atmosphere more conducive to making progress with more long-term challenges.

If there are two adults in parent roles, it is important to meet with them alone for a session or two to help them agree on setting limits with their son or daughter. This step is critical. The parents must be able and willing to use their authority, and they must cooperate in order to help a conduct disordered child. As is often the case, they will likely reveal other differences and sources of conflict that are not directly related to the child or adolescent's problem. The child or adolescent may be "triangulated," that is, become a target to which parents attribute difficulties they are having as a couple. Marital conflicts must be assessed thoroughly (see Chapter 10) and differentiated from problems the couple are having in their role as parents. If, for example, there is infidelity in the relationship, and one partner is angry and will not cooperate with the other on any other matters (e.g., money, parenting), then this problem must be addressed separately from their difficulties as parents. Parents will often agree in principle that it makes little sense to "take it out on the kids," even though they often, unwittingly perhaps, engage in scapegoating, sabotage, or other forms of triangulation. Substance abuse in one or both parents is often a problem in behaviorally disordered families. Without addressing it, little is likely to be accomplished by focusing on the child or adolescent's difficulties exclusively. Once parents agree to temporarily set aside their own difficulties and cooperate for the welfare of the child, the work can proceed. Once the child or adolescent is stabilized, other matters unique to the couple can be revisited. Sometimes, a success experience in parenting can reduce hopelessness, reduce tension in the household, and increase good will and a feeling that, as a couple, they may be better able to resolve some of their own difficulties.

The goals set for the child during this early period should also be achievable, and parents should be willing to reward partial successes. Of course, the goals depend on the type and severity of the problem and the age of the child. But small successes are important, and parents have to cooperate on helping the child achieve these. Optimism and the use of positive reinforcement are overwhelmingly more productive than sanctions and punitive measures. These should be used as a last resort. Parenting skills will be discussed in more detail below.

Effective coping skills with behaviorally disordered children and adolescents were developed partly on the premise that these children have deficits in the way they perceive and understand interpersonal relationships, difficulties understanding and regulating their own emotions, and a lack of problem-solving skills. Many children and adolescents, for reasons that include temperament, family history, and social circumstances, tend to see other people's behavior as potentially exploitive, harmful, or threatening. This distortion in understanding how "relationships work" is exacerbated by their own difficulties in coping with frustration, managing their own anger, and coping with a tendency to lash out verbally or physically when they feel threatened or challenged. For some children, these expectations and tendencies are further aggravated by the reality that, in their daily lives, violence and exploitation may be part of their community experience: drug dealing, violence, gang activities, and a culture steeped in violence and exploitation. Even the most even-tempered and well-loved child can face serious challenges when dealing with a daily reality where force and threats of violence are a frequent occurrence.

When working with the child or adolescent, it is important to engage in focused conversations about their daily encounters with others and pursue nonjudgmental questioning about their relationships. What do they think the other person expects of them? What does the young client offer the other person? How would another person, perhaps, deal with the same situation? For example, the child reports that someone knocked over their lunch tray in the cafeteria in school. How did that happen? What was your reaction? What did the other person say? Then what happened? Carefully examining the child or adolescent's thoughts, feelings, and behaviors in daily real-life scenarios will provide a blueprint (a cognitive schema) for the way they tend to interpret and deal with interpersonal relations.

Other questions should explore different types of relationships. Do you have any close friends? Who is your best friend? Why is that person your best friend? What do you have in common? Does that person think you are their best friend? Examining what the client's priorities are in that relationship, what they expect from the other person, what the client brings to the relationship, and what level of trust they have can go a long way toward understanding how the client relates to others and how the client sees himself in a relationship.

Gradually, a picture of the client's relationships will emerge. Given that the client has already been identified as behaviorally disordered, one should be prepared for a continuum of responses: either the client has the capacity for a prosocial and nonexploitive relationship with at least one other person, or (at the other extreme) tends to see all relationships as threatening and potentially harmful. Some "antisocial" children may have the capacity to engage in healthful prosocial relationships, but because of circumstances, these are limited in scope or opportunity. If, for example, they have witnessed or personally experienced much abuse at home, or they encounter much violence in their immediate community, they may keep any trusting relationships rather circumscribed. Adolescents in similar circumstances, may show little ability to engage in relationships unless there is some mutually agreed-upon "contract" that binds them to another: cooperating in criminal behaviors under pain of retaliation (e.g., gang affiliation), that is, relationships that are not generally considered healthful.

If the child or adolescent seems to have the capacity to relate to others on a more functional and empathic level, wants to get along with others, and reduce conflict in their life, there is much that practitioners can do. Cognitive-behavioral efforts that focus on social skills can help the child more accurately read and interpret the behavior and feelings of others in social situations and respond in ways that promote healthful relationships. Practitioners should discuss actual daily encounters that the client has in school and elsewhere, help the client assess those interactions and social situations, examine the possibility that they are negatively distorting the intent of the "other," and then suggest the possibility of trying out more prosocial cognitions. As with the "lunch tray" incident mentioned above, the practitioner should help the client carefully examine the situation: "What were your immediate thoughts and feelings about what happened?" "How did the other person respond?" "Did you think they were laughing at you?" "Could it be that they were just nervous?" "Did they say 'excuse me' or 'I'm sorry'?" "Do you think they did it on purpose?" and so on. Of course, there are a number of possibilities. Perhaps the class bully did do it on purpose. What then? The practitioner might then have to examine the client's options: "So, you thought of attacking him. What do you think that would have accomplished?" "What do you think the resulting consequences might have been?" "What if someone got seriously hurt?" "What if that person were you?" and so on.

Perhaps the adolescent was actually being targeted in that incident, perhaps not. In either case, it is critically important to help the young person to *stop, think about what just happened, identify their feelings, and consider the potential consequences of their behaviors before acting.* Children and adolescents who are categorized as oppositional, conduct-disordered, or antisocial tend to act impulsively before they think, and often do not allow for time to process their feelings and determine what really happened. Their negative "blueprint" that it's a "dog-eat-dog world" readies them to lash out and defend themselves rather than stop, think, feel, and decide calmly what a balanced response might be. In some cases, peer expectations demand an immediate, and often aggressive, response.

Once the problem is examined in detail, practitioners can help their impulsive clients to rehearse the "stop, think, feel, act" routine by modeling this cognitive process for them. Practitioners can guide them by modeling prosocial self-statements (i.e., self-talk) aloud in the presence of the child or adolescent, help the client rehearse these skills by prompting them with cues to practice the self-statements, track the problem over time, and reward themselves for showing self-control. The steps to follow should include the folowing: (1) identify the event (client was called a name, pushed, threatened by another, etc.), (2) stop and appraise the situation accurately, (3) identify one's feelings, and (4) consider the response that will best lead to a positive outcome for the client (preferably, a nonviolent resolution). Helping the adolescent to identify and control their anger and other related responses, and using constructive responses to avert aggressive encounters (e.g., calmly joking about it, changing the subject) can go a long way toward helping a young person avoid negative and sometimes tragic violent encounters.

Using guided meditation and other visualization techniques for covert practice often appeals to adolescents, and can be a low-anxiety approach to helping them walk through the "stop, think, feel, act" routine before practicing it in vivo. This exercise can help the young person relax and visualize themselves identifying, processing, and responding to a potential problem situation in a prosocial manner. The technique is similar to that described in general in Chapter 6. After having practiced the process "in the mind's eye," the practitioner can use role playing to act out scenarios that are likely to provoke the client, try variations of it, and gradually make it more challenging for the adolescent to respond in a constructive way. Interjecting humor now and then may be helpful in putting the young person in a constructive frame of mind and help them get some perspective on the problem. Although role playing is helpful, there is no substitute for practicing in the real world, and it is likely that the client will have more than sufficient opportunities to try out their new skills in everyday life. Although it is not practical to plan such events, the client should be ready to use their new skills when the opportunity naturally arises and log a few notes to evaluate their handling of the situation. Helping the adolescent to use monitoring and evaluation of their own reactions is essential if they are to make progress and maintain their gains over time. If family therapy is being employed and parents are supportive of the child's efforts, parents should be included in this part of the intervention as "consultants" to offer encouragement and reinforcement for the child's progress.

Improving Parenting Skills

The broader context of family therapy can greatly enhance cognitive-behavioral interventions with conduct-disordered children. Family sessions can be used to improve communication, work on problem solving, and improve interpersonal behaviors among family members. But a core aspect of effective family therapy for behaviorally troubled children and adolescents assumes the need to improve parenting skills. Parents have the responsibility to use their authority to both nurture their children as well as provide consistent, positive disciplining. Single parents, at times, face even greater challenges in caring for a behaviorally disordered child. Much of the content below describes the essentials of effective parenting in general, but *these are principles that apply to younger children with emerging behavioral disorders as well as adolescents who might meet criteria for conduct disorder.* When a child or adolescent comes for an intervention for a serious behavior problem, it is often the case that good parenting skills have not been applied consistently. At some point, however, if the adolescent's behaviors become potentially too dangerous and the parents have lost control over the child, the juvenile justice system may have to intervene in the role of surrogate parent. These interventions can range from court-ordered supervision and family therapy, to institutionalization in psychiatric care facilities, to juvenile detention centers depending on the severity of the disordered behavior.

Effective parenting, in principle, is not complicated: consistent, genuine caring and nurturance; providing for both the child's psychosocial and physical well-being; showing an interest in the child's ideas, thoughts, feelings, and experiences; being vigilant about their activities and companions inside and outside the home; and having clear policies about what behaviors are to be rewarded and which ones will be sanctioned as needed. In actual practice, however, being an effective parent with a conduct-disordered child is a challenge. For a variety of reasons, some parents are more skilled than others. Often, ineffective parents lack assertiveness, are uncomfortable using their authority, are immature, inexperienced, were subjected to ineffective parenting when they were children, were victims of abuse or neglect, had parents who had mental illnesses or substance abuse problems, or had parents who were simply overwhelmed by money problems and other life circumstances. Although these factors can affect anyone's skills when they become parents themselves, there is good reason to believe that most parents can learn to be more effective.

Practitioners should be clear and focused about identifying both the strengths and deficits that a parent brings with them to treatment when trying to cope with a behaviorally disordered child. As discussed earlier, if either parent has serious problems of their own, these may have to be addressed before parenting skills can be improved. A drug-impaired father or mother is not likely to be vigilant and attentive to a young adolescent who is testing his parent's limits. If mom is sleeping off heavy drinking every day when her daughter comes home, an opportunity to engage her daughter and discuss her day, deal with problems, give her support, and monitor her homework is lost. When these problems occur on a consistent basis, children and adolescents often begin to feel that their parents don't really care what they are doing during or after school.

Assuming individual or couple's problems within the family are mitigated to the point where the parents can focus their attention on improving parenting skills, there is much that a practitioner can do to help them make some positive adjustments. For starters, the social worker can demonstrate nurturance (e.g., emotional and physical caring and playing). This approach may be more helpful with parents who have young children and are anxious and overly concerned with their children being on their best behavior all the times. Sitting with the family and playing a game that includes the child can be a great way to develop a sense of family fun. The parents may see that, with a little investment in the nurturing side of family life, their efforts to enforce ordinary levels of discipline come with less effort.

Some parents become very anxious or even "freak out" as their children approach adolescence. Perhaps they recall some of their own risky behaviors (which they probably kept from their own parents), or perhaps they are afraid of unwanted pregnancy, getting into trouble, drinking alcohol and using other drugs, the dangers of driving, and so forth. However, rather than responding to the onset of adolescence with a sense of fun and engaging their older children in adult conversations about high-risk behaviors, some parents allow their anxiety to transform them into rigid disciplinarians. As a result, their adolescent children express resentment about being "treated like children" and are likely to rebel. Although reasonable limits are important and needed during this time, what is also needed is a lot more conversation about matters that parents lie awake at night worrying about. More conversation, more interest in what the adolescent is doing, and less arbitrary rule enforcement can reduce tensions and improve parent-teen relations markedly. Many parents are unwilling to engage their adolescent children as young adults, and, as a result, tensions, conflicts, and behavior problems remain unresolved.

Practitioners can help parents engage their adolescent sons and daughters by modeling this kind of "adult conversation" in front of the parents and then inviting the parents to join in. Many clients recall their adolescent years as a time when their parents were always yelling at them and threatening them with sanctions of one kind or another. Practitioners can help parents relax a bit by discussing the high-risk concerns associated with adolescence and helping parents engage their sons and daughters in frank discussions about sex, drugs, and other high-risk behaviors. Modeling and in-session practice can get things started, but parents need to continue these conversations at home.

There are occasions, however, especially with conduct-disordered children and adolescents, when talking is not enough. Nurturance and understanding is no guarantee that children and adolescents will not engage in serious problem behaviors. Parents have to be willing to use their authority in a constructive yet definitive manner. Using sanctions in a graduated way that "fits the crime" should be negotiated between parents. If both parents are available, disciplinary measures must be implemented in concert and without ambivalence. Single parents need to be reasonably consistent with their directives. With younger children, such interventions should occur as close to the infraction as possible and should not be done punitively. Brief time outs in their room or loss of TV privileges work well. If cooperation with reasonable tasks (e.g., picking up toys, doing homework) is not forthcoming, sanctions can be increased. For older children or adolescents, sanctions need to be commensurate with the infraction.

Practitioners can help parents understand that positive disciplining skills should not be delivered in a way that communicates disrespect or contempt for the child or adolescent. Positive disciplining should be delivered calmly through simple, clear communications. It is also important for the parent to give a clear reason why she is disciplining the child and to frame it in a way that focuses on long-term outcomes. Parents who say, "I don't have to give you a reason," are modeling authoritarian and unreasonable behavior. It is important that practitioners help parents understand that an arbitrary use of their authority only inspires frustration and contempt on the part of the child and overlooks the opportunity to communicate purposeful concern about the child's long-term well-being.

The following are specific procedures employed for teaching parents more effective parent management techniques. They should be adjusted to the specific problems and age-specific needs of children and adolescents. These essential skills include:

- Explaining the rationale for the approach to the parent (i.e., using positive efforts to increase prosocial behaviors, reduce negative behaviors, and improve the child-parent relationship)
- Demonstrating skills through role play
- Having the parent(s) explain the procedure (i.e., desired behavior) to the child until the child demonstrates an understanding of the procedure
- Having the child participate in role plays to demonstrate the procedure with the parent
- Directing the parent to demonstrate the approach with the child

while being observed by the practitioner (with the practitioner's direct coaching)

- Allowing the parent to practice without direct coaching
- Assigning homework for the parent to practice the new skills at home
- Reviewing the parent's performance in the following session
- To ensure continuation of progress, teaching parents how to pinpoint the problem behaviors and monitor them at home (e.g., recording compliance vs. noncompliance)
- Explaining how to shape the child's behavior by stringing together rewards and sanctions to increase the child's constructive and otherwise prosocial behaviors
- Teaching parents how to "monitor" their children at all times, even when they are away from home (This involves parents knowing where their children are, what they are doing, who they are with, and when they will be returning. Children must be held accountable for these "mini-contracts.")
- Demonstrating to parents how to be somewhat flexible, particularly with older children, and practicing problem-solving and negotiating strategies (Help them understand that being an effective parent does not always mean "winning" every battle decisively.)
- Assigning specific homework tasks as the child's progress dictates
- Directing parent management techniques toward improving the child's school behavior and performance if needed
- Arranging for regular communication between parent and teacher to compare notes regarding behaviors and school performance
- Helping parents to design goals for their children that are achievable and specific
- Encouraging the adults (e.g., parents, teachers) involved in the treatment to give praise and tangible rewards for prosocial behaviors

Behavioral Family Therapy Skills

Parenting skills are best applied within the context of behavioral and other similar family therapies (e.g., structural and strategic approaches):

- Identifying problem behaviors between family members, negotiate solutions, improve positive interactions (particularly by reducing coercive interactions)

- Demonstrating communication and problem-solving skills among all family members and continually monitoring and evaluating improvements
- Providing couples interventions to improve communication and problem solving (on issues other than parenting differences as well)
- Facilitating the style, direction, and intensity of communications, so they become increasingly constructive (e.g., one person speaking at a time, no interrupting, being specific about what you are saying, and no global accusations, characterizations, name calling, etc.)
- Negotiating straightforward contingency contracts to either facilitate the couple relationship or parent management skills

As discussed in Chapter 4 under "Assessment," the practitioner should continue to monitor communication patterns, alliances within the family, how well the parent or parents utilize their authority, and overall emotional tone of the family's communication. Practitioners need to work at all levels: with the individual client, the parent or parents as a couple, and with the whole family to improve and maintain the cooperation and consistency necessary to help the behaviorally disordered child or adolescent.

Case Management Skills: Engaging the Broader System and Employing Contingency Management

Even the most skilled efforts with the child and their family may not be sufficient to improve the child's behavior and improve overall family functioning. Often, when working with seriously conduct disordered adolescents, social workers must coordinate the intervention with other agencies: schools, criminal justice, primary health, and other community resources. The principles for working with the broader system within a case management framework include the need for professional initiative on the part of the social worker to enhance coordination of services, keeping all parties "on the same page" with a clearly communicated and negotiated intervention plan, and bolstering social and instrumental supports as needed. Intervention plans are likely to include contingencies for prosocial behavior (rewards) and antisocial behavior (sanctions). Specific skills are summarized as follows:

- Engaging in assertive case management with social systems as needed (i.e., schools, law enforcement, criminal justice, etc.) in addition to arranging for other instrumental and social supports

- Actively including teachers and other school personnel in the treatment plan to generalize and maintain prosocial behavioral improvements
- Encouraging all parties to work from the same intervention plan, particularly with regard to the contingency management strategy (Have a consistent list of the behaviors that are expected of the adolescent and clear consequences for both positive and negative behaviors. Various participants in the intervention must stick to the contingency management plan—that is, rewards and sanctions—*so responses can be swift, fair, and consistent.*)
- Making arrangements for long-term follow-up, "booster" sessions, and other needed services

For clients with co-occurring ADHD, interventions might also include:

- Psycho-education to teach parents about the causes, developmental course, and prognosis for ADHD (Books and videos may be recommended or provided to parents, so they can do some of this homework on their own time; parents are taught to understand that their child's difficulties can be either helped or hindered by the behavior of all family members.)
- Teaching parents to reduce stress in the household through the use of calm and clear communication skills, sound discipline practices, and enjoyable activities to reduce overall stress (Changes such as these can create a quieter atmosphere that is more conducive to relaxation and improved concentration for the child with ADHD.)
- Reviewing basic problem solving (i.e., defining the problem, developing a plan, anticipating obstacles, implementing and evaluating the plan) to approach daily problems in a more organized, focused, and systematic manner
- Discussing environmental management in the home (e.g., organized, uncluttered, a place to work privately) to reduce distractions, facilitate self-control, increase concentration, and improve problem solving
- Demonstrating for parents how to reduce the child's negative behaviors and increase task-focused behaviors (This strategy includes providing positive reinforcement to the child for productive behaviors and ignoring negative or distracting behaviors.)
- Showing parents how to attend to a child or adolescent's noncompliance by breaking down complex tasks, reducing distractions, and

giving simple, direct commands while providing immediate reinforcement for prompt compliance

- Discussing how to develop a token home economy with the child
by negotiating a menu of rewards for prompt compliance and sanctions or withheld rewards for noncompliance or negative behaviors
- Showing parents how to implement time-out procedures for noncompliance (Parents are encouraged to issue a command to the
child, wait a few seconds, and issue it again. Should the child not
comply, the child is directed to stay in time out—a few minutes for
young children, more time for older children. More time out may
be instituted should the child continue to be oppositional or
disruptive.)
- Encouraging cooperation between the parents and the child's
teacher in order to improve school behavior and academic performance (Parent and teacher are instructed to utilize a common "score
card" and implement rewards and sanctions based on those daily
school reports.)
- Consulting with the teacher on classroom contingency management plans (The plan is implemented in the classroom by the
teacher who sees that the child's work is broken down into smaller
increments and that the child's on-task behavior is consistently
rewarded. Disruptive behaviors are sanctioned with a time out or
temporary loss of privileges.)
- Reviewing and evaluating the ongoing results of the plan with the
parents, anticipating events that might lead to occasional setbacks,
and planning for possible "booster" sessions

Summary

Behaviorally disordered children, including those with co-occurring ADHD,
often require that social workers use their full complement of skills: supportive skills to maintain an often fragile working alliance with a difficult
adolescent or conflict-ridden family, coping skills to help parents deal
directly with disruptive behaviors in the home, and a comprehensive case
management plan to increase social and instrumental supports, coordinate
multiple services, and maintain consistency in implementing the intervention plan. By working directly with the individual child or adolescent,
improving parent coping skills and family functioning, and providing a
more coherent set of contingencies in the child's life across multiple systems, practitioners can make real progress in helping the oppositional child
or conduct-disordered adolescent and their family.

Case Study: Chi

The Comprehensive Service Plan (Assessment, Intervention, Evaluation)

Use all available information from the client and significant others, your observations, and input from other professionals to conduct both quantitative and qualitative aspects of this multidimensional-functional assessment.

Client identification data: (gender, age, marital status, sexual orientation; family composition; employment; racial, ethnic, cultural, religious/spiritual affiliation and identity, etc.)

Chi is a fifteen-year-old male from a Vietnamese family. He lives with his father, Quan, and his mother, Hue. His sister, Binh, is in her freshman year at college and lives in a dormitory. Quan and Hue left Vietnam (separately) for the United States in the mid-1970s after the fall of Saigon. Quan was an officer in the South Vietnamese army, and after arriving in the United States, worked a variety of jobs. In the last ten years, he has worked steadily managing an electronics store. His wife, Hue, has been a full-time homemaker but, in recent years, has begun to work part-time in local Vietnamese and other Asian restaurants as a waitress and receptionist. They identify themselves as Roman Catholic. Hue attends church. Quan and the children do not. They identify with Vietnamese and Chinese culture and celebrate both American and their own heritage during the holidays.

The presenting problem

Description of problem (client's view)

Chi states that he does not know why he was arrested or sent to the mental health center. He claims that he was arrested for no reason, just because the "police like to hassle me."

Description of problem (practitioner's view)

Chi was recently arrested after having beaten another teenager severely with a piece of steel pipe because the other boy failed to pay him money, presumably, in exchange for marijuana. The police report that witnesses have identified him as a rising young drug dealer with a penchant for violent retribution against those who don't pay up on time. Since this was his first arrest, the judge remanded him to a juvenile diversionary program where he is to receive family counseling and substance abuse treatment; his diversionary status is contingent on his cooperation, lack of further arrests, school attendance, and reports of progress from the social worker.

Psychosocial history with an emphasis on problem trajectory

After three interviews with Chi and his parents (i.e., an individual interview with Chi, a couples interview, and an interview with Chi and his parents together), the following facts have been determined. Quan and Hue met in the early 1980s at a church supper in a rural town in the northern United States. They soon became engaged. Hue became pregnant but lost her first child soon after birth. Hue was depressed for some time after that. During that time, Quan also become somewhat distant and (according to Hue) was also very depressed at times, drank a lot of alcohol, and had frequent violent outbursts of anger—smashing furniture or other objects, often after he had been drinking. He would often get up in the middle of the night, have a few drinks while sitting alone talking to himself, and return to bed. He would find it difficult to return to work the following day. After a time, the outbursts subsided somewhat, and he was able to moderate his drinking. He said that talking with other Vietnamese immigrants he worked with sometimes was upsetting but sometimes helped. He was clearly suffering from having witnessed many combat situations and related atrocities.

After conferring with a physician a few years after the death of their first child, Hue became pregnant with Chi to the delight of his parents. The parents report that Chi was somewhat of an oppositional boy early on and during grade school. Quan became increasingly strict with his son, insisting on certain rules of decorum regarding mealtime behaviors, cleaning and ordering his room, and strict obedience in every other way. As Chi entered adolescence, Quan became somewhat physical in response to Chi's verbal rebelliousness. Quan admitted having hit Chi on a fairly regular basis, always using on open hand but, nevertheless, hitting him hard enough to knock him down on several occasions. Chi responded by becoming increasingly aggressive and began hitting back. When things escalated about one year ago, Chi began missing school, spending days at a time living on the street, and keeping company with alleged gang members in the neighborhood. He did not complete his second year of high school and two months ago was arrested and referred to this clinic.

Attempts to resolve the problems, previous treatment, and relevant outcomes

Quan and Hue did try to get help for Chi. They attended pastoral counseling in their local church for a few visits, but Quan became angry when the counselor accused him of battering his son. Quan felt blamed and guilty, and decided not to return. Otherwise, no other treatments have been sought out. Quan mentioned that an elderly physician he saw when he was drinking heavily told him to get psychiatric help for "combat fatigue," but Quan never followed-up on that suggestion and wouldn't take the medication that the doctor recommended (he doesn't recall what it was).

The individual assessment

Mental status—cognitive disturbances: Describe the client's level of hallucinations, delusions, disorientation, bizarre behavior or speech, memory problems, serious confusion, or other symptoms of serious cognitive impairment. Include other troubling or dysfunctional beliefs or convictions.

Chi is clearly an angry, depressed, and suspicious young man. He sees the world as a very dangerous place, feels that he has to "prove" himself in his community, and that, if he does not demonstrate that he is fearless of others, they will "defeat me." He refuses to even look at his father during the interview but softens a bit when his mother addresses him. He sees no need to return to school and feels that he can make his own way without going to college like his sister. He feels very pessimistic about his own future. He says he prefers to live on the street and feels that the local gang is his "real family."

> How would you rate the client's overall mental status during the past month?
>
> POOR [0]   IMPAIRED [1]   MARGINAL [2]   GOOD [3]   EXCELLENT [4]

Mental status—emotional distress: Describe the client's level of depression, anxiety, and overall ability to regulate their emotions.

Chi is a very angry young man but he also appears to be very depressed. Although he does not report the usual classic signs of major depression (e.g., sleep, appetite, low energy), it is hard to sort out these matters since it appears that he is chronically using marijuana. He does not report any overt signs of suicidal ideation but claims that he can be fearless in his dealings with other gang members because he is not afraid to die. He stated, "Once you decide that you don't care if you die, you are capable of anything. That is why others fear me."

How would you rate your client's emotional well-being over the past thirty days?

POOR [0]   IMPAIRED [1]   MARGINAL [2]   GOOD [3]   EXCELLENT [4]

Behavioral problems: Describe your client's overall ability to regulate their behavior. Consider things such as their ability to express themselves effectively, ability to work at things patiently, tendencies to verbally or physically lash out at others, run away, harm themselves or proneness to impulsive, criminal, or substance-abusing behavior. How would you describe the client's overall impulse control?

Chi has long shown difficulty in school. Although he gives every impression of being highly intelligent, he has difficulty completing his work, he becomes impatient quite readily, and his frustration quickly leads to anger and taking some kind of physical action. He has trouble sitting still and prefers to "do things with my hands. I hate school. I can't sit there all day doing reading or listening to people. It makes me crazy." He says the only thing he likes about school is his shop class, and he reports liking his shop class teacher, Mike. "Mike is cool. He shows you how to do stuff, and he's nice, but he doesn't take any sh—from you either." Chi has been reported to have simply left school in the middle of class and wander the streets. When he was arrested recently, it was during school hours. He has also run away from home but usually returns after two or three days. He clearly is ready to fight, and though he claims to not carry weapons, he was found to have a short utility-type blade (box cutter) in his pocket. Based on his report, he seems to be quite ready to settle disputes or perceived slights with his fists. Chi appears to be an angry young man who sees the world as his personal battlefield, is easily offended by perceived slights, and is quite ready and willing to risk his life even when he is clearly outmatched and the odds are against him. He is also engaged in a criminal enterprise: selling marijuana. Although he was fortunate to be remanded to this diversionary program, he could easily transition in the next few years to selling narcotics and other drugs and become more involved with more violent and dangerous felons.

How would you rate your client's behavioral control generally over the past thirty days?

POOR [o]   IMPAIRED [1]   MARGINAL [2]   GOOD [3]   EXCELLENT [4]

Adaptive strengths and coping abilities: Describe your client's ability to cope with problems and everyday stressors. How would you describe the client's ability to assess problem situations, deal with "triggers," cope with stress, solve problems, and perhaps reach out to others for help in order to deal effectively with their difficulties?

Chi is quite resourceful, albeit in a way that is not really adaptive. He is, in a sense, brave and is willing to take on big challenges. His ability to channel that energy and initiative, however, is currently directed at the wrong things. If he were able to focus on some of his educational challenges or had the opportunity to focus on some technical training, these qualities might serve him better. Currently, he is not adapting well.

How would you rate your client's overall adaptive strengths and coping abilities over the past thirty days?

POOR [o]   IMPAIRED [1]   MARGINAL [2]   GOOD [3]   EXCELLENT [4]

Health problems: Describe the client's overall health. Aside from normal, transient illnesses, think about the client's general health habits (e.g., smoking, heavy drinking, exercise, weight), chronic primary health disorders, the client's opinion of their own health, ability to engage in their usual activities relatively free from discomfort, overall energy level, hospitalizations and treatments for illness other than psychiatric ones. Consider their documented medical history and any ongoing treatments.

He reports no health problems. Results of a recent physical reveal that he is in perfect health.

How would you rate your client's health over the past thirty days?

POOR [o]   IMPAIRED [1]   MARGINAL [2]   GOOD [3]   **EXCELLENT [4]**

Use of alcohol and other drugs: Describe the client's use of alcohol, illicit substances (cocaine, heroin, marijuana, hallucinogens, etc.) and abuse of prescription medication. How often do they use them, in what quantity, and how serious are the psychological, physical, or social consequences associated with their use?

Chi admits to chronic marijuana use, but no other drugs. His blood tests revealed no other drugs in his system, although enough time had elapsed after his arrest and confinement at home that this means little. He also claims that he has an occasional beer, although he does not really like it much. He reports that he does not use any illicit pharmaceuticals such as synthetic narcotics or barbiturates.

How would you rate the client's functioning in the past month with regard to substance use?

POOR [0]   IMPAIRED [1]   MARGINAL [2]   GOOD [3]   EXCELLENT [4]

Recreational activities: Consider what the client does for fun (alone or with others), hobbies, relaxation (reading, TV, video games, playing cards, etc.), and physical exercise (walking, jogging, biking, etc.). How would you describe the client's overall involvement in positive recreational activities?

Chi has been known to "hang out" at the local arcade. Many of his "customers" are there as well (he mostly sells pot to other teenagers). He likes video games, particularly those that act out military-type shooting adventures. He claims to have the highest score on one popular military shooting game. He finds this activity relaxing. Other than this activity and occasionally watching TV, he reports no other recreational outlets.

How would you rate the adequacy of the client's participation in healthy recreational activities over the past thirty days?

POOR [0]   IMPAIRED [1]   MARGINAL [2]   GOOD [3]   EXCELLENT [4]

Material resources: Describe your client's current or (if client is institutionalized) most recent living situation overall. Consider such things as adequacy of food, clothing, shelter, and safety.

Chi is well provided for. If he goes without food or adequate clothing, it is the result of a kind of ascetic self-denial as a self-styled "soldier."

How would you rate the overall adequacy of the client's material resources over the past month?

POOR [0]   IMPAIRED [1]   MARGINAL [2]   <u>GOOD [3]</u>   EXCELLENT [4]

Independent living/self-care: Describe how well your client manages their household, takes care of personal hygiene, eats, sleeps, and otherwise cares for their own basic needs.

As noted, Chi is cared for by his parents. Chi is resourceful, but this practitioner questions whether he could really take care of himself independently. I would not describe him as capable of adequately caring for himself.

How would you rate the client's ability to live independently and take care of their basic needs over the past thirty days?

POOR [0]   IMPAIRED [1]   <u>MARGINAL [2]</u>   GOOD [3]   EXCELLENT [4]

Work (role) satisfaction: Describe the client's current work-related or other important role-related activities (e.g., employed, student, homemaker, volunteer, retired person, disabled, etc.). Describe those activities and responsibilities that occupy the client in a productive manner.

At fifteen, Chi's predominant role is to obtain his education, and he is having extraordinary trouble doing that. As suggested earlier, he will probably have to do remedial work to complete enough "points" to finish his second year in high school.

How would you rate the client's work or role satisfaction over the past thirty days?

<u>POOR [0]</u>   IMPAIRED [1]   MARGINAL [2]   GOOD [3]   EXCELLENT [4]

Legal problems: Describe any legal problems the client has had or continues to have. These include minor infractions (e.g., public drunkenness, shoplifting inexpensive items, minor traffic violations, public disturbances) and more serious crimes (e.g., assault and battery, rape, burglary, driving under the influence, etc.). Consider their status (probation, awaiting imprisonment, parole). Also, consider any civil suits leveled at the client, pending financial judgments against them, and so on. Overall, how would you describe the client's current legal situation?

Chi is in serious trouble. If he fails to keep to the terms of this diversionary program, the judge assured him that he could be incarcerated in the juvenile detention facility until he is eighteen.

How would you rate the client's legal situation over the past thirty days?

POOR [0]   IMPAIRED [1]   MARGINAL [2]   GOOD [3]   EXCELLENT [4]

DSM-5 Diagnosis

Conduct disorder, adolescent onset type, 312.82
Cannabis use disorder, 304.30
Consider attention deficit/hyperactivity disorder, 314.01

Family relations: Describe the client's current family structure including authority, hierarchy, alliances, roles, rules, boundaries, subsystems (e.g., couple, siblings, parent-child alliances); patterns of interactions and quality of communications; specific problems within the family; specific adaptive strengths within the family; and how the family members describe their own racial, ethnic, cultural, and religious identities.

Chi's relationship with his father has clearly contributed to his current situation. Quan admits that "maybe I've been pretty rough on him at times." Hue tactfully suggested that Quan has always been "angry, upset, and sad" about the war and never left it behind. The hostility, anger, and violence that grew over the years between Chi and his father must clearly be resolved for both Chi's sake as well as for his father's. Hue has played the role of quiet intermediary but can do little more than try to comfort them both. However, Quan and Hue have remained close over the years and Chi does respond, somewhat, to his mother's interventions. Chi has expressed regret that he makes his mother worry about him. Chi is also fond of his sister Bihn and admits missing her since she left for college.

How would you rate the quality of the client's immediate family relationships over the past thirty days?

POOR [0]   IMPAIRED [1]   MARGINAL [2]   GOOD [3]   EXCELLENT [4]

Immediate social relationships (close friends and acquaintances): Describe the quality of your client's relationships with those available friends and acquaintances, as applicable. Over the past month, how would you describe the quality of the interaction overall between your client and them with respect to closeness, intimacy, general interpersonal satisfaction, effective communications, degree of conflict, level of hostility, aggression, and evidence of any emotional or physical abuse?

Chi's acquaintances are mostly younger teens who are "gang-banger wannabees," more mischief makers than criminals—at least not yet. Chi avoids the older male gang members, except in dealings as an intermediary to sell marijuana. Chi reports that some of his friends are "cool," and he seems to enjoy their company but does not bring them home, feeling that they would not be welcome or that his father would hassle them all the time. Thus, his parents have little idea about with whom he associates since they never meet their son's friends and acquaintances.

How would you rate the quality of the client's immediate social relationships over the past thirty days?

POOR [0]   IMPAIRED [1]   MARGINAL [2]   GOOD [3]   EXCELLENT [4]

Extended social relationships: Describe the type and quality of relationships between your client and others in the client's community (other than close friends and family). These people might include other families, law enforcement, human service agencies, school personnel, coworkers, and others from whom the client receives support or with whom the client is having serious conflict.

Chi's relations with local law enforcement, school personnel, and others in the community (e.g., shop owners) are somewhat contentious. Although he is seen as troubled and somewhat disruptive to those around him, consultation with the juvenile officer and his teachers reveals that he has likeable qualities as well.

> How would you rate the quality of the client's social relationships over the past thirty days?
>
> POOR [0]   IMPAIRED [1]   MARGINAL [2]   GOOD [3]   EXCELLENT [4]

A concise summary of the MFS assessment: Highlight the client's areas of distress and adaptive strengths. Emphasize those areas that are most likely to be emphasized in the intervention plan.

Chi is a troubled fifteen-year-old boy who appears to demonstrate many signs of a growing conduct disorder and chronic problem with marijuana abuse. He and his father have had a long-standing conflicted and often physically violent relationship. Chi has been emotionally and physically abused by Quan. Chi appears to be depressed (probably exacerbated by marijuana abuse), is quite hostile at times, shows poor impulse control, sees many in the world as his enemy but does appear to have the capacity to develop some genuinely caring relationships. He expresses some sense of remorse regarding the difficulty his behavior has caused his mother and feels badly that he has disappointed his sister as well. He looks up to her and misses her. He clearly has trouble concentrating in school and should be tested thoroughly by the school psychologist for ADHD and other specific learning disorders.

Recommendations for further focused assessment: Note recommended referrals to consultants or additional instruments to be used.

Refer to psychologist for additional assessment: ADHD, learning disabilities. Discuss the possibility of Quan participating in individual or couples sessions (as he prefers) to assess angry outbursts and depression; consider possibility of unresolved PTSD symptoms.

THE COMPREHENSIVE SERVICE PLAN SUMMARY

Assessment/Problems	Goals	Objectives	Interventions	Evaluation plan
(Briefly describe key problems to be addressed.)	(State desired outcome for each problem.)	(Describe specific "stepping stones" toward each GOAL. Update as client progresses.)	(Describe specific interventions to be used.)	(Describe indexes to be used for tracking progress.)
Behavioral impulsivity, aggression, fighting, running away; consequent legal problems	Reduce/eliminate aggressive behavior and associating with gang members and their acquaintances	Focus on one interaction per week in school; describe feelings of provocation, assessment, and how he reacted	*Supportive skills:* Develop a working relationship with Chi individually; focus on basic trust and identify some incentive for his participation (e.g., initially, to stay out of juvenile detention) and use a motivational posture to help engage him	Have Chi keep a chart and indicate the following per week:
Chi's interpersonal skill deficits	Develop nonviolent ways of resolving disputes	Identify and monitor negative thinking about himself, others; offer counterinterpretation	Join with Quan and Hue; avoid blaming Quan for "causing" Chi's behavior problems; focus on improving the situation "as a family"; plan to include Binh during semester break	Number of fights with others outside home
Depression, marijuana abuse	Improve overall mood; reduce to elimination of marijuana use	Monitor and report any marijuana use, how much, and what preceded his decision to use	*Therapeutic coping skills:* Individually, explore Chi's negative and hostile distortions regarding others; his readiness to overreact aggressively to every perceived slight; review his history with dad, make connections, and see if there is a chance for reconciliation; role play potential problem scenarios and	Number of angry encounters or fights with dad
Conflicts at home; ineffective parenting	Develop more effective parenting skills; eliminate physical abuse; use positive contingencies in concert with court mandates	Have two family discussions per week for twenty minutes; focus, initially, on each other's daily activities; monitor level of respect, awareness of careful listening, not interrupting; note indications of conflict and what occurred		Number of times he used marijuana
Educational/learning difficulties	Improve school attendance and performance	Achieve one full week of perfect attendance; 90% for a month		Rate his overall mood (0 "very bad," 1 "bad," 2 "neither good nor bad," 3 "good," 4 "great")
		Complete 90% of school work each week for a month		Have family rate their view of Chi's cooperativeness, respect (0 "very bad," 1 "bad," 2 "neither good nor bad," 3 "good," 4 "great")
				Summarize school reports and reports from juvenile officer
				Collate all data and share with Chi and his family weekly

model how to "stop, think, breathe, and evaluate" the situation before reacting; emphasize negative consequences of not "staying calm, being cool"; practice more effective communication skills

Apply similar coping skills to identifying "triggers" (e.g., frustration) to reduce and eventually eliminate marijuana use

Family sessions should focus on a "fresh start," calm, respectful communications in all directions; focus particularly on Chi and Quan's interactions, talking things out; encourage apologies, forgiveness, and mutual respect in the future; model effective communications, calm expression of feelings; practice at home and report in session; develop a few "new rules" around Chi's behavior while living at home; emphasize cooperation with some reasonable flexibility (e.g., homework, curfew, with whom he associates, etc.)

THE COMPREHENSIVE SERVICE PLAN SUMMARY (CONTINUED)

Assessment/Problems	Goals	Objectives	Interventions	Evaluation plan
(Briefly describe key problems to be addressed.)	(State desired outcome for each problem.)	(Describe specific "stepping stones" toward each GOAL. Update as client progresses.)	(Describe specific interventions to be used.)	(Describe indexes to be used for tracking progress.)
			Case management skills: Coordinate intervention plan with juvenile court, juvenile officer, school personnel; have Chi report to Juv. Off. Callahan weekly, in person; return school reports of attendance and completed work to parents and this social worker Referrals for psychological evaluation, medical evaluation for potential ADHD meds; consider individual therapy for Quan (PTSD?) or mutual help group in his community	

CHAPTER THIRTEEN

From Basic to Advanced Practice: Combining Essential Skills into EBPs

As discussed in Chapter 1, basic interventions are generally utilized with persons experiencing problems that tend to be mild to moderate in severity and relatively uncomplicated. These constitute the stressors and strains of everyday life: mild depression, relationship problems, stress and anxiety, and other transitory problems. These difficulties often respond well to basic counseling skills, including empathic listening, problem solving, and perhaps even some basic case management such as a referral to a support group. More advanced interventions (as in other professions) are those strategies that have been shown to be effective with problems that are more complex and are accompanied by a greater degree of psychosocial dysfunction. Social work intervention with these problems requires greater knowledge of human behavior, the use of more advanced assessment methods, and the ability to carry out more complex strategies. Providing assessment, intervention, and evaluation with major mental illnesses (i.e., schizophrenia, bipolar and major depression), addictions, disabling anxiety disorders, child abuse and neglect, childhood emotional and behavioral disorders, and eating disorders, among other problems can be very challenging even for seasoned practitioners.

As a result of decades of efforts of practitioners and practice researchers who share a commitment to practice research and evaluation, social workers now have many effective intervention options from which to choose. Evidence-based practices are interventions that have been shown repeatedly to be effective in controlled trials. Although the term "evidence-based" with regard to psychosocial interventions has been coined relatively recently, the term "evidence-based medicine" came into vogue in the early 1990s and has since been applied to the broader arena of psychosocial interventions, hence the more generic term "evidence-based practice."

However, the movement toward "empirically supported practice" has been around since (at least) the early 1960s. This term is a bit more ambiguous and applies to two related aspects of evidence-based practice: (1) using controlled research (i.e., experimental designs) to test psychosocial interventions and also to see how these approaches compare with no intervention or alternative intervention methods, and (2) evaluating how interventions are implemented in everyday treatment settings. These evaluation efforts are typically naturalistic, that is, not conducted under controlled circumstances (e.g., compared with alternative interventions).

Most academic, professional, and governmental agencies that have a vested interest in advancing evidence based practices use the first criterion to define evidence-based practices: psychosocial interventions that have been tested repeatedly in controlled trials and shown to be effective with clients experiencing serious psychosocial problems. These studies tend to be methodologically rigorous and include the following design criteria: the clients who are recruited to participate in these studies must be "real" clients (as opposed to graduate students, for example, playing the role of clients); the participants are usually randomly assigned to the experimental intervention group or comparison group (to rule out treatment expectancy bias); the practitioners who provide the interventions are trained specifically to provide the experimental or comparison approach; and multiple scales and related measures are utilized to see that the two groups are generally equal (in problem severity and other characteristics) at baseline (the beginning of the study) and to see if one group gains more benefit from treatment than the other group. After a few studies demonstrating that a particular approach is reasonably effective when compared with "no treatment" (i.e., delayed treatment) or some alternative approach, the intervention method is then published as a "manualized intervention," so practitioners can become acquainted with the basic guidelines and learn how to implement the approach. There is now a host of evidence-based practices available for working with clients who have severe mental illnesses, major affective disorders, anxiety disorders, substance use disorders, eating disorders, and childhood emotional and behavioral disorders, among other problems.

However, the second rubric of evidence-based practices is also important. Just because a practitioner claims to be using an "EBP," it does not necessarily follow that the practitioner is implementing it well or that the client will improve as a result of the intervention. In order to ensure that EBPs are well utilized, it is important that practitioners evaluate their own practice. Evaluating one's own practice means as follows: defining and measuring the client's presenting difficulties, defining the intervention to be used (e.g., an EBP), and monitoring the client's progress over the course of the intervention. Measuring key indicators can include both qualitative and quantitative measures. The evaluative procedure includes utilizing such indexes and scales beginning at baseline, at intervals during treatment, and at termination to monitor whether the client is improving or not on key indicators. This approach, as described in Chapter 4, is referred to as naturalistic single-subject evaluation. On a practical level, this is the only single-subject evaluation method that can be routinely used in everyday practice. Other approaches that include planned changes to the intervention (to see if a change in the intervention will yield more benefit for the client) constitute a form of controlled clinical research that requires special approval from an institutional review board (IRB) before implementing.

Evaluative research falls between the randomized controlled trial and naturalistic evaluation on the continuum of experimental control. In evaluative research, practitioners are testing hypotheses about the use of a novel intervention approach, and these designs usually take place in "real world" intervention environments. Thus, the purpose is primarily knowledge building to determine what treatments work best. The easiest way to distinguish naturalistic evaluation from evaluative research is by answering the following question: Does the evaluation procedure I am about to implement alter the way services would otherwise be provided to the client under current agency treatment procedures? If the answer is "yes," then the client should be made aware of that modification and be given the opportunity to voluntarily participate (i.e., give informed consent). However, if collecting qualitative and quantitative data at baseline, at specified intervals during the intervention, and at termination is part of routine service (to which clients are given the opportunity to approve voluntarily upon admission as clients to the agency), then the activity is considered routine (i.e., naturalistic) evaluation and no additional special permissions are required.

In summary, EBPs are currently defined as a consensus of findings from controlled outcome research. "Evaluating one's own practice" is a form of uncontrolled naturalistic design used to see that these approaches are implemented well (e.g., Gibbs & Gambrill, 2002; O'Hare, 1991; O'Hare, 2015; Proctor, 2003; Rosen, 2003; Thyer, 2004). Although selecting an EBP does not guarantee a good outcome for clients, evaluating the implementation of it can help to fine-tune the approach by considering ongoing evaluative feedback from clients and other collaborators (i.e., family members, teachers, etc.). Thus, rather than simply implementing EBPs by strict adherence to the manual, practitioners should make modifications based on clinical judgment informed by evaluative feedback (from the client and others) in order to implement these approaches with a reasonable balance of flexibility and fidelity (i.e., congruence) to the "ideal" model. In principle, the basic elements of EBPs are commensurate with the most recent Council on Social Work Education guidelines for social work education (see www .cswe.org). These guidelines call for students to develop "competencies" in the understanding and application of matters relating to the reliance on behavioral sciences and practice outcome research to inform and guide assessment and the selection of interventions. To wit:

> Social workers understand quantitative and qualitative research methods. Social workers know the principles of logic, scientific inquiry, and ethical approaches to building knowledge. Social workers understand that evidence that informs practice derives from multidisciplinary sources. They also understand the processes for translating research findings into effective practice. Social workers:
>
> 4a. use practice experience to inform scientific inquiry and research;
>
> 4b. engage in critical analysis of quantitative and qualitative research methods and research findings; and
>
> 4c. use and translate research findings to inform and improve practice, policy, and service delivery. (www.cswe.org, May 2014)

These guidelines, in a nutshell, are the driving rationale for this introductory practice text. Without a body of interdisciplinary scientific knowledge to guide both assessments and the selection of intervention strategies, social workers' professional decision making is then left to resort to tradition, argument by authority, intuition, practice fads, and a lot of guesswork. These criteria are no longer acceptable for supporting professional, ethical, and accountable social work practice.

Although this author does not claim to have the last word on what constitutes the definitive criteria for determining whether an intervention is an evidence-based practice or not, evidence-based social work practice is defined here as *the planned use of empirically supported assessment and intervention methods combined with the judicious use of monitoring and evaluation strategies for the purpose of improving the psychosocial well-being of our clients* (O'Hare, 2015).

EBPSW is primarily characterized by:

- Conducting qualitative assessment informed by current human behavior research and augmented by the use of reliable and valid quantitative assessment instruments (i.e., scales, indices). These instruments also provide a baseline for further monitoring and evaluation (thus, assessment and evaluation processes are inextricably linked).
- Selecting and implementing interventions that have been shown to be efficacious in controlled outcome research. Reasonable flexibility in implementing evidence-based practices is usually necessary to accommodate client needs and situational factors.
- Implementing evaluation methods as part of practice at the individual and program level. This includes the use of repeated measures (i.e., that which makes sense given the treatment context) and use of data to determine client outcomes.

Testing Combinations of Essential Skills: The Role of Controlled Outcome Research

The main thrust of this text has been two-fold: (1) to articulate the "essential skills" of social work practice, and (2) to describe how those basic skills can be combined to form more advanced effective practices. So, how do we know what combinations of essential skills have been shown to be effective with moderate to severe psychosocial conditions? That is where the role of clinical practice theory and research comes in. In the past, practitioners and practitioner-researchers used both theoretical and pragmatic (i.e., experiential trial and error) guidelines to develop what they thought would be effective intervention methods. Some of these approaches have worn well and still inform effective practice. However, after fifty years or so of methodological developments in research and evaluation, researchers have come to rely on more rigorous research designs to guide the development of evidence-based practices. The randomized controlled trial has come to represent the "gold standard" for demonstrating the efficacy of psychosocial interventions.

Using controlled experimental designs to test psychosocial interventions really came into its own in the 1960s, and this type of research has grown in quality and quantity to the present day. Early efforts tended to focus on mild to moderate psychosocial problems typical of out-patient therapy practices. For these problems, a number of different approaches were shown to have comparable results, leading some to erroneously conclude that "anything works." However, as practice researchers began to examine the effects of specific interventions on more specific and more challenging problems, differences began to emerge. Traditional insight-oriented psychotherapies, which dominated the helping professions through the 1970s, came to be seen as theoretically interesting but often no more effective than basic counseling. For more serious problems, including major depression, schizophrenia, serious anxiety disorders (including posttraumatic stress disorder), borderline personality disorder, addictions, eating disorders, couples and family problems, and serious childhood and adolescent disorders, cognitive-behavioral interventions have been shown repeatedly to result in better and more cost-effective outcomes and often have longer-lasting effects. Interpersonal psychotherapies based on a more "here and now" pragmatic focus on role conflicts, losses, and interpersonal difficulties have also been shown to demonstrate substantially positive results when applied to depression, couples' problems, and eating disorders. Emotion-focused therapy has also accumulated significant findings to support its use with depressed clients and conflicted couples. Behaviorally oriented family therapies that emphasized the application of behavioral skills for work with mentally ill members, conduct-disordered and substance abusing adolescents, and those dealing with childhood disorders are now considered to be the most effective among the different family therapies. Case management skills are often included as an important component of social work interventions but have also been packaged as comprehensive strategies to intervene with serious psychosocial disorders where coordination of complex cases is required (e.g., severe mental illness, child maltreatment, conduct disorders, and substance use disorders. *In short, effective practices for social workers are now eclectic combinations of supportive skills to engender an empathic and motivational working relationship, cognitive-behavioral coping skills to enhance existing strengths and learn new ways of effective coping, and case management skills to reduce social and environmental barriers and coordinate complex interventions.*

Objections to Evidence-Based Practices

Practitioners who prefer a more "intuitive" or "creative" approach to selecting interventions often object strenuously to the assertion that controlled research is the best strategy for determining intervention efficacy. Objections raised include the following: (1) "If my client improves, why can't I conclude that my intervention was effective? Don't my clients just know when a treatment has worked?" (2) "After thirty years of practice experience, I think I know which interventions are effective!" (3) "Why can't I just use the interventions that I like best? Why can't I just be creative with my clients?" and (4)"Don't evidence-based practice manuals make practice too technical and robotic?"

Responses to these arguments might include the following:

Argument #1

Simply observing that a client has improved does not rule out the possibility that they would have improved without treatment and for other reasons. The same is true if the client reports improvement and attributes the change to the intervention. Clients will certainly, under most circumstances, know whether they feel better, whether their problems have improved, and whether they are coping better. However, the client or the practitioner may not be in a position to determine *whether their improvement was the result of the intervention or some other factor.* It is simply not an easy thing to know. If the client likes the practitioner, they may attribute their improvement to the intervention, but that is not the same as knowing that their improvement was *the result* of the intervention.

Many clients' problems are transitory, and clients sometimes improve with the passage of time for a variety of personal or circumstantial reasons. You also don't know if the client would have improved even more if you had used some other intervention. Positive outcomes in an individual case prove little indeed about the general effectiveness of any intervention. As an experienced practitioner, I was always very happy when a client improved, but I rarely assumed that it was necessarily the result of my efforts. (Keep in mind that, if a practitioner takes most of the credit for a client's improvement, then, likewise, the practitioner is obliged to shoulder most of the responsibility of failure, including tragic and sometimes unpreventable outcomes such as suicide.) Conversely, if clients do not improve, we should also not be too quick to conclude that we have done a poor job. As in medicine, the practitioner can apply the intervention with considerable skill, but the outcome might still be a poor one. How is this so? There is much that we still do not know about psychosocial problems and psychiatric disorders and how to intervene with them successfully. In addition, some problems may simply be beyond our ability to help.

Argument #2

As for the second objection (the "experience" argument), there is good reason to believe that practitioners can continue for years engaged in the same practice approach without considering new alternatives. Practice experience is certainly important, but it does not, by itself, guarantee expertise. Experience is an important vehicle of learning, but without the guidance of an empirical knowledge base, it is simply that—experience—and does not tell us whether those years of experience have resulted in more effective interventions. Expertise is experience that is guided by a body of research findings. As Eileen Gambrill, a leading social work scholar, has opined, social workers often use argument-by-authority to justify their choice of theories and practices rather than critical thinking informed by an empirical knowledge base. As most competent professionals are aware, selection of theories and practices must now be based on sound research evidence, not claims to tradition or experiential authority.

Argument #3

As for the argument that social work practitioners should simply use the interventions they like best, students should be reminded that social work is a profession guided by laws and state health regulations, licensing, certifications, and ethical guidelines. Human behavior knowledge and interventions are informed through scientific methods. Practitioners will purchase liability insurance annually to protect themselves from the costs of potential civil lawsuits and criminal charges. Although a career in social work can be personally enriching, social work is not primarily a personal enrichment hobby; neither is it a form of performance art. Working with clients does not give practitioners unlimited prerogative to exercise what they consider to be their own creativity (e.g., a former colleague of mine likened his mental health practice to playing "jazz"). Practicing social workers put themselves and their clients at considerable risk by simply trusting their own intuition or applying their own judgment without the benefit of a professional knowledge base.

Fortunately, guidelines for what constitutes evidence-based practices are improving all the time. Social workers have a large and well-codified body of knowledge regarding human behavior problems and effective practices to help guide assessment and intervention methods. That process of using the best evidence to support practice is an essential quality of a competent and ethical professional social worker. Simply following one's own personal convictions without reference to a representative body of scientific research evidence to support one's practice approach is no longer considered ethical practice, and it certainly increases liability risk.

Argument #4

One of the arguments leveled against proponents of EBPs is that engaging in assessment and intervention informed by a knowledge base is somehow "robotic," "technical," or "inhuman." Actually, it is quite easy to argue that practitioners who simply use an approach that they find personally appealing might be engaged in substandard practice. As with physicians, psychologists, and professionals, social workers, at their best, bring their humanity to their work, give the utmost priority to engaging their clients on a personal but "real" level, and dedicate themselves to keeping abreast of the current knowledge in their field so they can do their best work for the sake of their clients.

Coming Challenges for Evidence-Based Practices

Many in social work and the other helping professions opine that evidence-based practice guidelines are too rigid and do not reflect how practice actually unfolds. To some degree, these objections and concerns are justified. Part of the constraining force behind the development of EBPs is the use of diagnostic criteria to categorize people's often complex problems. Although the scientific developments that have driven revisions of the DSM since the 1950s have contributed greatly to advances in modern mental health care, the diagnostic approach has some serious limitations in the way people's mental health problems are conceptualized. First, the "signs and symptoms" in these categories often overlap quite a bit among diagnoses suggesting considerable ambiguity. Second, many people have serious situational stressors that are not well considered in the DSM. Given that the DSM is rooted in the medical model, disorders are defined by what is *within* the individual, a position that presents serious limitations to conducting a thorough assessment. Third, there is a substantial amount of "comorbidity" in the mental health treatment population (i.e., people meet the criteria for two or more psychiatric disorders) that begs the question, "Which EBP guidelines should I follow?" Although some members of the committees that compiled the DSM-5 (APA, 2013) recognize the need to move toward a more dimensional approach (i.e., people have a variety of signs and symptoms across a range of severity that do not fit neatly into categories), such changes are still on the horizon.

However, "guidelines" for practice are not intended to be followed by rote. Guidelines for practice are no more actual practice than a map is an actual place or a meal cooked at home will reflect exactly what the author of a cookbook had in mind. Guidelines are just that: a recommended procedural framework to guide what is understood to be a complex human process fraught with indeterminacy. This lack of predictive certainty is due to a range of factors: client differences in age, gender, sexual orientation, race and culture, life experiences, treatment expectations, temperament, overall health, and so on, not to mention those that characterize the practitioner as well. The list of factors that can affect treatment process and outcome is quite long. In addition, comorbidity complicates the clinical picture greatly and adds more complexity to assessment and intervention given that EBPs are conducted by using relatively strict diagnostic criteria when selecting participants for randomized controlled trials. To some degree, the recruitment of homogeneous samples for RCTs and documented training of the practitioners is done to "rule out" alternative explanations for treatment outcomes implied by the list of "client factors" or differences in practitioners listed above.

Practitioner-researchers committed to developing evidence-based practice guidelines are acutely aware of these practical and methodological challenges. However, there is a growing chorus of practice scholars calling for a more pragmatic approach to the training, research, testing, and evaluation of evidence-based practices that capitalizes on common causal and maintenance factors associated with a range of psychiatric disorders and related psychosocial conditions (Barlow, Allen, & Choate, 2004; Glasgow, 2009; O'Hare, 2009; Westen, Novotny, & Thompson-Brenner, 2004). In addition, it has been recognized for some time that, while confirming common change processes across different approaches is difficult and remains undetermined, most effective interventions are comprised of *a relatively fixed set of effective practice skills* that in combination constitute various evidence-based practices (Goldfried, 2010; Lambert & Bergin, 1994; O'Hare, 2015; Orlinsky, Grawe & Parks, 1994; Taylor & Clark, 2009). In this text, those have been roughly categorized as supportive-relationship building skills, cognitive-behavioral coping skills, and case management skills. (Others might suggest variations on this taxonomy.) Rather than teaching a variety of relatively similar methods as discrete practice approaches for each and every different diagnostic group, many are calling for teaching *readily accessible skill sets* that can be applied flexibly to a range of problems and disorders across different treatment modalities (e.g., couples, family, and groups) (Barlow, 2008; Glasner-Edwards & Rawson, 2010; O'Hare & Geertsma, 2013). However, beginning practitioners should probably learn a few key approaches "by the book" and, later, learn to adapt them to complex psychosocial problems with the judgment and flexibility that can result from experience. Although this may sound reasonable in theory, relatively little is currently known about how practitioners make these judgments "on the fly," an area in need of more research (McCracken & Marsh, 2008; Schottenbauer, Glass, & Arnkoff, 2007).

EBPSW in a Broader Service Delivery Context

Despite some ambivalence, support for the adoption of evidence-based practices in social work and the allied professions is growing. Evidence-based practices are being promoted by a wide range of influential professional and governmental bodies, and, thus, the evolution and implementation of evidence-based practices in behavioral health and social services is now well on its way. Refinement and integration of policy, academic research, practice, and evaluation will continue for the foreseeable future and will be the result of interdisciplinary efforts across the helping professions. However, despite the growing support, the actual implementation of EBPs lags (Glasgow, 2009; Lehman, 2010).

Figure 10, at the end of this chapter, illustrates a working model of the interrelationships among policy and administration, research and education, practice and evaluation, and consumer expectations. The arrows suggest influence from one sphere to another. The model does not imply a primary origin or clear linear process of dissemination to the end point of clinical practice. It is understood that inputs into what is more abstractly referred to as *evidence-based practice* can originate from any sector, and all parts interact reciprocally to one extent or another with mutual influence. In brief, the working model suggests, first (as an arbitrary starting point), that practice scholars in research and academia are primarily responsible for knowledge development and dissemination of evidence-based practices. Practice scholars can directly influence policy makers and administrators and help guide them in developing optimal programming. Second, policy makers and administrators are responsible for service delivery and evaluation of services. They must respond directly to the needs of consumers, funding sources, accreditation bodies, and regulatory agencies. However, administrators and policy makers also have valuable insights into the complexities of program implementation and must work closely with practice-scholars to refine the real-world application of evidence-based practices. Third, with the support of social work educators and agency supervisors, practitioners become the linchpin for implementation of evidence-based practices. Without proper training and support through continuing education and supervision, evidence-based practices will not be implemented effectively at the individual client level. This task can be facilitated through the judicious use of fidelity and outcome measures to see that EBPs are implemented with an acceptable degree of faithfulness to EBP guidelines and effectiveness. Practitioners, in concert with their clients, also generate "from the ground up" special insights into the finer points of implementing EBPs, and must work with practice researchers and evaluators to develop more effective interventions (i.e., "practice-based evidence"). It is also understood that most researchers conducting practice research are trained practitioners themselves, thus underscoring the direct input practitioners have into defining and developing evidence-based practices. Thus, the process of knowledge building becomes a collaborative effort that cycles continuously through theory, practice, research, evaluation, and policy implementation and refinement. These processes are complex, and the evolution of evidence-based practice models will be accompanied by debate for some time (Gambrill, 2006; Johnson & Austin, 2006; O'Hare, 1991, 2015).

Policy, Administration, and Research

Although the use of scientific knowledge to guide practice is not new in principle, the medical profession formalized the term "evidence-based" in the early 1990s by promulgating its use in daily delivery of medical care (The Evidence-Based Medicine Working Group, 1992; Sackett, Straus, Richardson, Rosenberg, & Haynes, 2000). Since that time, the literature on evidence-based medicine and evidence-based practices in mental health and related fields has grown exponentially. To date, scores of professional organizations have offered practice guidelines for mental health and substance abuse interventions for adults and children (Bond, Drake, & Becker, 2010; Soydan, Mullen, Alexandra, Rehnman, & Li, 2010; Stuart, Rush, & Morris, 2002). A few of the more prominent organizations include the American Psychological Association, American Psychiatric Association, the American Academy of Child and Adolescent Psychiatry, the American College of Mental Health Administrators, the Cochrane and Campbell Collaborations, various branches of the National Institutes of Health, and the Agency for Healthcare Research and Quality. Although these and many other academic, governmental, and private-sector organizations actively play a variety of roles (e.g., funding relevant research, compiling and distributing resources, engaging in evaluation), all, in principle, support the use of practices that have been supported by controlled research. However, members of these agencies and supporters of EBPs in general are likely to continue debating what constitutes adequate methodological standards for determining "evidence-based practice." Debates that emphasize methodology rather than ideology are likely to drive the research and administrative processes that result in the increased use of evidence-based practices in social work.

Goldman and colleagues (2001) made a number of points regarding the implementation of evidence-based practices that are still relevant: (1)

evidence-based practice is now seen as a driving force for improving intervention quality and service accountability; (2) evidence-based practices are underutilized; (3) since there are gaps in "best practices" research for some problem areas as well as for more complex co-occurring problems, there remains plenty of room for informed clinical judgment when implementing evidence-based practices in the field; and (4) research on the development, dissemination, and implementation of evidence-based practices must and will continue. To date, there are few empirical guidelines for implementing evidence-based practices in human service agencies. Nevertheless, there is a growing expectation that implementing EBPs in community practice settings will require a flexible synthesis of science and consensus-building that results in high-quality programming amenable to continuous monitoring, evaluation, troubleshooting, and incremental refinement (O'Hare, 2015; Wandersman, 2003). Although observers of the EBP scene like to opine that local values, clinical judgment, and other nonspecific factors will undoubtedly be part of the decision-making process regarding how to adopt and implement EBPs, there is little research at this point on how these factors influence implementation and client outcomes.

Evidence-based guidelines are now increasingly tied to accreditation standards promoted by organizations such as the National Committee on Quality Assurance (NCQA), the Joint Commission on the Accreditation of Healthcare Organizations (JCAHO), and the Commission on the Accreditation of Rehabilitation Facilities (CARF). Although these organizations emphasize a range of process and performance indicators, *they are increasingly emphasizing the use of evidence-based practices.* In addition, with regard to malpractice claims, the courts have been increasingly referencing these evidence-based guidelines as "standards of care."

Consumer Expectations and Relations

The direct and indirect influences of consumers will be increasingly felt as evidence-based practices evolve and are disseminated. Client advocacy groups such as the National Alliance for the Mentally Ill are becoming more educated about evidence-based practices and are becoming involved in advocacy efforts to deliver "best practices" (Bond, Salyers, Rollins, Rapp, & Zipple, 2004). A simple "Googling" of "best practices in mental health" and "consumers" will reveal an exponential proliferation of organizations (e.g., national, state, private, and private nonprofit) devoted to informing consumers about evidence-based practices. Consumer groups, in turn, will enhance their influence by seeking the assistance of academic researchers and other informed advocates who can help consumer representatives keep abreast of current developments in evidence-based interventions and obtain access to better care. As a result of the growth of evidence-based practices, "informed consent" guidelines relevant to services in adult and child mental health, substance abuse, gerontology, and other fields will have to be improved to more explicitly educate everyday consumers about the availability of evidence-based intervention methods. It has long been understood that consumers have an ethical right to know what the medical and social science communities know about best practices (Meyers & Thyer, 1997). Because many practitioners have not been trained in EBPs, or because they reject them outright on personal or ideological grounds, many clients might not be receiving the best available care.

Practice and Evaluation

Becoming more knowledgeable about EBPs is one thing; consistent and effective implementation is quite another. To implement EBPs effectively, practice at the agency level must be accompanied by integrated evaluation processes whereby evaluation processes implemented at assessment, clinical review, termination, and follow-up provide data for both individual client and program-level evaluation. Naturalistic evaluation methods employing multidimensional measures of client well-being and consumer satisfaction can augment current clinical documentation requirements mandated by many accreditation agencies, as well as federal and state regulators and private insurers. Some degree of standardization (e.g., a statewide or federal common assessment/evaluation instrument package) will be required. Consultants from schools of social work can serve an invaluable role by providing requisite training, evaluation, and statistical skills to enhance quality assurance programs in human service agencies.

Social Work Education and Research

The fundamental role of full-time social work direct practice faculty is to teach, develop, and disseminate knowledge regarding human behavior, assessment, intervention, and evaluation methods. Traditionally, the helping professions, including social work, have maintained that they can create and enforce their own practice standards, and, as a result, practitioners have often felt entitled to exercise a high degree of professional autonomy. Nevertheless, there are considerable challenges ahead with regard to teaching, implementing, and evaluating the use of evidence-based practices by social workers.

How will social work academia respond to these challenges? There is considerable debate among social work educators regarding the nature of evidence, the types of methodologies employed in testing and evaluating interventions, and the proportionate role of "practice wisdom" in actual practice. Writing from the practice perspective of social services in Great Britain, Webb (2002) acknowledges these struggles, but concedes that the adoption of evidence-based practices as policy is a "foregone conclusion." He goes on to provide a reasonable framework for decision making that incorporates the use of evidence-based practice guidelines, but with full appreciation for the significant level of indeterminacy in day-to-day practice. His model includes the use of evidence-based protocols, clinical decision making, and feedback mechanisms based on clinical judgment to refine ongoing practice. These views are commensurate with others (e.g., Randall, 2002) who acknowledge that the implementation of evidence-based practices will have to come about as a reciprocal exchange between researchers and practitioners. At this point in social work's evolution, the debate no longer hinges on *whether* evidence-based practices will be adopted, but rather, *how they will be implemented.* To advance EBPs, social work educators will need to continue progress made in the following areas:

- Upgrade current human behavior curricula to critically reflect contemporary multivariate behavioral and social science theory and research
- Teach students how to judge the relative validity of such theories by critically analyzing the methodological quality of theory-driven research
- Teach valid qualitative and quantitative assessment methods
- Teach evidence-based *basic skills* (e.g., relationship building, cognitive-behavioral coping skills, and case management skills) for clients suffering from mild-to-moderate psychosocial distress
- Teach and give priority in the curriculum to *advanced evidence-based practices* (i.e., optimal combinations of basic skills) for working with moderate-to-severe psychosocial problems across all major fields of practice
- Teach students how to critically analyze the methodological components of outcome and evaluation research so they can better judge the efficacy and effectiveness of published practice research
- Teach students how to use an array of research and evaluation designs, to critically understand their relative strengths and weaknesses (i.e., threats to internal and external validity), and to use

the design that best addresses the right question under suitable circumstances

- Teach students to identify gaps in the current practice knowledge base
- Teach them to implement EBPs, maintain the integrity of the intervention, but apply them with reasonable flexibility by considering the unique needs of clients, co-occurring problems, problem complexity, and special circumstances of clients
- Teach evaluation methods for evaluating one's own practice that can be routinely employed in everyday practice environments (e.g., qualitative case analysis, nonexperimental single-subject designs, and naturalistic monitoring and evaluation of programs)
- Emphasize informed consent regarding the use of both the intervention and evaluation methods
- Model critical thinking for students as well as respect for the cumulative hard-wrought efforts of practitioner-research scholars; demonstrate a willingness to change one's mind when compelling evidence disconfirms one's favorite theories or practices; downplay the relevance of personalities in the field who emphasize marketing of their theories and practices over verification of their methods
- Expand academic-agency linkages to promote training, evaluation, and research on evidence-based practices (e.g., institutes for evidence-based social work practice)
- Improve standards for accrediting and licensing of social workers to reflect current knowledge of human behavior theory, empirically based assessment protocol, and evidence-based practices
- Provide training opportunities for field instructors and supervisors who need to upgrade their knowledge and skills with respect to EBPs
- Promote current advances in human behavior theory and evidence-based practices across social work curricula

Given the necessity of employing methodological rigor in human behavior research and in testing psychosocial practices, evidence-based practices for social workers (EBPSW) are less likely to go the way of other practice trends in the past. Evidence, not charisma, will be the watchword for future developments. For social workers to take on leadership roles in mental health, substance abuse, gerontology, child welfare, and other fields, employing rigorous methodological standards for developing and selecting psychosocial practices is no longer an option but a necessity.

Figure 10. A Model for Implementing Evidence-Based Social Work Practices

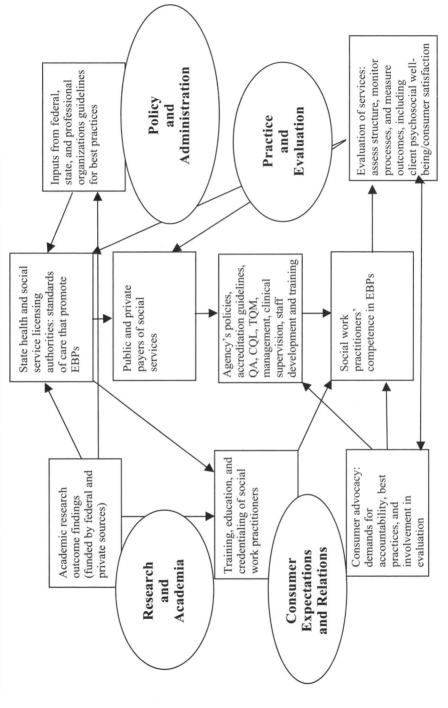

References

Abbott, P. J., Weller, S. B., Delaney, H. D., & Moore, B. A. (1998). Community reinforcement approach in the treatment of opiate addicts. *American Journal of Drug and Alcohol Abuse, 24,* 17–30.

Abramowitz, J. S., Brigidi, B. D., & Roche, K. R. (2001). Cognitive-behavioral therapy for obsessive-compulsive disorder. *Research on Social Work Practice, 11,* 357–372.

Aisenberg, E. (2008). Evidence-based practice in mental health care to ethnic minority communities: Has its practice fallen short of its evidence? *Social Work, 53,* 297–306.

Alessi, S. M., Rash, C., & Petry, N. M. (2011). Contingency management has also been shown to be efficacious with cocaine patients who engaged in pretreatment marijuana use. *Drug and Alcohol Dependence, 118,* 62–67.

Alexander, J. F., Waldron, H. B., Newberry, A. M., & Liddle, N. (1988). *Family approaches to treating delinquents.* Newbury Park, CA: Sage Publications.

Alford, B. A., & Correia, C. J. (1994). Cognitive therapy of schizophrenia: Theory and empirical status. *Behavior Therapy, 25,* 17–33.

American Psychiatric Association (2013). *Diagnostic and statistical manual of mental disorders* (5th ed.). Washington, DC: American Psychiatric Association.

Antony, M. M., & Swinson, R. P. (2000). *Phobic disorders and panic in adults: A guide to assessment and treatment.* Washington, DC: American Psychological Association.

Appelbaum, P. S. (1996). Law and psychiatry: *Jaffee v. Redmond*— Psychotherapist-patient privilege in the federal courts. *Psychiatric Services, 47,* 1033–1052.

Azrin, N. H., Sisson, R. W., Meyers, R., & Godley, M. (1982). Alcoholism treatment by disulfiram and community reinforcement therapy. *Journal of Behavior Therapy and Experimental Psychiatry, 13,* 105–112.

Bagley, C., & Mallick, K. (2000). Prediction of sexual, emotional, and physical maltreatment and mental health outcomes in a longitudinal cohort of 290 adolescent women. *Child Maltreatment, 5*(3), 218–226.

Bandura, A. (1986). *Social foundations of thought and action: A social cognitive theory.* Englewood Cliffs, NJ: Prentice-Hall.

Bandura, A. (1999). A sociocognitive analysis of substance abuse: An agentic perspective. *Psychological Science, 10,* 214–217.

Barlow, D. H. (Ed.). (2008). *Clinical handbook of psychological disorders* (4th ed.). New York, NY: Guilford Press.

Barlow, D. H., Allen, L. B., & Choate, M. L. (2004). Toward a unified treatment for emotional disorders. *Behavior Therapy, 35,* 205–230.

Barrett, B., Young, M. S., Teague, G. B., Winarski, J. T., Moore, K. A., & Ochshorn, E. (2010). Recovery orientation of treatment, consumer empowerment, and satisfaction with services: A mediational model. *Psychiatric Rehabilitation Journal, 34,* 153–156.

Bateman, A., & Fonagy, P. (2009). Randomized controlled trial of outpatient mentalization-based treatment versus structured clinical management for borderline personality disorder. *American Journal of Psychiatry, 166,* 1355–1364.

Beck, A. T. (1976). *Cognitive therapy and the emotional disorders.* New York: New American Library.

Beck, A. T. (1996). Beyond belief: A theory of modes, personality and psychopathology. In P. M. Salkovskis (Ed.), *Frontiers of cognitive therapy* (pp. 1–25). New York, NY: Guilford Press.

Becvar, D. S., & Becvar, R. J. (2009). *Family therapy: A systemic integration* (7th ed.). Needham Heights, MA: Allyn & Bacon.

Bedell, J. R., & Lennox, S. S. (1997). *Handbook for communication and problem-solving skills training: A cognitive-behavioral approach.* New York, NY: John Wiley & Sons, Inc.

Beedso, K., Knappe, S., & Pine, D. S. (2009). Anxiety and anxiety disorders in children and adolescents: Developmental issues and implications for DSM-V. *Psychiatric Clinics of North America, 32,* 483–524.

Begel, A. M., Dumas, J. E., & Hanson, R. F. (2010). Predicting child abuse potential: An empirical investigation of two theoretical frameworks. *Journal of Child and Adolescent Psychology, 39,* 208–219.

Beidel, D. C., & Turner, S. M. (2005). *Childhood anxiety disorders: A guide to research and treatment.* New York, NY: Routledge.

Bellack, A. S., Bennett, M. E., & Gearon, J. S. (2007). *Behavioral treatment for substance abuse in people with serious and persistent mental illness.* New York, NY: Routledge.

Bellack, A. S., & Hersen, M. (Eds.). (1998). *Behavioral assessment: A practical handbook* (4th ed.). Boston, MA: Allyn & Bacon.

Bellack, A. S., Mueser, K. T., Gingerich, S., & Agresta, J. (1997). *Social skills training for schizophrenia: A step-by-step guide.* New York, NY: Guilford Press.

Berg, I. K. (1999). Constructivist therapies: Solution-focused and narrative. In J. O. Prochaska & J. C. Norcross (Eds.), *Systems of psychotherapy: A transtheoretical analysis* (4th ed.) (pp. 437–456). Pacific Grove, CA: Brooks/Cole Publishing.

Beutler, L. E., Clarkin, J. F., & Bongar, B. (2000). *Guidelines for the systematic treatment of the depressed patient.* New York, NY: Oxford University Press.

Bieling, P. J., McCabe, R. E., & Antony, M. (2006). *Cognitive-behavioral therapy in groups.* New York, NY: Guilford Press.

Birchler, G. R., & Spinks, S. H. (1980). Behavioral-systems marital and family therapy: Integration and clinical application. *American Journal of Family Therapy, 8,* 6–28.

Birditt, K. S., Brown, E., Orbuch, T. L., & McIlvane, J. M. (2010). Marital conflict behaviors and implications for divorce over 16 years. *Journal of Marriage and Family, 72,* 1188–1204.

Bjorklund, D. F. (2000). *Children's thinking: Developmental function and individual differences* (3rd ed.). Belmont, CA: Wadsworth/Thomson Learning.

Blankers, M., Koeter, M. W. J., & Schippers, G. M. (2011). Internet therapy versus internet self-help versus no treatment for problematic alcohol use: A randomized controlled trial. *Journal of Consulting and Clinical Psychology, 79,* 330–341.

Bloom, M., Fischer, J., & Orme, J. G. (2009). *Evaluating practice: Guidelines for the accountable professional* (6th ed.). Upper Saddle River, NJ: Pearson.

Bolton, J. M., & Robinson, J. (2010). Population-attributable fractions of Axis I and Axis II mental disorders for suicide attempts: Findings from a representative sample of the adult, noninstitutionalized US population. *American Journal of Public Health, 100,* 2473–2480. doi: 10.2105/AJPH.2010.192252

Bond, G. R., Becker, D. R., Drake, R. E., Rapp, C. A., Meisler, N., Lehman, A. F., Bell, M. D., & Blyler, C. R. (2001). Implementing supported employment as an evidence-based practice. *Psychiatric Services, 52,* 313–322.

Bond, G. R., Drake, R. E., & Becker, D. R. (2008). An update on randomized controlled trials of evidence-based supported employment. *Psychiatric Rehabilitation Journal, 31,* 280–290.

Bond, G. R., Drake, R. E., & Becker, D. R. (2010). Beyond evidence-based practice: Nine ideal features of a mental health intervention. *Research on Social Work Practice, 20,* 493–501.

Bond, G. R., Salyers, M. P., Rollins, A. L., Rapp, C. A., & Zipple, A. M. (2004). How evidence-based practices contribute to community integration. *Community Mental Health Journal, 40,* 569–588.

Bouchery, E. E., Harwood, H. J., Sacks, J. J., Simon, C. J., & Brewer, R. D. (2011). Economic costs of excessive alcohol consumption in the U.S., 2006. *American Journal of Preventative Medicine, 41,* 516–524.

Bowlby, J. (1980). *Attachment and loss.* New York, NY: Basic Books.

Brown, R. T., Antonuccio, D. O., DuPaul, G. J., Fristad, M. A., King, C. A., Leslie, L. K., McCormick, G. S., Pelham, W. E., Piacentini, J. C., & Vitiello, B. (2008). *Childhood mental health disorders: Evidence base and contextual factors for psychological, psychopharmacological, and combined interventions.* Washington, DC: American Psychological Association.

Brown, S. A., Goldman, M. S., Inn, A., & Anderson, L. R. (1980). Expectations of reinforcement from alcohol: Their domain and relation to drinking patterns. *Journal of Consulting and Clinical Psychology, 48*(4), 419–426. doi: 10.1037/0022-006X.48.4.419

Browne, G., & Courtney, M. (2007). Schizophrenia housing and supportive relationships. *International Journal of Mental Health Nursing, 16,* 73–80.

Butler, A. C., Chapman, J. E., Forman, E. M., & Beck, A. T. (2006). The empirical status of cognitive-behavioral therapy: A review of meta-analyses. *Clinical Psychology Review, 26,* 17–31.

Caetano, R., Vaeth, P. A. C., & Ramisetty-Mikler, S. (2008). Intimate partner violence victim and perpetrator characteristics among couples in the United States. *Journal of Family Violence, 23,* 507–518.

Caplan, A. (2006). Ethical issues surrounding forced, mandated, or coerced treatment. *Journal of Substance Abuse Treatment, 31,* 117–120.

Carroll, K. M., & Onken, L. S. (2005). Behavioral therapies for drug abuse. *American Journal of Psychiatry, 162,* 1452–1460.

Castle, D., White, C., Chamberlain, J., Berk, M., Berk, L., Lauder, S., Murray, G., Schweitzer, I., Piterman, L., & Gilbert, M. (2010). Group-based psychosocial intervention for biplar disorder: Randomized controlled trial. *British Journal of Psychiatry, 196,* 383–388.

Chatterjee, S., Pillai, A., Jain, S., Cohen, A., & Patel, V. (2009). Outcomes of people with psychotic disorders in a community-based rehabilitation programme in rural India. *British Journal of Psychiatry, 195,* 433–439.

Chen, X., Thrane, L., Whitbeck, L. B., Johnson, K. D., & Hoyt, D. R. (2007). Onset of conduct disorder, use of delinquent subsistence strategies, and street victimization among homeless and runaway adolescents in the Midwest. *Journal of Interpersonal Violence, 22,* 1156–1183.

Chien, W. T., & Wong, K. (2007). A family psychoeducation group program for Chinese people with schizophrenia in Hong Kong. *Psychiatric Services, 58,* 1003–1006.

Chorpita, B. F., & Southam-Gerow, M. A. (2006). Fears and anxieties. In E. J. Mash & R. A. Barkley (Eds.), *Treatment of childhood disorders* (3rd ed.) (pp. 271–335) . New York, NY: Guilford Press.

Chow, W., Law, S., Andermann, L., Yang, J., Leszcz, M., Wong, J., & Sadavoy, J. (2010). Multi-family psycho-education group for Assertive Community Treatment clients and families of culturally diverse background: A pilot study. *Community Mental Health Journal, 46,* 363–371.

Clark, D. A., & Beck, A. T. (with Alford, B. A.). (1999). *Scientific foundations of cognitive theory and therapy of depression.* New York, NY: John Wiley & Sons, Inc.

Clarkin, J. F., Levy, K. N., Lenzenweger, M. F., & Kernberg, O. F. (2007). Evaluating three treatments for borderline personality disorder: A multiwave study. *American Journal of Psychiatry, 164,* 922–928.

Clavarino, A., Hayatbakhsh, M. R., Williams, G. M., Bor, W., O'Callaghan, M., & Najman, J. M. (2011). Depression following marital problems: Different impacts on mothers and their children? A 21-year prospective study. *Social Psychiatry and Psychiatric Epidemiology, 46,* 833–841.

Coffey, D. (2003). Connection and autonomy in the case management relationship. *Psychiatric Rehabilitation Journal, 26,* 404–412.

Collins, P. H. (2000). *Black feminist thought: Knowledge, consciousness, and the politics of empowerment.* New York, NY: Routledge.

Compton, S. N., Burns, B. J., Egger, H. L., & Robertson, E. (2002). Review of the evidence base for treatment of childhood psychopathology: Internalizing disorders. *Journal of Consulting and Clinical Psychology, 70,* 1240–1266.

Compton, B. R., & Galaway, B. (1999). *Social work processes* (6th ed.). Pacific Grove, CA: Brooks/Cole Publishing.

Compton, W. M., Thomas, Y. F., Stinson, F. S., & Grant, B. F. (2007). Prevalence, correlates, disability, and comorbidity of DSM-IV drug abuse and dependence in the United States: Results from the national epidemiologic survey on alcohol and related conditions. *Archives of General Psychiatry, 64*(5), 566–576.

Connor, B. D., & Lochman, J. E. (2010). Comorbid conduct disorder and substance use disorders. *Clinical Psychology: Science and Practice, 17,* 337–349.

Cooper, M. L. (1994). Motivations for alcohol use among adolescents: Development and validation of a four factor model. *Psychological Assessment, 6*(2), 117–128.

Corcoran, J. (2008). A meta-analysis of parent-involved treatment for child sexual abuse. *Research on Social Work Practice, 18,* 453–464.

Craighead, L. W., Craighead, W. E., Kazdin, A. P., & Mahoney, M. J. (Eds.). (1994). *Cognitive and behavioral interventions: An empirical approach to mental health problems.* Boston, MA: Allyn & Bacon.

Crisp, D., Griffiths, K., MacKinnon, A., & Bennett, K. (2014). An online intervention for reducing depressive symptoms: Secondary benefits for self-esteem, empowerment and quality of life. *Psychiatry Research, 216,* 60–66.

Davidson, K., Tyrer, P., Gumley, A., Tata, P., Norrie, J., Palmer, S., Millar, H., Drummond, L., Seivewright, H., Murray, H., & Macaulay, F. (2006). A randomized controlled trial of cognitive-behavior therapy for borderline personality disorder: Rationale for trial, method, and description of sample. *Journal of Personality Disorders, 20,* 5, 431–449.

Dixon, L. B., Adams, C., & Lucksted, A. (2000). Update on family psychoeducation for schizophrenia. *Schizophrenia Bulletin, 26,* 5–20.

Dixon, L. B., Dickerson, F., Bellack, A. S., Bennett, M., Dickinson, D., Goldberg, R. W., Lehman, A., Tenhula, W. N., Calmes, C., Pasillas, R. M., Peer, J., & Kreyenbuhl, J. (2010). The 2009 Schizophrenia PORT Psychosocial Treatment Recommendations and Summary Statement. *Schizophrenia Bulletin, 36,* 48–70.

Dixon, L. B., McFarlane, W. R., Lefley, H., Lucksted, A., Cohen, M., Falloon, I., Mueser, K., Miklowitz, D., Solomon, P., & Sondheimer, D. (2001). Evidence-based practices for services to families of people with psychiatric disabilities. *Psychiatric Services, 52,* 903–910.

Dobson, K. S. (Ed.). (2009). *Handbook of cognitive behavioral therapies* (3rd ed.). New York, NY: Guilford Press.

Dobson, K. S., & Craig, K. D. (Eds.). (1996). *Advances in cognitive-behavioral therapy.* Thousand Oaks, CA: Sage Publications.

Dohrenwend, B. P. (1998). Overview of evidence for the importance of adverse environmental conditions in causing psychiatric disorders.

In B. P. Dohrenwend (Ed.), *Adversity, stress and psychopathology* (pp. 523–538). New York, NY: Oxford University Press.

Dolgoff, R., Loewenberg, F. M., & Harrington, D. (2005). *Ethical decisions for social work practice* (7th ed.). Toronto, Canada: Thomson/Brooks Cole.

Drake, R. E. (1998). Brief history, current status, and future place of Assertive Community Treatment. *American Journal of Orthopsychiatry, 68,* 172–175.

Drake, R. E., McHugo, G. J., Clark, R. E., Teague, G. B., Xie, H., Miles, K., & Ackerson, T. H. (1998). Assertive Community Treatment for patients with co-occurring severe mental illness and substance use disorder: A clinical trial. *American Journal of Orthopsychiatry, 68,* 201–215.

Dumaine, M. L. (2003). Meta-analysis of interventions with co-occurring disorders of severe mental illness and substance abuse: Implications for social work practice. *Research on Social Work Practice, 13*(2), 142–165.

Duncan, B. L., & Parks, M. B. (1988). Integrating individual and systems approaches: Strategic-behavioral therapy. *Journal of Marital and Family Therapy, 14,* 151–161.

D'Zurilla, T. J., & Goldfried, M. R. (1971). Problem solving and behavior modification. *Journal of Abnormal Psychology, 78,* 107–126.

Eack, S. M., Hogarty, G. E., Greenwald, D. P., Hogarty, S. S., & Keshavan, M. S. (2011). Effects of cognitive enhancement therapy on employment outcomes in early schizophrenia: Results from a 2-year randomized trial. *Research on Social Work Practice, 21,* 32–42.

Epstein, E. E., McCrady, B. S., Morgan, T. J., Cook, S. M., Kugler, G., & Ziedonis, D. (2007). Couples treatment for drug-dependent males: Preliminary efficacy of a stand-alone outpatient model. *Addictive Disorders & Their Treatment, 6,* 21–37.

Evidence-Based Medicine Working Group (1992). Evidence-based medicine: A new approach to teaching the practice of medicine. *JAMA, 268,* 2420–2425.

Fabiano, G. A., Pelham, W. E., Coles, E. K., Gnagy, E. M., Chronis-Toscano, A., & O'Connor, B. C. (2009). A meta-analysis of behavioral treatments for attention-deficit/hyperactivity disorder. *Clinical Psychology Review, 29,* 129–140.

Fals-Stewart, W., Lam, W., & Kelly, M. L. (2009). Learning sobriety together: Behavioral couples therapy for alcoholism and drug abuse. *Journal of Family Therapy, 31,* 115–125.

Fals-Stewart, W., O'Farrell, T., & Lam, W. (2009). Behavioral couple therapy for gay and lesbian couples with alcohol use disorders. *Journal of Substance Abuse Treatment, 37*, 379–387.

Farmer, E. M. Z., Compton, S. N., Burns, B. J., & Robertson, E. (2002). Review of the evidence base for treatment of childhood psychopathology externalizing disorders. *Journal of Consulting and Clinical Psychology, 70*, 1267–1302.

Fischer, J. (1981). The social work revolution. *Social Work, 26*, 199–207.

Fisher, W. H., Packer, I. K., Grisso, T., McDermeit, M., & Brown, J. K. (2000). From case management to court clinic: Examining forensic system involvement of persons with severe mental illness. *Mental Health Services Research, 2*, 41–49.

Foster, S. L. (1994). Assessing and treating parent-adolescent conflict. In M. Hersen, R. Eisler, & P. Miller (Eds.), *Progress in behavior modification* (pp. 53–72). New York, NY: Academic Press.

Frankl, V. (1963). *Man's search for meaning: An introduction to logotherapy.* New York, NY: Pocket Books.

Franklin, C., & Jordan, C. (2003). An integrative skills assessment approach. In C. Jordan & C. Franklin (Eds.), *Clinical assessment for social workers: Quantitative and qualitative methods* (2nd ed.) (pp.1–52). Chicago, IL: Lyceum Books, Inc.

Franklin, M. E., & Foa, E. B. (2011). Treatment of obsessive-compulsive disorder. *Annual Review of Clinical Psychology, 7*, 229–243.

Freud, S. (1938). *The basic writings of Sigmund Freud.* New York, NY: Random House.

Gambrill, E. (1990). *Critical thinking in clinical practice.* San Francisco, CA: Jossey-Bass.

Gambrill, E. (2006). Evidence-based practices and policy: Choices ahead. *Research on Social Work Practice, 16*, 338–357.

Geisen-bloo, J., van Dyck, R., Spinhoven, P., van Tilberg, W., Dirksen, C., van Asselt, T., Kremers, I., Nadort, M., & Arntz, A. (2006). Outpatient psychotherapy for borderline personality disorder: Randomized trial of schema-focused therapy vs. transference-focused psychotherapy. *Archives of General Psychiatry, 63*, 649–658.

Gendreau, P. (1996). The principles of effective intervention with offenders. In A. T. Harland (Ed.), *Choosing correctional options that work: Defining demand and evaluating the supply* (pp. 117–130). Thousand Oaks, CA: Sage Publications.

Gibbs, L. E., & Gambrill, E. (2002). Evidence-based practice: Counterarguments to objections. *Research on Social Work Practice, 12*, 452–476.

Glasgow, R. E. (2009). Critical measurement issues in translational research. *Research on Social Work Practice, 19*, 560–568.

Glasner-Edwards, S., & Rawson, R. (2010). Evidence-based practices in addiction treatment: Review and recommendations for public policy. *Health Policy, 97*, 93–104.

Gold, P. B., Meisler, N., Santos, A. B., Carnemolla, M. A., Williams, O. H., & Keleher, J. (2006). Randomized trial of supported employment integrated with Assertive Community Treatment for rural adults with severe mental illness. *Schizophrenia Bulletin, 32*, 378–395.

Goldfried, M. R. (2010). The future of psychotherapy integration: Closing the gap between research and practice. *Journal of Psychotherapy Integration, 20*, 386–396.

Goldman, H. H., Ganju, V., Drake, R. E., Gorman, P., Hogan, M., Hyde, P. S., & Morgan, O. (2001). Policy implications for implementing evidence-based practices. *Psychiatric Services, 52*, 1591–1597.

Goldstein, H. (1986). A cognitive-humanistic approach to the court-ordered vs. voluntary hard-to-reach client. *Social Casework, 67*, 27–36.

Goodheart, C. D., Kazdin, A. E., & Sternberg, R. J. (2006). *Evidence-based psychotherapy: Where practice and research meet*. Washington, DC: American Psychological Association.

Goodman, C. C., Potts, M. K., & Pasztor, E. M. (2007). Caregiving grandmothers with vs. without child welfare system involvement: Effects of expressed need, formal services, and informal social support on caregiver burden. *Children and Youth Services Review, 29*, 428–441.

Gottman, J. M. (1993a). A theory of marital dissolution and stability. *Journal of Family Psychology, 7*, 57–75.

Gottman, J. M. (1993b). The roles of conflict engagement, escalation, and avoidance in marital interaction: A longitudinal view of five types of couples. *Journal of Consulting and Clinical Psychology, 61*, 6–15.

Gottman, J. M. (1998). On the etiology of marital decay and its consequences: Comments from a clinical psychologist. In T. N. Bradbury (Ed.), *The developmental course of marital dysfunction* (pp. 423–426). New York, NY: Cambridge University Press.

Grant, B. F., Dawson, D. A., Stinson, F. S., Chou, S. P., Dufour, M. C., & Pickering, R. P. (2004). The 12-month prevalence and trends in DSM-IV alcohol abuse and dependence: United States, 1991–1992 and 2001–2002. *Drug and Alcohol Dependence, 74*, 223–234.

Grant, B. F., Stinson, F. S., Hasin, D. S., Dawson, D. A., Chou, S. P., et al. (2005). Prevalence, correlates and comorbidity of bipolar I disorders and Axis I and II disorders: Results from the National Epidemiologic Survey on Alcohol and Related Conditions. *Journal of Clinical Psychiatry, 66*, 1205–1215.

Greenberg, L. S., Warwar, S., & Malcomb, W. (2010). Emotion-focused couples therapy and the facilitation of forgiveness. *Journal of Marital and Family Therapy, 36*, 28–42.

Greenberg, L. S., & Watson, J. C. (2006). *Emotion-focused therapy for depression.* Washington, DC: American Psychological Association.

Gregory, R. J., Chlebowski, S., Kang, D., Remen, A. L., Soderberg, M. G., & Stepkovitch, J. (2008). A controlled trial of psychodynamic psychotherapy for co-occurring borderline personality disorder and alcohol use disorder. *Psychotherapy: Theory, Research, Practice, Training, 45*, 28–41.

Grote, N. K., Swartz, A., Geibel, S. L., Zuckoff, A., Houck, P. R., & Frank, E. (2009). A randomized controlled trial of culturally relevant, brief interpersonal psychotherapy for perinatal depression. *Psychiatric Services, 60*, 313–321.

Gryczynski, J., Mitchell, S. G., Peterson, T. R., Gonzales, A., Moseley, A., & Schwartz, R. P. (2011). The relationship between services delivered and substance use outcomes in New Mexico's Screening, Brief Intervention, Referral and Treatment (SBIRT) initiative. *Drug and Alcohol Dependence, 118*, 152–157.

Gutierrez, L. M. (1990). Working with women of color: An empowerment perspective. *Social Work, 35*, 149–153.

Hare, R. D., Harpur, T. J., Hakstian, A. R., Forth, A. E., Hart, S. D., & Newman, J. P. (1990). The Psychopathy Checklist: Reliability and factor structure. *Psychological Assessment: A Journal of Consulting and Clinical Psychology, 2*, 338–341.

Hare, R. D., & Neumann, C. S. (2009). Psychopathy: Assessment and forensic implications. *The Canadian Journal of Psychiatry, 54*, 791–802.

Hargreaves, W. A., Shumway, M., Hu, T.-W., & Cuffel, B. (1998). *Cost-outcome methods for mental health.* San Diego, CA: Academic Press.

Harkness, D. (2011). The diagnosis of mental disorders in clinical social work: A review of standards of care. *Clinical Social Work Journal, 39*, 223–231.

Harned, M. S., Chapman, A. L., Dexter-Mazza, E. T., Murray, A., Comtois, K. A., & Linehan, M. M. (2008). Treating co-occurring Axis I disorders in recurrently suicidal women with borderline personality disorder: A 2-year randomized trial of dialectical behavior therapy versus community treatment by experts. *Journal of Consulting and Clinical Psychology, 76*, 1068–1075.

Hasking, P. A., & Oei, T. P. S. (2007). Alcohol expectancies, self-efficacy and coping in an alcohol-dependent sample. *Addictive Behaviors, 32*, 99–113.

Hasin, D. S., Goodwin, R. D., Stinson, F. S., & Grant, B. F. (2005). Epidemiology of major depressive disorder: Results from the national epidemiologic survey on alcoholism and related conditions. *Archives of General Psychiatry, 62,* 1097–1106.

Hasin, D. S., Stinson, F. S., Ogburn, E., & Grant, B. F. (2007). Prevalence, correlates, disability, and comorbidity of DSM-IV alcohol abuse and dependence in the United States: Results from the National Epidemiologic Survey on Alcohol and Related Conditions. *Archives of General Psychiatry, 64,* 830–842.

Henggeler, S. W., Schoenwald, S. K., Borduin, C. M., Rowland, M. D., & Cunningham, P. B. (1998). *Multisystemic treatment of antisocial behavior in children and adolescents.* New York, NY: Guilford Press.

Henggeler, S. W., Schoenwald, S. K., Borduin, C. M., Rowland, M. D., & Cunningham, P. B. (2009). *Multisystemic therapy for antisocial behavior in children and adolescents* (2nd ed.). New York, NY: Guilford Press.

Herman, D. B., Susser, E. S., & Struening, E. L. (1998). Homelessness, stress and psychopathology. In B. P. Dohrenwend (Ed.), *Adversity and psychopathology* (pp. 132–141). New York, NY: Oxford University Press.

Higgins, S. T., Budney, A. J., Bickel, W. K., Hughes, J. R., Foerg, F., & Badger, G. (1993). Achieving cocaine abstinence with a behavioral approach. *American Journal of Psychiatry, 150,* 5, 763–769.

Higgins, S., Sigmon, S., Wong, C., Heil, S., Badger, G., Donham, R., Dantona, R., & Anthony, S. (2003). Community reinforcement for cocaine-dependent outpatients. *Archives of General Psychiatry, 60,* 1043–1052.

Hill, C. E., Nutt, E. A., & Jackson, S. (1994). Trends in psychotherapy process research: Samples, measures, researchers, and classic publications. *Journal of Counseling Psychology, 4,* 364–377.

Hill, C. E., & O'Brien, K. M. (2004). *Helping skills: Facilitating exploration, insight, and action.* Washington, DC: American Psychological Association.

Holahan, C. J., & Moos, R. H. (1994). Life stressors and mental health: Advances in conceptualizing stress resistance. In W. R. Avison & I. H. Gotlib (Eds.), *Stress and mental health: Contemporary issues and prospects for the future* (pp. 213–238). New York, NY: Plenum Press.

Hollon, S. D., & Beck, A. T. (1994). Cognitive and cognitive-behavioral therapies. In A. E. Bergin & S. L. Garfield (Eds.), *The handbook of psychotherapy and behavior change* (4th ed.) (pp. 428–466). New York, NY: John Wiley & Sons, Inc.

Hopkins, M., & Ramsundar, N. (2006). Which factors predict case management services and how do these services relate to client outcomes? *Psychiatric Rehabilitation Journal, 29,* 219–222.

Horvath, A. O., & Greenberg, L. S. (1989). Development and validation of the working alliance inventory. *Journal of Counseling Psychology, 36,* 223–233.

Houston-Vega, M. K., & Nuehring, E. M. (1997). *Prudent practice: A guide for managing malpractice risk.* Washington, DC: NASW Press.

Howard, M. O., & Jenson, J. M. (1999). Clinical practice guidelines: Should social work develop them? *Research on Social Work Practice, 9,* 283–301.

Humphreys, K. (1999). Professional interventions that facilitate 12-step self-help group involvement. *Alcohol Research and Health, 23,* 93–98.

Jacobson, N. S., & Addis, M. E. (1993). Research on couples and couple therapy: What do we know? Where are we going? *Journal of Consulting and Clinical Psychology, 61,* 85–93.

Jacobson, N. S., & Margolin, G. (1979). *Marital therapy: Strategies based on social learning and behavior exchange principles.* New York, NY: Guilford Press.

Johnson, M., & Austin, M. J. (2006). Evidence-based practice in the social services: Implications for organizational change. *Administration in Social Work, 30,* 75–104.

Johnson, S. M. (2007). The contribution of emotionally focused couples therapy. *Journal of Contemporary Psychotherapy, 37,* 47–52.

Johnson, S. M., & Greenberg, L. S. (1995). The emotionally focused approach to problems in adult attachment. In N. S. Jacobson & A. S. Gurman (Eds.), *Clinical handbook of couple therapy* (pp. 121–141). New York, NY: Guilford Press.

Joutsenniemi, K., Moustgaard, H., Koskinen, S., Ripatti, S., & Martikainen, P. (2011). Psychiatric comorbidity in couples: A longitudinal study of 202,959 married and cohabiting individuals. *Social Psychiatry and Psychiatric Epidemiology, 46,* 632–633.

Kazdin, A. E. (1978). Methodological and interpretive problems of single-case experimental designs. *Journal of Consulting and Clinical Psychology, 46,* 629–642.

Kazdin, A. E. (1998). *Research design in clinical psychology* (3rd ed.). Boston, MA: Allyn & Bacon.

Kazdin, A. E., & Weisz, J. R. (1998). Identifying and developing empirically supported child and adolescent treatments. *Journal of Consulting and Clinical Psychology, 66,* 19–36.

Kendall, P. C. (1992). *Anxiety disorders in youth: Cognitive behavioral interventions*. Boston, MA: Allyn & Bacon.

Kendall, P. C. (1994). Treating anxiety disorders in children: Results of a randomized clinical trial. *Journal of Consulting and Clinical Psychology, 62*, 100–110.

Kernberg, O. F. (1976). *Object relations theory and clinical psychoanalysis*. New York, NY: Jason Aronson.

Kerrigan, D. L., Fonner, V. A., Stromdahl, S., & Kennedy, C. G. (2013). Community Empowerment among female sex workers is an effective HIV prevention intervention: A systematic review of the peer-reviewed evidence from low- and middle-income countries. *AIDS and Behavior, 17*, 1926–1940.

Kessler, R. C., McGonagle, K., Zhao, S., Nelson, C., Hughes, M., Eshleman, S., Wittchen, H., & Kendler, K. (1994). Lifetime and 12-month prevalence of DSM-III-R psychiatric disorders in the United States. *Archives of General Psychiatry, 51*, 8–19.

Kessler, R. C., Rubinow, D. R., Holmes, C., Abelson, J. M., & Zhao, S. (1997). The epidemiology of DSM-III-R bipolar I disorder in a general population survey. *Psychological Medicine, 27*, 1079–1089.

Klerman, G. L., & Weissman, M. M. (1993). *New applications of interpersonal psychotherapy*. Washington, DC: American Psychiatric Association.

Kohut, H. (1971). *The analysis of the self: A systematic approach to the psychoanalytic treatment of narcissistic personality disorders*. New York, NY: International Universities Press.

Kolves, K., Ide, N., & de Leo, D. (2010). Suicidal ideation and behavior in the aftermath of marital separation: Gender differences. *Journal of Affective Disorders, 120*, 48–53.

Koolaee, A. K., & Etemadi, A. (2010). The outcome of family interventions for the mothers of schizophrenia patients in Iran. *International Journal of Social Psychiatry, 56*, 634–646.

Kreyenbuhl, J., Buchanan, R. W., Dickerson, F. B., & Dixon, L. B. (2010). The Schizophrenia Patient Outcomes Research Team (PORT): Updated treatment recommendations 2009. *Schizophrenia Bulletin, 36*, 94–103.

Kroger, C., Schweiger, U., Sipos, V., Arnold, R., Kahl, K.G., Schunert, T., Rudolf, S., & Reinecker, H. (2006). Effectiveness of dialectical behavior therapy for borderline personality disorder in an inpatient setting. *Behaviour Research and Therapy, 44*, 1211–1217.

Kulhara, P., Avasthi, A., Grover, S., Sharan, P., Sharma, P., Malhotra, S., &

Gill, S. (2010). Needs of Indian schizophrenia patients: An exploratory study from India. *Social Psychiatry and Psychiatric Epidemiology, 45,* 809–818.

Kuno, E., Rothbard, A. B., Averyt, J., & Culhane, D. (2000). Homelessness among persons with serious mental illness in an enhanced community-based mental health system. *Psychiatric Services, 51,* 1012–1016.

Kurtz, M., & Mueser, K. T. (2008). A meta-analysis of controlled research on social skills training for schizophrenia. *Journal of Consulting and Clinical Psychology, 76,* 491–504.

Lamb, H. R., & Weinberger, L. E. (1998). Persons with severe mental illness in jails and prisons: A review. *Psychiatric Services, 49,* 483–492.

Lamb, H. R., & Weinberger, L. E. (2008). Mental health courts as a way to provide treatment to violent persons with severe mental illness. *JAMA, 300,* 722–724.

Lambert, M. J., & Bergin, A. E. (1994). The effectiveness of psychotherapy. In A. E. Bergin & S. L. Garfield (Eds.), *The handbook of psychotherapy and behavior change* (4th ed.) (pp. 143–189). New York, NY: John Wiley & Sons, Inc.

Lazarus, R. S. (1999). *Stress and emotion.* New York, NY: Springer Publishing Co.

Lazarus, R. S., & Folkman, S. (1984). *Stress, appraisal and coping.* New York, NY: Springer Publishing Co.

Lebow, J. (2000). What does the research tell us about couples and family therapies? *Psychotherapy in Practice, 56,* 1083–1094.

Lehman, A. F. (2010). Adopting evidence-based practices: Our hesitation waltz. *Schizophrenia Bulletin, 36,* 1–2.

Lehman, A. F., Steinwachs, D. M., & the Co-Investigators of the PORT Project (1998). At issue: Translating research into practice—the schizophrenia patient outcomes research team (PORT) recommendations. *Schizophrenia Bulletin, 24,* 1–10.

Leischenring, F., Leibing, E., Kruse, J., New, A. S., & Leweke, F. (2011). Borderline personality disorder. *Lancet, 377,* 74–84.

Leschied, A. W., Chiodo, D., Whitehead, P. C., & Hurley, D. (2006). The association of poverty with child welfare service and child and family clinical outcomes. *Community, Work and Family, 9,* 29–46.

Levy, L. B., & O'Hara, M. W. (2010). Psychotherapeutic interventions for depressed, low-income women: A review of the literature. *Clinical Psychology Review, 30,* 934–950.

Linehan, M. M. (1993). *Cognitive-behavioral treatment of borderline personality disorder.* New York, NY: Guilford Press.

Linehan, M. M., Comtois, K. A., Murray, A. M., Brown, M. Z., Gallop, R. J.,

Heard, H. L., et al. (2006). Two-year randomized controlled trial and follow-up of dialectical behavior therapy vs. therapy by experts for suicidal behaviors and borderline personality disorder. *Archives of General Psychiatry, 63*(7), 757–766.

Lu, W., Fite, R., Kim, E., Hyer, L., Yanos, P. T., Mueser, K. T., & Rosenberg, S. D. (2009). Cognitive-behavioral treatment of PTSD in severe mental illness: Pilot study replication in an ethnically diverse population. *American Journal of Psychiatric Rehabilitation, 12*, 73–91.

Lum, D. (2007). *Culturally competent practice: A framework for understanding diverse groups and justice issues* (3rd ed.). Belmont, CA: Thomson/ Brooks/Cole.

Lutzker, J. R., Bigelow, K. M., Doctor, R. M., Gershater, R. M., & Greene, B. F. (1998). An ecobehavioral model for the prevention and treatment of child abuse and neglect: History and applications. In J. R. Lutzker (Ed.), *Handbook of child abuse research and treatment* (pp. 239–266). New York, NY: Plenum Press.

Lyons, S. J., Henly, J. R., & Schuerman, J. R. (2005). Informal support in maltreating families: Its effect on parenting practices. *Children and Youth Services Review, 27*, 21–38.

Magill, M., & Ray, L. A. (2009). Cognitive-behavioral treatment with adult alcohol and illicit drug users: A meta-analysis of randomized controlled trials. *Journal of Studies on Alcohol and Drugs, 70*, 516–527.

Mahler, M. S., Pine, F., & Bergman, A. (1975). *The psychological birth of the human infant: Symbiosis and individuation.* New York, NY: Basic Books.

Makely, A. T., & Falcone, R. A. (2010). Posttraumatic stress disorder in the pediatric trauma patient. *Seminars in Pediatric Surgery, 19*, 292–299.

May, R. (1969). *Love and will.* New York, NY: Norton.

McCracken, S. G., & Marsh, J. C. (2008). Practitioner expertise in evidence-based decision-making. *Research on Social Work Practice, 18*, 301–310.

McCrady, B. S., Epstein, E. E., Cook, S., Jensen, N., & Hildebrandt, T. (2009). A randomized trial of individual and couple behavioral alcohol treatment for women. *Journal of Consulting and Clinical Psychology, 77*(2), 243–256.

McFarlane, W. R., Dixon, L., Lukens, E., & Lucksted, A. (2003). Family psychoeducation and schizophrenia: A review of the literature. *Journal of Marital and Family Therapy, 29*, 223–245.

McGuire, J., & Hatcher, R. (2001). Offense-focused problem solving: Preliminary evaluation of a cognitive skills program. *Criminal Justice and Behavior, 28*, 564–587.

McGurk, S. R., Mueser, K. T., DeRosa, T. J., & Wolfe, R. (2009). Work, recovery, and comorbidity in schizophrenia: A randomized controlled trial of cognitive remediation. *Schizophrenia Bulletin, 35,* 319–335.

McMahon, R. J., & Forehand, R. (1984). Parent training for the non-compliant child: Treatment outcome, generalization, and adjunctive therapy procedures. In R. F. Dangel & R. A. Polster (Eds.), *Parent training: Foundations of research and practice* (pp. 298–328). New York, NY: Guilford Press.

McMahon, R. J., & Frick, P. J. (2005). Evidence-based assessment of conduct problems in children and adolescents. *Journal of Clinical Child & Adolescent Psychology, 34*(3), 477–505.

McMahon, R. J., Wells, K. C., & Kotler, J. S. (2006). Conduct problems. In E. J. Mash & R. A. Barkley (Eds.), *Treatment of childhood disorders* (3rd ed.) (pp.137–268). New York, NY: Guilford Press.

McMain, S. F., Links, P. S., Gnam, W. H., Guimond, T., Cardish, R. J., Korman, L., & Streiner, D. L. (2009). A randomized trial of dialectical behavior therapy versus general psychiatric management for borderline personality disorder. *American Journal of Psychiatry, 166,* 1365–1374.

Mechanic, D. (1996). Emerging issues in international mental health services research. *Psychiatric Services, 47,* 371–375.

Meichenbaum, D. (1974). *Cognitive behavior modification.* Morristown, NJ: General Learning Press.

Merikangas, K. R., He, J. P., Brody, D., Fisher, P. W., Bourden, K., & Koretz, D. S. (2009). Prevalence and treatment of mental disorders among U.S. children in the 2001–2004 NHANES. *Pediatrics, 125,* 75–81.

Meyers, L. L., & Thyer, B. A. (1997). Should social work clients have the right to effective treatment? *Social Work, 42,* 288–298.

Miklowitz, D. J., Simoneau, T. L., George, E. L., Richards, J. A., Kalbag, A., Sachs-Ericsson, N., et al., (2000). Family-focused treatment of bipolar disorder: 1-year effects of a psycho-educational program in conjunction with pharmacotherapy. *Biological Psychiatry, 48,* 582–592.

Miller, J. C. (2008). 12-step treatment for alcohol and substance abuse revisited: Best available evidence suggests a lack of effectiveness or harm. *International Journal of Mental Health and Addiction, 6,* 568–576.

Miller, W. R., Meyers, R. J., & Hiller-Sturmhofel, S. (1999). The community-reinforcement approach. *Alcohol Research and Health, 23,* 116–120.

Miller, W. R., & Rollnick, S. (2013). *Motivational interviewing: Helping people change* (3rd ed.). New York, NY: Guilford Press.

Minuchin, S. (1974). *Families and family therapy*. Cambridge, MA: Harvard University Press.

Monti, P. M., & Rohsenow, D. J. (1999). Coping-skills training and cue-exposure therapy in the treatment of alcoholism. *Alcohol Research and Health, 23*, 107–115.

Morrison, J., & Anders, T. F. (1999). *Interviewing children and adolescents: Skills and strategies for effective DSM-IV diagnosis*. New York, NY: Guilford Press.

Morsette, A., Swaney, G., Stolle, D., Schuldberg, D., van den Pol, R., & Young, M. (2008). Cognitive Behavior Intervention for Trauma in Schools (CBITS): School-based treatment on a rural American Indian reservation. *Journal of Behavior Therapy and Experimental Psychiatry, 40*, 169–178.

Mueser, K. T., Bond, G. R., Drake, R. E., & Resnick, S. G. (1998). Models of community care for severe mental illness: A review of research on case management. *Schizophrenia Bulletin, 24*, 37–74.

Mueser, K. T., Corrigan, P. W., Hilton, D. W., Tanzman, B., Schaub, A., Gingerich, S., Essock, S. M., Tarrier, N., Morey, B., Vogel-Scibilia, & Herz, M. (2002). Illness, management and recovery: A review of the research. *Psychiatric Services, 53*, 1272–1284.

Mueser, K. T., Drake, R. E., & Bond, G. R. (1997). Recent advances in psychiatric rehabilitation for patients with severe mental illness. *Harvard Review of Psychiatry, 5*, 123–137.

Mueser, K. T., & Glynn, S. M. (1999). *Behavioral family therapy for psychiatric disorders* (2nd ed.). Oakland, CA: New Harbinger Publications, Inc.

Mueser, K. T., Meyer, P. S., Penn, D. L., Cancy, R., Clancy, D. M., & Salyers, M. P. (2006). The illness management and recovery program: Rationale, development, and preliminary findings. *Schizophrenia Bulletin, 32*, s32–s43.

Mueser, K. T., Noordsy, D. L., Drake, R. E., & Fox, L. (2003). *Integrated treatment for dual disorders: A guide to effective practice*. New York, NY: Guilford Press.

Mueser, K. T., Rosenberg, S. D., Goodman, L. A., & Trumbetta, S. L. (2002). Trauma, PTSD, and the course of severe mental illness: An interactive model. *Schizophrenia Research, 53*, 123–143.

Mueser, K. T., Rosenberg, S. D., Jankowski, M. K., Hamblen, J. L., & Descamps, M. (2004). A cognitive-behavioral treatment program for post-traumatic stress disorder in persons with severe mental illness. *American Journal of Psychiatric Rehabilitation, 7*, 107–146.

Mueser, K. T., Rosenberg, S. D., Xie, H., Jankowski, M. K., Bolton, E. E., Lu,

W., Hamblen, J. L., Rosenberg, H. J., McHugo, G. J., & Wolfe, R. (2008). A randomized controlled trial of cognitive-behavioral treatment for posttraumatic stress disorder in severe mental illness. *Journal of Consulting and Clinical Psychiatry, 76,* 259–271.

Mueser, K. T., & Jeste, D. V. (Eds.). (2008). *Clinical handbook of schizophrenia.* New York, NY: Guilford Press.

Nasr, T., & Kausar, R. (2009). Psychoeducation and the family burden in schizophrenia: A randomized controlled trial. *Annals of General Psychiatry, 8.* (Online: no page numbers given.)

Nathan, P. E., & Gorman, J. M. (Eds.). (2007). *A guide to treatments that work.* New York, NY: Oxford University Press.

National Association of Social Workers (2007). Code of Ethics. NASW.org.

Ngo, V., Langley, A., Kataoka, S. H., Nadeem, E., Escudero, P., & Stein, B. D. (2008). Providing evidence-based practice to ethnically diverse youth: Examples from the Cognitive Behavior Intervention for Trauma in Schools (CBITS) program. *Journal of the Academy of Child and Adolescent Psychiatry, 47,* 858–862.

Nichols, M. P., & Schwartz, R. C. (2006). *Family therapy: Concepts and methods.* Boston, MA: Pearson/Allyn & Bacon.

Nisbett, R. E., & Ross, L. (1980). *Human inference: Strategies and shortcomings of social judgment.* Englewood Cliffs, NJ: Prentice-Hall.

Northey, W. F., Wells, K. C., Silverman, W. K., & Bailey, C. E. (2003). Childhood behavioral and emotional disorders. *Journal of Marital and Family Therapy, 29,* 523–545.

Nusslock, R., Abramson, L., Harmon-Jones, E., Alloy, L., & Coan, J. (2009). Psychosocial interventions for bipolar disorder: Perspective from the behavioral approach system (BAS) dysregulation theory. *Clinical Psychology Science and Practice, 16,* 449–469.

Nygaard, R. L. (2000). The dawn of therapeutic justice. In D. H. Fishbein (Ed.), *The science, treatment, and prevention of antisocial behaviors: Application to the criminal justice system* (pp. 23–1 to 23–18). Kingston, NJ: Civic Research Institute.

O'Farrell, T., & Fals-Stewart, W. (2003). Alcohol abuse. *Journal of Marital and Family Therapy, 29,* 121–146.

O'Farrell, T. J., & Schein, A. Z. (2011). Behavioral couples therapy for alcoholism and drug abuse. *Journal of Family Psychotherapy, 22,* 193–215.

O'Hanlon, W. H., & Weiner-Davis, M. (1989). *In search of solutions: A new direction in psychotherapy.* New York, NY: Norton.

O'Hare, T. (1991). Integrating research and practice: A framework for implementation. *Social Work, 36*(3), 220–223.

O'Hare, T. (1996). Court-ordered vs. voluntary clients: Problem differences and readiness for change. *Social Work, 41,* 417–422.

O'Hare, T. (2009). *Essential skills of social work practice: Assessment, intervention and evaluation.* Chicago, IL: Lyceum Books, Inc.

O'Hare, T. (2015). *Evidence-based practices for social workers: An interdisciplinary approach* (2nd ed.). Chicago, IL: Lyceum Books, Inc.

O'Hare, T., & Collins, P. (1997). Development and validation of a scale for measuring social work practice skills. *Research on Social Work Practice, 7*(2), 228–238.

O'Hare, T., & Geertsma, J. (2013). Using the Practice Skills Inventory in real time: Implications for evaluating evidence-based practices. *Best Practices in Mental Health, 9*(2), (published online).

O'Hare, T., Shen, C., & Sherrer, M. (2013). Differences in trauma and posttraumatic stress symptoms in clients with schizophrenia spectrum and major mood disorders. *Psychiatry Research, 205,* 85–89.

O'Hare, T., Sherrer, M. V., Connery, H., Thornton, J., LaButti, A., & Emrick, K. (2003). Further validation of the Psycho-Social Wellbeing Scale. *Community Mental Health Journal, 39,* 115–129.

O'Hare, T., Sherrer, M. V., Cutler, J., McCall, T., Dominique, K., & Garlick, K. (2002). Validating the psychosocial well being scale among mentally ill clients with substance abuse problems. *Social Work in Mental Health, 1,* 15–30.

O'Hare, T., Tran, T. V., & Collins, P. (2002). Validating the Practice Skills Inventory: A confirmatory factor analysis. *Research on Social Work Practice, 12,* 653–668.

O'Leary, E. M. M., Barrett, P., & Fjermestad, K. W. (2009). Cognitive behavior family treatment for childhood obsessive-compulsive disorder: A 7-year follow-up study. *Journal of Anxiety Disorders, 23,* 973–978.

Ollendick, T. H., & King, N. J. (1998). Empirically supported treatments for children with phobic and anxiety disorders: Current status. *Journal of Child Psychology, 27,* 156–167.

Orlinsky, D. E., Grawe, K., & Parks, B. K. (1994). Process and outcome in psychotherapy—Noch Einmal. In A. E. Bergin & S. L. Garfield (Eds.), *The handbook of psychotherapy and behavior change* (4th ed.) (pp. 270–376). New York, NY: John Wiley & Sons, Inc.

Orlinsky, D. E., & Howard, K. I. (1986). Process and outcome in psychotherapy. In S. L. Garfield & A. E. Bergin (Eds.), *The handbook of psychotherapy and behavior change* (pp. 311–384). New York, NY: John Wiley & Sons, Inc.

Pagura, J., Stein, M. B., Bolton, J. M., Cox, B. J., Grant, B., & Sareen, J. (2010). Comorbidity of borderline personality disorder and posttraumatic stress disorder in the U.S. population. *Journal of Psychiatric Research, 44,* 1190–1198.

Pecora, P. J., Whittaker, J. K., Maluccio, A. N., & Barth, R. P. (2000). *The child welfare challenge: Policy, practice, and research* (2nd ed.). New York, NY: Aldine de Gruyter.

Perlman, H. H. (1957). *Social case work: A problem-solving process.* Chicago, IL: University of Chicago Press.

Powers, M. B., Vedel, E., & Emmelkamp, P. M. G. (2008). Behavioral couples therapy (BCT) for alcohol and drug use disorders: A meta-analysis. *Clinical Psychology Review, 28,* 952–962.

Prochaska, J. O., & DiClemente, C. C. (1984). *The transtheoretical approach: Crossing the traditional boundaries of therapy.* Homewood, IL: Dow Jones/Irwin.

Prochaska, J. O., DiClemente, C. C., & Norcross, J. C. (1992). In search of how people change: Applications to addictive behaviors. *American Psychologist, 47,* 1102–1114.

Proctor, E. (2003). Research to inform the development of social work interventions. *Social Work Research, 27,* 3–5.

Putnam, F. W. (2003). Ten-year research update review: Child sexual abuse. *Journal of the American Academy of Child and Adolescent Psychiatry, 42,* 269–278.

RachBeisel, J., Scott, J., & Dixon, L. (1999). Co-occurring severe mental illness and substance use disorders: A review of recent research. *Psychiatric Services, 50,* 1427–1434.

Rahman, A., Sikander, S., Malik, A., Ahmed, I., Tomenson, B., & Creed, F. (2012). Effective treatment of perinatal depression for women in debt and lacking financial empowerment in a low income country. *British Journal of Psychiatry, 201,* 451–457.

Randall, J. (2002). The practice-research relationship: A case of ambivalent attachment? *Journal of Social Work, 2,* 105–122.

Randolph, F. L., Ridgway, P., & Carling, P. J. (1991). Residential programs for persons with severe mental illness: A nationwide survey of state-affiliated agencies. *Hospital and Community Psychiatry, 42,* 1111–1115.

Raskin, N. J., & Rogers, C. R. (1995). Person-centered therapy. In R. J. Corsini & D. Wedding (Eds.), *Current psychotherapies* (5th ed.) (pp. 128–161). Itasca, IL: Peacock Publishers.

Reamer, F. (1995). Malpractice claims against social workers: First facts. *Social Work, 40,* 595–601.

Reamer, F. G. (1998). *Ethical standards in social work: A critical review of the NASW Code of Ethics.* Washington, DC: NASW Press.

Reamer, F. G. (2001). *The social work ethics audit: A risk management tool.* Washington, DC: NASW Press.

Reamer, F. G. (2003). *Social work malpractice and liability* (2nd ed.). New York, NY: Columbia University Press.

Reamer, F. G. (2006). *Social work values and ethics* (3rd ed.). New York, NY: Columbia University Press.

Reamer, F. G. (2012). *Boundary issues and dual relationships in the human services.* New York, NY: Columbia University Press.

Resick, P. A., Monson, C. M., & Rizvi, S. L. (2008). Posttraumatic stress disorder. In D. H. Barlow (Ed.), *Clinical handbook of psychological disorders* (4th ed.) (pp. 65–122). New York, NY: Guilford Press.

Richmond, M. (1918). *Social diagnosis.* New York, NY: Russell Sage Foundation.

Robbins, S. P. (2011). Oppression theory and social work treatment. In F. J. Turner (Ed.), *Social work treatment: Interlocking theoretical approaches* (5th ed.) (pp. 343–353). New York, NY: Oxford University Press.

Rogers, C. R. (1951). *Client-centered therapy.* Boston, MA: Houghton Mifflin.

Rolfsnes, E. S., & Idsoe, T. (2011). School-based intervention programs for PTSD symptoms: A review and meta-analysis. *Journal of Traumatic Stress, 24,* 155–165.

Rooney, R. H., & Bibus, A. A. (2001). Clinical practice with involuntary clients in community settings. In H. E. Briggs & K. Corcoran (Eds.), *Social work practice: Treating common client problems* (pp. 391–406). Chicago, IL: Lyceum Books, Inc.

Rosen, A. (2003). Evidence-based social work practice: Challenges and promise. *Social Work Research, 27,* 197–208.

Rossi, P. H., & Freeman, H. E. (1993). *Evaluation: A systematic approach.* Thousand Oaks, CA: Sage Publications.

Rothbaum, B. O., Meadows, E. A., Resick, P., & Foy, D. W. (2000). Cognitive-behavioral therapy. In E. B. Foa, T. M. Keane, & M. J. Friedman (Eds.), *Effective treatments for PTSD: Practice guidelines from the International Society for Traumatic Stress Studies* (pp. 60–83). New York, NY: Guilford Press.

Roysircar, G. (2009). Evidence-based practice and its implications for culturally sensitive treatment. *Multicultural Counseling and Development, 37,* 66–82.

Ryan, C. S., Sherman, P. S., & Judd, C. M. (1994). Accounting for case manager effects in the evaluation of mental health services. *Journal of Consulting and Clinical Psychology, 62,* 965–974.

Saavedra, L. M., Silverman, W. K., Morgan-Lopez, A. A., & Kurtines, W. M. (2010). Cognitive-behavioral treatment for childhood anxiety disorders: Long-term effects on anxiety and secondary disorders in young adulthood. *Journal of Child Psychology and Psychiatry, 51,* 924–934.

Sackett, D. L., Straus, S. E., Richardson, W. S., Rosenberg, W., & Haynes, R. B. (2000). *Evidence-based medicine: How to practice and teach EBM.* New York, NY: Churchill Livingstone.

Sadock, B. J., & Sadock, V. A. (2003). *Kaplan and Sadock's synopsis of psychiatry: Behavioral sciences/clinical psychiatry* (9th ed.). Philadelphia, PA: Lippincott, Williams and Wilkins.

Safren, A. A., O'Cleirigh, C., Tan, J. Y., Raminani, S. R., Reilly, L. C., Otto, M. W., & Mayer, K. H. (2009). A randomized controlled trial of cognitive behavior therapy for adherence and depression (CBT-AD) in HIV-infected individuals. *Health Psychology, 28,* 1–10.

Saleeby, D. (1996). Strengths perspective in social work practice: Extensions and cautions. *Social Work, 41,* 296–305.

Salyers, M. P., McGuire, A. B., Rollins, A. L., Bond, G. R., Mueser, K. T., & Macy, V. R. (2010). Integrating Assertive Community Treatment and illness management and recovery for consumers with severe mental illness. *Community Mental Health Journal, 46,* 319–329.

Sanchez-Meca, J., Rosa-Alcazar, A. I., Marin-Martinez, F., & Gomez-Conesa, A. (2010). Psychological treatment of panic disorder with or without agoraphobia: A meta-analysis. *Clinical Psychology Review, 30,* 37–50.

Schonbrun, Y. C., & Whisman, M. A. (2010). Marital distress and mental health care service utilization. *Journal of Consulting and Clinical Psychology, 78,* 732–736.

Schottenbauer, M. A., Glass, C. A., & Arnkoff, D. B. (2007). Decision-making and psychotherapy integration: Theoretical considerations, preliminary data, and implications for future research. *Journal of Psychotherapy Integration, 17,* 225–250.

Scott, J. E., & Dixon, L. B. (1995). Assertive Community Treatment and case management for schizophrenia. *Schizophrenia Bulletin, 21,* 657–668.

Seghal, B., Young, A., Gillem, A. R., Saules, K., Grey, M. J., & Nabors, N. A. (2011). Practicing what we know: Multicultural counseling competence among clinical psychology trainees and experienced multicultural psychologists. *Cultural Diversity and Ethnic Minority Psychology, 17,* 1–10.

Sexton, T. L. (2011). *Functional family therapy in clinical practice: An evidence-based treatment approach for working with troubled adolescents.* New York, NY: Routledge.

Shadish, W. R., & Baldwin, S. A. (2005). Effects of behavioral marital therapy: A meta-analysis of randomized controlled trials. *Journal of Consulting and Clinical Psychology, 73,* 6–14.

Sherrer, M. V., & O'Hare, T. (2008). Clinical case management. In K. Mueser & D. Jeste (Eds.), *Clinical handbook of schizophrenia.* New York, NY: Guilford Press.

Shiraev, E., & Levy, D. (2007). *Cross-cultural psychology: Critical thinking and contemporary applications* (3rd ed.). Boston, MA: Pearson/ Allyn & Bacon.

Shulman, L. (1999). *The skills of helping individuals, families, groups, and communities* (4th ed.). Itasca, IL: Peacock Publishers.

Siegel, D. (1984). Defining empirically based practice, *Social Work, 29,* 325–331.

Silverman, W. K., & Berman, S. L. (2001). Psychosocial interventions for anxiety disorders in children: Status and future directions. In W. K. Silverman & P. D. A. Treffers (Eds.), *Anxiety disorders in children and adolescents: Research, assessment and intervention* (pp. 313–334). New York, NY: Cambridge University Press.

Simpson, E. B., Pistorello, J., Begin, A., Costello, E., Levinson, J., Mulberry, S., Pearlstein, T., Rosen, K., & Stevens, M. (1998). Use of dialectical behavior therapy in a partial hospital program for women with borderline personality disorder. *Psychiatric Services, 49,* 669–673.

Skodol, A. E., Bender, D. S., Morey, L. C., & Oldham, J. M. (2013). The ironic fate of the personality disorders in DSM-5. *Personality Disorders: Theory, Research, and Treatment, 4,* 342–349.

Smith, B. H., Barkley, R. A., & Shapiro, C. J. (2006). Attention-deficit/hyperactivity disorder. In E. J. Mash & R. A. Barkley (Eds.), *Treatment of childhood disorders* (3rd ed.) (pp. 65–136). New York, NY: Guilford Press.

Smith, D. W., Witte, T. H., & Fricker-Elhai, A. E., (2006). Service outcomes in physical and sexual abuse cases: A comparison of Child Advocacy Center-based and standard services. *Child Maltreatment, 11*(4) 354–360.

Smokowski, P. R., & Wodarski, J. S. (1996). The effectiveness of child welfare services for poor, neglected children: A review of the empirical evidence. *Research on Social Work Practice, 6,* 504–523.

Snyder, D. K., Castellani, A. M., & Whisman, M. A. (2006). Current status and future directions in couple therapy. *Annual Review of Psychology, 57,* 317–344.

Sommers-Flannagan, J., & Sommers-Flannagan, R. (2003). *Clinical interviewing.* Hoboken, NJ: John Wiley & Sons, Inc.

Soydan, H., Mullen, E. J., Alexandra, L., Rehnman, J., & Li, Y. (2010). Evidence-based clearinghouses in social work. *Research on Social Work Practice, 20,* 690–700.

Stanton, M. D., & Shadish, W. R. (1997). Outcome, attrition, and family-couples treatment for drug abuse: A meta-analysis and review of the controlled, comparative studies. *Psychological Bulletin, 122,* 170–191.

Stark, K., Sander, J., Hauser, M., Simpson, J., Schnoebelen, S., Glenn, R., & Molnar, J. (2006). Depressive disorders during childhood and adolescence. In E. J. Mash & R. A. Barkley (Eds.), *Treatment of childhood disorders* (3rd ed.) (pp. 336–407). New York, NY: Guilford Press.

Stein, L. I., & Test, M. A. (1980). Alternative to mental hospital treatment. I: Conceptual model, treatment program, and clinical evaluation. *Archives of General Psychiatry, 37,* 392–397.

Steketee, G. S. (1993). *Treatment of obsessive-compulsive disorder.* New York, NY: Guilford Press.

Stout, E. S., & Hayes, R.A. (2005). *The evidence-based practice: Methods, models and tools for mental health professionals.* Hoboken, NJ: John Wiley & Sons, Inc.

Strom-Gottfried, K. (2007). *Straight talk about professional ethics.* Chicago, IL: Lyceum Books, Inc.

Stuart, G. W., Rush, A. J., & Morris, J. A. (2002). Practice guidelines in mental health and addiction services: Contributions from the American College of Mental Health Administration. *Administration and Policy in Mental Health, 30,* 21–33.

Stutzman, S. V., Bean, R. A., Miller, R. B., Day, R. D., Feinauer, L. L., Porter, C. L., & Moore, A. (2011). Marital conflict and adolescent outcomes: A cross-ethnic group comparison of Latino and European-American youth. *Children and Youth Services Review, 33,* 663–668.

Sue, D. (2005). *Multicultural social work practice.* New York, NY: John Wiley & Sons, Inc.

Sue, D. W., & Sue, D. (1999). *Counseling the culturally different* (3rd ed.). New York, NY: John Wiley & Sons, Inc.

Swartz, M. S., Swanson, J. W., Hiday, V. A., Borum, R., Wagner, H. R., & Burns, B. J. (1998). Violence and severe mental illness: The effects of substance abuse and nonadherence to medication. *American Journal of Psychiatry, 155,* 226–231.

Tandon, M., Cardeli, E., & Luby, J. (2009). Internalizing disorders in early childhood: A review of depressive and anxiety disorders. *Child and Adolescent Psychiatric Clinics of North America, 18,* 593–610.

Taylor, S., & Clark, D. A. (2009). Transdiagnostic cognitive-behavioral treatments for mood and anxiety disorders: Introduction to the special issue. *Journal of Cognitive Psychotherapy: An International Quarterly, 23*, 3–5.

Tehrani, J. A., Brennan, P. A., Hodgins, S., & Mednick, S. A. (1998). Mental illness and criminal violence. *Social Psychiatry and Psychiatric Epidemiology, 33*, s81–s85.

Tenhula, W. N., Bennett, M. E., & Kinnaman, J. E. S. (2009). Behavioral treatment of substance abuse in schizophrenia. *Journal of Clinical Psychology: In Session, 65*, 831–841.

Thomas, C., & Corcoran, J. (2001). Empirically based marital and family interventions for alcohol abuse: A review. *Research on Social Work Practice, 11*, 549–575.

Thyer, B. A. (1995). Effective psychosocial treatments for children: A selected review. *Early Child Development and Care, 106*, 137–147.

Thyer, B. A. (2004). Science and evidence-based social work practice. In H. E. Briggs & T. L. Rzepnicki (Eds.), *Using evidence in social work practice: Behavioral perspectives* (pp. 74–89). Chicago, IL: Lyceum Books, Inc.

Truax, C. B., & Carkhuff, R. R. (1967). *Toward effective counseling and psychotherapy*. Chicago, IL: Aldine.

Tversky, A., & Kahneman, D. (1974). Judgment under uncertainty: Heuristics and biases. *Science, 183*, 1124–1131.

Uba, L. (1994). *Asian Americans: Personality, patterns, identity and mental health*. New York, NY: Guilford Press.

U. S. Department of Health and Human Services (2000). *10th special report to Congress on alcohol and health*. Washington, DC: Government Printing Office.

U. S. Department of Health and Human Services (2003a). *The AFCARS report*. Washington, DC: Children's Bureau, Administration on Children, Youth and Families.

U. S. Department of Health and Human Services (2003b). *Assessing alcohol problems: A guide for clinicians and researchers* (2nd ed.). Washington, DC: National Institute on Alcohol Abuse and Alcoholism.

U. S. Department of Health and Human Services, Administration for Children and Families (2012). Child maltreatment 2011. Available from http://www.acf.hhs.gov/programs/cb/research-data-technology/stati stics-researc h/child-maltreatment.

Van Dorn, R. A., Elbogen, E. B., Redlich, A. D., Swanson, J. W., Swartz, M. S., & Mustillo, S. (2006). The relationship between mandated community treatment and perceived barriers to care in persons with severe mental illness. *International Journal of Law and Psychiatry, 29*, 495–506.

Verheul, R., van den Bosch, L. M. C., Koeter, M. W. J., de Ridder, M. A. J., Stijnen, T., & van den Brink, W. (2003). Dialectical behavior therapy for women with borderline personality disorder: 12-month randomized clinical trial in the Netherlands. *British Journal of Psychiatry, 182*, 135–140.

Wakefield, J. C. (1996). Does social work need the eco-systems perspective? *Social Service Review*, 1–32.

Waley, A. L., & Davis, K. E. (2007). Cultural competence and evidence-based practice in mental health services. *American Psychologist, 62*, 563–574.

Wandersman, A. (2003). Community science: Bridging the gap between science and practice with community-centered models. *American Journal of Community Psychology, 31*, 227–243.

Webb, S. (2002). Evidence-based practice and decision analysis in social work. *Journal of Social Work, 2*, 45–63.

Webster-Stratton, C., & Herbert, M. (1994). *Troubled families—problem children. Working with parents: A collaborative process.* New York, NY: John Wiley & Sons, Inc.

Wells, K. (2006). Child protection and welfare reform. *Child Abuse and Neglect, 30*, 1175–1179.

Weiss, J. (1995). Empirical studies of the psychoanalytic process. In T. Shapiro & R. N. Emde (Eds.), *Research in psychoanalysis: Process, development, outcome* (pp. 7–30). Madison, CT: International Universities Press.

Weissman, M. M., Markowitz, J. C., & Klerman, G. L. (2000). *Comprehensive guide to interpersonal psychotherapy.* New York, NY: Basic Books.

Westen, D., Novotny, C. M., & Thompson-Brenner, H. (2004). The empirical status of empirically supported psychotherapies: Assumption, findings, and reporting in controlled clinical trials. *Psychological Bulletin, 130*, 631–663.

Wexler, D. B. (1991). Inducing therapeutic compliance through the criminal law. In D. B. Wexler & B. J. Winick (Eds.), *Essays in therapeutic jurisprudence* (pp. 187–218). Durham, NC: Carolina Academic Press.

Wilson, C., & Powell, M. (2001). *A guide to interviewing children: Essential skills for counselors, police, lawyers, and social workers.* London, England: Routledge.

Wolfe, D. A., & Wekerle, C. (1993). Treatment strategies for child physical abuse and neglect: A critical progress report. *Clinical Psychology Review, 13*, 473–500.

Woods, M. E., and Hollis, F. (1999). *Casework: A psychosocial therapy* (5th ed.). New York, NY: McGraw-Hill.

Wynn, R. (2006). Coercion in psychiatric care: Clinical, legal, and ethical controversies. *International Journal of Psychiatry in Clinical Practice, 10,* 247–251.

Yalom, I. (2005). *The theory and practice of group psychotherapy* (5th ed.). New York, NY: Basic Books.

Young, J. E., Rygh, J. L., Weinberger, A. D., & Beck, A. T. (2008). Cognitive therapy for depression. In D. H. Barlow (Ed.), *Clinical handbook of psychological disorders: A step-by-step manual* (4th ed.) (pp. 250–305). New York, NY: Guilford Press.

Psychosocial Intervention Scale

*Client ID*_____ Date ___/___/___

Please check each of the skills below that you used during the most recently completed client visit.

Supportive Skills

1. Provided emotional support for my client (e.g., careful listening, empathy, positive regard).   _____

2. Made efforts to enhance the client's self-confidence, bolster morale (e.g., highlight strengths, emphasize opportunities for improvement and likely benefits of participating in the intervention).   _____

3. Listened carefully and showed that I understood the client's view of the problem clearly.   _____

4. Cultivated a collaborative working relationship with client to enhance participation in treatment (e.g., collaborate on goals, weigh pros and cons of changing, clarify respective roles in treatment).   _____

5. Actively motivated the client to increase his or her readiness to engage in treatment (e.g,, reduce substance use, improve social skills, seek employment, adhere to medication schedules).   _____

6. Actively tried to retain the client in treatment by, for example, reaching out, using motivational methods, contacting collaborators (e.g., law enforcement, health-care providers, significant others). _____

7. Helped client develop realistic goals for recovery at the client's own pace, avoided arguing with client about goals, and rolled with the client's resistance. _____

8. Used motivational strategies to help instill optimism and helped the client see how knowledge about the illness and improved coping skills could help the client achieve recovery goals. _____

Therapeutic Coping Skills

1. Helped client identify, examine, and challenge troubling or dysfunctional thoughts, cognitions, and beliefs (e.g., hallucinations and delusions as well as other common distortions, such as "My life is hopeless," "I'll never be able to stop using drugs," "Everyone is out to get me," "Nobody likes me," "Nothing good will ever happen for me," and other fears and worries). _____

2. Examined past experiences to help client learn from previous attempts to cope with problems. _____

3. Helped client put past experiences in a more positive light. _____

4. Explored past relationships to see how they affect client's current problems. _____

5. Provided psycho-education for my client about the problems he or she is experiencing (e.g., psychosis, depression, anxiety disorder, substance abuse, parenting skills) by presenting information and then checking and reviewing it to ensure that the client understood it. _____

6. Provided family psycho-education and support so the family could cope more effectively with stress and emotional upsets. _____

7. Taught strategies to help client take psychiatric medication according to prescription. _____

8. Taught and helped client enhance coping skills to deal more effectively with symptoms of mental illness and/or other related problems. ⎯⎯⎯

9. Helped the client identify, express, and cope with troubling feelings/emotions (e.g., problematic anger, depression, fears and anxieties, envy, jealousy). ⎯⎯⎯

10. Taught stress/anxiety coping strategies for emotional distress (e.g., brief meditation, breathing, muscle relaxation). ⎯⎯⎯

11. Taught client to identify, assess, monitor, and regulate problem behaviors (i.e., identify triggers, attempt solutions, evaluate the results). ⎯⎯⎯

12. Taught client a specific problem-solving or coping skill to deal with a particular problem (e.g., used rehearsal, role play, or modeling to help client learn and practice the new skill at home, work, or other situation). Specific examples include assertiveness training, communication or other interpersonal coping skills, confronting an anxiety-provoking situation, saying no to the offer of alcohol or other drugs, and improving parenting skills or relationship communication skills. ⎯⎯⎯

13. Used positive reinforcement to help the client improve the use of a skill and achieve a goal. ⎯⎯⎯

14. Showed client how to manage contingencies (i.e., provide rewards or sanctions) to manage his or her own behavior (e.g., reward oneself for one month sobriety) or to influence another person in a positive way (e.g., improve a child's behavior, reduce conflict with a partner or coworker, resolve other disputes). ⎯⎯⎯

15. Collaborated with client on plans to cope with relapses of a problem (e.g., suicidal thoughts, psychotic symptoms, substance abuse, anxiety attacks, going off medication, anger- or impulse-control problems). ⎯⎯⎯

16. Coached client in specific lifestyle changes to enhance overall psychosocial well-being and physical health (e.g., stop smoking,

reduce/abstain from substances and other high-risk behaviors, improve diet, engage in moderate exercise). _____

Case Management Skills

1. Assessed and attended to the client's level of material resources (e.g., income, housing, food, medical, other basic needs). _____

2. Made efforts to enhance social supports (e.g., improve the client's natural social network; link to other community resources, mutual help groups, family members, employers, landlords). _____

3. Helped client to recruit significant others in his or her life to increase social supports. _____

4. Advocated on the client's behalf (e.g., attempted to represent client's rights with landlord, court, other agencies, neighbor, other community member). _____

5. Provided information and/or referral (e.g., health, substance abuse, social services). _____

6. Networked with other providers and coordinated services for client with other agencies. _____

7. Assessed the client's vocational potential (e.g., experience, abilities, strengths). _____

8. Made at least one direct effort to link the client with a potential employer. _____

The Comprehensive Service Plan

Use all available information from the client and significant others, your observations, and input from other professionals to conduct both quantitative and qualitative aspects of this multidimensional-functional assessment.

Client Identification Data

Describe client identification data (e.g., gender; age; marital status; sexual orientation; family composition; employment; racial, ethnic, cultural, religious, and spiritual affiliation and identity).

The Presenting Problem

Describe the client's problem from the client's view.

Describe the client's problem from your view as practitioner.

Describe the client's psychosocial history with an emphasis on problem trajectory.

Describe attempts to resolve the problems, previous treatment, and relevant outcomes.

The Individual Assessment

Mental Status: Cognitive Disturbances

Describe the client's level of hallucinations, delusions, disorientation, bizarre behavior or speech, memory problems, serious confusion, or other symptoms of serious cognitive impairment. Include other troubling or dysfunctional beliefs or convictions.

How would you rate the client's overall mental status during the past month?

    Poor (0)   Impaired (1)   Marginal (2)   Good (3)   Excellent (4)

Mental Status: Emotional Distress

Describe the client's level of depression, anxiety, and overall ability to regulate his or her emotions.

How would you rate your client's emotional well-being over the past thirty days?

    Poor (0)   Impaired (1)   Marginal (2)   Good (3)   Excellent (4)

Behavioral Problems

Describe your client's overall ability to regulate his or her behavior. Consider things such as ability to express effectively; ability to work at things patiently; tendencies to verbally or physically lash out at others, to run away, or to cause harm to him- or herself; and proneness to impulsive, criminal, or substance-abusing behavior. How would you describe the client's overall impulse control?

How would you rate your client's impulse control generally over the past thirty days?
  Poor (0)   Impaired (1)   Marginal (2)   Good (3)   Excellent (4)

Adaptive Strengths and Coping Abilities

Describe your client's ability to cope with problems and everyday stressors. How would you describe the client's ability to assess problem situations, deal with triggers, cope with stress, solve problems, and reach out to others for help to deal effectively with difficulties?

How would you rate your client's overall adaptive strengths and coping abilities over the past thirty days?
  Poor (0)   Impaired (1)   Marginal (2)   Good (3)   Excellent (4)

Health Problems

Describe the client's overall health. Aside from normal, transient illnesses, think about the client's general health habits (e.g., smoking, heavy drinking, exercise, weight), chronic primary health disorders, the client's opinion of his or her own health, ability to engage in usual activities relatively free from discomfort, overall energy level, and hospitalizations and treatments for illness other than psychiatric ones. Consider the client's documented medical history and any ongoing treatments.

How would you rate your client's health over the past thirty days?
  Poor (0)   Impaired (1)   Marginal (2)   Good (3)   Excellent (4)

Use of Alcohol and Other Drugs

Describe the client's use of alcohol, illicit substances (e.g., cocaine, heroin, marijuana, hallucinogens), and abuse of prescription medication. What is the usage frequency? In what quantity? How serious are the associated psychological, physical, or social consequences?

How would you rate the client's functioning in the past month with regard to substance use?
    Poor (0)   Impaired (1)   Marginal (2)   Good (3)   Excellent (4)

Recreational Activities

Consider what the client does for fun (alone or with others), hobbies, relaxation (e.g., reading, watching television, playing video games or cards), and physical exercise (e.g., walking, jogging, biking). How would you describe the client's overall involvement in positive recreational activities?

How would you rate the adequacy of the client's participation in healthy recreational activities over the past thirty days?
    Poor (0)   Impaired (1)   Marginal (2)   Good (3)   Excellent (4)

Material Resources

Describe your client's current or (if institutionalized) most recent living situation. Consider such things as adequacy of food, clothing, shelter, and safety.

How would you rate the overall adequacy of the client's material resources over the past month?
    Poor (0)   Impaired (1)   Marginal (2)   Good (3)   Excellent (4)

Independent Living and Self-Care

Describe how well your client manages his or her household; takes care of personal hygiene; and eats, sleeps, and otherwise cares for basic needs.

How would you rate the client's ability to live independently and take care of his or her basic needs over the past thirty days?

Poor (0)   Impaired (1)   Marginal (2)   Good (3)   Excellent (4)

Work (Role) Satisfaction

Describe the client's current work-related or other important role-related activities (e.g., employed, student, homemaker, volunteer, retired, disabled). Describe the activities and responsibilities that occupy the client in a productive manner.

How would you rate the client's work or role productivity over the past thirty days?

Poor (0)   Impaired (1)   Marginal (2)   Good (3)   Excellent (4)

Legal Problems

Describe any legal problems the client has had or continues to have, including minor infractions (e.g., public drunkenness, shoplifting inexpensive items, minor traffic violations, public disturbances) and more serious crimes (e.g., assault and battery, rape, burglary, driving under the influence). Consider the client's status (e.g., probation, awaiting imprisonment, parole). Consider any civil suits in which the client in involved, pending financial judgments against them, and so on. Overall, how would you describe the client's current legal situation?

How would you rate the client's legal situation over the past thirty days?

Poor (0)   Impaired (1)   Marginal (2)   Good (3)   Excellent (4)

DSM-5 Diagnosis

Family Relations

Describe the client's current family structure, including authority, hierarchy, alliances, roles, rules, boundaries, subsystems (e.g., couple, siblings, parent-child alliances); patterns of interactions, and quality of communications. Describe specific problems within the family and specific adaptive strengths within the family. How does the family describe its own racial, ethnic, cultural, and religious identities?

How would you rate the quality of the client's immediate family relationships over the past thirty days?

    Poor (0)   Impaired (1)   Marginal (2)   Good (3)   Excellent (4)

Immediate Social Relationships

With respect to close friends and acquaintances, describe the quality of your client's relationships with those available friends and acquaintances, as applicable. Over the past month, how would you describe the quality of the interaction overall between your client and friends and acquaintances with respect to closeness, intimacy, general interpersonal satisfaction, effective communications, degree of conflict, level of hostility, aggression, and evidence of any emotional or physical abuse?

How would you rate the quality of the client's immediate social relationships over the past thirty days?

    Poor (0)   Impaired (1)   Marginal (2)   Good (3)   Excellent (4)

Extended Social Relationships

Describe the type and quality of relationships between your client and others in the client's community (other than close friends and family), including other families, law enforcement, human service agencies, school personnel, coworkers, and others from whom the client receives support or with whom the client is having serious conflict.

How would you rate the quality of the client's social relationships over the past thirty days?

    Poor (0)   Impaired (1)   Marginal (2)   Good (3)   Excellent (4)

A Concise Summary of the MDF Assessment

Highlight the client's areas of distress and adaptive strengths. Emphasize those areas that are most likely to be emphasized in the intervention plan.

Recommendations for Further Focused Assessment

Note recommended referrals to consultants or additional instruments to be used.

THE COMPREHENSIVE SERVICE PLAN SUMMARY

Assessment/Problems	Goals	Objectives	Interventions	Evaluation plan
(Briefly describe key problems to be addressed.)	(State desired outcome for each problem.)	(Describe specific "stepping stones" toward each GOAL. Update as client progresses.)	(Describe specific interventions to be used.)	(Describe indexes to be used for tracking progress.)

Guide to Reviewing Research Reports

Critically Reviewing Human Behavior and Practice Research: A Brief Guide

The Introduction

- Most studies open with a brief paragraph or two about the problem to be addressed.
- A literature review follows: key studies are carefully reviewed for content and for the quality of the methods employed. The authors summarize what is known, what the quality of the existing body of research is, and what gaps there are in both knowledge and quality of methodology in the current literature.
- A new research question should logically flow from the review, and specific hypotheses may be posed (although some authors report hypotheses in the "Methodology" section as "statistical analysis strategy").

Methods

Sample

- A description of the sample is presented here, detailing how it was obtained (e.g., random sample, convenience sample) and the sample characteristics (e.g., gender, age, race—using APA style for univariate statistics).
- If the investigation is an intervention study, how the sample was recruited and assigned to different treatment groups is discussed.

Design and Data Collection Procedure

- Design is primarily concerned with how the main variables of the study are configured relative to one another. Is it a survey (e.g., cross-sectional, longitudinal), a pre-experimental (e.g., uncontrolled pre-post study), quasi-experimental (e.g., comparison group with no random assignment), or true-experimental design? Is it an exploratory qualitative study?
- For survey research, did the authors use a convenience sample or random sampling? What size sample did they hope to obtain, and what was the actual response rate (i.e., the number of people who actually responded to the authors' request to participate in the study)?
- For a practice outcome or evaluation study, were cases assigned randomly, or were cases in two groups matched by some other criterion?
- How were data collected? Face-to-face structured or unstructured interviews? Self-report questionnaires done at home? Mail, telephone, or Internet survey? Who collected the data? How was informed consent obtained? How was clients' confidentiality protected?

Instruments

- What type of instruments (e.g., scales, indexes) were used? What did they measure?
- Did the authors provide information regarding any relevant published psychometric data (e.g., reliability, validity, utility)?
- How were the scales scored?

Statistical Analysis Strategy

- As noted earlier, the authors might state (or restate) the study hypotheses here with specific reference to the relationship they expected to find between the key variables (no expected relationship is a *null hypothesis*).
- The authors should also discuss what types of statistical tests they plan to use and why they selected them.

Results

- Authors should report in text or tables all univariate descriptive data on the study sample (if this has not been done in the "Sample" section) and present univariate statistics (e.g., means, standard deviations, frequencies, percentages) for all key study variables.

- Authors should report any bivariate tests (e.g., chi square, *t*-tests, Pearson correlations) that test the relationship of two variables. These tests are often the first test of any study hypotheses. What are the basic findings?
- Last, authors should report the findings of any multivariate statistical tests (e.g., regression, analysis of variance, structural equation modeling). Try to find a clear verbal explanation of the results of those tests.

Discussion

- Some authors summarize their key findings briefly at the beginning of the "Discussion" section.
- Authors should then discuss what the findings mean with respect to theory, practice, or policy in the context of previous literature.
- Authors should discuss the limitations of their study (e.g., missing data, attrition in participant sample, small sample).
- Authors should then discuss questions for future research.

Critically Reviewing Human Behavior and Practice Research: A Longer Explanation

The following guidelines were generally developed by the American Psychological Association for the conducting and reporting of research, and they are accepted by most helping professions, including the National Association of Social Workers. Scholars who conduct research or critically review others' research to determine whether it merits publication use these guidelines.

The Introduction

Most research reports begin with an opening paragraph or two defining the problem or practice method of interest and then offer an argument to impress on the reader the importance of a particular social problem or psychosocial intervention. A review of the previous research on the subject area follows.

A representative review of the literature. Knowledge building does not happen in a vacuum. Researchers must build on and ideally improve on what has been done before. Therefore, all research begins with a reasonably representative review of prior research on the subject of the article. The subsequent discussion touches on the criteria that authors use to judge the quality of previous research.

Defining a theoretical framework, clarifying key concepts, and stating a research question and hypotheses. Whether studying a human behavior problem or studying the effectiveness of an intervention, researchers employ some kind of theoretical framework. In human behavior studies, a theoretical framework attempts to explain the relationship between two variables or among three or more variables. In a research study of expectancy theory, for example, an investigator may try to test the relationship between concepts related to adolescent drinking: (1) the expectancy that drinking results in enhanced social experience, and (2) low self-esteem. Proponents of the theory might test the hypothesis that young people who have a strong belief that drinking enhances interpersonal skills (an idea derived, perhaps, from parental, peer, or cultural and media influences) are more likely to lack confidence in themselves in social situations (one aspect of low self-esteem). Theories that purport to explain human behavior should be testable; that is, stated in such a way that relevant research questions and hypotheses can be proved wrong (i.e., falsifiability). Whether this theory about beliefs in the effects of alcohol and interpersonal relations is valid depends on testing this theory many times with many different groups of people.

The general research question might be stated as follows: Are young people with poor self-esteem more likely to drink abusively if they believe that drinking will enhance their social experience? To test this research question, it must be restated in the form of hypotheses, which are declarative statements that assert how two or more concepts are related. Hypotheses regarding human behavior usually come in one of two forms: (1) A (poor self-esteem) is correlated with B (the expectation of enhanced social relations)—for example, a young person who scores high on a scale measuring belief in the positive effects of alcohol on social experience is significantly likely to have lower self-esteem; and (2) A (poor self-esteem) causes B (the expectation of enhanced social relations)—a young person with low self-esteem is significantly more likely to score higher on a scale measuring belief in the positive effects of alcohol on social experience. Hypotheses such as these that test the relationship between two concepts are among the simplest. Other hypotheses can be much more complex and involve multiple concepts.

Each concept in the hypotheses must be clarified in the introduction.

Self-esteem, for example, is a fairly general concept about which there has been much research, and the authors of the study must stipulate how they will define it. In addition, each concept in human behavior research must be measurable; that is, quantifiable on some level with a scale. The specifics of the measurement of the main concepts in a study are typically explained in the "Methods" section of a research article.

If the study focuses on the efficacy of a type of intervention, it is essential that the authors define the actual intervention (as distinguished from an underlying theory). The authors should describe the practice interventions in the introduction and pose specific hypotheses to test their effectiveness. The hypotheses, however, will be of only the causal type: A (the intervention) causes B (a good outcome for the client). A hypothesis that tests an intervention might be stated as follows: with elderly, depressed clients, interpersonal psychotherapy plus medication will show a significantly greater reduction in depression (as measured by the Hamilton Depression Rating Scale) than will medication alone. The authors also give reasons why they believe this will, in fact, be the outcome in their study. Although research regarding interventions may be reviewed in the introduction, more details about how the intervention was carried out during the study are usually described in the "Methods" section of the article.

There is a subtle but important distinction between outcome research and evaluation research. Outcome research is designed to test and establish the efficacy of psychosocial practices; that is, to test whether interventions are effective when tested under controlled circumstances in which clients have been carefully recruited according to specific guidelines, practitioners are well trained in using well-defined interventions, and outcomes are carefully measured. Usually, the intervention of interest is compared with a control group (which receives treatment after a brief waiting period) or a treatment that is normally used in community treatment settings (i.e., treatment as usual). The purpose of evaluation, however, is to test the effectiveness of interventions; that is, to determine whether interventions can be implemented effectively under routine circumstances in everyday practice settings, environments that tend to be more fluid and less orchestrated than controlled trials. However, the difference between controlled outcome research and evaluation research is more a matter of degree. Both share the same goal of testing whether interventions actually result in improved outcomes for clients.

Methods

After posing a research question and one or more hypotheses, the authors then discuss how they will answer the research question and test their hypotheses. This section is referred to as the "Methods" or "Methodology" section of a research report. Methods include a sampling design, study design and data collection procedure, a description of measurement instruments used in the study, and a description of the planned statistical strategy. If the study is a test of an intervention, then the interventions used in the study must be described in greater detail than in the introduction, so readers understand the type of treatment being tested.

Sampling strategies. In human behavior research, the investigators must provide a thoughtful selection of study participants with a clear description of their characteristics (e.g., gender, age, race). Sampling designs are based on either nonprobability samples or probability samples. Nonprobability samples recruit participants who fit a certain predetermined criteria (e.g., twenty single mothers with a serious mental illness, forty-five young men recently released from prison, twenty-six homeless elderly men). Small nonprobability samples lend themselves to qualitative research and other small-sample survey studies (i.e., studies that often include both qualitative and quantitative measures). Other nonprobability samples may be larger: a survey of 400 recently graduated social workers, 350 mentally ill persons who attend a community support program, or 800 families served by a child welfare agency over the course of three years.

Probability samples are those that have been drawn randomly. *Random* means that every individual on a list of possible participants (e.g., all registered voters in the United States) has an equal chance of being selected. Using probability tables, statisticians have calculated how many people, if drawn randomly, are needed to approximate a sample that is representative of those people in the larger group. For example, to know how the typical registered social worker feels about evidence-based practices, one would identify all members of the National Association of Social Workers (say, 150,000) and randomly select about 1,000 of them. This sample would provide a sound basis for generalization to all registered social workers, but only if the number of people who respond (i.e., the response rate) is sufficiently high. The response rate is the percentage of people from the sampled list who respond to the survey. What is acceptable? At least 50 percent of those 1,000 people in the sample need to respond. However, even 50 percent may not be adequate if it can be demonstrated statistically that those who responded were in some way different in key aspects from those who did not. Such an analysis would, of course, assume that one had some information about those who did not respond (e.g., gender, age, race, years of MSW experience). A very good response rate is 60 percent, and 70 percent or greater is considered excellent. In short, the higher the response rate is, the stronger is the case the researcher can make that the sample is a representative picture of the larger group.

In practice outcome (efficacy) or evaluation (effectiveness) studies, characteristics of the client participants should be clearly described (e.g., age, sex, diagnosis, ethnicity, referral sources). Clients who participate in treatment studies are usually recruited through clinics and human services agencies. Clients in evaluation studies are often the actual clients of the agency being evaluated. In all theoretical research and intervention studies, clients should be voluntary participants, should be informed about the nature of the study, and should have their confidentiality protected. Researchers must apply for approval to conduct studies through institutional review boards to ensure that they followed sound procedures to obtain informed consent and to protect client confidentiality.

Design. The authors of a research article must select and describe a research design that can potentially answer a specific research question. Doing so assumes a clear understanding of the strengths and limitations of each respective design. In general, human behavior studies employ one of the following: uncontrolled qualitative observation, cross-sectional survey, and longitudinal survey. Research on the efficacy of psychosocial interventions usually employs some variation of the experimental design (using comparison or control groups), otherwise referred to as the *controlled trial.* Evaluation studies often use either qualitative research with small samples or uncontrolled naturalistic evaluation with larger samples. Some evaluation studies use comparison groups. These different designs are explained subsequently.

A variety of data collection procedures is used in human behavior and intervention research. Questionnaires may be used in face-to-face interviews, mailed to participants, or filled out on the Internet. Other studies may employ direct observation (e.g., children in a classroom, practitioners behind a one-way window with clients). Some studies use more than one method of data collection: qualitative (e.g., recorded narrative accounts), quantitative (e.g., a scale that measures depression), or both. In any event, high priority is given to the selection of measures for the key study concepts (e.g., depression, posttraumatic stress). The scales selected should have a track record of reliability and validity (see Chapter 4).

Research designs typically used in human behavior research. Qualitative studies of individuals and groups are generally used in exploratory research, an approach that lends itself to examining new or unusual phenomena (e.g., living with an apocalyptic cult for a year to better understand recruitment practices and worldview). It can also be used to examine new dimensions of commonly occurring problems (e.g., narrative accounts of living with agoraphobia or in abandoned subway tunnels for years, surveying key informants to examine mental health needs and services in the community). The researcher who conducts qualitative research is interested in the relatively unfiltered accounts of individuals who want to tell their stories. Thus, much of the data collected are written or recorded accounts of the participants who provide the information or narrate their experiences. Such data can provide clues to better understand a problem, raise new questions about a problem, and open new avenues of investigation in human behavior theory and research.

However, often in large qualitative studies, some coding scheme must be derived to categorize and even measure much of the content to reduce it to a more manageable data set. To draw some tentative conclusions from the data, some attempt must be made to summarize the accounts of, say, one hundred unstructured interviews with homeless people living on the street. Computer software has been developed to assist with these efforts. Although often emotionally compelling, qualitative research has some serious limitations: despite the best of intentions to be objective and not get in the way of participants, qualitative data are likely to be interpreted from the investigator's point of view. What is gained in textured and detailed accounts of individual lives may be lost in interpretive bias and the lack of generalizability to larger groups of people in similar circumstances. Nevertheless, qualitative research is a great place to begin investigating problem areas that are underrepresented in the research literature. However, these methods are a beginning point, not an end point, for human behavior research. Once major theoretical terms are defined and questions posed, survey methods with larger groups must be conducted to determine whether the insights gained through qualitative methods hold for more representative samples of the population.

Cross-sectional surveys (i.e., surveys with large samples at one point in time) are powerful ways to collect large amounts of data on representative groups of the general population. Because of the power of probability sampling, representative samples of participants can be surveyed by mail, phone, or Internet, or interviewed in person. Large cross-sectional surveys can provide invaluable descriptive data on the occurrence of mental disorders and other psychosocial problems nationally and internationally. They can also be used to study matters of theoretical interest, such as the relationship between beliefs about drinking and actual rate of alcohol use, race and use of mental health services, the association between poverty and child abuse and neglect, authoritarian beliefs and domestic violence, perceptions of media portrayals of women and severity of eating disorders, and so on. The subjects to be addressed by cross-sectional surveys are limitless, and students need merely employ a few keywords in a search engine that includes social science research journals to realize the extent of theory-driven cross-sectional research.

Longitudinal surveys may also include availability samples or randomly selected samples, but they are designed to follow a group of persons over time, sometimes for five, ten, or twenty years. Although cross-sectional surveys can be used to collect data on large groups of representative samples, they are generally limited to demonstrating correlational relationships among factors. The strength of longitudinal designs (because the passage of time becomes a measurable factor) is in determining cause-effect relationships. If, for example, one wishes to study the effects of early childhood trauma on adolescent and adult psychosocial well-being ten and twenty years in the future (in the same participants, over time), one can then measure both those events around the time they occur (or soon after) and a variety of other contributing factors (e.g., early temperament, socioeconomic level, parenting status, substance abuse, other family problems) throughout adolescence and into adulthood. Although challenging to conduct, longitudinal studies can provide powerful evidence to support or refute developmental theories.

Research designs used to demonstrate the practice efficacy and effectiveness. As noted earlier, research used to determine whether certain interventions actually help people with certain problems or disorders spans the continuum from controlled outcome studies to naturalistic evaluation. Along this continuum is a range of design variations that can be used to either control for factors other than the intervention (to determine whether it is the intervention itself that makes a substantive difference for the client) or to determine how interventions work in a treatment-as-usual environment. There are good reasons for doing both types of studies: randomized controlled trials (discussed in Chapter 2) show whether interventions can work under carefully controlled circumstances, and program evaluations demonstrate whether interventions previously proved effective in controlled trials can be implemented cost effectively in everyday practice.

Evaluating practice: Naturalistic program evaluation. Although controlled trials are important tools for testing whether interventions can work under well-controlled conditions, it is also important to evaluate the implementation of interventions in typical practice settings. Just because a practitioner claims to use an evidence-based practice does not mean that the practice will be implemented skillfully or effectively. Evaluating one's own practice is important to ensure that the intervention is implemented well and that the client improves. If, over time, the client does not improve, then modifications to the intervention plan or the whole program may be in order. Research reports of human service evaluations are fairly common in practice journals with an applied orientation. It should also be kept in mind that between controlled trials and naturalistic evaluation are studies that combine elements of both. For example, quasi-experimental designs can be used to compare different agency programs with clients that have a similar range of characteristics but some different program elements.

Controlled experimental trials are not used frequently as a method of routine evaluation in human service agencies. A much more feasible approach that accommodates everyday practice in human service agencies is naturalistic program evaluation (Hargreaves, Shumway, Hu, & Cuffel, 1998; Kazdin, 1998; O'Hare, 2015; Rossi & Freeman, 1993), otherwise referred to as *passive observational designs*. In naturalistic program evaluation, services are delivered without using control or comparison groups. Before engaging in evaluation, however, every effort is made to train staff in evidence-based practices (i.e., approaches already tested in controlled trials) and to incorporate the use of reliable and valid instruments to monitor client progress and evaluate whether clients benefit from the intervention. However, there is a cardinal rule of evaluation that is clear yet often ignored: before one can evaluate the intervention, one must define the intervention (a review of research reports of program evaluations reveals a frequent lack of clarity with regard to defining the intervention). Again, the intervention methods (i.e., combinations of skills) are to be distinguished from other aspects of practice theories, specifically change-process theories that purport to explain how the intervention works. These are different questions and require different research designs to answer them. Authors of research reports should take considerable pains to clearly define how the interventions were carried out; otherwise, the reader is left with the question, What are the researchers evaluating?

Naturalistic evaluation incorporates reliable, valid, and useful measures (e.g., scales and indexes) into routine practice as part of assessment and ongoing monitoring of client progress. Most social workers who have practiced in human service agencies are familiar with the myriad forms to fill out, including psychosocial assessments, progress notes, termination summaries, and so forth. Often, such forms are poorly designed and can be a costly administrative nuisance. Data collection in naturalistic evaluation is not much different in terms of execution, except that the standards for selecting quantitative instruments (e.g., scales for measuring psychiatric symptoms, substance abuse, and child and adolescent adjustment) are much higher than standards for typical agency forms. The scales must have a record of reliability (consistency) and validity (accuracy), and when well chosen they can be clinically useful. Such scales can help practitioners perform better assessments and service evaluations. The data are ideally collected at baseline (as part of the assessment), during the intervention at key intervals, and at termination. Some evaluators will also arrange for follow-up measures. These data are useful for monitoring progress with individual clients, and when data are aggregated, they can be used for program evaluation.

Guidelines for recruitment of participants are less stringent in routine evaluation. Most agencies obtain informed consent for clients at intake and let them know that data collection as part of routine record keeping may be used for program evaluation. Thus, most clients are automatically included in agency evaluation processes.

Thus, the guidelines for conducting naturalistic evaluation are simple: (1) use interventions that have been shown to be effective in controlled trials (this point may seem obvious, but many agencies continue to use untested intervention methods), (2) train staff in the use of the approach, (3) use reliable and valid instruments as part of routine monitoring, and (4) use the data from the multiple measures and qualitative reports over time to determine whether clients have improved. In this way, naturalistic evaluation fits seamlessly into the routine implementation of clinical processes and can provide a solid foundation for determining the quality of clinical programming. Authors of evaluative research reports should explicitly justify all these points in their description of the evaluation design.

Determining and Interpreting Results

An extensive discussion of statistics would go well beyond the purposes here. However, a brief discussion is in order to help students understand why critical interpretation of results is so important.

Statistical findings of human behavior and practice research generally fall into three categories: univariate, bivariate, or multivariate results. Univariate results are statistics that report the results of one variable at a time. These statistics usually include frequencies and percentages, means (i.e., average scores), and standard deviations (a measure of dispersal around the mean score). For example, in a human behavior study on the prevalence of drinking among a random sample of one thousand high school students, typical univariate results might include the frequency and percentage of males (450, 45%) and females (550/55%) in the sample, the frequency and percentage of students who ever drink (650/65%), and the average amount of alcohol that a student consumes in a typical week (mean = 6.5 drinks). Univariate statistics are essentially used for description and thus are often referred to as *descriptive statistics.*

Human behavior and practice researchers, however, typically want to know more than descriptive information. As discussed earlier, researchers want to test hypotheses; that is, they want to make logical inferences from their data on, say, differences between groups or differences in clients' well-being between the beginning and the end of an intervention. Hence, bivariate and multivariate statistics are usually used to test hypotheses and thus are referred to as inferential statistics (as they test logical inferences about the relationship between variables and whether the differences are due to chance or to real differences in the general population). Commonly used bivariate statistics include the Pearson correlation coefficient, *t*-tests, and chi-square tests. Determining which statistic to use depends on how each variable is measured and whether the group is normally distributed; that is, whether the group statistics simulate those of the general population.

A typical use of bivariate statistics is to test a hypothesis to determine whether there is an important relationship or difference between two variables. For example, in an evaluation program, bivariate statistics show whether the average depression score for a group of women significantly improved from the time they start treatment to the time they finish treatment. Looking at the differences in scores for individual participants would not reveal whether the whole group benefited; it is necessary to compare the average group scores at the beginning and end of treatment. Comparison of the two mean scores requires a bivariate test of the hypothesis to show that there was a difference.

Multivariate statistics determine the relationships among more than two variables. For example, researchers are interested in more than just the relationship between gender and alcohol consumption in a group of high school students. A research question might be, Is stress in high school students related to alcohol consumption, and does this relationship vary by sex? Now there are three variables: sex, stress, and alcohol consumption. All of these factors can be measured, and how the three variables are related can be tested. It could be, for example, that stress has a greater impact on women's drinking than it does on men's drinking. Other factors could be added to the theoretical model, such as parental influence, participation in sports, overall quality of social relationships, and so on.

A multivariate research question in a program evaluation may focus on client characteristics (e.g., race, sex), services received (e.g., number of visits, type of intervention), and outcomes (e.g., changes in scores on depression and substance abuse scales). Several different questions could be asked: Does the number of visits differ across racial groups? Are there differences in rates of depression between men and women? Is one form of intervention more effective than another? These are interesting and important questions, but so far they only look at bivariate relationships. To complicate things (as researchers seem to enjoy), the researchers could ask more complex multivariate questions: Is one form of intervention more effective than another, and is the relationship between the intervention and outcome different by sex and race? Now there are four different variables: sex, race, type of intervention, and changes in score on a depression scale. To determine the answers, the researchers would use a multivariate statistical design that would examine changes in depression level while controlling (i.e., holding constant) the other factors. There are many multivariate statistical models available to researchers, but two of the more commonly used ones are multiple linear regression and variations on analysis of variance. Although detailed descriptions of these statistical approaches go beyond the purposes here, readers should, at this point, develop a basic understanding of the purpose of these statistical models in their research courses to be better able to read and generally understand research reports. Most human behavior and intervention research uses these methods, and though an in-depth understanding of them is beyond the expertise of most practitioners, a basic understanding of their purpose and the ability to understand the results of such tests is now essential.

The Discussion

Researchers sometimes provide a summary of the results in either the "Results" section or in the first part of the "Discussion" or "Conclusion" section of a research report. Interpretations of the results should be balanced, and the researchers should avoid reading too much into their findings (i.e., going beyond the data) or overgeneralizing the results beyond the sample of study participants. In the discussion, the authors should examine the results in the context of existing theory and previous human behavior or intervention research. The authors should also discuss the extent to which the results can be generalized to other groups of clients or treatment environments. Generalization is a key point because readers want to know the extent to which a theory applies to other groups or if an intervention is likely to work as well with similar groups of clients. The authors should also discuss the inherent limitations of the study design and any problems in carrying out the study (e.g., how many people dropped out or refused to answer questions). Last, most researchers offer suggestions for further research in their area of inquiry.

Learning how to critically read human behavior research requires considerable skill and is not a form of expertise that students typically develop early on in their social work careers. However, as one develops some basic skills in critiquing and understanding human behavior research, one can better distinguish theories for which there is a body of scientific evidence from those based mostly on ideology, tradition, or personal beliefs. However, most students (or experienced practitioners, for that matter) will not have to undertake the arduous task of reviewing human behavior research on their own. Fortunately, researchers and many practitioner-researchers have taken on the task of critically reviewing and summarizing human behavior and practice research findings to disseminate it for practitioners and other researchers. The findings of theory-driven research regarding child development, child abuse and neglect, major mental illnesses and substance abuse, aging, and so forth, are compiled in a wide array of excellent texts. The student need only seek them out. Being able to critically review human behavior research and practice outcome research is now an essential skill for social workers, as it allows them to collectively advance social work as a knowledge-based (rather than an ideology-based) profession.

Index